American Literature
A Brief History

Revised Edition

American Literature
A Brief History

Walter Blair
University of Chicago

Theodore Hornberger
University of Pennsylvania

James E. Miller, Jr.
University of Chicago

Randall Stewart

SCOTT, FORESMAN AND COMPANY
Glenview, Illinois   Brighton, England

Acknowledgments

The authors are grateful to the publishers who have given permission to reprint excerpts
from the following poems: "A Supermarket in California" from *Howl and Other Poems*
by Allen Ginsberg. Copyright © 1956, 1959 by Allen Ginsberg. Reprinted by permission
of CITY LIGHTS BOOKS. "The Dance" copyright 1952 by The Atlantic Monthly
Company from the book *Collected Poems of Theodore Roethke*. Reprinted by permission
of Doubleday & Company, Inc. and Faber and Faber Ltd. "The Waking" copyright 1953
by Theodore Roethke from the book *Collected Poems of Theodore Roethke*. Reprinted
by permission of Doubleday & Company, Inc. and Faber and Faber Ltd. "The Death of
a Toad" from *Poems 1943-1956* by Richard Wilbur. Reprinted by permission of Harcourt
Brace Jovanovich, Inc. and Faber and Faber Ltd. "The Waste Land" by T. S. Eliot from
The Collected Poems 1909-1962. Reprinted by permission of Harcourt Brace Jovanovich,
Inc. and Faber and Faber Ltd. "The Love Song of J. Alfred Prufrock" by T. S. Eliot from
The Collected Poems 1909-1962. Reprinted by permission of Harcourt Brace Jovanovich,
Inc. and Faber and Faber Ltd. Poems 185 (" 'Faith' is a fine invention") and 1052 ("I
never saw a Moor—") by Emily Dickinson. Reprinted by permission of the publishers and
the Trustees of Amherst College from Thomas H. Johnson, Editor, *The Poems of Emily
Dickinson*, Cambridge, Mass.: The Belknap Press of Harvard University Press, Copyright,
1951, 1955, by The President and Fellows of Harvard College. "Mending Wall" from *The
Poetry of Robert Frost* edited by Edward Connery Lathem. Copyright 1930, 1939, ©
1969 by Holt, Rinehart and Winston, Inc. Copyright © 1958 by Robert Frost. Copyright
© 1967 by Lesley Frost Ballantine. Reprinted by permission of Holt, Rinehart and Winston, Inc., the Estate of Robert Frost and Jonathan Cape Ltd. "Patterns" by Amy Lowell
reprinted from *Collected Poems of Amy Lowell* by permission of Houghton Mifflin Company. "The Progress of Faust," by Karl Shapiro, from *Poems, 1940-1953*. Copyright
1947 by Karl Shapiro. Reprinted by permission of Random House, Inc. "Roan Stallion"
by Robinson Jeffers, from *Selected Poetry of Robinson Jeffers*. Copyright 1925, 1953
by Robinson Jeffers. Reprinted by permission of Random House, Inc. "To the Stone
Cutters" by Robinson Jeffers from *Selected Poetry of Robinson Jeffers*. Copyright 1924,
1951 by Robinson Jeffers. Reprinted by permission of Random House, Inc. "These Trees
Stand. . ." by W. D. Snodgrass from *Heart's Needle*. Copyright © 1956 by W. D. Snodgrass.
Reprinted by permission of Alfred A. Knopf, Inc. "Man Against the Sky" from *Collected
Poems* by Edwin Arlington Robinson. Copyright 1953 by The Macmillan Company. Re-
printed by permission of Charles Scribner's Sons.

The publisher wishes to thank the owners for the use of the following artwork: Cover
photograph: Detail from the "Caswell Carpet." The Metropolitan Museum of Art, Gift of
Katherine Keyes, 1938, in memory of her father, Homer Eaton Keyes. Pp. 2–3, "Plan of
Savannah" by Peter Gordon, 1734 (engraving). I. N. Phelps Stokes Collection, Prints
Division, The New York Public Library, Astor, Lenox and Tilden Foundations. Pp. 46–47,
"Corner of Greenwich Street," drawing by Baroness Hyde de Neuville, c. 1810. I. N.
Phelps Stokes Collection, Prints Division, The New York Public Library, Astor, Lenox
and Tilden Foundations. Pp. 80–81, "Picnic Scene" by Susan Merrett, 1845. Courtesy of
the Art Institute of Chicago. Pp. 142–143, "Brooklyn Bridge, New York," lithograph by
Currier and Ives, 1869–93. Reproduced from the collections of the Library of Congress.
Pp. 196–197, Frozen Lake and Cliff, Sierra Nevada, California 1934. Photograph by
Ansel Adams, from the International Museum of Photography at the George Eastman
House. Pp. 242–243, Marisol: Women and Dog. 1964. Wood, plaster, synthetic polymer
paint and miscellaneous items. 72 x 82 x 16″. Gift of the Friends of the Whitney Museum.
Collection of the Whitney Museum of American Art, New York. Photograph by Geoffrey
Clements.

Preface

This volume presents a brief historical survey of American literature. The two parts of each of the six chapters discuss (a) the intellectual background of American literature and (b) literary trends. Each chapter is followed by a chronological table of events important in their impact on American literature or in literary history. Brief biographies and evaluations of American writers are presented alphabetically in supplement to the historical material, and the index directs the student to further information in the text. Appended to each of the biographies is a bibliography of the major works of the author. The student can use these bibliographies as the starting point in developing a list of books that offer significant and enjoyable reading in American literature. New to this edition, "Guides to Further Reading," following the biographies, lists detailed histories of the literature of the United States and useful bibliographies of secondary sources.

Any teacher who is acquainted with the two-volume anthology *The Literature of the United States* will have no trouble seeing that this historical survey is derived from the interchapter material. But this is not simply a reprinting; in the course of two revisions, changes have been made throughout. The last chapter, particularly, has been revised to bring it up to date.

This history is, therefore, more than an excerpt from a larger work and more than a supplemental textbook. Despite its brevity, the authors have endeavored to make it complete and independently intelligible. Many of the specific works in American literature referred to in this *Brief History* have been printed in the three-volume paperbound edition of *The Literature of the United States*, which, unlike the two-volume anthology, does not reprint the interchapters. Both the history and the anthology will, we believe, prove to be valuable tools for the student.

Walter Blair
Theodore Hornberger
James E. Miller, Jr.

Contents

American Literature
A Brief History

Who can desire more content, that hath small means;
or but only his merit to advance his fortunes,
than to tread and plant that ground he hath purchased by the hazard of his life? . . .
What so truely su[i]tes with honour and honestie, as the discovering things unknowne?
erecting Townes, peopling Countries, informing the ignorant,
reforming things unjust, teaching virtue. . . ?
—John Smith

CHAPTER 1

"Plan of Savannah," an engraving done of the town in 1734 by Peter Gordon

The English Colonies

1588–1765

Intellectual Currents

The Pattern of Colonial Culture

Most Americans know the story of the colonial period of the United States. It extends from Columbus' first voyage in 1492 to the Stamp Act of 1765, which united in opposition to British policy thirteen decidedly dissimilar colonies, whose peoples had barely begun to be aware of common interests and growing strength.

Columbus, seeking a new route to the fabled gold and silks and spices of China and India, found instead what was quickly and appropriately called the New World. Upon the Americas were soon unleashed the ambitions of the nations arising from the ruin of medieval unity. Spain, Portugal, France, Holland, Sweden—every one of them looked westward across the Atlantic for more lands and strength. England entered rather belatedly into this contest for colonies. The voyages of John and Sebastian Cabot in the fifteenth century had given her some claim to the northern continent of the newly discovered hemisphere, but it was nearly a century before men like Walter Raleigh sought to make that claim good by actual occupation. As soon as it was clear that the eastern parts of North America offered no such easily portable loot as the gold and silver of Peru and Mexico, most Englishmen had little enthusiasm for colonization, and many were openly scornful of such costly failures as that at Roanoke Island in 1585. Ultimately, however, their patriotism (a curious blend of nationalism and Protestantism), their needs as a seafaring people, and their longings for land and wealth accounted for the establishment of permanent settlements at Jamestown in Virginia in 1607 and at Plymouth in Massachusetts in 1620.

The Pilgrims at Plymouth barely survived their first winter, and Jamestown came close to extinction in an Indian massacre in 1622. The future, however, remained doubtful for only a short time. Between 1628 and 1640, in what is known as the Great, or the Puritan, Migration, perhaps as many as twenty-five thousand persons settled in New England, giving to Massachusetts both a long-lasting economic and cultural leadership and the power to press effectively against the French in Canada and the Dutch in New Amsterdam. Virginian stability and growth were assured by a steadily growing taste for tobacco among Europeans, and by the end of the seventeenth century the plantation way of life was well established there. More color and variety in the growing colonial society came with the absorption of the Dutch along the Hudson and the Swedes on the Delaware, and from the determination of the Roman Catholic Lord Baltimore and the Quaker William Penn, who made Maryland and Pennsylvania havens from state-imposed religious conformity. Georgia, to cite one final example, was founded by James Edward Oglethorpe in part as a refuge for the poor and in part as a bastion against the Spaniards in Florida.

In short, villages and farms and plantations proliferated up and down the Atlantic coastline, and everywhere men sought to build that kind of life which seemed to them desirable, compromising always with the hard facts of their environment and the often conflicting ambitions of their neighbors. By 1700 the colonists numbered more than a quarter of a million; by 1765, approximately a million and three quarters. They had been fortunate in having been left largely to their own devices, or interfered with only sporadically and unsystematically. The difficulties of administering colonies from a distance of three thousand miles had been recognized by everyone, and all the colonies had their representative assemblies (the first of them in Virginia) comparable to the lower house of the English Parliament. For all their differences—and the colonies had many—they agreed upon one thing: they wanted to control their own affairs. We know now, as Americans in 1765 could not know, that the steps from such a conviction to Lexington and Bunker Hill and Independence Hall were inevitable, that the essential truth of the colonists' situation lay in Thomas Jefferson's epochal words: "When, in the course of human events, it becomes necessary for *one people*. . . ."

One people!—This was the ideal. It was never fully achieved, of course, but the American colonists did become sufficiently unified to win their political independence and create, rather surprisingly, a new nation. The divisive forces were as powerful in their way as those we see today. Sectionalism was fostered by the difficulties of land travel and communication; personal and commercial connections between one colony and England were often closer than those between colony and colony. Congregational New England and the Anglican South regarded each other with suspicion. Varying national and racial origins and economic interests accentuated the differences among the colonies. By 1765 one out of every three Pennsylvanians was German; every other North Carolinian was of Scotch-Irish stock. Negro slaves made up almost half the population of Virginia, and in South Carolina and Georgia the whites were in fact outnumbered. In those colonies where settlement was spreading westward the Indians were either natural enemies or the prey of traders seeking quick and large profits. Neither a national consciousness nor a national conscience is discernible on the eve of the Revolution.

Language, folklore, learning, the arts, literary tastes and types, legal, political, and educational institutions—everything except the land itself and a few skills acquired from the Indians—had been brought across the Atlantic Ocean. The process of transplantation had been sporadic, almost accidental; it had never been smoothly regular, almost never simple. Always involved in the process had been change, adaptation, modification to meet the peculiar circumstances of the new environment. The old ways never worked quite perfectly under the new conditions. Men came who knew how to build houses, but they had to work with the building materials they found—lime for plaster, for example, was hard to come by—and they had to meet the idiosyncrasies of climates unlike those to which they had been accustomed. Physicians arrived, their minds stored with botanical medicine, only to discover that America had a flora of its own, whose medicinal use had to be discovered by experiment or learned from the natives. Traditions lingered, but necessity forced the quicker-witted to improvisation and dependence on first-hand knowledge, and the problems in the lands from Maine to Georgia were so varied as to call forth all the ingenuity that experience could develop. Decade after decade the processes of transplantation and adaptation were repeated, with infinite variations. New men and women came from Europe, bringing new tools and talents and opinions and adapting them as best they could to what they found. Frontier succeeded frontier as immigrants pushed up the streams toward the mountains to find new farms and found new villages. Stability was short-lived, change incessant.

Nor was Europe static. In almost every realm of human thought the period was tumultuous, full of conflict and revolutionary change. In economics, the feudal system was giving way to modern capitalism. In politics, the theory of the divine right of kings was being superseded by constitutional and contractual concepts. In religion, the schisms and sectarian rivalries which were the aftermath of the Protestant Reformation were hardly yet softened by the principle of toleration, which was eventually to bring some degree of amity. In science, revolution was continuous as Copernicus, Galileo, Bacon, Descartes, Boyle, Ray, Newton, and their associates and disciples changed both the world-view of western man and his method of advancing his knowledge of the world in which he lived. In literature and the arts, the creative outpouring of the Renaissance was succeeded by the more orderly but far from barren reign of Neoclassicism.

The colonial era of the United States coincided, in other words, with the germinal period of what we call the modern world. Europe, of necessity the chief constant factor to the people who settled in America, was itself becoming a new world. The more intelligent colonists, busy though they were with their own affairs, never forgot that they were participants in affairs of mighty moment, in the rebuilding of an old society as well as in the creation of a new one.

Colonial literature was therefore written as often for European readers as for American, and its concerns—economic, religious, political—were matters of intellectual controversy on both sides of the Atlantic.

The Economic Promise

The first and the greatest promise which the New World held out to Europeans was freedom from want. To landless men whose ancestors had for centuries been bound to someone else's soil, America offered freeholds. Here was room for a man to raise, on his own land, his own food and the fibers for his own clothing, a new chance to attain the security of overflowing granaries and well-stocked barnyards. As Captain John Smith put it, "Who can desire more content, that hath small meanes; or but only his merit to advance his fortunes, then to tread and plant that ground he hath purchased by the hazard of his life?"

Colonial literature is understandably rich in accounts of the economic resources of the New World. The prospective immigrant wanted to know, in as much detail as possible, about his chances of earning a living. He did not always find accurate information, because the books about the colonies were often written by promoters whose evaluations were rosily optimistic rather than cautious. From the explorers, travelers, and settlers, however, as well as from the promoters, there came in time an enormous body of information on the climate, topography, soils, plants, animals, and minerals of the various regions of British America. These writings told what would and would not grow. They paid particular attention to timber, because England needed shipbuilding supplies and her great forests were playing out. They reported in detail on game and fur-bearing animals, on fisheries, on the prospects of mines.

The earliest English survey of a region now a part of the United States was Thomas Hariot's *Virginia* (1588). Hariot was Raleigh's protégé and a member of the Roanoke expedition of 1585; his book is not merely the first but also one of the fullest and most accurate prognostications of the various ways in which a living might be earned in the New World. Many of John Smith's writings are of the same nature as Hariot's, and both his *Map of Virginia* (1612) and his *Description of New England* (1616) were read carefully by men who were considering emigration. No colony was launched without a similar "Map" or "True Report" of economic possibilities, followed by a local literature of promotion which was in turn succeeded by reports of progress. Of the many other books which might be named, the most important are Francis Higginson's *New England's Plantation* (1630), William Wood's *New England's Prospect* (1634), Thomas Morton's *New English Canaan* (1637), John Hammond's *Leah and Rachel; or, The Two Fruitful Sisters, Virginia and Mary-Land* (1656), George Alsop's *Character of the Province of Mary-Land* (1666), Daniel Denton's *Brief Description of New-York* (1670), William Penn's *Brief Account of the Province of Pensilvania* (1681), Thomas Ashe's *Carolina* (1688), and Gabriel Thomas' *Historical and Geographical Account of the Province and Country of Pensilvania* (1698). These books all insist that the fundamental needs of food, clothing, and shelter could be satisfied rather more easily in America than in Europe, and they suggest over and over again that industry and ingenuity could produce an abundance of good things far beyond the experience of the common man in Europe.

That the New World was a land of marvels, of limitless economic opportunity, was taken almost for granted. The European mind had been prepared for this conviction over many centuries. The ancients had harbored traditions of wonderful western lands—the Elysian Fields where happy souls went after death and the Islands of the Hesperides where golden apples grew. In the west, too, lay Atlantis, the great island continent swallowed up by earthquakes and the sea long before the time of Plato. In medieval times, men had written of inconceivably wealthy islands —Antillia and O'Brazil—somewhere in the western ocean, and the news had slowly circulated that the Norsemen had found a new, rich, western continent called Vinland. These stories, combined with the ineradicable faith that America was close to the legendary treasures of the Orient, had prepared Europeans for wonders, and they were duly delighted with the strange new plants and animals of which the explorers wrote.

Only a few were skeptical. Samuel Purchas, for one, expressed the belief in *Purchas His Pilgrimes* (1619) that America was not so wonderful as some people seemed to think. "For what haue they," he asked, "to oppose to our Elephants, Rhinocerotes, Camels, Horses, Kine, &c. Neither are the naturall fruits of America comparable to those of our World. Whence are their Spices, and best Fruits, but from hence, by transportation or transplantation? As for Arts, States, Literature, Diuine and Humane, multitudes of Cities, Lawes, and other Excellencies, our World enjoyeth still the priuiledge of the First-borne. America is a younger brother, and hath in these things almost no inheritance at all, till it bought somewhat hereof of the Spaniards, with the price of her Freedome." In the eighteenth century there were other skeptics, such as the Comte de Buffon and the Abbé Raynal, who were convinced that the American climate was so enervating that men and beasts degenerated in the New World. Thomas Jefferson sought to refute Buffon by compiling tables of the comparative weights of European and American animals and by assembling the skeleton of an American mastodon in his Paris apartments.

Most Europeans, however, were eager to look at America with unbounded optimism, especially when, as often happened, they grew impatient with the state of things in their own civilization. The prevailing temper was that of the English philosopher, George Berkeley, who pictured a Muse disgusted with Europe, waiting a better time

In happy climes, where from the genial sun
  And virgin earth such scenes ensue,

> The force of art by nature seems outdone,
>   And fancied beauties by the true.

Man was to be better treated by Nature in the western hemisphere than in Europe. He was, indeed, to rise to new heights, far more impressive than mere economic abundance could attain.

> Westward the course of empire takes its way,
>   The four first Acts already past,
> The fifth shall close the Drama with the day;
>   Time's noblest offspring is the last.

Only the presence of the native inhabitants seemed to stand in the way of New World greatness. To the American Indians, the coming of the white man was not fulfillment but disaster, not a new beginning, but—by and large—a terrible end. It is estimated (William T. Hagan, *American Indians*, 1961) that orginally there were over 600,000 Indians, representing over 600 different cultures, in what was to become the United States of America. The culture the white man brought with him—his animals, his weapons, his tools—all radically affected the Indian cultures, destroying in waves the delicate balance among them. The white man exploited the Indians in the fur trade and in the pursuit of precious metals. Most important of all, he robbed them of their lands. In return, the white man gave the Indians devastating diseases—tuberculosis, syphilis, measles, and smallpox.

All of this somewhat sordid history was not, of course, recorded during the colonial period (much of it had to wait for the twentieth century to appear in print). The settlers preferred to overlook the distasteful reality and dwell upon the legends and myths they had created about the Indians.

For the early settlers, the novelty of Indian customs, the unsettled problem of their origin (were they, for instance, descendants of the Lost Ten Tribes of Israel?), their uncanny skill in woodcraft, their unfamiliar social and political organization, their stoic endurance of pain and their apparent pleasure in torture, their exotic religious practices—all created interest amounting to fascination. The Pocahontas legend, whether or not Smith invented it out of whole cloth, epitomizes the tendency to create a "noble savage." Out of this grew the attitude known as primitivism, which glorified the unspoiled simplicity of the "uncivilized." Primitivism was basically an objection to the complexities and maladjustments of life in Europe, and appears more frequently in books written by Europeans than in those by persons who had actually been in contact with the Indians, although Thomas Morton's *New English Canaan* is a noteworthy exception. Later in the eighteenth century, primitivism appeared in the poems

Philip Freneau, the essays of Michel Guillaume St. Jean de Crèvecoeur, and the *Travels* of William Bartram. It continued well into the nineteenth century and is an essential element in the philosophical background of James Fenimore Cooper's Leather-Stocking tales and Henry Wadsworth Longfellow's *Hiawatha*.

Colonial literature also records the economic processes by which simple home industries were gradually supplanted by a more specialized industrial system. The references to mining and ironworks in the writings of John Winthrop and William Byrd give us a glimpse of the beginnings of industrialization, which was not to become general until many years after the achievement of political independence.

For many immigrants the New World fulfilled its economic promise. Many others, however, were exploited by the few who brought, accumulated, or inherited the capital required for large-scale farming. Chief among the economically oppressed were the Negro slaves, who by 1700 numbered perhaps 25,000, by 1765 over 325,000. There were slaves in all the colonies, but about four fifths of them lived south of Pennsylvania, where large planters of tobacco, rice, and indigo wanted cheap and unskilled labor. Only a few voices were raised against the institution in the early stages of its development (a few Quakers and, in New England, Samuel Sewall are remembered for their unusual sensitivity), even though many whites knew something of the cruelties of the slave trade and both the formulation of shockingly inhumane legal codes and not infrequent insurrections testified to injustice and brutal oppression. The justification of slavery, as Dwight L. Dumond has said (*Antislavery: The Crusade for Freedom in America*, 1961), was an assumption of biological inequality and racial inferiority which flatly contradicted professions of belief in individual freedom and human rights, to say nothing of negating a number of the sayings in Christ's Sermon on the Mount, including the Golden Rule. What resulted from this contradiction gives American history its most tragic theme and episodes.

Color prejudice operated not only against slaves but also against the blacks who were technically free, almost 60,000 of whom were counted by the 1790 census. They found it impossible to compete on equal terms with their fellow citizens, even in the colonies where slaves were few in number.

The Religious Life

Next to getting a living, the chief concern of great numbers of the colonists was religion. Some of them, indeed, regarded the saving of souls—their own and those of other people—as the most meaningful activity of life. To understand the men and women who established the pattern of

American society, we need to know with some exactness their religious and theological background and its reflection in literature.

First it must be understood that most of the colonists, whatever their church, were keenly aware of the Reformation. The Bible in their own language had been in the hands of Englishmen only since 1535, and to most of them it was a fresh and inexhaustible revelation of the will of God. The persecutions of the reign of Queen Mary, the fear of a Spanish invasion (which it was believed would have been swiftly followed by an Inquisition in England), the memory of the Gunpowder Plot of Guy Fawkes, the vexing problem of the royal succession, and the endless debates about church government and ritual—all were closer to the English in the early seventeenth century than the hatreds of the Civil War are to present-day Americans.

The earliest attempts to colonize reflect the religious rivalry between British settlers and the Catholic colonies established by France and Spain. Both Hariot and Smith emphasized the heathenism of the Indians, implying that it was the sacred duty of the English to convert them to the true faith, that is, to Anglicanism, before they could be led astray by the Spaniards or French. Although the settlers who came to America with any such altruistic intentions were decidedly in the minority, a good deal of missionary work among the Indians was attempted. Harvard, William and Mary, and Dartmouth were all founded with an eye to the education of Indian youth, although in all of these colleges other purposes soon loomed much larger.

Six important settlements—Plymouth, Massachusetts Bay, Maryland, Rhode Island, New Haven, and Pennsylvania—were the work of religious groups or leaders to whom economic considerations were distinctly secondary. Some wanted the opportunity to organize and run a church-state, perhaps to improve upon John Calvin's experiment at Geneva; others wished only the toleration of nonconforming sects. All relate in one way or another to the peculiar circumstances of the Reformation in England.

Between Henry VIII's break with the Pope and the end of the reign of Elizabeth I, the Church of England had arrived at a *status quo* accurately described as moderate Protestantism. The break with Rome was complete. The ruler was the acknowledged head of the English church; monastic orders had been abolished, and most of the lands accumulated over the centuries by the Church had been seized and distributed by the Crown; church services were held in English rather than in Latin; and the people had been provided with the English Bible and the English *Book of Common Prayer*. On the other hand, much that seemed "papist" to the more extreme Protestants remained—the hierarchy of parish priests, bishops, and archbishops, intimately connected with the structure of the civil state; richly ornamented churches and vestments; and set forms of prayer and worship.

English dissent or nonconformity (the terms are used interchangeably, although the latter connotes a somewhat more active position) consisted of innumerable groups and individuals who believed that the Reformation had not gone far enough. Some wanted to remove all vestiges of Catholic practices and rituals, placing more emphasis upon the sermon and the Bible as the chief means of bringing souls to Christ—these were the first English Puritans. Others desired to substitute a measure of lay control for the system of benefices, bishops, and archbishops, for which they found no Biblical precedent—these were the Presbyterians. Still others wished each congregation to decide for itself what form of worship it should follow—these were the Separatists, Independents, or Congregationalists, also sometimes called Brownists, after their first spokesman, Robert Browne (1550?-1633). In addition, there were many shades of opinion regarding the proper forms of worship and the most desirable form of church government. With the passage of time, differences of opinion about these matters multiplied rather than diminished, and the term "Puritan" began to be applied rather indiscriminately to all nonconformists.

The Anglican leaders sought continuously to enforce conformity to the *status quo.* Almost everyone regarded the church as an essential element to the stability of the state and could not envision a society tolerating diverse religious opinions. James I, therefore, in 1604, speaking of the Puritans, could announce, "I shall make them conform themselves or I will harry them out of the land, or else do worse." With the accession of Charles I in 1625, the more militant bishops had the support of a king with absolutist leanings, and the pressure on the Puritans increased enormously. Under William Laud, Bishop of London from 1628 until 1633, and thereafter Archbishop of Canterbury until his execution in 1645, clergymen who failed to follow the prescribed forms of worship were brought into church courts, tried, and if found guilty punished, most often (as in the case of Thomas Shepard) by being forbidden to exercise any clerical functions. Among these suspended clergy were many of the men who became the leaders of the New England colonies.

The Pilgrims who came to Plymouth were Separatists. Some of them had first emigrated to Holland, found the atmosphere there too foreign for their taste, and determined to settle in America. They were poor people and would not have been able to make the voyage in the *Mayflower* had not the necessary capital been provided by a group of "merchant adventurers" of London. William Bradford was the mainstay of the settlement and church which they founded in Massachusetts. In 1692 Plymouth became a part of the Province of Massachusetts Bay.

The Puritans of the Massachusetts Bay Company came to New England when it became clear that further reform within the English Church, headed by Laud, was impossible. They took care to bring their charter with them, and they intended to establish a commonwealth in which the kind of church they wanted might thrive. In contrast to the Pilgrims, they were wealthy and well educated, many of them being substantial property owners or professional men, university-trained as was their first governor, John Winthrop. Furthermore, they were numerous. Not all of them were as earnest in their religion as Winthrop and the ministers, but the Bay Colony leadership was farsighted and effective. Social, political, and educational institutions were so securely established that no study of the genesis of American life can ignore the Puritan tradition. Before the Puritans had been long in New England, they agreed upon a form of church government which was more Congregational than Presbyterian. Whether the *Cambridge Platform* of 1649 was shaped by the example of the Separatist Pilgrims, or by Congregational tendencies among the Bay Colony leaders themselves, is a debatable question. By the time the *Cambridge Platform* was adopted, the Westminster Assembly had effected changes not wholly dissimilar within the Church of England, although they were largely annulled by the Restoration in 1660.

Puritanism, however, was more than an attitude toward forms of worship and church government. The term was used then, as it is now, to describe a straitlaced way of life, a concern with moral conduct so great as to lead some individuals to attempt what we now think of as unwarranted control of the personal lives of their neighbors, a rigid repression of acts and fashions that today are no longer considered evil. Such was Puritanism at its worst. At its best it provided men and women with a sense of social responsibility, an earnestness about life which had in it both intellectual conviction and intense, sometimes even mystic, piety.

Underlying Puritan earnestness was Calvinism, a stern and legalistic theology constructed by the Genevan reformer, John Calvin (1509-1564). Calvinism portrayed God as a sovereign whom man, in the person of Adam, had disobeyed, thereby breaking an inexpressibly sacred and solemn covenant. Upon Adam and all his race, retribution had justly fallen. Through Christ, however, man had been given a second chance, although that chance was extended only to those men whom God had "elected" to be saved. Most men were predestined to damnation, as they deserved. Although one could never be wholly sure of being among the fortunate few for whom salvation was foreordained, life was to be lived in a search for the divine will, as it might be expressed in one's own struggle for serenity, through one's spiritual growth, or as it might be interpreted from unusual events (or "special providences") in the external world. To walk uprightly in the sight of God and to seek to follow His will—these were the aims of the Calvinist and the origin, as has often been remarked, of the "New England conscience."

The "Five Points" upon which the Calvinists insisted were predestination, limited atonement, total depravity, irresistibility of grace, and perseverance of the saints. Although the vistas of human life which these terms represent are still observable today, most of us discuss them in other terms, such as those of the existentialists. The American Puritans never tired of debating about them, nor of the two covenants which lay at the heart of their special version of Calvinism, often called "federal" or "covenant" theology. The covenant of works, which Adam broke, and the covenant of grace, which God offered through His son Jesus Christ, were enormously important in New England. One can see the idea of a covenant in the Mayflower Compact, and the intense concern with grace in the writings of Michael Wigglesworth, Edward Taylor, and Jonathan Edwards.

From the first, Calvinism had its opposition. Of the many challenging opponents four are so important to the student of literature that their description is a necessity. These four—Antinomianism, Arminianism, Quakerism, and Deism—had one thing in common: they granted human nature a more dignified role than the Calvinists were willing to grant it. Otherwise, they were most dissimilar. Antinomianism and Arminianism were merely theological positions, not necessarily concerned with a particular church any more than was Calvinism itself. Quakerism was and is the doctrine of a religious society, the Friends. Deism was neither a theology nor a church, but a philosophical position.

Antinomianism has approximately the place in religion that anarchy has in politics; that is to say, it is the denial of any authority over the individual. The Antinomian controversy which shook the Bay Colony to its foundations in 1636 and 1637 ended with the banishment of Anne Hutchinson for spreading, among other heresies, the doctrine that God revealed himself directly to individuals, so that a person could know whether or not he was of the "elect." Such thinking challenged both the Calvinistic conception of the Bible as God's final revelation and the social control which was basic in the thought of such leaders as Winthrop. Hawthorne's *The Scarlet Letter* is one of the works of literary art which owes something to Anne Hutchinson and Antinomianism (when, for example, Hester exclaims to Dimmesdale, "What we did had a consecration of its own!").

Arminianism takes its name from a Dutch theologian, Jacobus Arminius (1560-1609), who held that one could achieve salvation in part through "good works," that is to say, though living a moral and upright life. It was regarded by the Calvinists as derogatory to the sovereignty of God and was one of the "errors" which Edwards was most anxious to refute in his *Freedom of Will*. Although Arminianism was condemned by the Synod of Dort (1618-1619), the body which established the "Five Points" of Calvinism, "good works" continued to appeal to the masses of men more widely than did the doctrines of abstruse theology, and when in the eighteenth century evangelical preachers took religion to the people, Arminianism flourished. The Methodist movement in particular had Arminian aspects.

Quakerism is the only one of the many radical Protestant opinions of the seventeenth century which has remained influential in its original form. The people who first called themselves "Children of Light," and later the Society of Friends, organized under the leadership of George Fox (1624-1691) in the late 1640's. Their popular name was given them in jest, after Fox had asserted in a courtroom that even magistrates would come to "tremble before the word of the Lord." The Friends believed that the duty of man is to follow the Bible and what was variously called "pure wisdom" or "the Inner Light," an "opening" from God. With a quietistic listening for God's guidance they combined the social control of "speaking out" in meeting, by which the promptings of the Inner Light were communicated to and passed upon by other Friends—a procedure which preserved them from the Antinomian lawlessness. They believed that all men are brethren, that all violence (and especially war) is evil, that worldly distinctions of class and dress are unfriendly, that the taking of oaths is blasphemous. They had no professional clergy, and they tended to distrust higher learning. Bitterly persecuted in New England as late as 1677, they established themselves in New Jersey and Pennsylvania, where they became a powerful force for the abolition of slavery and for many varieties of social reform. Although they wrote many narratives of their religious experience, they produced relatively few great writers (the best of them was John Woolman), but their equalitarianism and humanitarianism have always been powerful factors in American life. Whittier was their chief spokesman in nineteenth-century American literature, but the Quaker tradition is strong in the work of Walt Whitman and many lesser authors.

Deism is ordinarily dated from the *De Veritate* (1624) of Lord Herbert of Cherbury, an English philosopher. Herbert approached religion from a purely rational angle, similar to what we would now call the comparative method. He found that in all times, whether pagan or Christian, men had agreed upon five axioms: (1) that there is a God; (2) that He ought to be worshipped; (3) that piety and virtue are the essentials of worship; (4) that man ought to repent his sins; and (5) that there are rewards and punishments in a future life. In the latter part of the seventeenth century, rationalism spread rapidly, in part as a result of the advance of science, and there was widespread acceptance of the Deistic position that religious truth could be obtained by the use of reason. Veneration of the Bible as the revelation of God is wholly lacking in this view of religion; the distinguishing mark of Deistic thought is the rejection of revelation. The best-known Deistic work by a colonial American is Benjamin Franklin's *Dissertation on Liberty and Necessity, Pleasure and Pain* (1725). He later decided his youthful Deistic convictions were not "useful," but no reader of Franklin is long in doubt about his basic agreement with Lord Herbert of Cherbury.

Toleration and revivalism, probably the most distinctive features of

American religion, also had their beginnings in the colonial period. Both remain, after all these years, the frequent concern of many Americans. A leading colonial exponent of tolerance was Roger Williams. Banished from Massachusetts Bay, he founded Rhode Island in 1636 as a tiny refuge for those who might be persecuted by the civil state for their religious opinions. His only predecessor in the advocacy of liberty of conscience and the separation of church from state seems to have been an English Congregationalist, Leonard Busher, whose *Religious Peace* had been published in 1614. Rhode Island was far ahead of its time. Not until the chartering of Pennsylvania in 1681 was a second colony willing to receive all victims of religious persecution. Maryland, to be sure, passed a Toleration Act in 1649 as a protection for the Catholics, but Jews and Unitarians were not welcome. The other colonies, some of them reluctantly, bowed to the provisions of the Toleration Act passed by Parliament in 1689, and thereafter the principle of religious freedom received at least lip service. Nonconformists to the dominant pattern of religious life are by no means safe, however, even today, although in later years intolerance toward one group or another has been an aspect of economic competition as often, perhaps, as of religious conviction.

Revivalism, while not wholly native, has long been the most conspicuous emotional outlet of American Protestantism. Its origins may be found in the religious situation of colonies founded by earnest and pious folk who saw their children slipping away from religion as life became easier and more secular. This situation developed in New England shortly after 1650 and is signalized by the adoption of the Half-Way Covenant of 1662, which admitted the children of church members to church membership (although not to communion) without the previously required confession of "religious experience." For most of the sixty years thereafter, New England clergymen seized upon every possible opportunity to expound the decline and decadence of religion, the necessity of a return to the ways of the founders (a renewal of covenant), the dangers of apostasy, and the innumerable signs of divine disfavor in comets, witchcraft, earthquakes, fires, and storms. Mrs. Knight's *Journal* is evidence of the trends which were viewed with alarm in Samuel Sewall's *Diary* and in many tracts and sermons by the Mathers. Cotton Mather's *Magnalia Christi Americana* is the best-known and most sustained complaint of the decline of religion and the diminishing influence of the ministers.

After 1720, religion was reinvigorated by what is known as the "Great Awakening," a series of revivals which reached the young people and the lower classes in all the colonies. Through the Awakening, religion found new leaders and a somewhat broader base, becoming perceptibly less intellectual and more emotional. The excitement began in some Dutch Reformed churches of New Jersey in the 1720's. Similar revivals occurred in the Presbyterian churches of Pennsylvania, and by the 1730's appeared

in New England, where Edwards was soon absorbed in their strange phenomena. Six times between 1729 and 1770 the colonies were visited by
George Whitefield (1714-1770), an English evangelist with Calvinistic
convictions who had been associated with the Wesleys in the early days of
Methodism. Whitefield preached to vast crowds, often out-of-doors, and
invariably aroused great enthusiasm. The Baptists and the Methodists
found many converts through highly successful revivals, particularly in the
South, in the decades just before the Revolution. Later the camp meeting
and the brush-arbor church were to take revivalism westward.

The literature of revivalism is enormous; it is estimated that more than
thirty-five thousand pieces relate to the Awakening. Best known, probably,
are Edwards' *Some Thoughts Concerning the Present Revival of Religion
in New England* (1742) and Charles Chauncy's *Seasonable Thoughts on
the State of Religion in New-England* (1743).

The effect of revivalism was to make religion more the immediate
concern of the common man than it had been before. That the development of revivalism coincided with the spread of a new sense of responsibility for the poor and the unfortunate is no accident. Revivalism was a
democratizing phenomenon. It has remained typical of American Protestantism, despite the frowns of settled clergymen and of the higher economic levels of society. Although it may have tended to divide churches
and to lend itself to the self-seeking of some unscrupulous evangelists, such
as the one Sinclair Lewis portrayed in *Elmer Gantry*, revivalism has
retained its appeal because of its recognition of the importance of emotional involvement as a part of religious experience.

Prior to 1765 scant concern was expressed for the religion of Negroes,
and occasionally efforts to Christianize slaves were vigorously opposed.
Part of the rationale of white superiority was that the blacks were not
Christians. Some slave owners and white ministers brought Negroes into
family prayers and even into their churches (most often in segrated sections), and there were scattered attempts to teach slaves to read the Bible,
even though some colonies forbade such instruction by law. The effort to
Christianize the slave community was probably not general until the early
nineteenth century. By that time the free Negroes had their own churches,
some of which were to lead in the abolition movement.

Commonwealth Building

A third great concern of the colonists, and a major theme in colonial literature, was the political hope which the New World offered. Americans
were thinking, from the first, of the possibility of a new kind of state.

John Smith was not alone in observing a parallel between Europe in
his time and the declining years of the Roman Empire. Although England

had become a great and strong nation under Elizabeth I, there seemed to be more distressing poverty, more selfish wealth, more injustice and social unrest than there had ever been before. We now see, with the perspective of distance, that feudalism was still not wholly disintegrated, that hereditary and class privileges had survived longer than serfdom, and that capitalism had not yet generated sufficient social responsibility among men of wealth. Smith could say with conviction and a tinge of threat that "rich men for the most part are growne to that dotage, through their pride in their wealth, as though there were no accident could end it, or their life." In America, a land of greater plenty, merit and industry might find their fair rewards; and all men, Smith thought, might work together for the common weal.

Smith's frequent use of the word "commonwealth" is significant, for to his generation a commonwealth was a state in which all citizens—not merely a few—had an interest in the government. This is not to say that Smith was a democrat; he was not. He vaguely expressed the general dissatisfaction of his time with the political *status quo*. Men were dreaming of an ideal commonwealth, as they had not been dreaming since Plato in the fourth century B.C.

Thomas More's *Utopia* (1515-1516) and Francis Bacon's *New Atlantis* (*c.* 1617) suggest the political climate of opinion in the age of expansion to the New World. Such dreams of a new society were supported by the nostalgia of the primitivists, who looked back to a Golden Age in which men lived in amity, untroubled by such bickerings as those produced by the Reformation and the new national rivalries. Reformers in Switzerland, the Low Countries, and England were beginning to talk of church-states organized according to the Word of God and promising a speedy and complete reformation not merely of the church but of almost everything. In short, dreams of a "brave new world" were everywhere. So many were thinking of an ideal political organization that Shakespeare, in *The Tempest* (*c.* 1610), created an "honest old counsellor," Gonzalo, whose satirical remarks are worth recalling:

> I' th' commonwealth I would by contraries
>   Execute all things; for no kind of traffic
> Would I admit; no name of magistrate;
>   Letters should not be known; riches, poverty,
> And use of service, none; . . .
>   All things in common nature should produce
> Without sweat or endeavour; treason, felony,
>   Sword, pike, knife, gun, or need of any engine,
> Would I not have, all foison, all abundance,
>   To feed my innocent people. . . .
> I would with such perfection govern, sir,
>   T' excel the golden age.

Eight American colonies—Plymouth, Massachusetts Bay, Maryland, Rhode Island, New Haven, Carolina, Pennsylvania, and Georgia—give evidence that their founders were thinking in terms of an ideal commonwealth. In most of the colonies economic and religious reasons were also involved, but at that time these could scarcely be separated from political intentions. The communistic beginnings of the Pilgrims, the theocracy of Massachusetts Bay and New Haven, the principles of toleration of Rhode Island, John Locke's "ideal" constitution for Carolina, and Oglethorpe's notion of Georgia as a refuge for debtors—all had political implications. The most discussed experiment is that of Massachusetts Bay.

The full story of the transformation of the dream of an ideal commonwealth into the workaday institutions of British America, not ideal but on the whole far less aristocratic than those of Europe, is highly involved. We should remember, however, that colonial literature records at least three processes or developments: (1) the familiar pattern of transplantation and adaptation, in this case of English political and legal institutions; (2) the relative freedom from interference which was the result of unsettled problems of political authority in the mother country as well as of distance; and (3) the growth of democracy and local control, usually attributed to the influence of Separatism, which trained the humble to share in church government.

All are well illustrated in the picture which Winthrop gives us of the conflict between aristocracy and democracy in the Bay Colony. The aim of Winthrop and his associates was to found a theocracy, a state of which the head should be God and the fundamental law His word, the Bible. They wanted a commonwealth in which civil authority should contribute in every way possible to the welfare of the Puritan churches. As John Eliot said in *The Christian Commonwealth* (1659), "there is undoubtedly a form of Civil Government, instituted by God himself in the holy Scriptures." This conviction, rather than any statutory provision, accounts for the leadership of the clergy in the seventeenth century. The magistrates consulted the "elders," that is, the ministers, about every important question of policy. Yet Winthrop had too much of a lawyer's respect for statute and for precedent to throw overboard the common law and the example of England, and it was not long before Massachusetts had a bicameral legislature and a legal code drawn from experience rather than from the Bible (as some ministers thought it should be). Because the Bay Company founders had the foresight to bring their charter with them, their government survived the chaotic changes of the Civil War in England.

Bradford and Williams reveal in their writings much the same background. From Plymouth, the original Separatist community, we have the Mayflower Compact, earliest of American written constitutions and, like Winthrop's speech on liberty, a reflection of the covenant theology. In it the Pilgrims agreed to "solemnly & mutualy in ye presence of God, and one of another, covenant & combine our selves togeather into a civill body politick, . . . and by vertue hearofto enacte . . . such just & equall lawes . . . as shall be thought most meete & convenient for yᵉ general good of yᵉ Colonie, unto which we promise all due submission and obedience." The Compact has a well-deserved distinction. It was Separatism, too, which led Williams to assert his doctrine that the power of the civil state must not serve the purposes of a single church. The belief that government should rest upon the consent of the governed found practical application very early in American experience.

The conflict between the ideal of government by the few and the ideal of government by the many is reflected throughout American literature. In the colonial period it is best seen in the vast body of writings relating to the theocracy in Massachusetts. The belief of the ruling classes that things were not going well may be felt in Sewall's *Diary* and Mrs. Knight's *Journal* —both writers found the common people rowdy and obstreperous. William Byrd felt much the same way about the backcountry North Carolinians. Occasionally the common man found a defender, the most notable of whom was John Wise, a vigorous champion of Congregationalism and democracy.

The colonies did not achieve the ideal commonwealth, but they present a consistent pattern of the effort to serve the common interest of all citizens, according to the lights of the leaders. "Their Cheif Red Letter day," Mrs. Knight wrote of the inhabitants of Connecticut, "is St. Election, which is annually Observed according to Charter, to choose their Governor; a blessing they can never be thankfull enough for, as they will find, if ever it be their hard fortune to loose it."

Scientific Thought

Anyone reading colonial literature notices that the texts are often punctuated with "It pleased God" or "a special providence of God appeared." These recognitions of the immediate concern of the Deity for His universe and people, always conspicuous in the historical works and diaries of the Puritans, may be found almost as readily in the reports of such hard-bitten gentlemen of fortune as Captain John Smith.

In the writings of Bradford, Winthrop, Sewall, and Mather, however, such references are often felt to be superstitious by latter-day readers, who live in a world which takes for granted an uninterrupted order of nature. We need to reflect briefly, therefore, upon the place of science in the thought of colonial Americans. The age unquestionably accepted the providential order of nature, a world in which the Lord intervened not merely to mark the sparrow's fall but to reward and punish in accordance with His inscrutable ends. Commenting on Cotton Mather's pulpit exposition of the Copernican hypothesis, Sewall dismissed it with "I think it inconvenient to assert such Problems."

We must not conclude too easily, however, that the seventeenth and eighteenth centuries were antiscientific. After all, they produced Bacon, Boyle, Descartes, Newton, Laplace, and many other first-rate scientists, whose search for truth was emulated, although not of course with such brilliant success, on this side of the Atlantic. Benjamin Franklin was not the first American to study natural phenomena, although he remains the most famous early experimenter and scientific theorist.

Colonial literature shows both a persistent scientific curiosity and a strong economic motive for the investigation of nature. Hariot impressed the Indians with mathematical instruments, the lodestone, and spring clocks, and Smith claimed to have fascinated Opechankanough with a sign-language exposition of astronomy and geography. Both men, moreover, classified and described natural phenomena in accordance with the best methods at their command, as did a great many of their successors among the travel writers and promoters. Bradford, as likely as anyone to perceive the hand of God in all events, found room to "leave it to naturallists to judge" the value of his hypothesis of the cause of earthquakes, and did not find his acceptance of providence inconsistent with speculation on the natural causes of the immoralities at Plymouth in 1642. William Byrd's accounts of his travels in Virginia and North Carolina abound in botanical, zoological, and medicinal observations; Byrd, like Cotton Mather, was a Fellow of the Royal Society of London and a contributor to its *Philosophical Transactions*, the foremost British scientific journal.

The study of nature was not outlawed nor even greatly hampered by the prevalent sense of the nearness of God and the mysterious operations of His providence. Sewall's "inconvenient" was probably intended as an expression of the feeling that science and religion ought not to be mixed rather than as forthright opposition to scientific speculation. Actual mistrust of science is rarely encountered.

The Fine Arts

Architecture, painting, sculpture, and music, now often closely related to literature, were of relatively little interest to colonial writers. These arts are, however, a fascinating aspect of colonial culture as a whole, for they reveal its cosmopolitan origins, its inevitable pattern of transplantation and adaptation, and the centrality of religion in colonial society.

The most interesting of colonial arts is architecture, in which all three of the above elements are readily observable. The settlers learned little or nothing about house-building from the Indians and sometimes were far more uncomfortable in their first winters than they might have been had they looked about them. They had, of course, no architects and often no surplus of skilled artisans; so they built, in a sense, from memory. The more pretentious of the early New England houses imitated the half-timbered gables and overhangs of the late medieval English towns. New Amsterdam favored the small slanting dormer windows of the Dutch cottage. Along the Delaware the Swedes built log cabins—a type of structure which was to become the traditional makeshift shelter of the frontier. In the South the larger plantation houses reproduced the multiple-flued chimneys of the Jacobean period, and still further south Spanish St. Augustine introduced stuccoed walls and archways to North America. Many of these styles and a number of others, such as the Cape Cod cottage, are still being copied by conservative builders; American domestic architecture is a vast monument to our cosmopolitan origins.

Almost always, however, the transplanting of European styles had its difficulties. Chief among them was climate; England and indeed western Europe did not ordinarily have the extremes of heat and cold which characterize the eastern seaboard of North America. Materials varied, too; stone and brick were expensive and demanded a considerable degree of manual skill, but wood was plentiful, cheap, and fairly easily managed by amateur carpenters. Adaptation was therefore a necessity; to take a single example, the half-timbered and plaster house of England was almost immediately clapboarded in Massachusetts.

Finally, the dominance of religion in colonial culture is evident from the fact that the most conspicuous survivals of public architecture are the churches. In New England, especially, but to a degree in all the colonies, the church was the center of town and village life, its steeple the visible symbol of faith and aspiration.

Cosmopolitanism, adaptation, and the influence of religion are less obvious in the other arts, but there are traces of them everywhere. Painting was devoted almost exclusively to the portraiture of well-to-do families or much-loved clergymen. The really wealthy tended to have their portraits painted in England, but there were colonial "limners" from the middle of the seventeenth century who could turn out a portrait in an old-fashioned style or, if necessary, paint an inn sign or a coat of arms. One of the best known portraits is that of Samuel Sewall, by a native amateur. The first portrait engraving known to have been made in the British colonies was a woodcut of Richard Mather dating from 1670; the first line engraving on copper, a portrait of Increase Mather made about 1701; the first mezzotint for framing, a portrait of Cotton Mather made in 1727.

Sculpture was confined, prior to the nineteenth century, to the carving of angels and of death's-heads, hourglasses, scythes, and other symbols of mortality upon tombstones, and to carving in wood. The stroller in colonial graveyards comes away with a vivid sense of the fearlessness of death which accompanied profound faith, and visitors to museums containing ships' figureheads and other wood-carvings gain a first-hand impression of a seafaring, hand-skilled folk.

The first music consisted of the singing of psalms, in which the Puritans were deeply involved. The first book published in what is now th-

United States was the *Bay Psalm Book* (1640). With the Great Awakening
came a renewed interest in church music, with a concern for hymns and
choral singing. Even earlier, in Pennsylvania, the German pietistic sects had
introduced instrumental music into their services. Secular music was rare
before the Revolution, even in the South, and very little is known about
the music of the Negroes, beyond the fact that they brought both love of
that art and ancient melodic patterns from their native Africa.

The Circumstances of Literary Production

Because the state of printing and the book trade are closely related to the
health of literature, it is useful to recall something of the circumstances of
the author in the years before 1765. Of particular importance were his
close connection with Europe, his increasing opportunities as printing
presses multiplied and as periodicals were established, and the changing
nature of the reading public to which he addressed himself.

In the seventeenth century, as one would expect, most important
books written by or relating to the colonists were printed in Europe. The
colonial author wrote not so much for his immediate neighbors as for the
larger world of which he felt himself a part.

For a time, indeed, colonial printing presses were both few in number
and ill-equipped for book production. Printing was established in Massachusetts in 1639, but there were no presses in Maryland and Pennsylvania
until 1685, none in New York until 1693. By 1763, however, printing had
begun in all the thirteen original colonies. It was based upon the necessity
for copies of the laws and other public papers. Almanacs, school textbooks, legal and business manuals, newspapers, and other useful but
scarcely literary productions accounted for the bulk of the printed matter.
Lengthy books were expensive, and very few of them were printed. In
fact, to print a big book, such as Samuel Willard's *Compleat Body of
Divinity* (1726), required the cooperation and the type of several printers.
Sermons, pamphlets, and small volumes of poems were fairly common.
One common practice for those who admired a particular sermon was to
subsidize its printing and then distribute copies to appreciative friends, as
Samuel Sewall liked to do. Such distribution of a funeral sermon was
apparently regarded as a suitable memorial to the departed. Much material
was reprinted from English sources, sometimes, as in the case of textbooks,
over and over again. The quantity of theological literature was greatest in
New England, that of belles-lettres and political literature greatest in the
middle colonies, and that of legal literature greatest in the South. In general, the production of the colonial printers was heavily utilitarian. It was
not easy for colonial authors to rush into print. The book-buying public
was relatively small; the average edition of books and pamphlets in the
early part of the eighteenth century was probably between three and five

hundred copies. As a matter of fact, much of what we now read as colonial literature, including the works here mentioned from the pens of Bradford, Winthrop, Sewall, Mrs. Knight, Byrd, and Edward Taylor, was not even in print prior to the Revolution.

Newspapers, although almost nonexistent in the seventeenth century, constituted the staple work of colonial printers by 1750. *Publick Occurrences*, which appeared in Boston in 1690, was suppressed by the governor and council after a single issue, so that the *Boston News-Letter*, established in 1704, is usually regarded as the first American newspaper and the *Boston Gazette* (1719) as the second. Other important early newspapers include the *American Weekly Mercury* of Philadelphia (founded 1719), the *New-England Courant* of Boston (1721), the *New-York Gazette* (1727), the *Maryland Gazette* of Baltimore (1727), the *Pennsylvania Gazette* (1730)—Franklin's journal and the best of colonial newspapers— the *South Carolina Gazette* of Charleston (1732), and the *Virginia Gazette* of Williamsburg (1736). Most of these papers were of modest size at first, and it was many years before there was much space for literary material. Sometimes, as in the case of James Franklin's *New-England Courant*, a printing shop became the center of an informal club of literary-minded gentleman, and Benjamin Franklin used the *Pennsylvania Gezette* to promote the cooperative and political ends he had in mind. Gradually newspapers began to find room for letters to the editor, political articles, discussions of science and technology, even familiar essays and poetry. Magazines were even less significant than newspapers, although in 1741 both Benjamin Franklin and his chief rival, Andrew Bradford, issued short-lived magazines in imitation of London periodicals.

The colonial printer was often bookseller and postmaster as well. Many books were imported, and as time went on their distribution was accomplished by peddlers and auctions as well as by bookshop sales. A few of the more expensive books were sold by subscriptions obtained before they were actually printed. All in all, it seems certain that most readers, like most serious authors, looked abroad for their fulfillment of literary life.

American traditions about censorship and the control of the press had their beginnings in this time. There were incidents in which governors or councils brought action against printers, but probably the colonial press was as free or even freer than that of England. As early as 1696 a Massachusetts jury refused to convict a printer for publishing a work which had offended the officials and the clergy, and in 1735 the famous trial of Peter Zenger in New York enhanced the precedent that libel laws were not to be readily used to suppress freedom of speech and freedom of the press. By the beginning of the Revolutionary period the colonial press was in a position to play what from some points of view may be regarded as a decisive part in the drama of political action that would lead ultimately to the independence of the United States.

Literary Trends

Moses Coit Tyler, in his *History of American Literature, 1607-1765* (1878), divided colonial books into two groups: those written for English readers and those intended for the Americans themselves. In the former group Tyler found six types of material: (1) books whose purpose was to send home tidings of "welfare or ill fare"; (2) books written to appeal legal or financial matters to superior tribunals in England; (3) apologetics, designed to defend the colonies against injurious aspersions by their enemies; (4) writings particularly devoted to the Indians; (5) "descriptions of nature in America"; and (6) accounts of gradual innovations in politics, laws, creeds, and religious and domestic usages. Among the writings composed for the colonists themselves Tyler found four types of material: (1) sermons and religious treatises; (2) histories; (3) poems; and (4) prose with miscellaneous purposes.

Tyler's classification is still useful, but its fundamental division violates the conclusion of later scholars that the colonists seldom wrote merely for themselves. As we turn now to problems of literary forms and excellence, we can describe the bulk of colonial writings under seven heads. The principle of division is still content, but we shall consider particularly the structural problems which faced colonial writers, and their solutions in: (1) accounts of voyages; (2) promotion tracts; (3) sermons; (4) polemical tracts and treatises; (5) histories and biographies; (6) diaries and autobiographies; and (7) poems. A brief explanation of the absence of plays and novels in colonial America will conclude this introduction.

Accounts of Voyages

Of the literary types common in the colonies, the simplest in structure was the account of a voyage, from which developed the later literature of travel. At first such accounts were plain narratives written by plain and barely literate men. The organization was chronological, presenting a sequence of events as recorded in the writer's memory, journal, or whatever notes he had thought worth making. He could expand whenever his interests or those of his prospective readers seemed to make expansion desirable. The letter in which Columbus reported upon his first voyage is a good example of the type; another is John Brereton's *Briefe and True*

Relation of the Discouerie of the North Part of Virginia (1602), the earliest English account of the New England coast. The type dominates the great collections of voyages which were edited by Richard Hakluyt, Samuel Purchas, and John Harris (*Collection of Voyages and Travels*, 1705). Although written to provide information, the account of a voyage was seldom impersonal, and it sometimes achieved a sharpness of effect and a charm as great as if written by a literary artist.

Both Mrs. Knight's *Journal* and Byrd's "Progress to the Mines" adapt the type to a land journey with highly readable results. Byrd's versions of the *History of the Dividing Line* show how readily information and humor could be inserted into the elastic structure of the travel narrative.

Travel books constitute one of the largest classes of American literature. Although such books are closely related to the economic motives for colonization and westward migration, they are also valuable for the light they throw upon social life and customs. Often, moreover, they reveal interesting and lively personalities, some of them with a sense of humor and a talent for entertainment.

Promotion Tracts

The writer of a promotion tract almost invariably faced various organizational difficulties. To generalize attractively about the resources of the region he was describing required persuasive division of material with which he was not always intimately acquainted. Furthermore, he could make only limited use of narrative, and he needed to appear judicious and relatively objective. Promotion tracts therefore vary considerably in structure, according to the individual solutions of these problems.

Thomas Hariot wisely followed his main interest—economic resources —in his account of Virginia. First he described commodities already found or raised in Virginia in quantities sufficient to be marketable: useful plants, minerals, and furs. He then listed commodities known to be plentiful enough to sustain life: grains, vegetables, fruits, game animals, fowl, and fish. A third section listed miscellaneous commodities. His account of the Indians followed, and the whole was concluded by a few pages of persuasion.

John Smith's *Description of New England* and *Map of Virginia* employed a far commoner structure. They both began with the general geographical features and then described the climate, winds, soils, rivers, settled places, plants, animals, birds, fish, minerals, and Indians. The *Map* was the more carefully organized; in his *Description* Smith himself realized that his enthusiasm had carried him away, and at one point he asks his readers to bear with him, adding that he is not "sufficiently yet acquainted in those parts, to write fully the estate of the Sea, the Ayre, the Land, the

Fruites, the Rocks, the People, the Gouernment, Religion, Territories and Limitations, Friends and Foes: but as I gathered from the niggardly relations in a broken language to my understanding, during the time I ranged those Countries." Smith, one may note, had a list of topics arranged in an order proceeding from the general to the particular. This systematic approach he probably derived from the geographical literature of his day, which in turn reflects the almost invariable approach of the medieval schoolmen to the study of the external world.

Scientific education was based on the works of Aristotle, which were studied according to a settled system. A student began with the *Organon* and the *Physica*, which deal with logic and the general properties of natural bodies; next he examined the *De Caelo*, a description of the heavens; after that he took up the *De Generatione et Corruptione*, which treats the four elements—earth, water, air, and fire—and their various combinations and interactions; he then looked at the *Meteorologica*, which describes the various processes of change in the elements, and at various discussions of "perfectly mixed" and "imperfectly mixed" bodies of the inanimate kind (stones, metals, and minerals); and finally he came to the *De Anima* and the *Historia Animalium*, descriptions of animate bodies (plants and animals). Thus equipped, he could undertake the study of man.

Many promotion tracts besides Smith's were based upon this tradition, for it was the topical arrangement most familiar to educated men. Francis Higginson's *New England's Plantation* begins with the following statement: "And because the life and wel-fare of euerie Creature here below, and the commodiousnesse of the Countrey whereas such Creatures liue, doth by the most wise ordering of Gods prouidence, depend next vnto himselfe, vpon the temperature and disposition of the foure Elements, Earth, Water, Aire, and Fire. . . . Therefore I will indeauour to shew you what *New England* is by the consideration of these apart, and truly endeauour by Gods helpe to report nothing but the naked truth." Wood's *New England's Prospect* is similarly Aristotelian, in that it proceeds from the general to the particular. Morton's *New English Canaan* is less systematic.

Although the thoughtful reader will discover many minor variations, together with some amusing decisions about order and treatment, the promotion tracts are remarkably consistent in general outline. They are very numerous and are closely related to the "progress reports" sent back to those at home by actual settlers. Reports of progress contain a somewhat larger proportion of narrative, but do not differ greatly otherwise.

Sermons

The sermon was the most highly developed literary type in colonial literature, and a list of the sermons available in print and in manuscript would run literally into the thousands. Men and women listened to sermons every Sunday; often they went to lecture sermons during the week; they heard sermons on many public occasions—elections, thanksgiving and fast days, military training, funerals. The more serious kept diaries or notebooks, recording the texts and even the heads of the discourses to which they listened. Men and women who lived in an age when the pulpit was the center of intellectual life knew a good sermon when they heard one.

Only a few of the many sermons by the American Puritans have been reprinted. They are most readily available in a microcard series prepared by the American Antiquarian Society. A few early sermons have been reprinted in collected editions or in facsimile, and the interested student can find examples of the preaching of John Cotton, Roger Williams, Thomas Hooker, and Thomas Shepard. Not until we reach the early eighteenth century, however, do we find, in Jonathan Edwards, a preacher whose works are easily located.

The Puritan sermon was most often organized according to a set pattern. A Scriptural text was chosen, doctrines were derived from it, reasons given for these doctrines, and uses for the doctrines suggested. This logical framework was lightened by homely illustrations, questions and answers, bursts of eloquence, and by the frequent citation of parallel texts from the Bible.

Today's readers may find the "firstlys," "secondlys," etc., wooden and pedantic, but they should remember that earnest churchgoers wanted to know where they were, so that during the week they could discuss within the family the soundness of their minister's third "use." From Cotton to Edwards the pattern varied little in its larger outlines.

Some Puritan sermons reflect the system of logic developed by a sixteenth-century French humanist, Petrus Ramus, or Pierre de la Ramée. Ramus saw the world in terms of pairs or opposites, and he may well be responsible for the fondness for similitudes and antitheses which is evident in the sermons, even in those of Edwards.

The sermons raise questions, moreover, about prose style. The Puritans tended to favor the "plain" style, but some of them were fond of embellishing their discourses with tags of Latin, Greek, or even Hebrew, or with allusions to secular literature. Among the Americans, Cotton Mather was probably the most given to ornament. He seems to have had the idea that part of the preacher's job was to educate his unlettered congregation. A comparison of Thomas Shepard and Jonathan Edwards reveals a sharp contrast between an almost brusque vigor and a polished smooth-flowing eloquence. One man is clearly of the Renaissance, the other a child of the Enlightenment.

Their purpose, however, was the same: to persuade men to consider honestly the state of their souls. The minister was to preach the gospel of Jesus Christ, to awaken his hearers to the supreme importance of faith and generation and to the urgent necessity of assuming an active part in the eternal warfare within man's soul between good and evil, the spirit and the flesh, God and the Devil. The sermon was the essence of Protestantism, more important than any theological dogma or form of worship, perhaps even more important than the sacraments (although the Lord's Supper was of enormous significance to such a man as Edward Taylor). Among the Calvinists, the sermon was the chief means of preserving believers from fatalistic acceptance of their destiny. That most men were foreordained to sin and damnation and that there was nothing the individual could do about it: these were doctrines which might easily have led to despair or indifference. The sermons, however, were based upon the even more powerful doctrines that divine grace did come to some men, and that to those who received it grace was a constant growth, an increasing understanding of perfection, an endless enlarging of one's capacity to deal with doubt and sin and temptation. Hence the soul searching of the Puritans, the esteem and affection for "soul-ravishing" preachers like Shepard, the vast respect for the sublime certainty with which Edwards testified to the "spiritual Light" which is "the dawning of the Light of Glory in the Heart." Puritans found sermons thrilling because sermons guided the analyzing and strengthening of their inner life.

The sermon was both an appeal to man's imperfect reason and a stirring of his emotion, both an intellectual experience and a glimpse of magnificent poetic vistas, opened by God's promise to the regenerate soul. Whenever and wherever religion was a vital and absorbing concern it called forth some of the best available literary talent. The sermon remains, moreover, the key to the religious life of the colonial era.

Beginning of Controversial Writing

Theological and political discussion also produced an extensive literature of controversy. Decisions had to be made about church government, institutional organization, governmental policy, and theological positions, and there were often wide divergences of opinion. Men with convictions expressed them in numerous tracts and treatises, such as Roger Williams' *Bloudy Tenent*, Cotton Mather's *Manuductio ad Ministerium*, John Wise's *Vindication*, Jonathan Edwards' *Freedom of Will*, and Charles Chauncy's *Seasonable Thoughts*. These, and other works like them, vary widely in their structure, which ordinarily grew directly out of the controversial issues with which they dealt.

Williams' use of the dialogue is not uncommon, and has the virtue of lending some drama to the issues, but topical organization is probably more usual. Polemical tracts were frequently a point-by-point refutation of a preceding pamphlet or treatise. Sometimes they were constructed as a series of queries, to which the author gave his well-considered answers. The fiction of a "letter" to a friend was used many times. To generalize about the literary form of the literature of controversy is, therefore, extremely difficult. Its most striking difference from similar material of today is perhaps that little of it appeared in magazines. The development of periodicals as a forum for discussion came in a later period.

The volume and variety of tracts and treatises can best be suggested by listing a few of the better-known titles, in addition to those by Williams, Eliot, Cotton Mather, Wise, Edwards, and Franklin which have already been mentioned. Among the books which still find readers are the following: Richard Mather's *Church Government and Church Covenant* (1643); John Cotton's *Way of the Churches of Christ in New-England* (1645); Nathaniel Ward's *Simple Cobler of Aggawam in America* (1647); Thomas Hooker's *Survey of the Summe of Church Discipline* (1648); Increase Mather's *Cases of Conscience concerning Evil Spirits Personating Men* (1693); Samuel Sewall's *Selling of Joseph* (1700); Cotton Mather's *Essays to Do Good* (as *Bonifacius*, 1710) and *Christian Philosopher* (1721); Franklin's *Modest Inquiry into the Nature and Necessity of a Paper Currency* (1729) and *Proposals Relating to the Education of Youth in Pensilvania* (1749); Jared Eliot's *Essay on Field Husbandry in New England* (Part I, 1748); John Woolman's *Some Considerations on the Keeping of Negroes* (Part I, 1753); James Otis' *Vindication of the Conduct of the House of Representatives of Massachusetts* (1762) and *Rights of British Colonies Asserted and Proved* (1764). Religion, women's fashions, social reform, science, education, agriculture, politics—all are represented, and the list could easily be extended. This type of literature had its models in Europe, but its content is almost always peculiarly American. It is the basis of the tradition of free discussion and a free press and is perhaps, to the intellectual historian, the most significant part of colonial writing.

Histories and Biographies

History and biography are conspicuous in colonial literature because the settlers wanted, for several reasons, to preserve a record of what happened in the New World. In its simplest form such writing was annalistic, a simple statement of historical and biographical fact. The journals of Bradford and Winthrop and Nathaniel Morton's *New-England's Memoriall* (1669) follow the natural chronological order and set down the main facts of each year. This bare narration seldom satisfied the colonial writer of history, however; he conceived it his duty to interpret events, usually in terms of speculation about God's intentions.

Mixed motives appear in most colonial histories and biographies. John Smith's *The Generall Historie of Virginia* (1624) was both a justification of his own actions and a defense of the somewhat unpopular movement for colonization. Smith also had a remarkably modern grasp of the connection between history and geography. William Bradford's *The History of Plymouth Plantation* (1620-1647) was written for the children and grandchildren of the Pilgrims, that they might understand and perpetuate the piety of the little group of founders whose struggles had merited, so Bradford thought, the special favor of God. John Winthrop's *The History of New England* (1630-1649), strongly flavored with the same providential view of events as Bradford's book, had in it also both an element of self-justification and a lawyer's respect for exact knowledge of precedents and experiments in institutional organization. Cotton Mather's sixty-odd biographies in *Magnalia Christi Americana* show a tendency to defend the "New England Way," as well as to emulate the didactic purpose of Bradford. William Byrd's two works, *The Secret History* (1728) and *The History of the Dividing Line* (1728), and Samuel Peters' *General History of Connecticut* (1781) had axes to grind as well as information to convey.

Much colonial historical writing was tinged with the belief in a providential order of nature, and hence took on a distinctly theological quality. If events were to be interpreted as the working out of the divine plan, which man could never know in its entirety, a monstrous birth might be quite as instructive as a victory in battle or a momentous political or religious compromise. To the modern reader, Winthrop seems to jump easily from affairs of great moment to the most trivial events, and to be scarcely aware of the operation of economic, political, and social forces upon a changing society. He was more interested in looking for moral meanings in events. The same attitude characterizes most seventeenth-century histories, appearing most vividly in Edward Johnson's *The Wonder-Working Providence of Sion's Saviour in New England* (1654) and reaching its culmination in Cotton Mather's *Magnalia Christi Americana* (1702). For the providential theory the colonists had the example of the Book of Kings, the Roman historian Livy, and many ecclesiastical annalists from the time of St. Augustine.

More rationalistic tendencies may also be observed in colonial historiography. We have already noted Bradford's analysis of the possible causes for an outbreak of immorality in 1642. Judicious and objective methods were foreshadowed in Thomas Prince's *Chronological History of New England in the Form of Annals* (2 vols., 1736, 1755), in William Stith's *History of the First Discovery of Virginia* (1747), and most notably in Thomas Hutchinson's *History of the Province of Massachusetts Bay* (3 vols., 1764, 1767, 1828). These works likewise had European models, although Hutchinson's was the only one to show traces of the regard for institutional development which made Voltaire's *Age of Louis XIV* (1751) a landmark.

Diaries and Autobiographies

An amazing number of colonists kept diaries or wrote autobiographies. Their purpose was sometimes practical—the desire to have a record of the weather, the planting and harvesting of crops, business transactions, and personal affairs. More often, perhaps, and almost always in the case of the autobiographies, the aim was fundamentally religious. Earnest churchgoers wished to study the state of their souls, and one of the best possible methods was to preserve a day-by-day or systematic account of temptations, struggles, and meditations.

The best example of a Puritan diary is that kept between February 1653, and May 1657, by Michael Wigglesworth, not printed until 1951. Its agonizing concern for the shortcomings of its author (and of his neighbors!) is pathological but probably typical. Cotton Mather's diary, better known and much longer, gives the impression of being dressed up for possible publication. In the realm of autobiography, Jonathan Edwards' "Personal Narrative" is probably outstanding for its portrayal of a man absorbed in the problem of his relation to God. The autobiography and "Meditations and Spiritual Experience" of Thomas Shepard are earlier efforts in this genre. There are innumerable "testimonies" or spiritual autobiographies, especially among the Quakers, most of which concentrate on the experience of conversion. Two of the greatest of early American books—John Woolman's *Journal* (1774) and Benjamin Franklin's *Autobiography* (1771, 1784, 1790)—are in the direct line of descent from the simpler self-analyses. The type has been studied recently by Daniel G. Shea, Jr. (*Spiritual Autobiography in Early America*, 1968).

Those diaries which are most treasured by later generations are the ones in which soul-searching is leavened by an interest in temporal affairs. Winthrop's journal and the travel journal of Mrs. Knight have this interest, but the two chief diaries are those by Samuel Sewall and William Byrd. Both preserve for us the customs, manners, and personalities of relatively worldly people. We learn from them of the food, the drink, the social life, the household appointments, the gardens, the crimes, the births, marriages, and deaths—the external life, in short, of seventeenth- and eighteenth-century Americans.

Sewall's diary is the better of the two, even though it does not compare with the great English diaries of John Evelyn and Samuel Pepys, written at about the same time. Sewall's world was more circumscribed than theirs. Like all good diarists, however, Sewall has the virtue of revealing himself as a human being, beset by frailties and inadequacies and little vanities.

Byrd kept his diary in shorthand; and except for those portions of it which he chose to expand into travel accounts or histories of the running of the Dividing Line, it has been only recently available. Its three volumes cover the years 1709-1712 (published 1941), 1717-1721 (1958), and 1739-1741 (1942). Although the entries are sometimes repetitious and trivial, they provide the most intimate acquaintance we now have with a leading member of the Virginia oligarchy, which was closely allied in its ambitions with the landed gentry of England. Sewall went to London as a tourist, but for Byrd, London was a second home.

Poems

American poetry prior to 1765 is, when compared to that of England in the same period, small in quantity and, with few exceptions, inferior in quality. No colonial poet, with the possible exception of Edward Taylor, reached the level of George Herbert or Robert Herrick, and none remotely approached the artistic achievement of Donne, Milton, Dryden, or Pope.

Nevertheless, the attitude toward early American verse has become much less apologetic in the last thirty years, thanks to the discovery of Taylor by Thomas H. Johnson (ed., *The Poetical Works of Edward Taylor*, 1939), the investigation of Taylor's predecessors and contemporaries by Harold S. Jantz (*The First Century of New England Verse*, 1943), and the work of Harrison T. Meserole *(Seventeenth-Century American Poetry*, 1968). Poetry which nineteenth-century critics found either quaint or pedantic is now taken seriously and its tight-packed imagery admired. The style which Moses Coit Tyler spoke of as "fantastic perversion" is now labeled "Baroque" and studied with respect.

Seventeenth-century American verse can be divided roughly into two categories: that written to be memorized, and that written to dignify or embellish important occasions. The former is the best known and more naïve.

Puritan children apparently memorized maxims and stories in verse from the earliest days of the settlement. Among the pieces available for this purpose were rhymed accounts of English Protestant history by the Rev. John Wilson (see *Handkerchiefs from Paul*, ed. K. B. Murdock, 1927) and *The Day of Doom* (1662), the Rev. Michael Wigglesworth's famous summary of Calvinistic theology. Even the compilers of the *Bay Psalm Book* (1640), although their main purpose was to translate the Hebrew with the greatest possible exactness, chose to put the psalms to be sung in New England churches in English meter, that is to say in the ballad stanza of folk poetry:

> The Lord to mee a shepheard is,
>   want therefore shall not I.
> Hee in the folds of tender-grasse,
>   doth cause mee downe to lie.

> To waters calme me gently leads
>   Restore my soule doth hee:
> he doth in paths of righteousnes:
>   for his names sake leade mee.

The use of the ballad stanza reveals the strength of the popular tradition in the face of novel conditions—in this instance the Puritan respect for the Hebrew text of the Psalms. Poetry as art suffered, but the meter of "Barbara Allan" was the one most easily remembered. Also intended as aids to memorization, although essentially didactic in the same way as colonial historical writing, are the numerous historical poems of the period. Bradford himself tried his hand at this type of writing, but the best known examples are Benjamin Tompson's narratives of King Philip's War: *New Englands Crisis* (1676) and *New-Englands Tears for Her Present Miseries* (1676). Both display the providential theory of history in an elaborate form.

Many important events were commemorated in poetry (see *American Broadside Verse*, ed. Ola Elizabeth Winslow, 1930), but the one thing that most commonly called for the dignifying presence of verse was the death of a clergyman or other public figure. The anagrams and elegies thus evoked have been the butt of considerable humor, including Benjamin Franklin's recipe for the would-be elegist:

> For the subject of your Elegy, Take one of your Neighbors who has lately departed this Life; it is no great matter of what Age the Party dy'd, but it will be best if he went away suddenly, being *Kill'd, Drown'd*, or *Frose to Death*.
>
>   Having chose the Person, take all his Virtues, Excellencies, &c. and if he have not enough, you may borrow some to make up a sufficient Quantity. To these add his last Words, dying Expressions, &c. if they are to be had; mix all these together, and be sure you strain them well. Then season all with a Handful or two of Melancholly Expressions, such as, *Dreadful, Deadly, cruel cold Death, unhappy Fate, weeping Eyes*, &c. . . . let them Ferment for the Space of a Fortnight, and by that Time they will be incorporated into a Body, which take out, and having prepared a sufficient Quantity of double Rhimes, such as *Power, Flower; Quiver, Shiver; Grieve us, Leave us; tell you, excel you; Expeditions, Physicians; Fatigue him, Intrigue him;* &c. you must spread all upon Paper, and if you can procure a Scrap of Latin to put at the End, it will garnish it mightily; then having affixed your Name at the Bottom, with a *Moestus Composuit*, you will have an Excellent Elegy.

The quality of the Puritan funeral elegy no doubt deteriorated. In the early seventeenth century, however, it was, as Jantz has demonstrated, a

sophisticated form. A number of the elegists began with an anagram of
their subject's name (John Fiske, for example, took John Cotton [Iohn
Kotton] and got "O, Honie knott"), then used this anagram as a basic
image around which the elegy developed. The result was the kind of tight-
packed imagery which is so much admired in the poems of Edward Taylor.
Fiske's poem includes such passages as this:

> Hee who the knotts of Truth, of Mysteries
> sacred, most cleerely did ope' fore our eyes
> even hee who such a one, is ceas'd to bee
> 'twixt whose life, death, the most sweete harmony
> Knotts we doe meet with many a cue daily
> which crabbed anggry tough unpleasing bee
> but we as in a honi-comb a knott
> of Hony sweete, here had such sweetenes Gott
> the knotts and knobbs that on the Trees doe grow
> the bitterest excressences we know.

The mnemonic verses and the elegies loom large in the seventeenth
century, but they are not, of course, the whole story. Poets Anne Bradstreet and Edward Taylor range fairly widely for their subject matter and,
although they imitated French and English religious poets—the English
Spenserians, Du Bartas, Donne, Herbert, Quarles, and Richard Crashaw—
succeeded in conveying the intensity of their individual experience and
tell us much of the inner life of American Puritanism.

In the eighteenth century, American verse took on a more classical
orientation, as the number of colleges increased and educated gentlemen
followed the fashions set by Dryden and Pope. Latin verses continued to
be composed, and translations constituted a common exercise. The "high-
brow" versemaking reached its height in *Pietas et Gratulatio* (1761).
Harvard College's tribute to the new king, George III, it contained three
poems in Greek, sixteen in Latin, and twelve in English. Individuals trained
in the classics were also interested in the work of the English Neoclassical
school, and there were many colonial poems in the manner of the satires
of Dryden and Pope, the mock-heroics of Butler, and the philosophical
pieces of Thomson, Young, and Pomfret. These are often of interest for
their content, although it is disconcerting to find colonial poets expressing
boredom with court and city life, when, as someone said, five minutes'
walking would have taken any one of them into a cow pasture. We may
safely leave the works of Mather Byles, John Adams (the clergyman, not
the statesman), George Webb, William Livingston, the younger Thomas
Godfrey, Nathaniel Evans, Joseph Green, and other "wits" to the special-
ist, remembering, however, that they were the literati of their day and that
they cherished the tradition of belles-lettres in a world frequently too busy
for art.

Plays and Novels

Fiction and drama, which bulk large in later American literature, were
almost nonexistent in the colonial period. Both were distrusted by serious-
minded persons, in England as well as in America, although it is not just
to ascribe their absence entirely to Puritan influence. A theater requires
considerable capital and a public in the habit of playgoing, neither of
which is often to be found except in the largest centers of population. As
a class, moreover, actors were long mistrusted by civic authorities, as the
history of the London theater shows. These factors alone would be enough
to account for the antagonism to stage plays which appears in colonial laws
forbidding their public performance. Virginia was one of the few colonies
without such legislation, but the earliest mention of a play performed in the
colonies suggests some prejudice even there. In 1665 three citizens of
Accomac County were called upon to appear in costume and tell what
they said in *Ye Bare and Ye Cubb*. They were discharged and their accuser
forced to pay the court charges.

The Puritans, however, unquestionably delayed the development of an
American drama. Their influence had closed the theaters in England for
eighteen years, and many colonists shared the resentment of English
Puritans for the ridicule of Puritanism in Elizabethan drama. Remembered
also was the association of the theater with the immoralities of king and
court and the vigorous attack on the theater by the church fathers of the
latter days of the Roman empire. To the famous English attacks on the
theater by Stubbs (1583), Prynne (1632), and Collier (1698) there was
at least one American parallel: Increase Mather's *Testimony against Several
Prophane and Superstitious Customs, Now Practised by Some in New
England* (1687).

There was no effort to keep printed plays out of the college libraries,
and as time went on there seems to have been sporadic interest in them in
academic halls. There is some evidence that students at Harvard were
thinking of histrionic things in the 1690's—a doubtful tradition that
Benjamin Colman, later a prominent liberal clergyman, wrote a Latin play
entitled *Gustavus Vasa* in 1690, and an allusion to examining "several of
the Scholars about the Comedy" in Increase Mather's diary for 1698.
The students at William and Mary offered a "pastoral colloquy" before the
governor in 1702, and later in the eighteenth century undergraduates at
Philadelphia, Princeton, New Haven, and Cambridge were frequently
experimenting with dialogues and dramatic exercises. *The Prince of
Parthia*, by the younger Thomas Godfrey, one of the literary group centering in the College of Philadelphia, was written in 1759, published in 1765,
and actually produced on a professional stage in 1767. Imitative of the
English heroic drama, it was a natural outgrowth of the discovery of belles-
lettres by undergraduates and their friends.

New tastes and attitudes were accepted by the general public only gradually, despite the efforts of entranced amateurs, the visits of professional actors, and the changing tone of English drama. The first play to be printed was *Antroboros* (1714), a political satire published anonymously by Robert Hunter, governor of New York. Williamsburg built a theater in 1716, but there is no evidence that it was used until twenty years later. New York probably was entertained by a group of professional actors in 1732, and Charleston had a brief "season" in 1735. A company which performed Addison's *Cato* in Philadelphia in 1742 was arrested and forbidden to appear again. Going to New York, the company performed *Richard III*, *The Beggar's Opera*, and other plays in 1750. An amateur performance scandalized conservative Boston in that same year, although George Lillo's bourgeois tragedy, *George Barnwell* (1731), had been reprinted in *The New-England Weekly Journal* within a year after its appearance in London. American theatrical history is usually said to have begun in 1752, with the arrival of Lewis Hallam's "American Company," which had a continuous history of performance until 1774, when the Continental Congress forbade theatrical performances "for the duration." The American Company played at Williamsburg, New York, Philadelphia, Annapolis, Newport, Providence, Charleston, and several towns in Virginia, and succeeded (sometimes by such stratagems as offering *Othello* as a series of "Moral Dialogues") in familiarizing the more venturesome colonists with the plays of Shakespeare, Marlowe, Dryden, Congreve, Farquhar, Addison, Steele, Cibber, Ambrose Philips, and others. But there was no native drama.

Nor did colonial Americans produce either novels or novel-like narratives comparable to those of Bunyan, Defoe, and Swift. This is less surprising than that there should have been no drama, for the novel as a form had by no means reached its full maturity. The seriousness of the reading public left little time for long romances, although a good many of them appear on colonial book lists, and the pleasure in swift-moving narrative was partly provided for by the accounts of voyages and travels, the somewhat lurid accounts of captivity among the Indians, and other factual material such as reports of the experiences and final hours of pirates and murderers and the descriptions of remarkable providences and witchcrafts. Many works of fiction which supposedly portrayed life must have seemed dull in comparison to more direct reporting. The prevalent attitude toward fiction was probably that of Cotton Mather in *Manuductio ad Ministerium*, where he advises divinity students to enjoy the recreation of poetry but not to be so set upon it

as to be always poring on the *Passionate* and *Measured* Pages. Let not what should be *Sauce* rather than Food for you, Engross all your Application. . . . Indeed, not merely for the *Impurities* which they convey, but also on some other Accounts, the *Powers of Darkness* have a *Library* among us, whereof the *Poets* have been the most *Numerous* as well as the most *Venemous* Authors. Most of the modern *Plays*, as well as the *Romances* and *Novels*, and *Fictions*, which are a sort of *Poems*, do belong to the Catalogue of this cursed Library.

T.H.

Chronological Table of
LITERATURE AND HISTORY

1492 Columbus, discovering islands in the western ocean, believed he had reached part of Asia

1497 Cabot touched the North American coast, laying the foundation for English territorial claims in the New World

1507 ● Martin Waldseemüller's *Cosmographiae Introductio,* German treatise on geography, wherein the newly discovered western hemisphere was named "America" in honor of Amerigo Vespucci, Italian navigator

1535 ● The Bible first fully translated into English, by Miles Coverdale

1536 ● Calvin's *Institutes of the Christian Religion*

1539 De Soto landed in Florida and marched west toward Mexico; before his death in 1542 he had reached the Mississippi and explored as far north, perhaps, as what is now Kentucky

1540 Coronado began an expedition into what is now New Mexico, Arizona, and the Great Plains

1549 ● First *Book of Common Prayer* (revisions in 1552, 1559, 1604, 1662), criticized by those who wished to rid the English Church of "popish" ritual

Uniform church service prescribed in England

1562 John Hawkins made the first of three privateering voyages to the West Indies, bringing England into direct conflict with Spain for New World riches

1572 St. Bartholomew's Day Massacre of about 10,000 Huguenots strengthened anti-Catholic feeling in England

1577 Francis Drake began a voyage taking him through the Straits of Magellan, along the western coast of the Americas (where he took possession of New Albion—present-day California and Oregon—in the name of Queen Elizabeth), and back to England (1580) by way of Java and the Cape of Good Hope

1578 Charter for exclusive colonization in North America granted by the Queen to
Sir Humphrey Gilbert and associates, among them Gilbert's half brother,
Walter Raleigh

1582 ● Richard Hakluyt's *Divers Voyages*

1584 Charter granted to Raleigh (Gilbert's ventures having failed) guaranteeing to
colonists in North America the political rights of Englishmen

1585 Raleigh sent seven ships to America, landing 107 men on Roanoke Island

1586 Raleigh's colony returned to England by Drake's ships when needed supplies
failed to arrive on schedule · Decision that Chesapeake Bay area would be
better for colonization than Roanoke, where the Indians were hostile

1587 120 persons left on Roanoke through the treachery of a ship captain; when
a supply expedition finally arrived in 1590, this "lost colony" had vanished,
leaving no trace except the word "Croatan" carved on a tree

1588 ● Hariot's *Briefe and True Report of the New Found Land of Virginia*

Destruction of the Spanish Armada in the English Channel, marking
emergence of England as the chief sea power in the world

1602 The first of a series of expeditions (made during the years 1602-1605 under
Captains Gosnold, Pring, and Waymouth) to the coast between present-day
Maine and Martha's Vineyard; these explorations revived English interest in
North America

1603 ● Shakespeare's *Hamlet* printed

Death of Elizabeth (reigned 1558-1603); accession of James I · Champlain
made his first voyage to New France, exploring the St. Lawrence River

1606 Charters granted to two colonizing groups, the London and Plymouth
Companies, who divided the territory of Virginia between them

1607 Jamestown, first permanent English settlement in North America, founded by
the London Company

1608 ● John Smith's *True Relation*

Quebec founded by Champlain · Migration of the Scrooby congregation of
Separatists to Holland, the starting-point of William Bradford's *History of
Plymouth Plantation*

1609 Henry Hudson discovered the river now bearing his name

1611 ● The *King James Version* of the Bible

1612 ● Smith's *Map of Virginia*

1614 Northern part of Virginia explored by Smith for the Plymouth Company
and named by him "New England" · Colony established by the Dutch at the
mouth of the Hudson

1616 ● Smith's *Description of New England*

1619 First representative assembly convened in Virginia · First Negro slaves imported

1620 ● *Mayflower Compact* signed in Cape Cod Bay, 11 November

Charter granted by the London or Virginia Company to English capitalists, on behalf of the Separatists in Holland, for a settlement somewhere south of the Hudson · The *Mayflower,* driven off her course by storms, landed the Pilgrims on the shore of Massachusetts Bay

1621 Patent for the Pilgrims' settlement obtained from the Council for New England, successor to the Plymouth Company

1622 ● *Mourt's Relation,* by William Bradford and Edward Winslow, first authentic description of the Pilgrim settlement at Plymouth

1624 ● Smith's *Generall Historie* · Winslow's *Good News from New England*

Annulment of the Virginia charter, making that settlement the first royal colony

1627 Charter granted to the Massachusetts Bay Company · Thomas Morton arrested for his "scandalous" revelry at Merry Mount, deported by the authorities of the Plymouth Colony

1630 ● Smith's *True Travels* · Francis Higginson's *New England's Plantation*

"Great Migration" of the Puritans of the Massachusetts Bay Company, led by Governor John Winthrop, which by 1640 brought more than 20,000 persons to New England

1634 ● William Wood's *New England's Prospect*

Maryland settled

1636 Roger Williams founded Providence in Rhode Island · Harvard College founded (classes begun in 1638)

1637 ● Thomas Morton's *New English Canaan*

1640 ● *Whole Booke of Psalmes,* better known as the *Bay Psalm Book*

1641 ● Thomas Shepard's *Sincere Convert* · Massachusetts *Body of Liberties*

1642 Civil War in England precipitated by attempt of Charles I to impeach and imprison five members of the House of Commons

1644 ● Williams' *Bloudy Tenent of Persecution for the Cause of Conscience*

1649 Charles I tried and executed (reigned 1625-1649); Charles II crowned in exile in 1651 · England declared a commonwealth and the House of Lords abolished

1650 ● Anne Bradstreet's *Tenth Muse Lately Sprung Up in America*

1651 Parliament passed the first Navigation Act, designed to undermine the commercial supremacy of the Dutch; it provided that no goods should be imported from Asia, Africa, or America, except in English vessels; with supplementary acts in 1660 and 1663 it became one of the chief sources of friction between the American colonies and the British administration

1660 The Restoration brought Charles II to the English throne

1662 ● Michael Wigglesworth's *Day of Doom*

Act of Uniformity purged the Church of England of dissenting clergymen and sent another wave of ministers to America

1664 New Netherlands taken by the English

1667 Treaty of Breda, after the Second Anglo-Dutch War, gave all Dutch colonies in America to England and Acadia (later Nova Scotia) to France

1668 William Penn became a Quaker · Joliet explored the Great Lakes · La Salle explored the Ohio country, perhaps reaching the Mississippi

1674 ● Samuel Sewall's *Diary* begun

1675 Beginning of King Philip's War (1675-1676), marked by numerous massacres and the burning of frontier villages

1676 ● Benjamin Tompson's *New Englands Crisis,* a series of poems on the providential delivery of New England from the threat of King Philip · Increase Mather's *Brief History of the Warr with the Indians*

Bacon's Rebellion, an early instance of conflict between a royal governor (William Berkeley of Virginia) and those whom he governed

1678 "Popish Plot" to oust Charles II and place James, Duke of York, an avowed Catholic, on the throne; some thirty-five persons executed before it was discovered that the evidence was fabricated

1681 ● Penn's *Some Account of the Province of Pensilvania in America*

Charter obtained by William Penn for a new colony on the Delaware · Massachusetts called upon to surrender its charter

1685 Death of Charles II (reigned 1660-1685); accession of James II

1688 Connecticut and Rhode Island charters revoked · James II permitted to escape to France—the so-called "Glorious Revolution"

1689 ● Cotton Mather's *Memorable Providences relating to Witchcrafts and Possessions* · John Locke's *Treatise of Civil Government,* setting forth the contract theory of government which was to influence American political philosophy

Deposition of James II (reigned 1685-1689); accession to the throne of Mary (daughter of James II) and her husband, William of Orange

1691 New Massachusetts charter made property the basis of suffrage and destroyed the vestiges of direct church control in the government

1692 Sir William Phips made royal governor of Massachusetts · Special court appointed to investigate the witchcraft outbreak at the village of Salem

1693 ● Cotton Mather's *Wonders of the Invisible World*

William and Mary College chartered (classes begun about 1710)

1701 Yale College founded

1702 ● Cotton Mather's *Magnalia Christi Americana*

Death of William III (reigned 1689-1702; Mary died in 1694); accession of Anne · Beginning of the War of the Spanish Succession (1702-1713), Queen Anne's War in America

1704 ● Sarah Kemble Knight's *Journal* begun

1707 Formal union of England and Scotland under the name of Great Britain, with a single Parliament

1710 ● Cotton Mather's *Bonifacius* or *Essays to Do Good*

1713 Treaty of Utrecht, ending the War of the Spanish Succession, gave to Great Britain all French claims to Acadia, Newfoundland, and the Hudson Bay Settlement; France retained Canada

1714 Death of Anne (reigned 1702-1714); accession of George I, Elector of Hanover

1717 Compagnie d'Occident formed in Paris to colonize on the banks of the Mississippi; rumors of gold and silver mines led to furious stock speculation known as the "Mississippi Bubble," which collapsed in 1720

1718 New Orleans founded

1721 ● *New-England Courant* (1721-1726) established; contained Benjamin Franklin's first characteristic writing, the "Dogood Papers" · Cotton Mather's *Christian Philosopher*

1726 ● Cotton Mather's *Manuductio ad Ministerium*

1727 Death of George I (reigned 1714-1727); accession of George II

1728 ● William Byrd helped survey the boundary line between Virginia and North Carolina, keeping the diary which he later elaborated into his *History of the Dividing Line* and *Secret History of the Line*

1732 ● First issue of *Poor Richard's Almanack*

1733   Sugar Act, passed to protect British interests in the West Indies, threatened colonial trade

1734   ● Jonathan Edwards' *Divine and Supernatural Light*

1738   George Whitefield made the first of five evangelical tours of the American colonies · First spinning machines patented in Great Britain

1740   Charity school founded in Philadelphia, from which developed the College of Philadelphia and, eventually, the University of Pennsylvania

1741   ● Edwards' *Sinners in the Hands of an Angry God* · Bradford's *American Magazine* and Franklin's *General Magazine* established at Philadelphia

1742   ● Edwards' *Some Thoughts Concerning the Present Revival of Religion in New England*

1743   ● Charles Chauncy's *Seasonable Thoughts on the State of Religion in New England*

1744   Beginning of the War of the Austrian Succession (1744-1748), King George's War in America

1748   ● Montesquieu's *Esprit des lois,* French political treatise largely responsible for the separation of powers under the American Constitution

Treaty of Aix-la-Chapelle ended the War of the Austrian Succession but left control of the Ohio country undetermined

1749   ● Franklin's *Proposals relating to the Education of Youth in Pensilvania*

British grant of more than a half-million acres to the Ohio Company roused French fears that there were plans to separate Canada from Louisiana

1750   ● Jonathan Mayhew's *Discourse Concerning Unlimited Submission and Non-Resistance to the Higher Powers* asserted the right of revolution under conditions such as those of 1642 and 1688

1751   ● Franklin's *Experiments & Observations on Electricity*

1752   First regular theatrical company visited the colonies · Change of calendar from the Julian (Old Style) to the Gregorian (New Style)

1753   ● John Woolman's *Some Considerations on the Keeping of Negroes,* Part I

French seized the Ohio country

1754   ● Edwards' *Freedom of the Will* · Franklin presented his *Plan of Union* to the Albany Conference

State of undeclared war with France recognized by call for delegates from all the colonies to meet at Albany, New York, in June to discuss intercolonial organization · King's College (later Columbia University) founded

1755   British and American troops under General Braddock, advancing on Fort

Duquesne, totally defeated · Franklin active in getting supplies to Braddock's troops and in supervising the construction of forts to protect Pennsylvania from invasion · Acadians deported en masse from Nova Scotia

1756 ● John Woolman's *Journal* begun

1757 Fort William Henry captured by the French · Franklin sent to London by the Pennsylvania assembly, which desired full control of the expenditure of public funds · Seven Years' War (1756-1763) formally declared (French and Indian War in America)

1758 ● Franklin's *Way to Wealth,* in *Poor Richard Improved*

Tide of the French and Indian War turned toward the British · House of Commons resolved that "the claim of right in a colonial Assembly to raise and apply public money, by its own act alone, is derogatory to the crown and to the rights of the people of Great Britain"

1759 Ticonderoga, Niagara, and Quebec taken by the British and Americans

1760 ● Franklin's *Interest of Great Britain Considered with Regard to Her Colonies,* a plea for the annexation of Canada and a united Anglo-American empire

Death of George II (reigned 1727-1760); accession of George III

1761 Colonial administration reflected a general "tightening up" to help ease the financial strain of the war, which had concluded in America but not elsewhere · Attempt to give "writs of assistance" in the execution of general search warrants to Massachusetts customs officials angered James Otis, who in a famous speech asserted the inalienable rights of life, liberty, and property security

1762 ● Otis' *Vindication of the Conduct of the House of Representatives of the Province of Massachusetts Bay,* first public statement of the "no taxation without representation" argument

Spain secretly acquired from France all of Louisiana west of the Mississippi

1763 By the Treaty of Paris, ending the Seven Years' War, Great Britain received all of Canada from France, Florida from Spain · Rumors circulated that Parliament intended to tax the colonies for part of the cost of the war, and perhaps enforce the long-forgotten Navigation Acts (see 1651)

1764 ● Otis' *Rights of the British Colonies Asserted and Proved* asked for colonial representation in Parliament if that body was to levy taxes on America

Parliament modified the Sugar Act, with obvious intentions of taxing the colonies

1765 ● Stephen Hopkins' *Rights of Colonies Examined* · Martin Howard's *Letter from a Gentleman at Halifax to His Friend in Rhode Island,* first important Tory answer to Otis and Hopkins, arguing that the colonies were legally corporations, with privileges stated in their charters, and that the colonists were "virtually" represented in Parliament, which was not organized on a territorial principle · Daniel Dulany's *Considerations on the Propriety of Imposing Taxes in the British Colonies for the Purpose of Raising a Revenue by Act of Parliament* objected to Howard's argument

Stamp Act, March · Americans reacted to news of the Stamp Act with a pamphlet war, riots, and the mobbing of prominent Tories · Stamp Act Congress convened in New York, October; drew up a declaration of rights and grievances, petitioned the king, and sent memorials to both houses of Parliament

A watercolor drawing of Greenwich St., New York, by Baroness Hyde de Neuville, c. 1810

We, the people of the United States, in order to form a more perfect union,
establish justice, insure domestic tranquillity, provide for the common defense,
promote the general welfare, and secure the blessings of liberty
to ourselves and our posterity,
do ordain and establish this constitution for the United States of America.
—Constitution of the United States

CHAPTER 2

The New Republic
1765–1829

Intellectual Currents

A New and a Proud Nation

The most distinctive aspects of the second great stage of American development were the stabilization of independent political institutions and a fervent desire to outshine the older nations of Europe in every conceivable way. Just as republican government was to be better than monarchical, so republican society, republican art, and republican literature were expected to excel anything that the Old World had yet produced. In what has often been called the early national period (extending from the Stamp Act Congress in 1765 to the inauguration of Andrew Jackson as seventh President in 1829), the future destiny of America was almost incessantly discussed and in some ways determined. These years constituted the first great era of American nationalism, cultural as well as political. Behind it lay the age of colonialism, before it the period of a sectionalism which culminated in civil war.

Events between 1765 and 1829 crowded one upon another. The Stamp Act was the first of a series of political crises which showed Americans the power they had when they united. Then came the Revolutionary War itself, followed by Shays' Rebellion, the framing and ratification of the Constitution, the Whiskey Insurrection, the birth of the two-party system, the Louisiana Purchase, the War of 1812, the Monroe Doctrine, and the Missouri Compromise. Union and expansion went hand in hand, and few foresaw the grave danger in the unexpected and rapid spread of Negro slavery. In Europe, meanwhile, the industrial revolution transformed Great Britain, and the continent seethed with the destruction of the French monarchy and the rise and fall of Napoleon.

Like all periods of rapid change, this one was exceedingly complex. Many aristocratic institutions and philosophies were under attack, and in the arts neoclassicism was giving way to the almost indefinable but impressively power-charged mood which came to be called romanticism.

Politically, then as now, and in Europe as well as in America, the "haves" were ranged against the "have nots," the proponents of centralized control against those who wished more local autonomy, absolutists and authoritarians of all sorts against all varieties of individualists and democrats. Time-worn but perennial conflicts are discernible in all the familiar oppositions—Mercantilism or Protectionism *vs.* Free Trade,

Imperialism *vs.* Home Rule, Tory *vs.* Whig, and Federalist *vs.* Republican. Basic differences in political philosophies, such as those between the right and the left, are never decisively resolved. There are always compromises, and those made in the early national period were of crucial importance to Americans, because they so largely determined later lines of thought. However short of perfection they may have fallen, they embodied ideals that were considerably more democratic than was then common in other lands.

Consider first the assertions of the Declaration of Independence: that all men are created equal, and that government rests on the consent of the governed. Both notions seemed ridiculous and extremely dangerous to many Americans, and it is hard to know how fully they were believed in. Even Thomas Jefferson argued, in *Notes on the State of Virginia* (Query XIV) that Negroes were intellectually inferior to whites. In 1776, however, equality and a greater respect for the ordinary man were ideals to conjure with, and they have remained central in American thought.

Consider, on the other hand, the preamble to the Constitution, where the emphasis is upon the government and its functions—justice, the preservation of order, and the promotion of the general welfare. The "liberty" whose blessings the preamble proposed to secure was so abstract, so far perhaps from the ideals of the Declaration, that by 1791 ten amendments (the Bill of Rights) had been adopted. The framers of the Constitution were convinced that the unity, stability, and continuity of the nation— indeed its very survival—depended upon more effective control of divisive elements, including misguided majorities. The founding fathers so arranged things, therefore, that "the governed" could not possibly make a hasty or ill-considered change. This kind of conservatism has also remained a powerful American ideal, and the Constitution has been amended only sixteen times since 1791.

American nationalism, then, encompassed from the first widely divergent views of human nature and the role of government. The "American way" was democratic up to a point—but it did not extend the ideal of equality to Negroes or to women. It sought to keep government close to the people by maintaining a fine balance between the federal government on the one hand and the state governments on the other—but tipped the scales toward "big" government by specifying federal control of foreign affairs, coinage, foreign commerce, and military and naval forces. Two of the most persistent issues in American life—civil rights and states' rights— go back, in short, to the beginnings of the national experience.

It must be admitted, moreover, that emotion played a large role in the growth of nationalism. The Revolution was to a degree a social upheaval, in which distrust of British control was mingled with antipathy to the wealthy. Crèvecoeur's "The American Belisarius" vividly suggests the feelings which sometimes got out of control. The common man could take the ideal of equality seriously, and in his more aggressive moments take the law into his own hands. The idea of inferiority, and particularly of inferiority to Britain, was unendurable, and even the most thoughtful Americans were extraordinarily sensitive to criticism.

The events of the period contributed to the growth of nationalism. Such diverse factors as the Revolution itself, the conservative reaction to the events in France, the Napoleonic wars, and westward expansion helped to unify the young nation.

Many democratic tendencies were accentuated or set in motion by the Revolution. Large estates were confiscated and divided; small business and manufacturing were stimulated; church establishments were attacked; slavery, imprisonment for debt, and humiliating punishments were looked at with growing disfavor; the idea of universal education at state expense was seriously proposed. Americans were not of one mind about these matters, but they recognized that such tendencies differentiated the United States from the older nations of Europe. Americans agreed, more-over, in insisting that they were now ready to manage their own affairs, and in being sublimely confident that they could manage them better than the British had. The Americans were a "new" people, as Crèvecoeur put it. They were ready to teach the rest of the world; they were weary of being taught.

The assertion of the rights of man by the revolutionists in France seemed at first a gratifying compliment to the example set in America. The bloodbath of the Reign of Terror, however, evoked a strong reaction among the more conservative Americans, not yet sure that the Constitu-tion had really solved the problem of internal tranquility. The Federalists, who under the leadership of George Washington, John Adams, and Alexander Hamilton controlled the government from the adoption of the Constitution until 1801, were committed to a strong federal union, able to keep order at home and repel enemies from abroad. Events proved them right.

The Napoleonic wars, which disrupted commercial and diplomatic accord with Europe, made American isolation more complete than it had been since the Revolution and led to a second armed confrontation with Great Britain. Because the War of 1812 cut off the United States from the rest of the world, the nation achieved the economic self-sufficiency which had long been talked about. Textile and iron industries grew up quickly, and Americans faced westward expansion with assurance.

The West, despite its individualism, was even more nationalistic than the seaboard states. It looked to the federal government for its lands and the means of access to them, and its local ties were new and weak. The West tended to be least respectful of Europe, most certain that the United States could "lick" the entire Old World if necessary. The "war hawks" who favored the War of 1812 were westerners.

From the perspective of the twentieth century it is clear that the ties with Europe were not cut sharply, despite the powerful influence of nationalism. The old pattern of transplantation and adaptation continued as such immigrants as Albert Gallatin, Éleuthère Irénée Du Pont, and Samuel Slater brought their talents to the new nation. In finance and in manufacturing Americans had still much to learn.

In literature, however, nationalism led Americans to attempt the impossible—the creation, overnight, of a tradition of belles-lettres. To the cultural nationalist the possession of a first-rate literature of politics and a highly reputable literature of religion was not enough; if poetry, fiction, and the drama were the marks of a great civilization, America must have them. If, as Aristotle had asserted, epic poetry is the height of literary art, the United States must have epic poems comparable in grandeur to those of the continent and the superior political institutions of the Republic.

This quixotic attempt is reflected in the work of many of the writers of the period—Philip Freneau, the Connecticut Wits (see p. 68), William Cullen Bryant, Washington Irving, and James Fenimore Cooper most particularly. In orations delivered at college commencements or on the Fourth of July, and in short-lived magazines with "United States" or "Columbian" or the name of a state or city in their titles, Americans hammered at the theme of intellectual independence, the creation of a literary culture better than that of monarchical Europe. They did not succeed in their effort, but it was not for want of trying.

National pride led to many pleas for more generous support of American writers and to many defenses of America against the supercilious remarks of British editors and travelers. This outpouring of nationalistic literary fervor, most voluminous after the War of 1812, has been labeled the "Paper War" and was not of lasting interest, although both Cooper and Irving contributed to it. The "War" had, however, one very important effect: it focused the attention of American writers more sharply on the native scene. What, they asked themselves, was unique in American life? In their effort to answer that question they became concerned with native types, dialects, manners, scenery, and institutions. Despite their frequent failure to solve the problem of fresh or appropriate forms in which to clothe their new literary material, they left a body of writing notable both for its variety and for its interpretation of American life.

Political Thought

The literature of politics, generously represented in this period, may be conveniently summarized as it appeared in four stages of American history: (1) the debate about self-government which extended from the Stamp Act to the Declaration of Independence; (2) the Revolution itself; (3) the struggle for stability and an acceptable balance of the opposing political philosophies of Hamilton and Jefferson; and (4) the continuing battle of the common man for a share in the responsibilities and rewards of political office.

(1) The differences of opinion and of feeling which lay behind the Revolution may be seen in Franklin's "Edict by the King of Prussia" and "Rules by Which a Great Empire May Be Reduced to a Small One," as well as in Thomas Paine's *Common Sense* and the Declaration of Independence itself. Franklin provides a description of the economic and political irritations, enumerated also in the Declaration; Paine offers insight into the emotions of the period.

These writings are only a small part of the literary debate of 1765-1776. Pamphlets, speeches, sermons, and state papers appeared in profusion. Outstanding among the Whig writers were Samuel Adams, John Adams, James Otis, Daniel Dulany, and John Dickinson, along with the then youthful Jefferson and Hamilton. The Tory position was maintained by such writers as Martin Howard, Daniel Leonard, Samuel Seabury, and Joseph Galloway. Patrick Henry's "Give me liberty or give me death" speech of March 1775 is a part of the debate, as in Francis Hopkinson's *A Pretty Story* (1774). In a little more than a decade a large body of polemical prose appeared, offering arguments based both upon specific legal or constitutional positions and upon abstract philosophies of government. The Declaration includes both types.

The legal position of the Patriots—denial of the authority of Parliament to levy "internal taxes" on the colonies, assertion of the doctrine of "no taxation without representation," and demands that the colonial legislatures be recognized as the only just means of obtaining "consent of the governed"—proved in the end less defensible than direct appeal to the right of revolution. For that and other "natural rights" specifically named in the Declaration, the Patriots had the precedents of the revolutions which had driven Charles I and James II from the English throne. The Americans knew their history and their political philosophy; their writings show close study of the theories of Thomas Hobbes, Sir Robert Filmer, John Locke, and many other English and European thinkers. Americans had behind them, moreover, a solid tradition of theological disputation. It is impossible to read their presentations of their case without respecting their mental caliber and clarity of exposition.

(2) The "clash of resounding arms" at Lexington ended the constitutional debate and brought forward more emotional and persuasive writers —propagandists they would now be called. Their task was to unite and hold in line a Revolutionary party which was probably never more than a two-thirds majority of the population. Their method was to appeal to the interests and the prejudices of as many different groups as they could. Master of them all was Paine, whose *Crisis* series ranks with the most successful propaganda ever written. Newspapers and magazines printed

much similar material, including numerous poems, such as Freneau's "Memorable Victory" (1781), Francis Hopkinson's "Battle of the Kegs" (1778), and Dwight's "Columbia, Columbia, to Glory Arise" (1793). Popular songs, ballads, and hymns all had their place in the literary war. There were also lengthy verse satires, of which the most famous was John Trumbull's *M'Fingal* (Part I, 1775), an imitation of a popular English attack on the Puritans, Samuel Butler's *Hudibras* (1663-1678). The Loyalists also had their propagandists, the best known being Joseph Stansbury, Jonathan Odell, and Jacob Bailey. They show clearly the social cleavage of the Revolution, for they almost invariably assumed a snobbish tone toward the "rabble." Neither party was averse to name-calling or scurrility. The Loyalists, however, had few printing presses available, and their opinions must be sought in letters, diaries, parodies of Patriot songs, and such accounts of affairs as were published in England after the war. Of these last, the most notable is Jonathan Boucher's *A View of the Causes and Consequences of the American Revolution* (1797).

(3) In the literature of the years between the end of the war and the stabilization of the new government, a rational and deliberate tone is again uppermost, although undertones of emotion are often heard. The great monument of these times, outside of the Constitution itself, is *The Federalist*, in the main the work of Hamilton. Washington's *Farewell Address*, in which Hamilton had a hand, the inaugural addresses of Jefferson, and Freneau's "Stanzas to an Alien" (1799) reflect a few of the issues of the day. A fuller picture would include *The Anarchiad* (1786-1787) and numerous other works by the Connecticut Wits, most of whom were strongly Federalist in their convictions. Joel Barlow, author of *Advice to the Privileged Orders* (1791) and *The Conspiracy of Kings* (1792), was the great exception.

Especially interesting here is the repetition, with variations, of the age-old conflicts. Centralized control and local autonomy, government by the few and government by the many—these were again among the alternatives. Woodrow Wilson and others have suggested that the Constitution was based upon a political philosophy derived in part from Newtonian physics. Its framers, according to this view, sought to balance opposing political forces one against another, and conceived of the state as a matter of retaining equilibrium despite incessant change and movement. John Adams was the chief American spokesman for this philosophy; he distrusted unlimited democracy and believed that stable government required elaborate checks and balances among executive, aristocratic, and democratic forces. The French philosopher Montesquieu, a student of British constitutional development, had had much the same idea, and he is known to have been so widely read in America that he, rather than Newton, is often credited with the checks and balances theory.

(4) The Federalists, however right they may have been, were not

always astute politicians. Some of them failed to disguise their belief that the masses counted for little, the *aristoi* for much, and they sometimes ignored local loyalties and conditions which they would have done well to study. The voters were not to be denied the respect which the ideal of equality promised them, and toward the end of the period they were receiving from most successful politicians the flattery which has ever since been theirs. The common people wanted leaders they could identify with; diplomatic protocol and correct grammar mattered little to them. In 1828, they elected Jackson, and "the age of the common man" began.

The "common man" was the white adult male. Women could not vote, although when the Constitution was under debate Abigail Adams had urged her husband to deal more fairly with her sex. Nor could Negro slaves vote, although three fifths of them were counted in determining a state's representation in Congress. Nor could many free Negroes, for many states had legalized color discrimination. Nor could the Indians, who were regarded as members of foreign nations, and were being gradually settled upon reservations, chiefly in the West (a method backed by both Jefferson and Jackson).

Such writers as H. H. Brackenridge and James Fenimore Cooper had doubts of the wisdom of man in the mass. Cooper's political views are set forth in such novels as *The Pioneers* (1823), *Home as Found* (1838), and *The Crater* (1847), and more directly in a nonfictional discussion, *The American Democrat* (1838).

Jackson himself learned that a working democracy is not easily achieved. In the peroration of his *Farewell Address* (1837) he expressed pride in the national accomplishment and assurance that there was no longer danger from abroad. Then he said, "It is from within, among yourselves, from cupidity, from corruption, from disappointed ambition, and inordinate thirst for power, that factions will be formed and liberty endangered. It is against such designs, whatever disguise the actors may assume, that you have especially to guard yourselves."

Economic Development

The problem of earning a living was not so frequently or so fully the concern of literature after 1765 as it had been before. Nevertheless, the later writing can be better understood with some knowledge of the economic thought and conflicts which distinguished American life in the early national period. Fundamental, of course, was the desire of individuals to "get on" in the world. Simple living, thrift, and industry, the ideals preached by Poor Richard in Benjamin Franklin's *The Way to Wealth*, were the ideals of most men. They were praised by writers as diverse as Crèvecoeur, Washington, Jefferson, Dwight, and Barlow. "My Neighbor

Freeport" and Rip Van Winkle, both of whom were averse to hard work, were decidedly not heroes of the era. John Woolman, however, did not share the opinion that financial success was the chief end of life. Like Thoreau in a later generation, Woolman wished to know the result of the pursuit of wealth. He reached a thought-provoking conclusion: "Wealth desired for its own sake Obstructs the increase of Virtue, and large possessions in the hands of selfish men have a bad tendency, for by their means too small a number of people are employed in things usefull, and therefore some of them are necessitated to labour too hard." A few other observers —Crèvecoeur and Dwight, for example—expressed a similar concern lest money-getting end in too wide a discrepancy between the very rich and the very poor. Poor Richard's disciples, however, could scarcely admit the possibility that men could work too hard.

What were the main features of the American economy? In 1765 the Americans were primarily an agricultural people, and this was still true in 1829, but in the interval the nation's economy underwent great changes which had their due effect upon literature. Four such changes may be mentioned: (1) the shift from a colonial to a national economy, although with continuing conflicts between those who wanted a centralized control of commerce, manufactures, finance, and transportation, and those who wanted a large measure of local control; (2) the far-reaching development of industry and the factory system; (3) the creation, through expansion to the West, of an enormous domestic market; and (4) the unexpected expansion of slavery, as raw cotton, after Eli Whitney's perfection of the cotton gin in 1793, quickly became the most important American export.

The colonies in 1765 were dependencies of a nation which, insofar as it had a colonial policy, had accepted the mercantilist doctrine that overseas possessions should supply the home country with raw materials and serve as a market for manufactured products. Mercantilism was also partly responsible for the British desire to limit expansion to the West, where the control of markets would be more difficult. That attitude aroused as much antagonism, probably, as either the trade regulations or the taxation which was sought to help pay for the French and Indian War. The Virginians were particularly unwilling to give up the West to the Indians. As Paine's *Common Sense* shows, the Americans had come to think in "continental" terms, and they were determined to control not merely their internal affairs but their economic life as well.

The success of the Revolution permitted the development of home manufactures and the opening of the West. The federal government gradually acquired title to the western lands, and, with the Constitution, internal tariff barriers were removed. Washington's *Farewell Address* provides a good view of the hope that the natural economic rivalries of the various sections might be minimized, a hope echoed later by Jefferson and Jackson. Americans did not agree, however, on the extent to which the central government should aid the states in internal improvements or "protect" infant industries or control the financial structure of the nation. They never have agreed on these matters, but their disagreements were especially sharp in the age of Hamilton's *Report on Manufactures*, of the clamor of the West for roads and canals, and of Jackson's classic struggle against the Second Bank of the United States.

Industrialization was forced upon the United States by the war between France and Great Britain, waged almost continuously from 1795 to 1815. The unprecedented growth of American foreign trade involved the nation in its first attempt to make good its right to trade as a neutral with belligerent nations, in the face of Napoleon's Berlin and Milan Decrees and the British Orders in Council. The Embargo Act of 1807 and the War of 1812 are usually credited with effecting a large measure of self-sufficiency in manufactures, although the full effect of the factory system was not felt until several decades later.

The settling of the West began almost immediately after the Revolution, but it was enormously accelerated by the introduction of new means of transportation. The steamboat reached the Ohio River in 1811, only four years after Robert Fulton's first successful demonstration on the Hudson. Roads and canals followed swiftly; the Cumberland, or National, Road had reached Zanesville, Ohio, by 1825, the year in which the Erie Canal was completed. The railroad era was soon to come; construction of the Baltimore & Ohio began in 1828. The West soon had its own literature, reflecting the turbulence of the period, and from the time of the *Western Review* (1819-1821), published in Lexington, Kentucky, it had its own periodicals and a local literature. The early western writers, such as Morgan Neville and Peter Cartwright, are only half the story. The West was the scene of two of Cooper's novels (*The Prairie*, 1827, and *The Oak Openings*, 1848), and it fascinated other eastern authors, notably William Cullen Bryant (as in his poem "The Prairies," 1832).

Of the 2,900,000 Americans counted in the first census (1790), about 700,000 were slaves. Slavery was believed to be a dying institution; emancipation laws were passed by the northern states and many southerners were convinced, as was Jefferson, that with the exhaustion of the land by tobacco the system would be abandoned. Yet there were 3,000,000 slaves in 1830, out of a total population of 12,866,000. In the new cotton belt states the inequities of the anachronistic economic system intensified. In 1810 fewer than 50,000 people lived in the old Mississippi Territory; by 1830 Mississippi (admitted in 1817) contained 136,000 people and Alabama (admitted in 1819) 309,000. The profits of cotton had silenced most of the white opposition to slavery in the South, and in the North the antislavery movement, except among the Quakers, had just begun to gather strength. Black people, however, were beginning to speak out, as can be seen from David Walker's *Appeal* (1829), one of the first books of protest against slavery from the free Negro's point of view.

Religion

Religion remained vastly important to Americans, although it did not occupy quite so central a position as it had in the colonial period. The disruption and damage of the Revolution perceptibly weakened the position of many churches; Congress was forbidden by the Constitution to make any laws leading toward the establishment of a state church; and the Bill of Rights asserted the principle of complete religious toleration. Disestablishment followed in those states which had supported particular churches, and the period as a whole displays that wide variety of religious thought to which Americans are now accustomed. Nationalistic tendencies may be discerned in various denominations and in the continued dominance of Protestantism, but they are of minor significance.

This is not to say that religious fervor lessened, or that sectarianism disappeared. The vast majority of Americans continued to attend church, denominational rivalries were no less intense, and the literature of religion was still enormous. Calvinism remained a powerful force through the influence of such followers of Edwards as Dwight, and it may be seen in a watered-down form in certain lines of William Cullen Bryant's "Inscription for the Entrance to a Wood" (1817) and "To a Waterfowl" (1815). Revivalism flourished at intervals throughout the period, especially in the West, as the autobiography of Peter Cartwright, the circuit-riding Methodist preacher, shows; Quakerism found its best American exponent in John Woolman.

From the standpoint of literary history, however, the distinctive feature of the age is the emergence of the rationalistic and humanitarian doctrines of Deism and Unitarianism. Neither was new; neither was widely popular. The virulence with which they were both attacked gives us some hint of their effect upon the age, and from this distance it is clear that their confidence in the powers of the mind and their tendency to present a man-centered universe expressed something basic.

Deism (see Chapter One), which denied the revelation of God in the Bible, chose to seek religious truth through human reason. The chief religious duty, according to the Deists, was to serve one's fellow man. Franklin arrived at Deistic beliefs early in life and he seems never to have deserted them. After his *Dissertation on Liberty and Necessity* (1725), however, he never expounded them openly, having reached the conclusion, apparently, that the orthodox Christian churches operated as a desirable social control, doing more good than harm. Somewhat similar attitudes are to be seen in Crèvecoeur, Freneau, Jefferson, and even Washington. At the time of the French Revolution, Deism became momentarily a proselyting faith, spread by Deistic newspapers, magazines, and societies, as well as by more or less formal treatises. Three of the last are worth mention: Ethan Allen's *Reason the Only Oracle of God* (1784), for which the Revolutionary hero of Vermont was largely indebted to a Dr. Thomas Young; Paine's

The Age of Reason (1795), and Elihu Palmer's *Principles of Nature* (1802). These works were the object of violent attacks by such orthodox Christians as Dwight, who regarded Deism not only as the worst form of infidelity but also as the handmaiden of political radicalism. Deism fell into decline, for most people were unwilling to give up the authority of the Bible.

Unitarianism, the denial of the doctrine of the Trinity and the divinity of Jesus Christ, is fully explained in William Ellery Channing's sermon, "Unitarian Christianity." It had been common among the upper and more rationalistic classes in Boston and other large New England towns since the 1780's and became a matter for heated debate only after 1805, when a Unitarian was appointed to the professorship of divinity in Harvard College. Differing from Deism in its acceptance of revelation, Unitarianism is chiefly significant for its similar emphasis upon human nature and reason and for its humanitarianism. The genesis of the succeeding age of reform, insofar as that reform was triggered by transcendentalism, has often been found in Unitarianism. Closely related to it is Universalism, organized as a formal sect in 1794 with the central doctrine that God could never have intended other than that all men shall be saved. These doctrines, though not widely popular, challenged the dominance of Calvinism.

Science and Education

Americans were of two minds about science and education in the early national period. They usually spoke of them with respect, and some substantial steps were made in their development. Neither, however, was very generously supported, and one does not have to look far for evidence of anti-intellectualism.

This ambivalent attitude may be explained in part by the bitter party strife between the Federalists and the Republicans. Jefferson, a lifelong lover of gadgets and of science, helped to frame the Northwest Ordinance, which set the pattern for federal aid to schools (and forbade slavery in that region), encouraged the Lewis and Clark Expedition, one of the earliest of many government-sponsored surveys, and suggested the bureau which became the United States Coast and Geodetic Survey. Yet Jefferson was ridiculed as a "philosopher," unfit to run a government. "Go wretch," wrote William Cullen Bryant in *The Embargo* (1808),

> resign thy presidential chair,
> Disclose thy secret measures, foul or fair,
> Go, search with curious eyes for horned frogs,
> 'Mid the Wild wastes of Louisiana bogs;
> Or where the Ohio rolls his turbid stream
> Dig for huge bones, thy glory and thy theme.

The thirteen-year-old Bryant was echoing an opinion widely held in Federalist circles, as was Washington Irving when he lampooned Jefferson as Wilhelmus Kieft in the Knickerbocker *History of New York*. "I have known many universal geniuses in my time," Diedrich Knickerbocker says, "though to speak my mind freely I never knew one, who, for the ordinary purposes of life, was worth his weight in straw—but, for the purposes of government, a little sound judgment and plain common sense, is worth all the sparkling genius that ever wrote poetry or invented theories."

Scientific study was becoming more specialized and more technical, and the gulf between the educated and the unlearned was widening. The scientist, therefore, is sometimes portrayed as a comic figure in popular literature. In Cooper's *The Prairie*, for example, considerable space is given to Obed Bat, M.D., "fellow of several cis-Atlantic learned societies." The new species of animal which he discovers, *Vespertilio Horribilis Americanus*, turns out to be a jackass.

Nevertheless, American science was growing and, despite its allegiance to a worldwide community of learning, displaying distinctly nationalistic tendencies. To the single lasting scientific society of the colonial period, the American Philosophical Society, was added, in 1780, the American Academy of Arts and Sciences, as well as innumerable local and state organizations. Those devoted to the study of natural history were especially active. Scientific periodicals were established. One such journal, the *American Journal of Science and Arts*, was founded by Benjamin Silliman in 1818 with the express purpose of raising science to "the elevation of our national character."

Neither the common schools nor the universities were given much genuine state support before 1829; the democratization of education was to come somewhat later. The principle that the state should educate its citizens and exert itself for the diffusion of knowledge was, however, vigorously enunciated by Washington, Jefferson, John Adams, James Madison, and many others. At the Constitutional Convention, Charles Pinckney proposed to give Congress the control of education and to establish a national university. Many other schemes for nationalizing education were put forward; all of them failed to win popular support, probably because of the determination of the states to retain as many of their prerogatives as possible.

The Fine Arts

The fine arts, relatively unimportant in the colonial period, were especially susceptible to the later impulses toward nationalism. Their connection with literature became much more intimate than it had been before. While it cannot be said that they attained great distinction before 1829, their development was extraordinary and well worth remarking.

The piety which had supported portraiture in the earlier age now became patriotic, and the founders of the Republic were given generously such immortality as paint could provide. The many portraits of Washington by Gilbert Stuart (1755-1828) are the best known example of the demand which supported a dozen or more portrait painters at this time. Most of them were trained abroad, some under Benjamin West (1738-1820) in London. West, an expatriate from Pennsylvania, was President of the Royal Academy from 1792 until his death. Large historical paintings of events connected with the Revolution were also popular, although the best known (and in some eyes the worst), Emanuel Leutze's "Washington Crossing the Delaware," was painted somewhat later. The largest national commission, for four twelve-by-eighteen-foot paintings for the rotunda in the Capitol at $8000 each, was given to John Trumbull (1756-1843). His subjects were the surrender of Burgoyne at Saratoga, the surrender of Cornwallis at Yorktown, the Declaration of Independence, and the resignation of Washington.

More interesting to students of literature, because it paralleled the literary search for new material, is the development of landscape paintings by the Hudson River School and its successors. The interconnections of literature and landscape painting at this point are numerous and fascinating. Bryant addressed a characteristic patriotic sonnet ("To Cole, the Painter, Departing for Europe") to Thomas Cole (1801-1848), with whom he shared a delight in unspoiled nature and a propensity toward didacticism and allegory. "The Flood of Years" is a poem whose pictorial effect derives from a series of images markedly like those in Cole's ambitious series—the five paintings called "The Course of Empire" and the four entitled "The Voyage of Life." Cooper, too, had affinities with the landscape painters, most particularly a fondness for grand panoramic vistas; a good deal of the power of his wilderness scenes comes from his seeing them as a painter might.

As was the case with science, the period brought noteworthy cooperative enterprises by artists—short-lived academies and associations, art schools, and museums such as the one established about 1780 by Charles Willson Peale (1741-1827). The National Academy of the Arts of Design, which is still in existence, was established in 1826. Prominent among its founders was Samuel F. B. Morse (1791-1872), better known for his perfection of the electromagnetic telegraph. It was an age of versatility.

Sculpture had only begun to develop, although by 1829 a considerable number of Americans, among them Horatio Greenough (1805-1852), were studying that art in Rome. Many of them returned to help fill the halls of the Capitol at Washington with patriotic statuary. Greenough's own colossal statue of Washington, with one naked shoulder and the flowing lines of a Roman toga, was commissioned in 1833 and completed ten years later. It now seems less interesting than some of the ship figureheads of the period, the work of unpretentious artisans.

Music became somewhat more popular in the early national period, although it was still closely bound to religion. The "singing schools" proliferated after the Revolution, spreading out from New England as New Englanders moved westward. They produced one memorable composer, William Billings (1746-1800), author of a number of original hymns in what was called the "fuguing" manner. Revivalism was also the source of many popular hymns; some musicologists believe that the Negro spirituals were an influence on and owe a good deal to revivalist camp meetings. In the towns, music grew more sophisticated as time went on. Choral societies were organized as far west as Cincinnati; opera was introduced in the 1820's; and music had a conspicuous place in the theater of the period. In all these developments immigrants played a conspicuous part, and the music was, for the most part, imported. Nationalism in music was largely confined to patriotic songs, which were numerous. It is instructive to recall that both "Hail Columbia" and "The Star-Spangled Banner" (as well as "America") were probably imports, so far as their melodies go. The lyrics were written by Joseph Hopkinson (1770-1842) and Francis Scott Key (1779-1843).

In no area is cultural nationalism more obvious than in the architecture of public buildings from about 1790 down through the following century. Classical models were for the most part triumphant, partly because the founding fathers thought them most proper for a Republic and partly because they wanted impressive facades. Much of the enthusiasm stemmed from Jefferson, who fell in love with the Roman remains at Nîmes in southern France, and with the Maison Carré in particular. His taste is evident in the Virginia state capitol at Richmond, in his own home, Monticello, and in the old ranges of the University at Charlottesville. The extension of the classical forms to domestic architecture was much less happy, especially in northern climates. Greek revival houses were sometimes mere boxes with impressive columned fronts, which kept light from the interior and collected snow and ice on the roof. Colonial and Georgian styles survived, however, especially in the seaboard towns, and the great architect of the period is now acknowledged to have been Charles Bulfinch (1763-1844), designer of the State House at Boston.

The Circumstances of Literary Publication

The literate American between 1765 and 1829 had great advantages over his colonial ancestors. He benefited from an enormous expansion of printing, the establishment of a periodical press scarcely rivaled elsewhere in the world, and the American copyright system, which protected literary property to a degree previously unknown. None of these developments had reached its height by 1829, but their collective importance to literature can scarcely be overemphasized.

Many of the books of the period were printed in America for American readers. Some of the exceptions—certain pieces by Franklin, Crèvecoeur's *Letters*, and Paine's *Age of Reason*—are those whose circumstances of publication were peculiar. Irving and Cooper, chief among the few writers who had audiences on both sides of the Atlantic, developed the profitable system of nearly simultaneous editions in London and New York.

The spread of printing can be suggested by statistics. In 1810 the census found 202 paper mills in the United States. Charles Evans, who in the late nineteenth century sought in his *American Bibliography* to list all American imprints before 1820 (and did not complete the task), discovered 35,854 items before 1800, of which 25,634 were printed between 1766 and 1799 inclusive, as against 10,220 items between 1639 and 1765. He listed 329 imprints for 1765 and 784 for 1799. Nor was this steady increase concentrated in one locality: the chief center of printing prior to the Revolution was Boston; Philadelphia then held the lead until the 1820's, when it went to New York. But there were presses in all the larger towns, including those in the West, and many of them printed books as well as newspapers and political material. All printing was still by hand, on flat-bed presses, but improvements and industrialization were in the offing. The Columbian Iron Press, developed about 1807, substituted the principle of the fulcrum for that of the screw. Steam and revolving cylinder presses were soon to be available; and one American, William Church (1778-1853), had patented in London in 1827 a typesetting and composing machine.

The stimulation to printing was primarily political, for this was the age of party journalism. Much of the political writing by Franklin, Adams, Paine, Jefferson, Hamilton, and Freneau first appeared in newspapers, which, despite paper shortages and military occupations, played an important role in the Revolution. After the war ended, newspapers multiplied; it is said that about 200 were published simultaneously by 1801. Dailies appeared in Philadelphia and New York in 1783 and 1785, when those cities had about 25,000 inhabitants. In the Hamilton-Jefferson period, party journalism swiftly came to maturity with the help of Freneau. Newspapers survived the Alien and Sedition Acts (1798); their place in political controversy is clarified by Jefferson's attention to them in his *Second Inaugural*. Bryant made his fortune as editor and part owner of the New York *Evening Post*, founded by Hamilton in 1801. Throughout the period, in short, newspapers increased rapidly in number (by 1829 there were probably more than a thousand of them), in size, and in influence.

Magazines developed more slowly. F. L. Mott, in *The History of American Magazines* (1938), has estimated that about seventy-five were begun between 1783 and 1801, and several hundred more during the first third of the nineteenth century. Most of them were short-lived, but they played a large part in the rise of belles lettres. Among the most influential were the *United States Magazine* (Philadelphia, 1779, edited by

H. H. Brackenridge), the *New-York Magazine* (1790-1797), and the *North American Review* (Boston, 1815-1939). Other important literary outlets included the *Farmer's Weekly Museum* (Walpole, N.H., 1793-1810, edited chiefly by Joseph Dennie), the *Columbian Magazine* (Philadelphia, 1786-1792), the *American Museum* (Philadelphia, 1787-1792), the *Massachusetts Magazine* (Boston, 1789-1796), and the *Port Folio* (Philadelphia, 1801-1827, edited by Dennie). These periodicals, and others like them all over the nation, provided a market for poems, essays, fiction, and literary criticism on a scale previously unknown. They were the background for the magazine world which supported Edgar Allan Poe in the next decade.

The American author, moreover, was favored after 1790 by a national copyright law protecting him from the unauthorized use of his work within the United States (but not, it will be noted, abroad) for a period of fourteen years, with the possibility of an extension for another fourteen. This law, based upon the similar statute passed in Great Britain in 1710 and upon legislation in Connecticut in 1783, was a great boon, although it did not protect American writers from the competition of pirated British books. International copyright was not achieved until 1891.

The book trade developed rapidly after the Revolution, and before the end of the period publishing, as now understood, was replacing the older methods of bridging the gap between author and reader. Bookstores and printing establishments transformed themselves into publishers, and some of the familiar names of present-day publishing appeared. The firm of Wiley was founded by Charles Wiley, a bookseller, in 1807; that of Harper by J. and J. Harper, printers, in 1817; that of Appleton by Daniel Appleton, who began business by keeping a general store, in 1825. Americans, nevertheless, were still largely dependent upon Great Britain for their reading; it has been estimated that American presses supplied only twenty percent of current books in 1820, only thirty percent in 1830.

Literary Trends

The content of American literature between 1765 and 1829 was largely determined by the peculiar circumstances of American life and, as we have seen, reflects clearly the dominant nationalistic thought of the period. When we turn, however, to problems of literary intention and method, we are at once impressed by a quite dissimilar if not conflicting factor—the continuing influence of European and particularly British literary fashions. This is reflected in the rise to greater importance than ever before of poetry, the essay, drama, and fiction—those forms in which the ideas of the writer are shaped within a fairly well-defined aesthetic pattern. It cannot be said that Americans uniformly displayed, within these forms, that cultural independence which they thought so desirable. The rise of belles-lettres nevertheless reflects the appearance of a class of writers who thought of themselves as literary artists, and of a reading public ready for literature other than the merely informational or utilitarian.

Romanticism

Our early national literature was written at approximately the same time as that of the romantic resurgence abroad, and its connections with that widespread movement are so numerous that many scholars have preferred to describe it as the early stage of American romanticism.

Romanticism is difficult to define. Most readers feel that Freneau, Bryant, Irving, and Cooper, when compared to the neo-classicism of the Connecticut Wits, represent something new, just as Cowper, Burns, Wordsworth, Coleridge, Scott, Byron, Shelley, and Keats represent something new when one compares them to Pope and Johnson. This "newness" is exceedingly difficult to describe because it is a compound of many separate elements, no single one of which is an adequate means of differentiation. Yet there is a perceptible difference, both in degree and in the prevailing conception of a man's relation to the universe in which he lives. This difference, whether it be described in terms of mood or in terms of literary method, is what is called romanticism.

Like other large generalizations, the term *romanticism* has been used so loosely that some critics have wished to discard it altogether. A majority, however, has found it indispensable, and a great deal of effort has been expended in the attempt to find an acceptable definition. René Wellek has recently surveyed these labors and concluded that the "peculiarity" of romanticism lies in "that attempt, apparently doomed to failure and abandoned in our time, to identify subject and object, to reconcile man and nature, consciousness and unconsciousness by poetry which is 'the first and last of all knowledge.' "*

Wellek's definition works beautifully with the major American writers of the 1829-1860 period: Emerson, Thoreau, and Whitman; Poe, Hawthorne, and Melville. Their writings are shaped by poetic symbolism (one of the chief means of identifying subject and object), by a faith in intuition, and by an exhilarating determination to place man in a satisfying relationship to nature and to God.

One can make a case for Cooper as another fairly complete romanticist by Wellek's definition, although the task is not as easy as with the writers just listed. Freneau, Bryant, and Irving, however, fit the definition only imperfectly. They use many of the themes which preoccupied their successors—nature and the picturesque, the common man, the legendary past— but they lack the underlying philosophy, the urge to identify and reconcile which Wellek isolates. This is why they are commonly called pre-romantics, corresponding to such British writers of the eighteenth century as Thomson, Crabbe, and Cowper.

Some American literary historians have lamented a tendency toward calling Bryant the "American Wordsworth" and Cooper the "American Scott." There can be no doubt, however, that American writers were deeply influenced by the literary fashions of Great Britain. The imitation, however, was far less slavish than it was in the case of many works by the Connecticut Wits. Freneau, Bryant, Irving, and Cooper all had a fondness for native materials and occasional flashes of original insight. Americans contributed to romanticism as much, perhaps, as they derived from it. The interplay of forms, ideas, and mood was simply the continuation of a cultural bond with Europe which no degree of national pride could wholly sever. Always the American writer was drawn in two directions: to his own land, which usually furnished him with the unique materials of his writing; and to that cosmopolitan tradition which ordinarily furnished him with the forms and methods within which he worked.

*"Romanticism Re-examined," in *Romanticism Reconsidered: Selected Papers from the English Institute*, edited with a Foreword by Northrop Frye (New York and London: Columbia University Press, 1963), p. 133. The phrase quoted by Wellek is from the Preface to the second edition of Wordsworth and Coleridge's *Lyrical Ballads*. Professor Wellek's excellent survey of the vast literature on romanticism is also available in his *Concepts of Criticism* (New Haven, Yale University Press, 1963)

Types of Diminishing Importance

With the advent of more polished and more self-consciously "literary" writers, the distinctive ideas of the age were much more likely to find expression in belles lettres than had previously been common. Accounts of voyages on land and sea, promotion tracts, sermons, histories, and biographies continued to be written, but their characteristics changed somewhat and they no longer held a separate place. Two such pieces which are still of interest today are Crèvecoeur's *Letters* (1782) and William Bartram's *Travels* (1791). The former is really a series of essays, and Bartram's book too has an essaylike flavor if one skips judiciously. Other examples of this type are such works as Jonathan Carver's *Travels* (1778), Jefferson's *Notes on the State of Virginia* (written about 1782), Timothy Flint's *Geography and History of the Mississippi Valley* (1827), and the travel books of Bryant, Cooper, and Irving.

Sermons, while still innumerable, became freer and more polished, under the influence of ideals of composition like those expressed by William Ellery Channing: "An easy, unbalanced, unlabored style should be the mode of expression. . . . Simple truth, in plain, perspicuous words, should form the body of the discourse . . ." (c. 1819). Timothy Dwight's Calvinistic sermons are probably more typical of the time than Channing's, but the sermons of both men and the hundreds of others published during the period are now seldom read. The methods of oral discourse developed in the pulpit had their influence upon political oratory, which, as we shall see, now came into great favor.

As one might expect, the nationalistic temper of the period had an immediate effect upon history and biography. The events of the Revolution were recorded, its heroes immortalized in such works as John Marshall's *Life of Washington* (1804-1807), and there was a flood of local histories, headed by Jeremy Belknap's *History of New Hampshire* (1784-1792). Little of this work was objective, and Irving's burlesque of antiquarianism and parochial pedantry in the Knickerbocker *History of New York* was doubtless needed. Not for several decades was history of literary merit and sound scholarship to be popularized by Prescott, Motley, and Parkman. Cooper's history of the United States Navy and Irving's many biographies should not be forgotten, however. These writings were thoroughly characteristic of the period in which these men matured.

Polemical Tracts and Treatises

The literature of persuasion was, of course, predominant in an age of continuous political discussion. It had a conspicuous place from the first, as we have seen; now it reached a very high level indeed in such examples as Franklin's "Edict" and "Rules," John Adams' *Novanglus*, Paine's *Common Sense*, *American Crisis*, and *Age of Reason*, Barlow's *Advice to the Privileged Orders*, and *The Federalist*. Many other works from the period might be named, for the great bulk of political writing belongs to this class, as do many theological treatises. Closely related to the tract and treatise on the one hand, and to the sermon on the other, are the innumerable political addresses and orations, such as Washington's *Farewell Address* and Jefferson's inaugural speeches.

The structure of this material varies so greatly that few generalizations are possible. Certain new tendencies are evident, however. The development of newspapers and magazines made place for short pieces like Franklin's, and for lengthy series of essays and letters such as those by John Adams, Paine (in the *Crisis*, for example), and Hamilton. Such series were quite obviously imitative of the numerous British periodical essays.

Topical arrangement continued to dominate, with the nature of the controversy determining the pattern. Of especial interest is the meticulous planning of *The Federalist*, described in the first number of that series, and the variety which was achieved by Paine, both in *Common Sense* and in the *Crisis* series. The addresses and orations will be found to have remarkably similar structure, except that to the topical arrangement are added the speaker's invariable exordium (introduction) and peroration (conclusion). The modest beginning and the highly dignified conclusion, often embodying an appeal to divine guidance, which characterize all of the political speeches, are still a part of the pattern of discourse expected of our national leaders.

The rhetorical height of the period was unquestionably the Declaration of Independence, which combines the topical structure of the tract with the tones and methods of oratory. The revisions of Jefferson's first draft provide an opportunity to study the standards of the Revolutionary period. The careful balance of emotion and reason makes the Declaration a model of its kind, and it is not surprising that its phrases have never lost their vividness. Paine's writings have a similar oratorical ring, as do many of Hamilton's. Unfortunately we have no authentic texts of the speeches with which James Otis and Patrick Henry electrified their audiences, but we know that they too were masters of persuasion.

Diaries and Autobiographies

Franklin's *Autobiography* and Woolman's *Journal* will be found in any list of the great books of the period. They form a remarkable contrast, although both are related to the tradition of self-examination which goes back to the recitals of religious experiences which both the Puritans and the Quakers once required. These recitals, usually chronological in structure and didactic in purpose, depended on the attractiveness of the self-revealed personality for their relative success. Woolman is of course the outstanding spiritual autobiographer; he should be compared with Jonathan Edwards as a witness to the reality of religious experience. Franklin, by contrast, reveals the secularization of American life; as a matter of fact, he did his reputation a disservice by telling so unblushingly the ways he devised to get ahead in the world. More than one reader has been repelled by the flavor of self-centeredness in Franklin's story, even though he was probably more civic-minded and socially useful than the vast majority of men in his time.

Poems

Poetry had been written in America from the first, but it now began to bulk much larger. The work of two poets of this period—Freneau and Bryant—would be included in most lists of major American writers. Worthy of note are the poets of the Revolution, two of the Connecticut Wits (Dwight and Barlow), and two sentimentalists (Wilde and Woodworth).

The "singers" of the Revolution were more concerned with propaganda than with artistic finish, but the relatively greater sophistication of their work, when one compares it to the *Bay Psalm Book* or *The Day of Doom*, is immediately evident. Popular ballad meters were retained, together with such ballad devices as repetition and refrain, but both "Yankee Doodle" and "The Battle of the Kegs" consistently use feminine rhymes and "Nathan Hale," probably the finest of the anonymous ballads, has a subjectivity unusual in the type.

The Revolutionary songs are, in fact, somewhat more free and fresh in their forms than most of the poems by the Connecticut Wits, who regarded themselves as the "highbrows" of their time. The Wits had studied English literature (most of them at Yale) and accepted the classical "rules," including that respect for established types which is sometimes described as the "tyranny of the genres." Timothy Dwight thought so highly of Denham, Pope, Thomson, and Goldsmith that he incorporated whole lines from their poetry in *Greenfield Hill* and deliberately imitated their forms and diction, even though he was dealing with American themes and problems. Joel Barlow, least conservative of the Wits, felt most at home in the mock-heroic and the iambic pentameter couplet perfected by Alexander Pope. A reverence for the classical forms vitiated the sometimes original ideas of the Connecticut Wits. Their efforts in the epic—Dwight's *Conquest of Canaan* (1785) and Barlow's *Columbiad* (1807)—are the best known evidence of misguided nationalistic endeavor.

Religious poetry continued to be written, often in imitation of English models. Interesting examples can be seen in *Poems on Various Subjects*,

Religious and Moral (London, 1773) by Phillis Wheatley, a Boston slave girl who had been born in Africa.

We may leave sentimentalism for later discussion; such pieces as "The Lament of the Captive" and "The Old Oaken Bucket" merely foreshadow the reign of tears and self-pity in the holiday gift-books of the 1830's and 1840's.

Freneau and Bryant, taken together, look forward to the triumph of romanticism. Both were precursors of the new mood, rather than consistently a part of it. Freneau began as an admirer of the classics, Milton, and Ossian (see "The Power of Fancy"), and was never really very venturesome in his verse forms. His political and religious views, on the other hand, were liberal for his time, and a number of his poems (such as "The Indian Burying-Ground") have the dreamlike, "soft focus" quality which is one of the characteristics of romanticism. Bryant similarly had deep roots in English poetic theory of the eighteenth century; his concept of the imagination and his emphasis upon the moral quality of beauty sometimes conflicted with his more romantic glorification of emotion. Bryant was forward-looking, also, in his experiments with anapestic substitutions in iambic meter.

Examination of the minor poetry written between 1765 and 1829 will strengthen any reader's impression of the transitional nature of the period. Such examination may be easily made in anthologies: Elihu Hubbard Smith's *American Poems, Selected and Original* (1793), *The Columbian Muse* (1794), and Samuel Kettell's *Specimens of American Poetry* (1829). The transition was far from over by 1829.

Essays

Newspapers and magazines played their part in the increase of poetic production, but they were most fundamental to the American development of the literary essay. The essay form had firmly established itself in England with *The Spectator* (begun 1717) of Addison and Steele, and its prestige was much enhanced by Samuel Johnson, Oliver Goldsmith, and later authors. The essay's brevity and variety, together with the ease to which it could be adapted to didactic purposes, made it very attractive to Americans, who had had nothing quite like it before except the squibs in the almanacs. As early as 1722 Franklin was imitating *The Spectator* in his brother's newspaper, over the signature of "Silence Dogood." For many years thereafter the newspaper or magazine which lacked its "Theodore, the Hermit" (William Smith), "Tomo Cheeki" (Freneau), "Jonathan Oldstyle" (Washington Irving), or "Oliver Oldschool" (Joseph Dennie) was a rarity. The effectiveness of these essays was limited somewhat by the authors' attempts to maintain their anonymity. The type depends for its success on the personality, even the idiosyncrasy, of the author, but these early American attempts achieved only a dignified sameness. In Irving's *Sketch Book*, however, the essay achieved genuine distinction. Crèvecoeur, also, has some claim to regard as an essayist; he was among the first to write what might be called the nature essay.

Newspaper and magazine requirements were likewise responsible for the beginnings of American literary criticism, in reviews and leading articles. Much of William Cullen Bryant's literary criticism took the form of the review; his lectures on poetry, though prepared for oral delivery, could also be considered reviews in form. The earliest American reviewers learned their trade from the British quarterlies, much as they deplored the strictures of those journals on American politics and culture.

Plays

In the drama, also, imitation and adaptation of European models was combined with the all-pervading nationalism. Royall Tyler's *The Contrast* (1787) is an admirable illustration of this process. Tyler is supposed to have written his comedy within three weeks of seeing a play for the first time. What he saw was Richard Brinsley Sheridan's *The School for Scandal*; the play that he wrote had as one of its characters Jonathan, a rural New Englander and the first of many "stage Yankees." The hero of *The Contrast*, Colonel Manly, is a patriotic former officer of the Revolutionary army.

Important changes in the theatrical situation should be noted. The repertoire company system which had grown up during the colonial period survived the closing of the principal theaters in the decade after 1774, but before 1829 it was giving way to the "star" system, which throughout the nineteenth century brought famous English actors to tour major American cities. Prejudice against the theater lessened, as is evident from the opening of an undisguised playhouse in Boston in 1794 and the repeal in 1789 of a long-ignored Pennsylvania law against stage plays. The theater became firmly established, with an ever increasing number of native-born actors, managers, and playwrights; neither public support nor copyright laws, however, yet favored a native drama.

Some native plays, now lost, may have been produced in the years just before the Revolution. During the conflict itself some political use was made of dramatic dialogues and satires, but few of them were actually acted. H. H. Brackenridge's *Battle of Bunkers Hill* (1776) is typical of such closet drama. Beginning with Tyler, however, American playwrights began to see their work on the stage. Many of them were amateurs like Tyler and James Nelson Barker of Philadelphia. Two—William Dunlap and John Howard Payne—made the theater their profession, writing plays which were traditional in structure. A brief description of their work will provide an impression of theatrical affairs and of the difficulties which lay in the way of native drama.

Dunlap, born in New Jersey in 1766, was a boy in New York City during the Revolution. Between 1784 and 1787 he was in London, studying painting under Benjamin West and seeing as many plays as he could. He began writing soon after his return to New York and had his first play produced in 1789. Before his death he wrote at least twenty-nine original plays, adapted and translated twenty-one more from the German and the French, and published, in 1832, the first history of the American theater. As manager of the Park Theater, New York, in 1796-1805, he turned largely to foreign themes and fashions, although his most famous tragedy, *André* (acted in 1798), was based upon the well-known spy story of the Revolution and exemplifies the tendency to use nationalistic material.

Payne's chief distinction rests upon his being the first successful actor to be trained in the American theaters. Like Washington Irving, he did most of his writing for the English audience and was inclined to be critical of the failure of his countrymen to support native authors. He went to England in 1813 and did not return for nineteen years. More than sixty plays have been attributed to Payne, the best known of which are the tragedy *Brutus* (1818), which became one of the widely popular plays of the nineteenth century; *Clari or the Maid of Milan* (1823), an adaptation from the French containing Payne's most famous composition, "Home, Sweet Home"; and *Charles the Second* (1826), a farce written in collaboration with Irving. As the titles indicate, Payne looked abroad for his themes and models.

At home, Tyler had numerous successors in the attempt to glorify the Revolutionary struggle and native American character types. Not many native playwrights had sufficient theatrical sense to succeed; however, it may be added in their defense that the drama everywhere in western Europe was in the doldrums.

Novels and Short Stories

The prejudice against fiction which had marked the colonial period did not disappear in America until well after 1800. Jefferson, Dwight, and Noah Webster are only a few of the many who expressed the belief that stories gave wholly false notions of life to impressionable youth. Nevertheless, fiction grew steadily more popular. In the late eighteenth century circulating libraries specializing in fiction prospered with the support of young ladies who demanded romance; and the new magazines, although expressing a pious editorial concern about the possible moral effect of fiction, could not afford to bar it from their pages. By the 1780's American authors were helping to supply the market, often meeting the anticipated criticism by protestations that their tales were drawn from "real life," or pointing out that they invariably portrayed the awful consequences of sin and the fair rewards of virtue. That sin was made attractive was purely coincidental.

The prevailing nationalism was evident in the quest for American settings and characters, but the American novel in its first stages was nevertheless heavily indebted to British models. Three distinct trends may be discerned, in an order which is roughly chronological. (1) The earliest American novels were adaptations of the fiction of sentiment and sensibility which had made the reputations of Samuel Richardson and Laurence Sterne; Mrs. Hannah Webster Foster's *The Coquette* is generally regarded as the best example of the type. (2) Americans next imitated the sensationalism of the so-called Gothic romance, as practiced in its latter stages by Mrs. Ann Radcliffe, and the mystery-laden propaganda novel of which William Godwin's *Caleb Williams* (1794) is typical; this trend is illustrated by the work of Charles Brockden Brown (1771-1810) and, so far as propaganda is concerned, by H. H. Brackenridge's *Modern Chivalry*. (3) Finally the society or domestic novel, for which Fanny Burney and Jane Austen were famous, and the historical romance as developed by Sir Walter Scott became naturalized; in these forms James Fenimore Cooper achieved the first really striking success.

Sentiment and sensibility—alike in their release of the "tender" emotions but differing in that sentimentalism was didactic and moral, sensibility deliberately throat-filling and tear-jerking—can scarcely be separated in *The Power of Sympathy; or, The Triumph of Nature* (1789), written "to expose the dangerous Consequences of Seduction and to set forth the advantages of female Education." Usually regarded as the first American novel, it was long attributed to Mrs. Sarah Wentworth Morton, but is now believed to have been the work of William Hill Brown. Mrs. Susanna Haswell Rowson's *Charlotte Temple, a Tale of Truth* (1791) was more popular. Many other sentimental novels might be named, and seduction and suicide and floods of tears filled many pages of fiction far into the nineteenth century. For most readers, however, *The Coquette* will be a sufficient introduction to the type. Its form—a series of letters—was derived from Richardson's *Pamela* and *Clarissa Harlowe* and, while not universal, was characteristic.

Charles Brockden Brown made use of the epistolary form in *Jane Talbot* (1801) and *Clara Howard* (1801), but he is better known for his "thrillers": *Wieland* (1798), *Ormond* (1799), *Arthur Mervyn* (1799-1800), and *Edgar Huntley* (1799). These are remarkable for their use of such mysteries as ventriloquism and sleepwalking, as well as for wonder-working heroes and deep-dyed villains. Brown's imitation of the Gothic romance and of Godwin is unmistakable but far from slavish. He learned how to tell a good story, and some of his methods and materials were borrowed later by Edgar Allan Poe. Brown's work also shows traces of social purpose, although that theme was best used by Brackenridge, whose models were *Don Quixote* and Henry Fielding. His *Modern Chivalry* is a rambling book, partly a satirical tract on the times and partly a picaresque romance, with Teague O'Regan as its rogue hero.

The work of Cooper, although in some respects feeble, was a clear improvement over earlier attempts in the novel. His first effort, *Precaution* (1820), was an imitation of the Jane Austen type of domestic fiction, and foreshadowed his lifelong concern with social distinctions. *The Spy* (1821) was doubtless suggested by the success of the then unidentified author of *Waverley* (1814) and *Ivanhoe* (1820) in combining history with fiction. Nationalism helped to make Cooper's work popular, but he deserves credit for his skill in obtaining suspense in those parts of his novels in which physical action dominates, and with advances in characterization and the use of setting. He excelled in the escape-pursuit pattern of adventure, which dominates the Leather-Stocking series; unfortunately he often tried to mix with it over-elaborate mysteries, as in *The Pioneers* and *The Prairie*. But he made the American novel respectable, and his work was paralleled by Lydia Maria Child (1802-1880), Catherine Maria Sedgwick (1769-1867), and James Kirke Paulding (1778-1860).

Unlike the novel, the short story was largely dependent upon the magazines. Its beginnings are closely connected with those of the essay and with "characters" (delineations of unusual or typical personalities). Franklin came close to the short story in "The Way to Wealth" and "The Ephemera," while Crèvecoeur's "The American Belisarius" is half-essay, half-story. The British magazines, although full of Oriental and moral tales, widely imitated in America, had not perfected the short story by 1819, nor had the German and French storytellers. Irving's *The Sketch-Book*, therefore, is something of a landmark in world literature as well as in American. The story-sketches retained many of the characteristics of the essay: a sense of the author's presence and manipulation, leisurely movement, a fullness of detail that is sometimes almost digression, and the achievement of atmosphere rather than suspense and sharp climax. Although few of his contemporaries rivaled him, one can argue convincingly that with the short story American literature first came of age. "Rip Van Winkle" and "The Legend of Sleepy Hollow" are America's first fictional masterpieces.   T. H.

Chronological Table of
LITERATURE AND HISTORY

1766 ● Numerous pamphlets relating to the Stamp Act and the right of Parliament to tax the colonies

Benjamin Franklin appeared before the House of Commons, 28 January · Declaratory Act, 7 March, affirmed the right of Parliament to legislate for the colonies "in all cases whatsoever" · Stamp Act repealed, 18 March

1767 ● John Dickinson's *Letters from a Farmer in Pennsylvania* arguing against British regulation of colonial trade

Townshend Acts, effective 20 November, imposed duties on paper, tea, glass, and painter's lead · The Earl of Hillsborough became secretary of state responsible for American affairs

1768 ● *Circular Letter,* drafted by Samuel Adams for the Massachusetts House of Representatives, urged all colonial assemblies to resist the policies of the British ministry

Massachusetts House dissolved after defying Hillsborough's order that it rescind the *Circular Letter* · British troops moved to Boston from Halifax to impress the Whig "extremists"

1769 ● Samuel Adams and others, *An Appeal to the World, or a Vindication of the Town of Boston*

Nonimportation agreements adopted throughout the colonies caused British merchants to press for the repeal of the Townshend Acts

1770   Boston Massacre, 5 March · Townshend Acts repealed, with the exception of the duty on tea · Population (estimated) about 2,000,000

1771 ● Franklin wrote first part of his *Autobiography*

First spinning-mill established by Samuel Arkwright in Derbyshire, England

1772 ● Philip Freneau and H. H. Brackenridge, *Rising Glory of America*

Local committee of correspondence formed in Boston by Samuel Adams · The *Gaspee,* a revenue cutter, burned by Rhode Island citizens

1773 ● Franklin's "Edict by the King of Prussia" and "Rules by Which a Great Empire May be Reduced to a Small One"

Hutchinson Letters, sent to Boston by Franklin, undermined the little remaining colonial confidence in the British ministry · Intercolonial committees of correspondence established · Boston Tea Party, 16 December

1774 ● John Woolman's *Journal* · John Adams' "Novanglus" letters in the Boston *Gazette* · Thomas Jefferson's *Summary View of the Rights of British America* · Alexander Hamilton's *Vindication of the Measures of Congress* · Francis Hopkinson's *Pretty Story* · Edmund Burke's *Speech on American Taxation,* best example of the British Whig support for American complaints

Five "Intolerable Acts" passed by Parliament as a result of Boston Tea Party ·
First Continental Congress met in Philadelphia, 5 September, demanded the
repeal of the "Intolerable Acts," and formed a "Continental Association" for
administering nonimportation and nonexportation agreements · Sharp division
of Americans on the question of resistance to British policy

1775 ● Samuel Seabury's *Westchester Farmer* pamphlets, most important exposition
of the Loyalist position · Hamilton's *The Farmer Refuted* · John Trumbull's
M'Fingal, first part · Burke's *Speech on Conciliation with America*

General Gage marched from Boston to seize military supplies at Concord, 18
April, his intention being announced by Paul Revere · Skirmishes at Lexington
and Concord, 19 April · Second Continental Congress convened at Philadelphia, 10 May · Battle of Bunker Hill, 17 June · Washington assumed command
of the Continental army besieging Boston, 3 July · Americans captured
Montreal, November, but were eventually forced to withdraw from Canada

1776 ● Thomas Paine's *Common Sense* · *The Declaration of Independence*

Boston evacuated by the British, 17 March · Sentiment for independence
culminated in the *Declaration,* signed 4 July and 2 August · British army
landed on Long Island, 22 August, and soon occupied Manhattan Island ·
Nathan Hale executed, 22 September · Washington and his troops forced to
retreat across New Jersey · Americans heartened by victory at Trenton, 26
December · Organization of state governments begun

1777 ● Hopkinson's *Political Catechism*

First supplies received from France · British occupied Philadelphia, September
· General Burgoyne, after marching from Canada, surrendered to the Americans under General Gates at Saratoga, 17 October · Articles of Confederation,
legalizing the Continental Congress, submitted to the states for ratification;
adopted in 1781 · "Conway Cabal" to displace Washington as commander-in-
chief failed · Winter quarters at Valley Forge

1778 American independence recognized by France and a military alliance effected
· Unofficial aid received from Spain · Philadelphia evacuated by the British,
18 June

1779 ● Hopkinson's *Battle of the Kegs*

Spain declared war on Great Britain, 16 June · The British warship *Serapis*
captured by the *Bon Homme Richard,* commanded by John Paul Jones, 23
September

1780 British captured Charleston · Spaniards took Mobile · Benedict Arnold's
treason discovered, 26 September · Major John André executed, 2 October ·
Various military actions in North Carolina and Virginia, hereafter the chief
battle area · Population (estimated) about 2,800,000

1781 ● Philip Freneau's *British Prison-Ship* · Samuel Peters' *General History of
Connecticut*

British campaign in the South ended with surrender of Cornwallis and his
troops at Yorktown, Virginia, 19 October

1782 ● Crèvecoeur's *Letters from an American Farmer*

Provisional peace treaty signed at Paris, 30 November

1783 End of the war proclaimed by Washington, 19 April · Treaty of Paris, 3 September, recognized American independence, restored Florida to Spain · New York evacuated by the British, 25 November

1784 Ordinance providing for the survey and sale of public lands in the West, later supplemented by the Ordinance of 1785 and the famous Northwest Ordinance of 1787

1785 ● Timothy Dwight's *Conquest of Canaan*

John Adams appointed minister to Great Britain, with instructions to negotiate commercial agreements and settlement of Western land question, the British being still garrisoned in the forts at Detroit, Niagara, and elsewhere.

1786 ● The Connecticut Wits' *Anarchiad* · Freneau's *Poems*

Shays' Rebellion in Massachusetts, first Populist uprising · Annapolis Convention, September, dominated by Hamilton, issued call for a convention to consider amending the Articles of Confederation

1787 ● Royall Tyler's *Contrast* acted · John Adams' *Defence of the Constitutions of Government of the United States*

Constitutional Convention held at Philadelphia, 14 May-17 September · Constitution submitted for state ratification, nine votes being sufficient

1788 ● Alexander Hamilton, James Madison, and John Jay, *The Federalist* · Freneau's *Miscellaneous Works*

Constitution ratified by the ninth state, New Hampshire, 6 April

1789 ● Washington's *First Inaugural* · John Adams' *Discourses on Davila* begun

Constitution in effect, 4 March · Washington and Adams elected President and Vice-President, 6 April · Washington inaugurated in New York City, 30 April · Fall of the Bastille, Paris, 14 July · Declaration of the Rights of Man, 4 August

1790 ● Susanna Haswell Rowson's *Charlotte Temple*

First United States census: population approximately 4,000,000

1791 ● William Bartram's *Travels* · Joel Barlow's *Advice to the Privileged Orders* · Paine's *Rights of Man,* first part · Hamilton's *Report on Manufactures* · *National Gazette* founded, with Freneau as editor

First ten amendments to the Constitution (Bill of Rights) · First Bank of the United States chartered · Vermont admitted as the fourteenth state

1792 ● H. H. Brackenridge's *Modern Chivalry,* first part · Barlow's *Conspiracy of Kings*

Kentucky admitted as the fifteenth state · Paine imprisoned in Paris · Capitol at Washington begun · Washington reelected President

1793   Louis XVI executed · France declared war on Great Britain, Holland, and Spain, being already at war with Austria and Prussia · "Citizen" Genêt landed in the United States · United States proclaimed neutrality despite alliance of 1778 with France · Reign of Terror in France · Cotton gin invented by Eli Whitney

1794   ● Dwight's *Greenfield Hill* · Paine's *Age of Reason,* first part

Whiskey Insurrection in western Pennsylvania

1796   ● Barlow's *Hasty-Pudding* · Washington's *Farewell Address*

Tennessee admitted as the sixteenth state · John Adams elected second President, with Jefferson as Vice-President · British troops finally withdrawn from the western forts

1797   ● Tyler's *Algerine Captive*

Anti-French feeling increased by the attempt of Talleyrand, foreign minister for the Directory, to bribe American emissaries—"X.Y.Z. Affair"

1798   ● Charles Brockden Brown's *Wieland*

Alien and Sedition Laws, an expression of the Federalist fear of "French principles" · States' rights asserted by Virginia and Kentucky Resolutions

1800   Jefferson elected third President · United States census: population nearly 5,500,000

1801   John Marshall became Chief Justice of the Supreme Court · Jefferson inaugurated in the new capital city, Washington · Tripoli declared war on the United States, who refused to pay increased tribute to halt piracy

1802   Ohio admitted as seventeenth state

1803   Congress authorized expedition under Meriwether Lewis to the Northwest · Louisiana purchased from Napoleon for $15,000,000 · John Marshall established doctrine of "judicial review" in the case of *Marbury vs. Madison*

1804   Death of Hamilton · Jefferson reelected President

1807   ● Washington Irving and others, *Salmagundi* · Barlow's *Columbiad*

Seamen were taken off an American man-of-war by British in *Chesapeake* affair, June · Jefferson, by proclamation, forbade the entrance of British warships into American harbors · Embargo Act, 21 December, prohibited all ships from leaving American ports

1808   ● William Cullen Bryant's *Embargo*

Importation of slaves into the United States forbidden · Economic distress caused by the Embargo Act made Jefferson highly unpopular · James Madison elected fourth President

1809   ● Irving's *Knickerbocker History of New York*

Embargo Act repealed · Non-Intercourse Act passed, permitting American shipping to destinations other than French and English ports

1810   United States census: population of approximately 7,240,000

1811   United States broke off diplomatic relations with Great Britain, after failing to obtain agreement on the rights of neutrals

1812   Louisiana admitted as the eighteenth state · United States declared war on Great Britain · Madison reelected President

1813   Blockade of American ports established by the British · American fleet under Perry victorious at Put-in-Bay, on Lake Erie, 10 September

1814   Washington captured by the British, 24 August · Hartford Convention assembled, 15 December, to express New England disapproval of the war · Treaty of Ghent, 24 December, ended the War of 1812 but failed to resolve the major issues

1815   ● *North American Review* established · Freneau's *Poems on American Affairs*

British defeated in the Battle of New Orleans, 8 January · Napoleon returned from Elba, 1 March, was defeated at Waterloo, 18 June, and banished to St. Helena, 8 August

1816   Indiana admitted as the nineteenth state · James Monroe elected fifth President

1817   ● Bryant's "Thanatopsis," in the *North American Review*

Mississippi admitted as the twentieth state

1818   Illinois admitted as the twenty-first state · Boundary between the United States and Canada defined

1819   ● Irving's *Sketch Book*

Alabama admitted as the twenty-second state · Tallmadge amendment to the bill for the admission of Missouri brought the slavery question to the forefront in national affairs · Florida acquired from Spain

1820   ● James Fenimore Cooper's *Precaution*

Missouri Compromise adopted · Maine admitted as the twenty-third state · United States census: population of more than 9,500,000 · Monroe reelected President

1821   ● Bryant's *Poems* · Cooper's *Spy*

Missouri admitted as the twenty-fourth state

1822   ● Irving's *Bracebridge Hall*

1823   ● Cooper's *Pilot, Pioneers*

1824 ● Irving's *Tales of a Traveller*

John Quincy Adams elected sixth President

1826 ● Cooper's *Last of the Mohicans*

1827 ● Cooper's *Prairie* · Edgar Allan Poe's *Tamerlane and Other Poems,* published anonymously

1828 ● Nathaniel Hawthorne's *Fanshawe* · Irving's *Life and Voyages of Christopher Columbus* · Noah Webster's *American Dictionary of the English Language*

"Tariff of Abominations," high protective tariff unacceptable to the South · Doctrine of nullification stated by John C. Calhoun in the "South Carolina Exposition," adopted by the legislature of that state · Andrew Jackson elected seventh President

CHAPTER 3

The American Renaissance

"Picnic Scene," a watercolor by Susan Merrett, mid-nineteenth century

1829–1865

*We will walk on our own feet;
we will work with our own hands;
we will speak our own minds.*
—Ralph Waldo Emerson

Intellectual Currents

Between the triumph of the frontier in Jackson's election and the days of the Civil War, the United States emerged as a flourishing nation—a nation of the common man, a nation with a culture, a nation of promises, but a nation increasingly divided by the presence of Negro slaves in a society which glorified the freedom of the individual to rise to whatever level his talents permitted.

In literature, this was the period of renaissance, the period of awakening and development, when Americans at last began speaking their own minds. Most of the writers of the era were New Englanders, although Poe, Melville, and Lincoln were outside the New England orbit. Even they were mindful of New England, for Poe was sharply critical of transcendentalists and abolitionists; Melville was profoundly affected by New England's chief writer, Nathaniel Hawthorne; and Lincoln was the spokesman for the cause which New England's writers eloquently supported.

This period in New England has been given a variety of happy designations. Barrett Wendell called it "The Renaissance of New England," Lewis Mumford, "The Golden Day." By whatever name it is known, it was the greatest literary period in the history of New England. In their works the writers of Boston and Cambridge, Concord and Salem set forth their all-embracing ideas having to do with democracy and the common person, industry and the expanding frontier, science and human progress, religion and human nature, and slavery and the Civil War. These concerns reflect the ideological turmoils of an ever increasing self-awareness in a seemingly boundless nation.

Democracy, Industrialism, Expansion

From 1829 to 1860 the two major political parties in the United States were the Whigs and the Democrats. Conservative men of property in New England were likely to be Whigs; liberals and men of little or no property were likely to be Democrats.

The election of Andrew Jackson of Tennessee by the Democrats in 1828 is one of the great landmarks in the evolution of American democracy. The common man, whether backwoodsman, farmer, or small merchant, regarded Jackson, the conqueror of the Creek Indians and the hero of New Orleans, as a popular champion. Jackson's Whig opponent, the "aristocratic" John Quincy Adams, carried only New England and the North Atlantic states; the South and West went solidly for "Old Hickory." During the Jacksonian period, government in America became more democratic. The movement toward democracy, which had begun with the War of Independence but which had been arrested somewhat in the 1790's owing to apprehension caused by the excesses of the French Revolution, now resumed its onward course. State constitutions were liberalized. Religious tests and property qualifications for holding office were at last removed, and manhood suffrage was adopted generally, within the limits already described (see p. 54).

The Price of Manifest Destiny

In 1829 the Union consisted of twenty-four states, in half of which Negro slavery was legal. During the next three decades nine more states were added: Arkansas (1836), Michigan (1837), Florida (1845), Texas (1845), Iowa (1846), Wisconsin (1848), California (1850), Minnesota (1858), and Oregon (1859). As the names suggest, this was the period in which the United States became a vast continental nation, facing the two greatest oceans of the world. To some this was an appropriate fulfillment of the promise of American grandeur; to others—the Indians, the blacks, and the Mexicans from whom a great part of the new territory was wrested by force—it was further cause for rankling resentments.

During Andrew Jackson's presidency the Cherokees were a major topic of debate, and they provide a classic instance of a minority group entangled in conflicts between state and federal authority and between the judicial and executive branches of American government. By treaties made after the Revolution they held large tracts of land in northwestern Georgia. In 1820 they adopted a form of tribal government based on the white man's, providing for an elected chief, senate, and house of representatives. In 1827 they established themselves as the Cherokee Nation, under a constitution, and they were, in fact, considered an autonomous people by the United States Supreme Court. However, since the time of Jefferson federal policy had been to settle all Indian tribes west of the Mississippi, accomplishing this by negotiation and supposedly just compensation. Some Cherokees had gone to the Indian Territory, but most of the tribe was content to stay on its Georgia lands, which were made the more valuable by the discovery of gold. After Jackson's election the Georgia state legislature enacted a series of measures designed to force the Cherokees to move. The Indians carried their contention that these acts were invalid to the Supreme Court, but no counsel for Georgia appeared and the opinions handed down by John Marshall, the chief justice, were, to say the least, curious. One (to which Justice Story of Massachusetts dissented) was that the Cherokees were not after all a sovereign nation but wards of the federal government, for whose welfare the President was responsible.

Despite much harassment, the Cherokees stayed on their lands until they were evicted by force in 1838. Their march to the Indian Territory was an extreme hardship; thousands died, and today the route is known as "the trail of tears." Emerson was moved to speak up for them at a protest meeting in Concord and to write a letter to President Van Buren. Thoreau predicted that unless the Indian wished to be pushed into the Pacific he should become a husbandman and put aside his bow and arrow, fish-spear, and rifle. "What detained the Cherokees so long," he wrote, "was the 2923 plows which that people possessed; and if they had grasped their handles more firmly, they would never have been driven beyond the Mississippi. No sense of justice will ever restrain the farmer from plowing up the land which is only hunted over by his neighbors." John Quincy Adams, looking back from 1841, decided that the whole business was a "sickening mess of putrefaction." The states within whose borders the Cherokees had lived, he wrote, "broke down all the treaties which had pledged the faith of the nation. Georgia extended her jurisdiction over them, took possession of their lands, houses, cattle, furniture, negroes, and drove them out of their dwellings. All the Southern States supported Georgia in this utter prostitution of faith and justice; and Andrew Jackson, by the simultaneous operation of fraudulent treaties and brutal force, completed the work." Jackson and the Georgians did not see it that way, to be sure, but the Indians did, and for that matter still do. The pattern of the Cherokee dispossession was all too often followed later.

At about the same time justice and expediency also clashed in Texas, beyond the western boundary of the United States. Slavery had been the main issue in the Missouri Compromise of 1821, reached after a two-year-long debate during which the breakup of the Union into two or three confederacies was often predicted. The agreement was that Missouri should be admitted as a slave state, Maine separated from Massachusetts to retain the balance in the Senate, and slavery forbidden in that part of the Louisiana Purchase north of 36° 30′ latitude.

Two years later Stephen F. Austin established a colony near the mouths of the Brazos and Colorado rivers, on lands granted legally by the Mexican government, and by 1835 about 30,000 Anglo-American settlers were in Texas. The region was ideal for cotton production, thinly populated by Indians and settlers from Mexico, and feebly administered from a remote and unstable capital. As early as 1830 Jackson seems to have hoped that it might be purchased. In 1836 the Texans refused to accept the Mexican dictatorship and the rule of General Santa Anna, and although defeated at the Alamo secured their independence by Sam Houston's victory at San Jacinto. The question of eventual annexation of the Republic of Texas at once arose. It was to divide Americans for the next decade.

New England Looks at the New Democracy

To many New Englanders Jackson and his supporters seemed the dregs
of democracy. Emerson wrote to Thomas Carlyle, "A most unfit person in
the Presidency has been doing the worst things; and the worse he grew,
the more popular." Like many educated men, Emerson doubted at times
the wisdom of the uneducated masses. "The mass," he wrote in a skeptical
moment, "are animal, in state of pupilage, and nearer the chimpanzee."
But it would not be fair to Emerson to suppose that his snobbish statements represent his real attitude. Despite moments of skepticism, he held
firmly to his faith in the ultimate wisdom of the people. The belief that
"God is in every man" was to him "the highest revelation." And he said
in another passage on the subject, "The great mass understand what's
what." It should be remembered that Emerson took sharp issue with his
friend Carlyle on the subject of democracy: when Carlyle advocated what
we today should call a fascist doctrine, Emerson vigorously dissented. He
could think of many benefits that might come from even the "rank rabble
party, the Jacksonism of the country." For one thing, this new democracy
of the West might cure America of its abject dependence upon Old World
literature and Old World traditions, might "root out the hollow dilettan-
tism of our cultivation." And he came ultimately to an admiration of
Jackson himself. Writing in 1862 of the truly memorable things which he
associated with the national capital, he mentioned along with the eloquence of Daniel Webster and the "sublime behaviour" of John Quincy
Adams, the "fine military energy of Jackson in his presidency."

Jackson's fine military energy appealed also to James Russell Lowell,
who wrote in his "Latest Views of Mr. Biglow":

Ole Hick'ry wouldn't ha' stood see-saw
  'Bout doin' things till they wuz done with,—
H'd smashed the tables o' the Law
  In time o' need to load his gun with;
He couldn't see but jest one side,—
  Ef his, 'twuz God's, an' thet wuz plenty;
An' so his *'Forrards'* multiplied
  An army's fightin' weight by twenty.

It must have required a great adjustment for the New England mind to
appreciate a man like Andrew Jackson. Emerson and Lowell were capable
of making the necessary accommodation, and Nathaniel Hawthorne, alone
among the major New England writers, was a loyal member of the Democratic party and a staunch supporter of Jackson. Late in life he recorded in
his journal the considered judgment, "Surely Jackson was a great man."
But despite the personal challenge of Jackson himself, Emerson spoke for
the generality of educated New Englanders when he said that the Whig

party had the "best men"; the Democratic party, he added, had the "best cause."

Many New Englanders were dubious, too, about the consequences of westward expansion. Some deplored the loss of energetic and ambitious young people. Others were depressed or angered by the political maneuvering which led to the war with Mexico and by the greed and violence of the mining camps in the far West. Like all eras, New England's "golden day" was hard upon men and women with tender consciences.

Of the nine new states, only three allowed slavery, and five (Michigan, Iowa, Wisconsin, Minnesota, and Oregon) were virtually an extension of New England, closely tied to her by their schools, colleges, churches, and cultural attitudes. The appeal of the upper Midwest to young New Englanders lay in the fact that 80- or 160-acre farms could be purchased from the government for $1.25 per acre. Some of the emigrants were of course speculators, but many were genuine dirt farmers who found the soil of Iowa, for example, decidedly more tractable than that of Vermont. Few shared Whittier's admiration of the austerity of life in New England:

> Then ask not why to these bleak hills
> I cling, as clings the tufted moss . . .
> Better with naked nerve to bear
> The needles of this goading air,
> Than, in the lap of sensual ease, forego
> The godlike power to do, the godlike aim to know.

Even Emerson, who at one point observed that "The wise man stays at home," did some day-dreaming, late in life, about what he had missed. Writing home from California in 1870, he said "if we were all young—as some of us are not,—we might each of us claim his quarter-section of the Government, & plant grapes & oranges, & never come back to your east winds and cold summers."

The West had its imaginative as well as economic and climatic attractions. William Dean Howells, on a pilgrimage from Ohio to Concord and Boston, found Hawthorne "curious about the West, which he seemed to fancy more purely American, and said he would like to see some part of the country on which the damned shadow of Europe had not fallen." Lowell expressed a similar view when writing of Nature's creation of Lincoln ("Commemoration Ode," 1865):

> For him her Old-World moulds aside she threw,
>   And choosing sweet clay from the breast
>   Of the unexhausted West,
> With stuff untainted shaped a hero new . . .
>   Nothing of Europe here . . .

"I believe," Thoreau wrote in his journal in 1851, "that Adam in paradise was not so favorably situated on the whole as is the backwoodsman in America. You all know how miserably the former turned out,—or was turned out,—but there is some consolation at least in the fact that it remains to be seen how the western Adam in the wilderness will turn out.

> In Adam's fall
> We sinned all.
> In the new Adam's rise
> We shall all reach the skies."

The political turmoil of the years of westward expansion seldom gave New Englanders more than brief moments of such optimism. The idealists among them were shocked by the treatment of the Indians, bitter about the extension of slavery furthered by the Mexican War and the annexation of Texas, and horrified by the spectacle of the California gold rush.

The Industrial Revolution

Like the Jacksonian revolution, the industrial revolution affected the entire country; its effects, however, became especially conspicuous in New England. After the War of 1812, business capital and initiative in New England were diverted from commerce to manufacturing, and the abundance of water power and skilled labor guaranteed the success of the factory system. The most striking new feature of the New England landscape about 1820 was the factory village, built near a waterfall and consisting of mills and houses for the "operatives." Workers in the early New England factories were mostly farmers' daughters from the surrounding country. Hawthorne in one of his rambles about the countryside remarked on the bright, cheerful faces looking out through the factory windows. A notable instance was Lowell, Massachusetts (founded in 1822), where the factory girls dressed neatly, were properly chaperoned, and published a literary weekly. By 1840 there were some 1200 cotton factories in the United States, two thirds of which were in New England. The raw material for this industry came, of course, from the plantations of the South.

One result of the industrial revolution in New England was the accumulation of wealth, a good deal of which was used for cultural purposes. Many New Englanders studied in Europe. The colleges of New England grew in resources and prestige. Almost every town had its free public library and its Lyceum, where an instructive course of lectures was given during the winter. Emerson, and even Thoreau, lectured on many Lyceum platforms. In the cities, mechanics' institutes offered vocational training. The Lowell family might be cited as illustrating the happy marriage of wealth and culture: one uncle of James Russell Lowell founded the manufacturing city which bears his name; another uncle established the famous

Lowell Institute in Boston, where lectures have been given for more than a century by distinguished scientists, scholars, and men of letters.

To most New England writers of the period the industrial revolution no doubt seemed more beneficent than otherwise. One major writer, however—Henry David Thoreau—spoke out loud and bold against the mechanization of American life. Thoreau's objection was based upon the fundamental principle, Emerson's principle, of self-reliance. A man ought to do for himself the things which more and more were being done by machines: he ought to walk instead of riding on the train; he ought to build his own house, make his own clothes, bake his own bread. The machine brought on the division of labor which reduced men from integers to fractions. "Where is this division of labor to end?" Thoreau cried in *Walden*; and he added a statement the force of which is only today becoming apparent: "No doubt another *may* also think for me; but it is not therefore desirable that he should do so to the exclusion of my thinking for myself."

Compared with Thoreau's, the comments of other writers on the advancing machine age seem less decisive. Emerson entered a mild demurrer in *Self-Reliance* (1841), warning that "the harm of the improved machinery may compensate its good"; but, in the long run, he was willing to accept the machine as part of the "beneficent tendency." Hawthorne seems to have been apprehensive of evil results; to him, apparently, the machine was a malevolent monster. One finds in his journal the following note for a story: "A steam engine in a factory to be supposed to possess a malignant spirit; it catches one man's arm and pulls it off; seizes another by the coat-tails, and almost grapples him bodily; catches a girl by the hair, and scalps her; and finally draws a man and crushes him to death." Here was a conception out of which Hawthorne might easily have developed a tale of Gothic horror, and perhaps also of social prophecy.

A conspicuous and characteristic product of the industrial revolution in America was the man of big business, the captain of industry. The subject received scant attention in the literature of the period. One passage, however, is of particular interest—a passage in Emerson's *Journals* which expresses the writer's great admiration of John M. Forbes, a builder of railroads in the West in the 1860's:

> He is an American to be proud of. Never was such force, good meaning, good sense, good action, combined with such domestic lovely behaviour. . . . Wherever he moves, he is the benefactor. It is of course that he should shoot well, ride well, sail well, administer railroads well, carve well, keep house well, but he was the best talker also in the company. . . .

The type has suffered at the hands of later writers. Perhaps Emerson was naïve; or possibly the type deteriorated in the post-Civil War period; or, quite likely, Americans have grown more aware of the inequity of the co-existence of great wealth and great poverty.

Science and Human Progress

Natural science advanced with remarkable rapidity in the nineteenth century, and its effects became more and more pervasive. In England—to mention only two of many notable publications in the scientific field—Sir Charles Lyell's *Principles of Geology* (1830-1833, 3 vols.) established the antiquity of the earth and the gradual evolution of its surface, and Charles Darwin's *Origin of Species* (1859) presented the theory of evolution through the process of natural selection. In New England and elsewhere in America, scientific activity in all fields kept pace with developments in the Old World. Benjamin Silliman at Yale published his *Elements of Chemistry* in 1830; Asa Gray at Harvard brought out a notable *Manual of the Botany of the Northern United States* in 1848; Louis Agassiz of Switzerland began in 1846 a distinguished career at Harvard in the field of comparative zoology. The Harvard Astronomical Observatory in 1846 was equipped with the world's largest telescope; and in 1847 the American Association for the Advancement of Science was organized in Boston "to promote intercourse between American scientists, to give a strong and more systematic impulse to research, and to procure for the labors of scientific men increased facilities and wider usefulness." New England writers were aware of these scientific developments, and their writings reflect, in various ways and degrees, the influence of the new facts and the new theories of experimental science.

Emerson greeted the scientific movement with enthusiasm. "One of the distinctions of our century," he wrote, "has been the devotion of cultivated men to natural science; the benefits thence derived to the arts and to civilization are signal and immense." Late in life he declared, "If absolute leisure were offered me, I should run to the college or the scientific school which offered the best lectures on Geology, Chemistry, Minerals, and Botany." Although one cannot be sure that Emerson read all of the scientists to whom he refers in his writings, his scientific reading was remarkably wide and certainly included, among other things, the works of Newton, Linnæus, Buffon, Lamarck, Lyell, Gray, Agassiz, and Darwin. But Emerson was not himself a scientist, nor was he interested in science for its own sake. Science was of value to him for the moral and spiritual implications which scientific fact and theory suggested to his mind—a quite unscientific reason. He liked to draw illustrations of spiritual truth from physical phenomena ("The axioms of physics translate the law of ethics," he said), and his pages abound in analogies between natural and spiritual laws. He was delighted, furthermore, by the doctrine of evolution, particularly by the earlier evolutionary theory of the French naturalist, Chevalier de Lamarck, which seemed to him to confirm his optimistic view of humanity. Paraphrasing Lamarck, he wrote as a motto for *Nature:*

> And striving to be man, the worm
> Mounts through all the spires of form.

If the worm might become man, if the caterpillar might evolve into a philosopher, then the future of the constantly evolving human race became glorious to contemplate.

Thoreau's relation to science was much more intimate than Emerson's. Thoreau was interested in nature for its own sake quite as much as for its transcendental meanings. A student of botany and zoology, he liked to use the Latin names of plants and animals when he wrote about them. He sent to Agassiz, for identification, specimens of fish and turtles, some of which were unknown to the Harvard professor. Thoreau did not have, however, either the equipment or the temperament of the genuine scientist. He did not go beyond description of behavior and classification. He would not murder to dissect. A hawk could be best studied, he maintained, not as a "dead specimen," but free and soaring above the fields. In short, Thoreau was, to use the phrase of his friend Ellery Channing (a nephew of William Ellery Channing), "the *poet*-naturalist."

Among the Brahmins (the "aristocracy" of Boston, so named by Oliver Wendell Holmes), Longfellow and Lowell gave little attention to science, though Longfellow shared the general faith in the contributions of science to human progress. Lowell, on one occasion, twitted the Darwinians upon their arrogant assumption that evolution had supplanted God in the modern world (see his "Credidimus Jovem Regnare"). A third Brahmin, however, achieved a real distinction in science. Oliver Wendell Holmes studied medicine in Paris and from 1847 to 1882 was professor of anatomy and physiology in the Harvard Medical School. His most famous contribution to medical science was his essay on "The Contagiousness of Puerperal Fever" (1842), which materially aided the efforts of the medical profession to reduce the mortality of women in childbirth. Holmes' medical training gave him a scientific approach to his literary subjects. He became particularly interested in the problem of the bearing of heredity upon moral responsibility and the physical causes of mental aberrations, which is the subject of his novel *Elsie Venner* (1861) and of other writings. He stated the problem as follows in the preface to the novel:

> Was Elsie Venner, poisoned by the venom of a crotalus [rattlesnake] before she was born, morally responsible for the 'volitional' aberrations, which translated into acts become what is known as sin, and, it may be, what is punished as crime? If, on presentation of the evidence,

she becomes by the verdict of the human conscience a proper object of divine pity and not of divine wrath, as a subject of moral poisoning, wherein lies the difference between her position at the bar of judgment, human or divine, and that of the unfortunate victim who received a moral poison from a remote ancestor before he drew his first breath?

Holmes anticipated by at least a generation the approach of modern neurology. He was the author of many volumes of popular novels, essays, and verse, but he nevertheless considered his article on childbed fever his best title to fame.

Hawthorne, once again, is found perversely at odds with this self-confident, progressive, optimistic age. He discovered a danger in the new emphasis upon experimental science. In "Rappaccini's Daughter," in "Ethan Brand," and elsewhere, he examined the scientist and discovered that the scientist had been dehumanized. Of Dr. Rappaccini, "as true a man of science as ever distilled his own heart in an alembic," Hawthorne wrote: "His patients are interesting to him only as subjects for some new experiment. He would sacrifice human life, his own among the rest, or whatever else was dearest to him, for the sake of adding so much as a grain of mustard seed to the great heap of his accumulated knowledge." Likewise, Ethan Brand, a scientist in the field of experimental psychology, became "a cold observer, looking on mankind as the subject of his experiment"; he "lost his hold of the magnetic chain of humanity"; he became "a fiend." Hawthorne, like some other writers after him, seemed to think that the exclusive cultivation of the scientific faculty produces atrophy of soul, and creates and lets loose in the world an agent which is "fiendish" because utterly unmoral, a viewpoint that still persists in spy stories of "mad scientists" and science fiction, as well as more serious works.

New England: Changing Concepts of God and Man

The most important development in the religious thought of New England in this period was the break with Calvinism. Boston clergymen had become increasingly liberal in the eighteenth century (as shown in the opposition between Chauncy and Edwards), but it was not until the beginning of the nineteenth century that Unitarianism was strongly established. The appointment in 1805 of an avowed Unitarian to the chair of Divinity at Harvard, hitherto occupied by staunch Calvinists, may be taken as marking the transition. And yet the change from Calvinism to Unitarianism was perhaps not so complete, even in eastern Massachusetts, as some have supposed. That William Ellery Channing, the most influential of the early Unitarians, should have delivered his famous "Moral Argument Against Calvin-

ism" as late as 1820 would seem to suggest the tenacity of the old orthodox beliefs. Preaching from his Unitarian pulpit in 1831, Emerson desig-
nated the Calvinistic and Unitarian groups as the "rigid" and the "liberal"
parties, respectively, and urged his hearers to "borrow something of eternal
truth from both of these opinions."

The chief points of difference between Calvinism and Unitarianism as
expounded by Channing and his successors can be summarized briefly: (1)
The two beliefs differed in their conceptions of the Deity. Calvinism emphasized God's inexorable justice; Unitarianism stressed His benevolence.
The Unitarians questioned the justice of the doctrine of election: a God
who said (according to Michael Wigglesworth) "I do save none but mine
own elect" seemed arbitrary and capricious. (2) The two beliefs differed
in their conceptions of Christ. According to Calvinism, Christ is literally
the Son of God, the second member of the Holy Trinity. According to
Unitarianism, Christ is divine only in the sense in which all men are divine
or have an element, however small, of divinity in their nature. The difference between Christ and ordinary mortals becomes one of degree, not of
kind. (3) The two beliefs differed in their conceptions of man. Calvinism
asserted the innate depravity of man, his predestination, and the necessity
of his salvation through the atoning death of Christ. Unitarianism insisted
upon man's innate goodness and his spiritual freedom. The Atonement
became unnecessary to Unitarians, who preferred to point to Christ's life
as an example to be emulated by men already potentially good.

As a young man Channing lived for two years in Virginia, where he
presumably absorbed much of French romantic philosophy. From
Rousseau and writers of his school, Channing probably derived, and imported into Boston in the early 1800's, the ideas of the excellence of
human nature and its infinite perfectibility. The inscription on the base of
Channing's statue in Boston aptly summarizes his contribution to the
religious thought of New England: "He breathed into theology a humane
spirit and proclaimed anew the divinity of man." In his *The Flowering of
New England* Van Wyck Brooks justly declares, "By raising the general
estimate of human nature, which the old religion had despised, Channing
gave a prodigious impulse to the creative life."

By 1820 Channing could say, "Calvinism is giving place to better views.
We think the decline of Calvinism one of the most encouraging facts in our
passing history." Unitarianism became the religion particularly of the fashionable and the well-to-do in and around Boston. "Whoever clung to the
older faith," remarks Barrett Wendell, "did so at his social peril." Unitarianism, however, did not conquer the whole of New England. There were
scattered Unitarian outposts, such as the parish of Sylvester Judd in
Augusta, Maine, but the older faith continued to dominate in the regions
west and north of Boston.

Apart from both Calvinists and Unitarians, the Quakers were a compar-

atively small but important group. In early New England, Quakers were apt
to be obstreperously fanatical, but by the time of John Woolman their
fanaticism had diminished, and in nineteenth-century New England they
were, in the words of one historian, "inconspicuous and inoffensive." The
Quakers, however, were always active in social reform movements such as
abolitionism and pacificism.

Like the Calvinists, the Quakers believed in the divinity of Christ and
in the Bible as the inspired word of God. Like the Calvinists, too, they
insisted upon the essential sinfulness of man: "Too dark ye cannot paint
the sin," said John Greenleaf Whittier, their chief representative in literature, in "The Eternal Goodness," his best poetical statement of Quaker
belief. But Whittier in the poem objects to the "iron creeds" of the Calvinists and to their emphasis upon God's wrath; he prefers to think of "our
Lord's beatitudes." The Quakers emphasized the "Inner Light," which
God, they believed, gave to all human beings and which afforded an infal-
lible guide to the righteous life. Quakerism was more benevolent and
humanitarian than Calvinism, and more pietistic than Unitarianism. A
mere layman might experience some difficulty in distinguishing between
the doctrine of the Inner Light and the Emersonian doctrine of intuition.

Emerson, after less than three years in the Unitarian ministry, resigned
his pulpit in 1832 because of a growing dissatisfaction with the official
role of the clergyman and the formalities of the church. Unitarianism, he
felt, was good as far as it went; but it did not go far enough toward the
rehabilitation of the individual. The new doctrine of which Emerson became the chief interpreter is known as transcendentalism. Emerson's
Nature, published in 1836, was the bible of the early transcendentalists,
and the "Transcendental Club" was, from 1836 until about 1844, a center
of activity. Another focus was a quarterly magazine, *The Dial* (edited
1840-1842 by Margaret Fuller, and 1842-1844 by Emerson), which published many contributions by transcendentalists during its four-year existence. The group as a whole was greatly influenced by the idealistic philosophies of other lands and ages: by Plato and the Neo-platonists, by the
Oriental scriptures, by Kant and other German idealists—particularly as
interpreted by Coleridge and Carlyle.

Transcendentalism has been defined philosophically as "the recognition in man of the capacity of knowing truth intuitively, or of attaining
knowledge transcending the reach of the senses." It has been described
historically as having been "produced by the importing of German idealism
into American Unitarianism." The last definition indicates an important
relation between transcendentalism and Unitarianism and requires a consideration of the similarities and differences between the two.

Unitarianism prepared the way for transcendentalism by insisting that
man is essentially good and may trust his own perceptions of religious
truth. Channing spoke of "the confidence which is due to our rational and

moral faculties in religion" and said that "the ultimate reliance of a human being is and must be on his own mind." But it is important to observe two points of difference: (1) Channing, the Unitarian, expressed confidence in "our *rational* faculties." Emerson, the transcendentalist, drew a sharp distinction between the "Understanding," by which he meant the rational faculty, and the "Reason," by which he meant the suprarational or intuitive faculty; and he regarded the "Reason" as much more authoritative in spiritual matters than the "Understanding." (2) The transcendentalists carried this reliance upon the intuitive perceptions of the individual much further than conventional Unitarianism would warrant—carried it so far as to set aside even the authority of the Christian Bible. "Make your own Bible," said Emerson. "Select and collect all the words and sentences that in all your reading have been to you like the blast of a trumpet, out of Shakespeare, Seneca, Moses, John, and Paul." Emerson would renounce all authority, all standards and laws externally imposed: "Nothing is at last sacred but the integrity of your own mind." He proclaimed this glorification of intuition and the repudiation of all external religious authority to a Unitarian audience at Harvard in 1838: "Thank God for these good men [meaning the Saints and the Prophets] but say 'I also am a man.'" The result was a storm of protest. Emerson's transcendentalism had gone far beyond the bounds even of liberal Unitarianism.

Transcendental thought in the abstract can be best studied in Emerson. His disciples, of whom there were many, were usually interested more in practice than in theory and attempted to apply Emerson's individualistic doctrines in various practical ways. Many of them, finding that they could not effect the social changes they wanted singlehandedly, turned to collective action and founded societies of like-minded people. If the membership grew large enough, considerable political pressure could be—and was—exerted, as will be seen shortly.

Many passages in Henry David Thoreau seem echoes of Emerson, though Thoreau's expression of the thought is always more concrete than Emerson's. "The fact is," Thoreau wrote in his journal in 1853, "I am a mystic, a transcendentalist, and a natural philosopher to boot"—meaning by "natural philosopher" a scientific student of nature. The emphasis in the statement is significant. Mystical, transcendental passages abound in Thoreau, especially in his earlier writings, as they abound everywhere in Emerson. But as Thoreau grew older, his interest in the observation and description of the world of nature became more and more absorbing. He became—as his journals of the 1850's attest—more of the natural philosopher and somewhat less of the transcendentalist.

Transcendental ideas scarcely touched the writers of Boston and Cambridge. Influenced by his medical studies, Dr. Holmes approached religious problems from the scientific point of view. He objected to the Calvinistic condemnation of sinners because he believed that wrongdoing is often the result of an unfortunate heredity; bad men, he thought, should be treated as if they were insane. On the positive side, he had no transcendental ardor, but rather a rationalistic belief in the ability of the soul, in favorable circumstances, to "build more stately mansions." Henry Wadsworth Longfellow's religious thought—such as it was—was mildly Unitarian, pleasantly optimistic about life and death. And James Russell Lowell, although he could write appreciatively of the stimulating effect of Emerson (". . . he made us conscious of the supreme and everlasting originality of whatever bit of soul might be in any of us"), was not a disciple; nor was he in sympathy with transcendental ideas. "The word 'transcendental,' " he declared in the unsympathetic essay on Thoreau, "was the maid of all work for those who could not think." The men of Boston and Cambridge found the Concord air too rarefied for their mundane needs.

The chief spokesman of the opposition to transcendentalism, however, was Nathaniel Hawthorne, who returned, in part at least, to the Calvinist position. He satirized utopian reforms on the ground that superficial reform measures avail nothing so long as the human heart, which is innately sinful, remains unregenerated. "Purify that inward sphere," he advised in "Earth's Holocaust," "and the many shapes of evil that haunt the outward will vanish of their own accord." He satirized Unitarianism and transcendentalism in "The Celestial Railroad"; Bunyan's arduous pilgrimage seemed to him still the best way of reaching the Celestial City. In stories and novels he showed that evil is an ever present reality, not an illusion to be brushed aside, and that self-reliant individualism alone does not save man from disaster. Hawthorne is a striking example of the persistence of the Puritan point of view in an age of liberalism and progressivism.

But it would be a mistake to suppose that the Puritan inheritance affected Hawthorne alone. It was everywhere present, giving native roots and indigenous strength to New England's flowering. The religious emphasis was a Puritan trait, as was the emphasis on books and reading. The transcendental pursuit of perfection was the old Puritan pursuit of perfection in a new guise and on different terms. The diaries of Emerson, Thoreau, and Hawthorne continued an old Puritan practice; and the soul searchings in Emerson and Thoreau recall passages in Cotton Mather and Jonathan Edwards. When Emerson said that the poet "must drink water out of a wooden bowl," he was quoting the most austere of English Puritans, John Milton. The austerity of Emerson and Thoreau, and of Hawthorne, too, was of the essence of Puritanism. If this Puritan essence was considerably diluted in the other writers of the period, it nevertheless made itself felt. It came out in the ethical earnestness of Longfellow and Lowell and in their native attachments. In sum, the great period of New England literature would have been impossible without the two centuries of Puritan inheritance. It is hardly an accident that the three New England writers of the period whose works seem most likely to endure—Emerson, Thoreau, and Hawthorne—are the writers whose roots were deepest in New England's Puritan past.

Herman Melville: Explorer of the World and Enigmas

After a boyhood in New York City and Albany, a voyage to Liverpool,
three years in the South Seas, a brief second residence in New York City,
and a journey to London and Paris, the much-traveled Herman Melville
settled in 1850, at the age of thirty-one, at "Arrowhead" near Pittsfield,
Massachusetts. Obviously he was not a product of Massachusetts nor a part
of the literary movement of New England, but his Massachusetts residence
—which lasted, with interruptions for other travels, for more than twenty
years—brought him within the sphere of influence of the New England
Renaissance. He met in the Berkshires many of the New England writers
and struck up a stimulating and sympathetic friendship with Hawthorne,
who in 1850-1851 resided at nearby Lenox. It is significant that Melville
wrote his greatest book, *Moby Dick*, during the months of his close association with Hawthorne and that he dedicated the book to Hawthorne.

Like Hawthorne, Melville was concerned with the darker side of human
fate. Both insisted upon the reality of evil in the world; both were skeptical of the optimism of Emerson and his benevolent theory of the Universe;
both presented the tragedies of the mind and soul. Hawthorne agreed with
Bunyan's *Pilgrim's Progress*, where man is represented as going through life
weighed down by a burden of sin. Melville called Ecclesiastes "the truest
of all books . . . the fine hammered steel of woe."

Melville had seen at first hand the brutality of ship captains, the depravity of Old World cities, the vices brought to the South Sea islanders by
"civilized" invaders. More than that, evil appeared triumphant (as in
Pierre), even when man's motives were virtuous. Why, Melville asked, did a
good God—if indeed He is good—permit evil in His world? Melville could
not accept the Universe with as much resignation as his friend Hawthorne.
He persisted in challenging the riddle, courageously, defiantly.

In *Moby Dick*, which is a compendium of Melville's metaphysical spec-
ulations, Captain Ahab relentlessly pursues the White Whale only to be
destroyed in the end. The allegory is susceptible of many interpretations.
To Ahab "all evil was visibly personified and made practically assailable in
Moby Dick." Ahab, however, is not the embodiment of unmixed good:
his conduct is irrational and foolhardy; it is contrary to the well-being of
others; it is motivated by revenge. Elsewhere, Ahab (and perhaps Melville)
saw in Moby Dick "outrageous strength with an inscrutable malice sin-
ewing it," and he hated chiefly the *inscrutability* of the whale. The story
perhaps represents man's hopeless but heroic attempt to search out the
inscrutable, to know the unknowable; the tragedy of man becomes the
tragedy of his limited comprehension. But whatever the interpretation—
and each reader must make his own, for the allegory with its countless
ramifications is too complex to admit of a simple, categorical explanation
—Melville's Ahab, like Ethan Brand and other characters of Hawthorne,

becomes completely obsessed with this one pursuit and sacrifices everything else to it. If the tragedy of man is his inability to possess complete
knowledge of himself and his destiny, Ahab's tragedy is his monomania,
the narrow range of his passion.

Melville's chief concern was with profound enigmas—the nature of God
and man, the mystery of "Providence, Foreknowledge, Will and Fate"
—and like Milton's philosophers he "found no end, in wandering mazes
lost." He was not, however, indifferent to the more mundane problems of
modern society, and scattered through his works one finds abundant evidence of his awareness of contemporary social questions.

His own observation of tyranny on shipboard and the exploitation of
the native population on the Pacific islands had awakened in him a flaming
passion for social justice in a truly democratic society. This passion was
expressed angrily in *White-Jacket*, where he condemned the naval practice
of flogging, and philosophically and satirically in *Mardi*, where he surveyed
the governments, beliefs, and manners of much of the nineteenth-century
world.

The latter book is of special importance for the student of Melville's
social ideas with reference to his own country. He was critical of America's
faults. "Vivenza [the United States] was a braggadocio": boastfulness was
getting to be a national habit; after all, God should be given some credit
for our mountains and rivers. The existence of slavery nullified our noble
Declaration of Independence. The war against Mexico was foisted upon
the nation by the imperialistic action of the President. The California of
the gold rush was a "golden Hell." And speaking more radically, Melville
pointed out the incompleteness of our freedom: political freedom alone
was not enough, for "freedom is more social than political." But despite
these and many other imperfections, the young American democracy
inspired in Melville an ardent faith. The West was a source of fresh hope—
Westerners "were a fine young tribe; like strong new wine they worked
violently in becoming clear." "In its better aspect," he declared, "Vivenza
was a noble land": "Like a young tropic tree she stood, laden down with
greenness, myriad blossoms, and the ripened fruit thick-hanging from one
bough. She was promising as the morning. Or Vivenza might be likened to
St. John, feeding on locusts and wild honey, and with prophetic voice,
crying to the nations from the wilderness. Or, childlike, standing among
the old robed kings and emperors of the Archipelago, Vivenza seemed a
young Messiah, to whose discourse the bearded Rabbis bowed." Like
Hawthorne, Melville was a philosophical pessimist and a political optimist.
It was possible to believe in original sin and still be a democrat.

Religion and Politics: Southern Versions

The greatest writer of the ante-bellum South, Edgar Allan Poe, has usually been thought of as completely aloof from the intellectual currents of his time. V. L. Parrington confirmed this view in his famous pronouncement, "The problem of Poe, fascinating as it is, lies quite outside the main current of American thought. . . ." It is true that Poe was not a philosopher, like Emerson, or a political propagandist, like Lowell, or a critic of society, like Thoreau. But it does not follow that he was without ideas and attitudes which are relevant both to his own work and to the history of American thought.

The late Professor Margaret Alterton summed up Poe's social and political attitudes as follows:

> Poe rejected democracy, social reform, and the doctrine of progress. . . . He had no faith in democratic institutions and no belief in human perfectibility or natural goodness. He despised the mob. . . . He endorsed and defended the institution of slavery, and regarded the abolition movement with horror as an envious attack on the rights of property.

Poe, in short, went to the aristocratic extreme.

One reason for Poe's attitudes, no doubt, was his proud, fastidious temperament; another, his desire to identify himself with, and be accepted by, the aristocracy of his adopted region, the South. His repeated attacks on New Englanders seem to have been motivated, in part, by regional prejudice—the following attack on Lowell, for example: "Mr. Lowell is one of the most rabid of the abolition fanatics, and no Southerner who does not wish to be insulted . . . should ever touch a volume of this author."

If Poe's aristocratic sentiments seem a little artificial and stagey, they nevertheless colored his view of life and conditioned the kind of fiction he wrote. "The House of Usher" is a typical Poe symbol of an aristocracy decadent but beautiful. The decay of the Usher line contained no seeds of a democratic birth. The attitude is, at bottom, perhaps the Gothic-aristocratic admiration of a noble and picturesque ruin.

Poe was so completely the artist that any discussion of his ideas and attitudes is likely to impinge upon the discussion of his literary achievements, for his ideas and attitudes can hardly be treated apart from their embodiment in his poetry and fiction. Two aspects of his thought, however, may be mentioned. These aspects are separable, and yet in the ultimate reaches of Poe's thought they seem to unite in a mystic union.

One is a scientific rationalism which is best illustrated in *Eureka*. In this quasi-philosophical work, Poe attempted an analysis of the universe based upon Newtonian principles. He was concerned with such philosophical pairs as repulsion-attraction, diffusion-gravitation, and variety-unity. The universe, Poe believed, had a mathematical beauty and precision in which one might catch a glimpse of the divine. He said, characteristically: "The plots of God are perfect. The Universe is a plot of God." Poe may have thought that in his own plot structures he was embodying a divine principle.

Another aspect of Poe's thought might be called imaginative idealism. It is instructive to compare the idealisms of Poe and Emerson; though both owed something to Coleridge, they are essentially different. "Beauty," Emerson said with staid Puritan accent, "is the mark God sets upon virtue." Poe, on the other hand, spoke of "the human aspiration for Supernal Beauty," in the contemplation of which one experiences "an elevating excitement of the soul." Poe thought poetry could give a vision of this supernal beauty: in the reading of poetry, he said, "we are often made to feel, with a shivering delight, that from an earthly harp are stricken notes which cannot have been unfamiliar to the angels." Although it may not be true that he was confusing an excitement of the nerves with a true vision of the Ideal, it seems fair enough to say that whereas Emerson's idealism was profoundly moral, Poe's was narrowly, possibly morbidly, aesthetic.

Poe's social and political conservatism was buttressed by the scientific analogy of a perfect and stable universe; as such, it was representative of an important facet of American thought during the period. His concept of the Idea was a union of mathematics and music—a "supernal beauty" pure and unearthly. His aestheticism was, on its negative side, a protest against the Puritan overemphasis on the moralistic in literature; and Poe himself became the chief symbol of the American artist who is at odds with the crass world about him.

Religious questions were not nearly so vital in Southern literature as in the literature of New England and in the writings of Melville. Southern writers, in general, did not concern themselves with spiritual laws, like Emerson; or with remorse for sin, like Hawthorne; or with metaphysical speculation, like Melville. Indeed, in religious matters the cultivated Southerner was likely to be tolerant to the point of indifference. John Pendleton Kennedy's account of Frank Meriwether in *Swallow Barn* (1832) may be regarded as fairly typical of the gentry of the Old South:

If my worthy cousin be somewhat over-argumentative as a politician, he restores the equilibrium of his character by a considerate coolness in religious matters. He piques himself upon being a high-churchman, but is not the most diligent frequenter of places of worship, and very seldom permits himself to get into a dispute upon points of faith. If Mr. Chub, the Presbyterian tutor in the family, ever succeeds in drawing him into this field, as he occasionally has the address to do, Meri-

wether is sure to fly the course; he gets puzzled with scripture names,
and makes some odd mistakes between Peter and Paul, and then generally turns the parson over to his wife, who, he says, has an astonishing
memory.

Good form, however, required a decent respect for the outward obser-
vances of religion. Among the aristocracy, the Episcopal Church was the
best form; the Presbyterian, though less good, was socially acceptable.
Meanwhile, it should be noted, the revivalistic evangelism of the Methodists and Baptists flourished on the frontiers west of Charleston and Richmond, and by the time of the Civil War had enlisted such a large following
as to change materially the religious complexion of the South.

The conservative Southerner was likely to consider the Puritan a dis-
agreeable fellow—crabbed in temperament, morbid in the pursuit of virtue.
William Gilmore Simms preferred the Cavalier type. If religious ideas became articulate in the Charleston of Simms or the Baltimore of Kennedy,
they were likely to take on a rationalistic, eighteenth-century flavor. A
statement by Kennedy on his sixty-fifth birthday might have come from
Franklin or Jefferson: "I endeavor to avoid the uncharitableness of sectarian opinion, and maintain an equal mind toward the various forms in
which an earnest piety shapes the divisions of the world of believers—tolerating honest differences as the right of all sincere thinkers, and looking
only to the kindly nature of Christian principle as it influences the personal lives and conduct of men, as the substantial and true test of a sound
religion."

Politics, however, were another matter. The Old South had a genius
for politics, and nothing delighted the Charleston lawyer or the Virginia
planter more than a political discussion. The hero of *Swallow Barn* was a
Jeffersonian Democrat who supported the rights of the states and preferred the agrarianism of the South to the mercantilism and industrialism
of the North. In early life Kennedy doubtless agreed with his hero; but he
later opposed the new Jacksonian Democracy, satirizing it vigorously in
Quodlibet (1840). As a result of his connections with the business interests
of Baltimore, he became a Whig advocate of the protective tariff for manu-
facturers and ended a staunch Unionist and Republican.

Simms' political course was the reverse of Kennedy's: he began as a
Unionist and became an ardent champion of states' rights. New occasions
teach new duties, Simms might have said. When he opposed nullification
of federal law in South Carolina in 1832, he was supporting Jackson and
the issue was the tariff. When he advocated nullification in South Carolina
twenty years later, he was supporting Calhoun and the issue was slavery.

Although Simms was more democratic in his sympathies than Kennedy
—possibly because of youthful experiences on the Southwestern frontier—
the two men agreed that the business of government belonged in the abler

hands of the ruling class, ordinarily the planter aristocracy. As to the subject races—the Indian and the Negro—writers like Kennedy and Simms
believed that their state of subjection argued their intrinsic inferiority and
that their superiors should maintain them in humane tutelage until some
distant time when emancipation might prove feasible. Kennedy painted a
disarming picture of the master-slave relationship at Swallow Barn, where
he found "an air of contentment and good humor and kind family attachment." He looked forward to gradual emancipation and the possible success of colonizing experiments. Simms' early view was substantially the
same. His later violent championship of slavery as "a wisely devised institution of heaven" can be understood only in the light of the sectional controversy of the 1850's.

New England's Reformers

"We are all a little wild here with numberless projects of social reform,"
Emerson wrote to Carlyle in 1840. "Not a reading man but has a draft of a
new community in his waistcoat pocket."

The impetus to remake society was in part economic. A period of road-
and canal-building, in which many states had overextended their credit,
together with widespread land speculation and "wildcat" banking, had
ended in the Panic of 1837, which was followed by five or six years of
hard times. Religion, however, was perhaps an even greater force in a
movement which often combined the forces of Quakers and transcendentalists for the betterment of a world they thought sick in many ways.

Transcendentalism's best-known attempt to construct a model with
which to contrast the inadequacies of the capitalist system was Brook
Farm, organized in 1841 and dissolved in 1847. Its foremost leader was a
Unitarian clergyman, George Ripley. The community, he wrote, was "to
guarantee the highest mental freedom, by providing all with labor adapted
to their tastes and talents, and securing to them the fruits of their industry;
to do away with the necessity of menial services by opening the benefits of
education to all; and thus to prepare a society of liberal, intelligent, and
cultivated persons, whose relations with each other would permit a more
wholesome and simple life than can be led amidst the pressure of our com-
petitive institutions." In its last years, Brook Farm adopted the organization into phalanxes proposed by the French socialist F. M. C. Fourier and
followed in numerous other American Utopian communities. The Christian
idealism which Ripley represented constituted, however, Brook Farm's
main strength.

Most of the transcendentalists, and indeed most of the New England
clergy, were much interested in the effort to bring together on common
ground the worker and the thinker. Among the many visitors were

Emerson, Margaret Fuller, Theodore Parker, Elizabeth Peabody, Orestes Brownson, and Bronson Alcott. Hawthorne resided at Brook Farm for some months; *The Blithedale Romance* is a distillation of some of his memories of an experiment whose intentions he respected, however unhappy he was about pitching manure as one of his chores.

Brook Farm was conservative in comparison with Fruitlands, the community founded in the spring of 1843 by Alcott and a mystical English friend, Charles Lane. Their ideal was to use nothing which has caused wrong or death to man or beast. Outlawed, therefore, were sugar, molasses, tea, and cotton, all products of slavery or peonage. Milk, butter, cheese, meat, fish, and whale oil were forbidden, since they involved the exploitation of innocent animals. Wool was felt to be the theft of the lawful property of sheep and silk no better than "worm-slaughter." Some substitute for shoe leather was envisioned, and only by subterfuge did Joseph Palmer bring in cattle to plow the land to be used for raising vegetables. (Palmer, by the way, wore a beard because he felt it given him by God, and had spent some time in prison for assaulting some of his smoothshaven tormentors.) Alcott is said to have preferred to subsist upon "aspiring" vegetables such as peas, beans, and corn, rather than upon those which mundanely chose to grow in the dirt. The tensions which developed within this small group of dreamers (or lunatics, as many called them) are described in a sketch by Louisa May Alcott ("Transcendental Wild Oats," *Silver Pitchers*, 1876), who was eleven when Fruitlands collapsed in January 1844.

Most reformers wanted some kind of change, as quickly as possible, and had little wish to form model communities. Their method was to organize societies to promote their causes. Local at first, then statewide, and eventually national or even international in structure, these organizations consolidated their positions at conventions, and often moved into politics by exerting pressure upon Congressmen, public officials, and newspaper editors. What usually began in the consciences of a few concerned individuals was by this process changed into powerful collective action. The classic examples are the abolition movement, which had favored the quiet persuasion of men like John Woolman before its metamorphosis into a militancy which generated violence, and the antiliquor campaign, which abandoned the goal of temperance in favor of prohibition.

Although New Englanders were not alone in their desire for social improvement, a surprisingly large number of leaders came from that region. Among Emerson's contemporaries who worked for various causes were Margaret Fuller and Susan B. Anthony (equal rights for women), Louis Dwight (more humane treatment of prisoners), Dorothea Dix (greater sympathy for the insane), Thomas Hopkins Gallaudet (the education of deaf-mutes), Samuel Gridley Howe (the education of the blind), Horace Mann (the education of youth in general), Neal Dow (prohibition of spirituous liquors), Elihu Burritt (the outlawing of war), and William Lloyd Garrison (the abolition of slavery). Few reformers, however, limited themselves to a single task. Garrison, for example, crusaded at one time or another not only for abolition but also for woman's suffrage, prohibition, justice for the Indians, stricter observance of the Sabbath, the elimination of capital punishment and of imprisonment for debt, limitation of the use of tobacco, and pacifism. He was on hand, of course, for the Chardon Street Convention in Boston in 1840, called together by the Friends of Universal Reform. So many good causes were being urged upon Americans, and so great was the confidence of the more radical that a new world was on the verge of creation, that Hawthorne was stirred to mild satire of the reform movements in "Earth's Holocaust" (1844).

The abolition of slavery was of course the most immediately important of these many crusades, and the most far-reaching in its effects. The centrality of the slavery question in the westward expansion of the nation and the concomitant struggles for political power will be described in the next section. Two events which occurred in Boston in 1829 should be mentioned, however, because they mark a highly significant change in attitudes toward Negro slavery.

One was the publication of David Walker's *Appeal*, the first literary expression of the convictions of a free Negro about the oppression of his race. Walker was what we call today a black nationalist. He had a profound contempt for "white Christians," was convinced that the destruction of a nation which not only tolerated but even fostered racism was not far off, and advocated whatever violence was necessary to give blacks control of their own destiny. Needless to say, Southern officials did their best to see that Walker's pamphlet was kept out of circulation.

Militancy also marked the 1829 Fourth of July address by Garrison—his first public demand for immediate, complete emancipation, the theme of the periodical he would found in 1831, *The Liberator*. Garrison had no political or economic program (he is said to have voted only once in his life), but he was determined to right a moral wrong with the greatest possible speed. For the next thirty years he was to attack with equal outrage the owners of slaves and the government which protected an immoral institution.

Garrison had a part in the founding of the New England Anti-Slavery Society in 1831 and of the American Anti-Slavery Society in 1833. Not all abolitionists shared his distaste for political activity, and in 1839 those who favored working to change the laws and amend the Constitution formed the American and Foreign Anti-Slavery Society, in which Whittier was a leader for some years. The Liberty Party polled many thousands of votes in the presidential elections of 1840 and 1844; numerous abolitionists supported the candidates of the Free-Soil Party in 1848 and 1852; and many of them had a share in the formation of the new Republican Party,

which ran John Charles Fremont for President in 1856 and Abraham
Lincoln in 1860. The power thrust of abolitionism was, however, more
moral than political, as a review of events will show.

Toward Civil War

The debate over Texas coincided in time with the abandonment of apolo-
gies for slavery by Southern whites, who by 1835 were glorifying their "peculiar institution" as the best possible solution to the economic and moral
problems of a biracial and agricultural society. Their militancy was in part
a reaction to the abolitionism of Walker and Garrison, but its real basis was
probably economic. Cotton was now the chief export of the United States
and the demand for slaves was so great that unscrupulous owners were
breeding Negroes for sale like cattle. Whatever may have been the reason,
proslavery books and pamphlets now became numerous. The white South
obviously was on the offensive.

Its leaders, of whom John C. Calhoun is the most notable, were skillful
politicians, influential in national politics and in the halls of Congress.
They argued vigorously, of course, for the sovereign powers of the States
and against an overcentralized government. For many years they were
successful.

The antislavery forces were particularly horrified that slavery and trade
in slaves existed in the District of Columbia. For years petitions had poured
in for Congress to do something about it. In 1836 the House adopted a
rule that all petitions relating to slavery should be tabled. Other "gag"
rules followed; their effect was to increase rather than lessen political ten-
sion. The petitions multiplied; on a single day (February 14, 1838) John
Quincy Adams presented 350 to the House, 158 of them against the most
recent gag-rule, 54 against the annexation of Texas.

In this atmosphere Martin Van Buren, who became President in 1837,
opposed annexation, believing that it would lead to war. A treaty was
drawn up in John Tyler's administration only to be rejected in the Senate
by a vote of more than two to one. John Quincy Adams rejoiced at this
defeat of the proslavery interests; "I record this vote as a deliverance, I
trust, by the special interposition of Almighty God, of my country and
human liberty from a conspiracy comparable to that of Lucius Sergius
Catalina." (Calhoun was the Catiline Adams had in mind, Sam Houston a
fellow-conspirator!) "The annexation of Texas," Adams continued, "is the
first step in the conquest of all Mexico, of the West India islands, of a mari-
time, colonizing, slave-tainted monarchy, and of extinguished freedom."

The expansionists, however, were not long restrained. In 1844 Van
Buren had been rejected as leader of the Democrats, and Henry Clay and
the Whigs virtually destroyed, both largely because of their opposition to

the annexation. James K. Polk, a "dark-horse" Democratic nominee, was President-elect, and before his inauguration a joint resolution of the two houses of Congress authorized the administration to invite Texas to join the Union, with the right of subdividing into five states if the Texans so decided.

"The annexation of Texas," Emerson wrote in his journal, "looks like one of those events which retard or retrograde the civilization of ages. But the World Spirit is a good swimmer, and storms and waves cannot easily drown him. He snaps his fingers at laws." Most New Englanders, for all their faith in divine providence, were more perturbed. All the political know-how of Daniel Webster, all the editorials of Whittier, all the shouting of Garrison had failed them.

The war with Mexico, which began in 1846 with a skirmish over the disputed western boundary of Texas, was an even greater blow to New England idealists. James Russell Lowell, in the first series of *The Biglow Papers* (1847-1848), expressed the prevailing opinion that Polk's intention was the extension of slavery. Lowell also was aware of how the unequal contest would appear to later generations of Yankee-hating Latin-Americans. One of Lowell's characters, Birdofredum Sawin, the Massachusetts rustic unwary enough to have enlisted in the army, writes home of the Mexicans:

> I'd an idee that they were built arter the darkie fashion all.
> An' kickin' colored folks about, you know, 's a kind of national;
> But wen I jined I worn't so wise ez thet air queen of Sheby,
> Fer, come to look at 'em, they aint much diff'rent from wut we be,
> An' here we air ascrougin' 'em out o' thir own dominions,
> Ashelterin' 'em, as Caleb sez, under our eagle's pinions,
> Wich means to take a feller up jest by the slack o' 's trowsis
> An' walk him Spanish clean right out o' all his homes an' houses;
> Wal, it doos seem a curus way, but then hooraw fer Jackson!
> It must be right, fer Caleb sez it's reg'lar Anglo-saxon.

The "Mexican Polka" (as Homer Wilbur called it) created a familiar dilemma between patriotism and conscience. Governor George N. Briggs of Massachusetts, a devout Baptist committed to abolition, temperance, and other liberal causes, had to cooperate with the administration in Washington and raise troops and taxes. Thoreau, on the other hand, spent a night in the Concord jail in the summer of 1846 for refusing to pay his poll tax; the result was the world-renowned *Civil Disobedience* (1849), a classic treatment of its subject.

That Polk wished to acquire far more territory than Texas was clear to everyone. The antislavery forces therefore supported a rider proposed by Congressman David Wilmot of Pennsylvania to an administration bill asking $2,000,000 to arrange a peace. The Wilmot Proviso, intended to prohibit slavery in any territory acquired from Mexico, passed the House in 1846 and 1847, but was defeated in the Senate. Among its supporters were Abraham Lincoln in the House and Daniel Webster in the Senate.

The war lasted longer than had been expected, but it was over by the autumn of 1847 and the Treaty of Guadalupe Hidalgo was signed early in 1848. For $15,000,000 and the assumption of responsibility for claims by Americans against Mexico, the United States added the vast area which today comprises the states of California, Nevada, and Utah, and parts of Arizona, New Mexico, Colorado, and Wyoming. With this new territory came the problems of dealing with additional minorities not readily assimilable to "Anglo" culture: the southwestern Indians and the Spanish-speaking Roman Catholics living from Texas to California.

At the time, however, the paramount issue was slavery. If the line of latitude adopted in the Missouri Compromise were to be maintained, over half of the area would be open to slavery. If Congress were to adopt the Wilmot Proviso, slavery would be confined to Texas, which claimed all the lands east of the Rio Grande, including well over half of present-day New Mexico.

Acrimonious debates which ended with the short-lived Compromise of 1850 were precipitated by the discovery of gold in California in 1848. Immigrants, most of them males, poured in from all over the world. Within a year more than 40,000 got there by wagon train across the plains and mountains; thousands more made the trip by way of the Isthmus of Panama. By the end of 1849 these newcomers had drawn up and adopted a state constitution prohibiting slavery, held elections, and asked for admission to the Union.

Calhoun, although he realized that most of the newly acquired land was unsuitable for plantation labor, took the position that all territories were the common property of the several states, to be administered by the central government as a trusteeship. Further, any citizen of any state had the right to take his property (slaves included) to any territory and have federal protection for it until that territory became a state. This argument proved to be no more than a delaying action, but it shows how sensitive the white South had become about its way of life.

Early in 1850 Henry Clay introduced a series of eight resolutions in the Senate, hoping to reach an amicable settlement of the issue. The debate which followed has been called the greatest in Congressional history; it was not finally concluded until the latter part of September. Calhoun's speech of March 4 and Webster's of March 7 are among the best-known statements of position on the issues which were to bring on civil war.

Among the measures eventually agreed to were the admission of California as a free state, the organization of New Mexico and Utah as territories which would decide the question of slavery for themselves when ready for statehood, the payment of $10,000,000 to Texas for giving up her claim to eastern New Mexico, and a much more stringent law to assure the return of escaped slaves to their owners. Webster's concurrence with the last of these provisions brought him the contempt not only of abolitionists but also of many former admirers. "The word *liberty* in the mouth of Mr. Webster," Emerson wrote, "sounds like the word *love* in the mouth of a courtezan."

In accordance with Article IV, Section 2, of the Constitution, laws requiring the free states to return fugitive slaves had existed since 1790. They had not, however, been obeyed. Thousands of slaves—precisely how many thousands no one knows—had gained their freedom by running away, and if they reached a free state they were more and more likely to find shelter, clothing, and means of transportation to Canada. The Underground Railroad was in operation early in the century; after 1830 its surreptitious but efficient defiance of the law became, as Calhoun phrased it, "notorious and palpable."

The Quakers, clergymen, and others who saw freeing slaves as a duty higher than that of complying with laws protecting slaveowners had no intention of changing their ways. On the contrary, their efforts to assist fugitives redoubled. They invaded courtrooms and freed escapees by force. With every instance of a slave being returned to the South, antislavery feeling intensified. As Emerson once hinted, a standing army would have been required to enforce the Fugitive Slave Law.

The successful escape of slaves to Canada provided the climax for Mrs. Stowe's *Uncle Tom's Cabin* (1852), a novel enormously popular in the North and in England and almost immediately dramatized in various forms. Its portrayal of slavery, although in some respects highly sentimental (Uncle Tom's Christian meekness has irritated black readers for over a century), infuriated Southern whites. William J. Grayson, in *The Hireling and the Slave* (1854), charged Mrs. Stowe with possessing a "venal pencil and malignant heart." She wrote, he thought, for profit and British recognition. In his preface, Grayson spoke for most slaveholders: "What have the Abolitionists done, what have they given, for the Negro race? They use the slave for the purposes of self-glorification only, indifferent about his present or future condition. They are ambitious to bring about a great social revolution—what its effects may be they do not care to inquire."

The most colorful figure of the 1850's was "Old Brown of Ossawatomie." Thoreau thought John Brown a man of "rare common sense" and compared him to Oliver Cromwell. Emerson wrote that he was "a pure idealist of artless goodness." The more general opinion was that he was insane, and unquestionably his schemes for liberating the Negroes were somewhat less than practical. The end, for him, justified any necessary means, and he proved quite willing to die for his convictions.

"John Brown's Body," the marching song of Northern soldiers in the

Civil War, is thought to have been based on the tune of a Negro camp-meeting hymn. Julia Ward Howe used the same tune for her "Battle Hymn of the Republic," also inspired by Brown. She caught as well as anyone the spirit of a man with one flaming conviction:

> Mine eyes have seen the glory of the coming of the Lord;
> He is trampling out the vintage where the grapes of wrath are stored;
> He has loosed the fateful lightning of His terrible swift sword,
> His truth is marching on.

John Brown was born in Connecticut and brought up in Ohio. He had little education aside from learning his father's trade, tanning. Twice married, he fathered twenty children. Markedly unsuccessful in business, he moved with his family many times, spending brief periods in Pennsylvania, Massachusetts, Virginia, and New York. From his youth he was an abolitionist, active in the Underground Railroad, organizing free Negroes, and fostering educational projects which he hoped would hasten emancipation. His family shared both his intense hatred of slavery and his religious zeal.

Brown's fame was an aftermath of the Kansas-Nebraska Act of 1854, a compromise measure which organized the two territories on the same basis as Utah and New Mexico, allowing the settlers to decide for themselves whether or not to permit slavery. Behind this annulment of the Missouri Compromise was the rivalry of Chicago and St. Louis for control of the route of the transcontinental railroad which everyone knew was soon to be built. Stephen A. Douglas wanted to make sure that Nebraska was not left to the Indians; David R. Atchison wished to clear the way for the expansion of the Missouri railroads to the West. The decision about slavery, one of the results of these men's horsetrading in Congress, was bitterly attacked by the abolitionists. They acted quickly to see that antislavery settlers would outnumber the proslavery Southerners, organizing such societies as the New England Emigrant Aid Company, which financed the establishment of a Free-Soil colony at Lawrence. Among the settlers were five of John Brown's sons.

They recognized almost at once that the issue was not likely to be settled peacefully, and sent word to their father that arms and ammunition were needed. He filled a wagon with weapons, topped the load with surveying instruments, and drove to Kansas. He reached Ossawatomie in the autumn of 1855 and, rightly anticipating guerilla warfare, became the leader of an armed militia. In May 1856 the town of Lawrence was attacked and its hotel and newspaper offices burned. Brown decided upon retaliation. He made a list of those whose extermination seemed most likely to give proslavery men a "restraining fear," and during the night of May 24 led a party of six, including four of his sons, in the killing of five of his enemies. Not surprisingly, Ossawatomie was attacked and burned in

August, despite Brown's vigorous defense. Terrorism and reprisal gave a new dimension to the abolition movement.

Thinking himself an instrument of God, Brown next attempted a plan he had long had in mind: the establishment of a mountain stronghold for fugitive slaves, free Negroes, and militant abolitionists. His idea was that they should arm themselves and make periodic raids into the slave states to free as many Negroes as possible, perhaps in time all in the South. Brown raised some money to support this scheme and in the summer of 1859 rented a farm near Harper's Ferry, Virginia, at the juncture of the Shenandoah and Potomac rivers, fifty-five miles from Washington. There he secretly assembled a tiny army of about twenty men, who in the night of October 16 seized the United States arsenal and armory in the town. Militia quickly blocked Brown's retreat, and a detachment of marines commanded by Col. Robert E. Lee captured Brown after an engagement which cost the lives of half of Brown's men, including two of his sons. He was tried for treason, convicted, and hanged at Charlestown on December 2.

On October 19 Thoreau had begun to record in his journal his views on John Brown, "the bravest and humanest man in all the country." No current event ever stirred the author of *Walden* more deeply than the Harper's Ferry incident; it was for him "the best news that America has ever heard." "A Plea for Captain John Brown," an address derived from the journal, was delivered in Concord on October 30; it flatly contradicted the opinion of editors and townspeople that Brown was insane. Thoreau spoke again at the memorial service held in Concord the day of Brown's execution and prepared remarks for a burial service which he was unable to attend. That Thoreau, whose strategy was usually that of passive resistance, should so admire John Brown is remarkable evidence of the depth of feeling about slavery by 1859. From a staunch refusal to associate himself with the abolition societies he had reached the point of writing, "I do not complain of any tactics that are effective of good, whether one wields the quill or the sword, but I shall not think him mistaken who quickest succeeds to liberate the slave. I will judge of the tactics by the fruits."

Lincoln spoke less kindly of John Brown in his famous Cooper Union speech of February 27, 1860. "An enthusiast," he said, "broods over the oppression of a people till he fancies himself commissioned by Heaven to liberate them. He ventures the attempt, which ends in little else than his own execution." Assassination and bomb-throwing would not, he asserted right the wrongs of society.

The War Years

The election to the Presidency in 1860 of Abraham Lincoln precipitated the secession movement in the South. The new Republican Party was

exclusively the party of the North; political lines were more completely
sectional than ever before. Since Lincoln had declared that "this government cannot endure permanently half slave and half free," and the Republican Party vigorously opposed the extension of slavery, Southern extremists believed that they were forced to choose between abolition and secession. South Carolina seceded from the Union in December 1860, and by
February 1861, Georgia, Alabama, Florida, Mississippi, Louisiana, and
Texas had followed her example. Shortly thereafter, the Confederate
States of America was organized in Montgomery, Alabama, with Jefferson
Davis as president. On April 12, 1861, the Confederate batteries in Charles-
ton harbor fired on the federal garrison in Fort Sumter, which surrendered
the next day. Soon after this decisive event marking the opening of the war,
Virginia, Arkansas, Tennessee, and North Carolina joined the Confederacy.

The choice between state and nation was a difficult one for many
Southerners to make. The old constitutional argument that the states were
older than the Union (true of course of only the original thirteen) and that
the Union consequently derived its authority from the states was no doubt
intellectually convincing to some. But loyalty is based in the emotions
rather than in the intellect. The most distinguished officer of the Confederate army, Robert E. Lee, resigned his commission in the United States
Army when Virginia seceded because, as he put it, "I have been unable to
make up my mind to raise my hand against my native state, my relatives,
my children, and my home." In New England, Nathaniel Hawthorne
expressed sympathy with Lee's view when he said, with a touch of irony:
"If a man loves his own State and is content to be ruined with her, let us
shoot him if we can, but allow him an honorable burial in the soil he
fights for."

At the outset of the war, the South believed that cotton alone was a
guarantee of victory; that if deprived of cotton, the textile industry—and
therefore the entire economy—of the North and of England would collapse. The Southern expectation was not realized. England, though on the
point of doing so in 1862, never recognized the Confederacy. The issue
was to be decided by arms alone, and the overwhelming superiority of the
North in population and resources permitted little doubt of the eventual
outcome. It is hardly necessary here to recount the shifting tides of battle
during the four years of war. The turning point came in July 1863, when
Lee was defeated at Gettysburg and Vicksburg capitulated after a long
siege. The surrender of Lee to Gen. Ulysses S. Grant at Appomattox,
Virginia, on April 9, 1865, in effect terminated the war.

Lincoln's *Second Inaugural Address*, delivered a little more than a
month before Lee's impending surrender and the author's death, regarded
the war as the righteous judgment of God on both North and South for
the sin of slavery. The task before us, he said, was to proceed, "with malice
toward none, with charity for all . . . to bind up the nation's wounds . . . to

do all which may achieve and cherish a just and lasting peace among ourselves, and with all nations." Lincoln's humane and wise view of postwar
policy might, but for his assassination, have led to far happier relations
between blacks and whites in the reconstruction years which followed.

R. S.

T. H.

Literary Trends

The period from 1829 to 1865 was rich not only in ideas but also in artistic expression. Although New England produced more than its share of great artists, other sections also nurtured authors of note. The Southwest was represented notably by a great group of humorists. Both the South and the East were the background for Edgar Allan Poe. New York was represented by Herman Melville, whose best fiction ranks with the finest our country has produced, and also by a preeminent poet, Walt Whitman. Whitman, whose career began near the end of this period and extended until 1892, will be considered in a later section.

In designating this period "the American Renaissance," critics have had in mind certain similarities it bore to the English Renaissance. The English period, which preceded the American by about two and a half centuries, produced a host of great writers and literary masterpieces. In its literary productions, whether created by giants such as Marlowe, Spenser, and Shakespeare or by lesser writers, two impulses had been operative, one foreign and the other native. The exciting discovery of foreign literary works, both old and new, had accounted in part for such works as Shakespeare's *Julius Caesar*, based upon the *Lives* by the Greek biographer-historian Plutarch (translated by North in 1579), and his *Othello*, derived from an Italian *novella* by Cinthio which had first appeared during Shakespeare's lifetime. The patriotic enthusiasm of the day, which had soared during the reign of Queen Elizabeth, found expression in Shakespeare's historical plays such as *Henry IV* and *Henry V* as well as in many of his dramas with foreign settings.

Similarly, during the American Renaissance both foreign and domestic influences, old and new, were notable. Respectful study of ancient and contemporary foreign literature and travel abroad, which acquainted authors with European culture, left their marks upon not only the stuff but also the form of our literature. At the same time, proud of their own vast nation and its unique democratic system, many authors recounted American history and depicted native scenes and characters.

The Essay—A Standard Form Takes on New Qualities

In this period, as in the preceding one, the essay was an important literary form; but a combination of old and new influences, as well as the personal predilections of each author, gave the type distinctive qualities.

Poe: Critic and Journalist

Poe's essays and articles show kinship with those foreign writers in two ways. For one thing, he was in the tradition of European authors who alternated between the role of critic and that of creator. Such German predecessors as Goethe (1749-1832), Schlegel (1767-1845), Tieck (1773-1853), and Schelling (1775-1854) were critics and philosophers as well as poets. And so were several British authors known by Poe: Coleridge, who wrote his literary autobiography and several fine lyrics; Wordsworth, who theorized about his own poems in critical prefaces; Shelley, who wrote a *Defence of Poesy* in addition to his poetry; and Byron, who wrote *English Bards and Scotch Reviewers*, as well as lyrics which Poe admired greatly. Poe, similarly, philosophized about literature, justifying poetry in general and his own poetry in particular in works such as "Letter to B—" (1831) and "The Philosophy of Composition" (1846) and in numerous published reviews.

Poe worked frequently in the tradition of important Britons and Scots who were reviewers for influential periodicals such as *Blackwood's Magazine, The Quarterly Review*, and *The Edinburgh Review*. Such men as Francis Jeffrey (1773-1850), William Hazlitt (1778-1830), Leigh Hunt (1784-1859), and Thomas De Quincey (1785-1859) were journalists whose work for magazines enhanced their literary reputations. Poe's reviews of current books, such as *Twice-Told Tales*, were journalistic contributions resembling overseas reviews in procedure and tone. At times they were as ferocious as any in the notoriously stern British reviews, but generally they were intelligent estimates which augmented Poe's fame as a critic.

Lowell: Critical, Reminiscent

Of the famous Massachusetts men, perhaps the nearest to traditional essayists was James Russell Lowell. Yet the patterns he followed were not those of relatively impersonal essays such as some British authors had written in the eighteenth century. What he wrote was, as a rule, quite personal. A large share of his prose, which dealt with issues of the day—candidacies, governmental policies, political theories—might have appeared in newspapers and did appear in magazines which took stands on current affairs.

Such prose, though it served its purpose in its time, has interest now for political rather than literary historians. Most important as literature is Lowell's critical or reminiscent prose—"Shakespeare," "Keats," "A Good

Word for Winter," "Cambridge Thirty Years Ago," and the like. In all these essays an important factor is the revelation of Lowell's personality—his wit, his learning, his enthusiasm, his sensitivity, his novel way of putting things. One of his volumes bore a title which might have been used for many—"Fireside Travels." He wrote as if he were putting on paper the sort of talk an informed professor, blessed with humor, might deliver to an intelligent student who had dropped in for an evening chat by the library fire in Elmwood. Lowell poured out enthusiasms, drove home points by quoting now and then from old books pulled down from towering tiers of shelves, frolicked with classical allusions or Latin quotations, rolled felicitous phrases over his tongue. In particular, he was a master of the epigram—a condensation of his observation and judgment into witty or striking phrases and sentences. Despite some unevenness in his achievements, Lowell's work in the field of the personal essay was outstanding.

Holmes: Conversational, Neoclassical

Oliver Wendell Holmes, like Lowell, wrote much prose of a frankly utilitarian kind—in his case, prose which made use of the doctor's scientific interests and training (e.g., "Mechanism in Thought and Morals"). However much such writing contributed to the thought of the period—many believe a great deal—the prose which showed Holmes at his inimitable best was more like the informal talk of a New England drawing room or boarding house than like a medical school lecture. Such work took the unique form employed in the *Breakfast-Table* series.

The literature which Holmes knew as a boy did its part to shape his essays. He was fond of remarking how much it had meant to him to have been born and reared "among books and those who knew what was in books," to have had a chance, as a youngster, to page through first editions of eighteenth-century classics in the large library which his forebears had collected. "All men are afraid of books," he claimed, "who have not handled them from infancy." The form of his essays had its parallels with those of the period with which he felt a spiritual kinship—the eighteenth century. This had been the age of his boyhood idols, Addison and Steele, authors of *The Spectator*, which, as *The New Yorker* of its day, reviewed, laughed at, and philosophized about people and events of eighteenth-century London.

The Autocrat, the Professor, and the Poet of Holmes' series were Spectators commenting upon contemporary manners; and boarding-house society, like the club to which the Spectator had belonged, was "very luckily composed of such persons as were engaged in different ways of life, and deputed as it were out of the most conspicuous classes of mankind." Holmes' sketches, like *The Spectator's*, portrayed characters as humorous types—the landlady's daughter, for instance: "(Aet. 19 +. Tender-eyed blonde. Long ringlets. Cameo pin. Gold pencil-case on a chain.

Locket. Bracelet. Album. Autograph book. Accordeon. Reads Byron,
Tupper, and Sylvanus Cobb, Junior, while her mother makes the puddings.
Says 'Yes?' when you tell her anything.)" Essays in the form of conversation—dialogues—had been used frequently in the eighteenth century: by
Shaftesbury to comment upon ethics; by Berkeley, on philosophy; and by
Franklin, on a variety of subjects. In a similar manner the *Autocrat* papers
record conversations of the boarding-house members. James Boswell
(1740-1795) had reported the sparkling talk and what Holmes called the
"bow-wow manner" of Samuel Johnson; and Holmes acknowledged his
indebtedness in the subtitle of the *Autocrat—Every Man His Own Boswell.*
In *Tristram Shandy* (1760) Sterne had recorded meandering talk interspersed with personal essays and punctuated in a manner foreshadowing
Holmes' eccentric punctuation.

Nineteenth-century publications, too, probably suggested devices
which gave the *Autocrat* papers novelty. Possibly magazines and annuals
(which achieved remarkable popularity in this period), with their alterna-
tion of stories, essays, and poems, suggested a similar intermingling of
types. The dramatic interplay between personalities common to fiction
may have influenced Holmes' habit of giving his conversations a dramatic
quality and of running a plot (like one in a magazine serial story) through
his papers. Like Lowell, Holmes no doubt was following the example of
nineteenth-century English essayists such as Lamb and Hazlitt in talking
intimately of his life, personal prejudices, and feelings. The Autocrat is, in
effect, Holmes airing his own views to fellow boarders. "He was a well-
behaved gentleman at table," testified the Autocrat's landlady, "only
talked a good deal, and pretty loud sometimes, and had a way of turnin'
up his nose when he didn't like what folks said. . . . Many's the time I've
seen that gentleman keepin' two or three of the boarders settin' round the
breakfast table after the rest had swallered their meal, and things was
cleared off . . . and there the little man would set . . . a-talkin' and a-talkin',
—and sometimes he would laugh, and sometimes the tears would come into
his eyes. . . . He was a master hand to talk when he got a-goin'."

Thoreau and Emerson: Philosophical, Transcendental
A kind of discourse distantly related to informal talk left its imprint
upon Henry David Thoreau's prose works, whether short pieces or longer
ones, such as *Walden,* in which numerous essays were linked. Thoreau kept
a detailed journal in which, from day to day, he set down experiences,
observations, and thoughts, and from this he drew materials as needed.
These diaries were written with artistic care, the passages in them were
carefully integrated with other parts of essays in which they were used,
and the sentences were scrupulously polished, so that in the end there
was less improvisation than there appeared to be. In learning to shape sentences to his needs—by studying the metaphysical poets, by translating

Greek dramas and passages from Greek poems, by aping English prose masters—Thoreau became indebted to earlier authors. "Every sentence," he wrote, with these models in mind, "is the result of long probation, and should be read as if its author, had he held a plough instead of a pen, could have drawn a furrow deep and straight to the end."

Since the conveying of rich personal experience and meaning by straight furrow expressions was, in Thoreau's opinion, the chief task of the writer, what shaped his prose style more than anything else was his philosophy. To see what Thoreau was trying to do, the reader must understand that, despite all his accumulations of scientific data, Thoreau's way of thinking led him to care little for strictly scientific writing. He attempted, instead, in his finished works, to write in the role of a philosopher. The scientist, according to transcendental beliefs, recorded the workings of the mere intellect—the "Understanding." The great writer, the man of vision, by contrast, recorded the discoveries of a faculty above mind and more important—the "Imagination" or the "Reason," which intuitively perceived in natural objects the truth of which they were symbols. Said Thoreau:

> It is the subject of the vision, the truth alone, that concerns me. The philosopher for whom rainbows, etc., can be explained never saw them. With regard to such objects, I find that it is not they themselves (with which men of science deal) that concern me; the point of interest is somewhere *between* me and them (i.e., the objects). . . .

Seeing the inner meanings of natural phenomena, the great writer employed those phenomena, Thoreau believed, to communicate those meanings. "My thought," he explained, "is a part of the meaning of the world, and hence I use a part of the world to express my thought."

When he filled his pages with vivid details, he attempted to make them illuminating in the transcendental sense: he wanted to set down particular instances of the universal law so that readers might find his sense of "reality"—the higher kind—in them. His stay at Walden was a search "for the essential facts of life," and his circumstantial record of the experience (or more precisely of an ideal experience based upon sixteen years of records in his journal) was an attempt to convey his insights in meaningful symbols. And elsewhere than in *Walden* his practice was to show the eternally true in terms of the particular. "There was an excellent wisdom in him, proper to a rare class of men, which showed him the material world as a means and a symbol," wrote Emerson. "To him there was no such thing as size. The pond was a small ocean; the Atlantic, a large Walden Pond." Certain that the small stood for the large, Thoreau at times used paradoxes and philosophical generalizations, but mainly he trusted minute, concrete details on page after page to convey his meaning.

Ralph Waldo Emerson's patterns of thought, though extraordinarily concrete for a philosopher, were more abstract than Thoreau's. "In reading Thoreau," he said, "I find the same thought, the same spirit that is in me, but he takes a step beyond and illustrates by excellent images that which I should have conveyed in a sleepy generality." In speeches such as "The Divinity School Address" and in essays often largely derived from his lectures, Emerson's training as a minister and lecturer can be seen. Like some orators, he was most interested in generalizing, in following lines of reasoning. Perhaps it is not inaccurate to say that while Thoreau's emphasis was particularly on concrete things, Emerson's was on philosophical relationships.

Emerson set forth what he conceived to be the task of the philosopher in his study of his idol Plato: it was to follow the natural course of the mind as it related the One which was the Oversoul to the Many, or as it related the Many to the One.

> The mind [he wrote] is urged to ask for one cause of many effects; then for the cause of that; and again the cause . . . self-assured that it will arrive at an absolute and sufficient one,—a one that shall be all. . . . Urged by an opposite necessity, the mind returns from the one to that which is not one, but . . . many; from cause to effect; and affirms the necessary existence of variety, the self-existence of both, as each is involved in the other. These strictly-blended elements it is the problem of thought to separate and reconcile.

Such was the idea Emerson had of the method of his essays, and a reader who has patience and skill in dialectic can, indeed, see that the essays are constructed according to this pattern.* It is difficult, however, to follow the involvements of his peculiar transcendental structure. Although some of Emerson's essays have structures such as are found in more conventional compositions, most appear to lack coherence and unity. Many readers have agreed with Thomas Carlyle's remarks to Emerson in a letter about the *Essays: First Series:*

> The sentences . . . did not . . . always entirely cohere for me. Pure genuine Saxon; strong and simple; of a clearness, of a beauty—But they did not, sometimes, rightly stick to their foregoers and their followers: the paragraph not as a beaten *ingot,* but as a beautiful square *bag of duckshot* held together by canvas!

For many readers, the virtue of the essays will be found chiefly in individual sentences—excellent for their extraordinary proverbial quality, for

---

*For some analyses of Emerson's essays according to this principle see W. T. Harris, "Ralph Waldo Emerson," *Atlantic*, 1882, CL, 238-252, and Walter Blair and Clarence Faust, "Emerson's Literary Method," *Modern Philology*, 1944, XLII, 79-95

their compact expression of profound thoughts. Even such small units as sentences, however, show that Emerson, like other essayists of his day, combined old materials and methods with newly discovered ones, thereby making his purposeful writing seem a new thing.

American Fiction Comes into Its Own

When authors of the period 1829-1865 wrote fiction, they were inclined to consider whether the setting of their narratives should be remote or near at hand in time and space. Both kinds of settings were popular. German and British Gothic romances—or tales of terror—utilizing exotic backgrounds were extremely popular; so were Sir Walter Scott's historical novels, the last of which appeared in 1832. Across the ocean, in addition, fiction which portrayed the manners and talk of common folk flourished. This fiction had a large audience in the United States: Sir Walter Scott, Maria Edgeworth (1767-1849), and Charles Dickens (1812-1870), who wrote about such folk, were the most popular authors in this country—native authors included—during this period. American authors adapted both types of settings and characterizations to their own purposes.

Poe: Skilled Craftman

Early in his career as a fictionist, Poe wrote a letter to T. W. White, owner of the *Southern Literary Messenger,* explaining how he had happened to write one of his weird stories. He had been reading successful magazines, foreign and American, and had found that a certain kind of story was in demand. He mentioned "The Spectre in the Log Hut" *(Dublin University Review),* "The Last Man" *(Blackwood's),* "The Suicide" and "The Dance of Death" *(Godey's),* and "The Spectre Fire Ship" *(Knickerbocker).* All these were in the tradition of the Gothic tale of terror, which had flourished since the mid-eighteenth century. The most popular tales, Poe said, represented "the ludicrous heightened into the grotesque; the fearful colored into the horrible; the witty exaggerated into the burlesque; and the singular heightened into the strange and mystical." Poe could turn out stories with any of these effects, but he was at his best in creating the second and fourth of them. Such spine-tingling tales as "The Fall of the House of Usher," "Ligeia," "The Man of the Crowd," "The Masque of the Red Death," and "The Cask of Amontillado" owe much to the Gothic romances.

They also owe much to Poe's self-conscious craftmanship. Thinking in terms of contemporary psychological theories and of the "science" of phrenology (the study of the shape of the skull), widely accepted during his day, Poe devised a theory about writing tales which, fortunately, retained much of its validity after these "sciences" had lost theirs. Poe conceived of two elements in a tale—incident and tone—as stimuli to a response by the reader. The skillful artist, therefore, was one who carefully formulated the effect he wished to achieve, then invented and combined incidents and related them in words chosen to establish the preconceived effect. A tale so wrought, he felt, could not fail to "leave in the mind of him who contemplated it with a kindred art, a sense of the fullest satisfaction." The process, some have thought, was a somewhat mechanical one; but Poe's skill in both invention and execution led him to unsurpassed achievements in this genre. Subordinating everything in the tale to the effect, Poe skillfully utilized the characteristic backgrounds, characters, and incidents of Gothic romance.

Hawthorne: Romance and Allegory

In believing that the most soul-stirring effect could be achieved by blurred rather than precise details, Poe differed from Nathaniel Hawthorne, whom he greatly admired and at times rather badly misread—differed, as a matter of fact, from most New Englanders. In this period, one who saw a Yankee village from a distance noticed first of all the tidy white-spired churches which were an important and recurrent motif in the quiet green landscape—and which exerted a great force in the life of the region. Founded by zealots, New England for decades had produced moralizing literature, and it continued to produce it even when its authors turned to fiction. For Hawthorne, preeminent among New England fictionists, the theme of the tale was tremendously important. Although the Gothic influence was almost as pronounced on Hawthorne as it was on Poe and though sentimental fiction and allegorical narrative were important in shaping his fiction, these devices were subordinated to Hawthorne's own New England purpose.

As has frequently been noticed, paraphernalia of the tale of terror—animated ancestral portraits, fiendlike villains, men who sold their souls to the devil, witches, unnatural portents—figured prominently in this author's tales and novels. The influence of sentimental fiction, too, is clear, even in such a masterpiece as *The Scarlet Letter.* The penalty of seduction, a chief stock in trade of the sentimentalists, is the chief substance of this great romance. Hester's daughter, little Pearl, resembles a typical character of the fiction of sensibility—a child bringing sunshine into the home and gently leading parents to virtue. The misled feminist and the ministering angel popular in fourth-rate novels are combined in the portrayal of Hester. Stereotypical Calvinistic villainy is bestowed upon Chillingworth. The sensibility of the minister and his dying glimpses of heavenly glory are hackneyed motifs in the sentimental pattern. And in the tales, as in the longer works, one familiar with the fiction of feeling will see its stuff transmuted by Hawthorne.

Hawthorne was further influenced by an older, traditional type of fiction—the allegorical narrative, which, from childhood, he had read with much pleasure. When in 1843 he listed the authors he considered most notable, along with such conventional choices as Homer, Cervantes, Shakespeare, and Milton, he named masters of fable and allegory: Aesop, Ariosto, Spenser, and "Bunyan, moulded of homeliest clay, but instinct with celestial fire." Other influences in addition to his liking for these authors encouraged him to borrow from them. Like Emerson, he had ideas about the artist's duty to give meaning to natural objects when he depicts them. The artist, he felt, cannot exactly reproduce the grandeur of nature which itself suggested truth. His "only recourse," he decided, was to substitute something "that may stand instead of and suggest the truth." His Preface to *The House of the Seven Gables* suggested that a great advantage of a Romance was that it "has fairly a right to present . . . truth under circumstances, to a great extent, of the author's own choosing or creation." This truth, moreover, might be the unifying element. "In all my stories, I think," he remarked, "there is one idea running through them like an iron rod, and to which all other ideas are referred and subordinate. . . ." Lowell's comment noted the same ideational unity: "It is commonly true of Hawthorne's romances that the interest centres in one strongly defined protagonist,—perhaps we should rather say a ruling Idea, of which all the characters are fragmentary embodiments."

Subtly adapted devices of allegorical fiction—for the portrayal of background and character and the selection of incidents—made possible Hawthorne's amalgamation of Gothic and sentimental elements in impressive fiction. Reminiscent of Spenser's Forest of Error or Bower of Bliss, in which details of background are made to stand for the author's concepts, are Hawthorne's descriptions of the Pearson cottage in "The Gentle Boy," for example, and of the garden in "Rappaccini's Daughter." Hawthorne's characters, too, are embodiments of ideas according to allegorical formulas. Sometimes older allegorists associated significant articles or details of dress with a character: in *Pilgrim's Progress* Christian labors under his heavy burden; in *The Faerie Queene* the knight has his "bloudie crosse." In "The Minister's Black Veil," Minister Hooper wears his meaningful bit of crepe. Again, older allegorists at times showed physical deformities which betokened spiritual deformities, as in the cases of Bunyan's Giant Despair and Spenser's Malbecco. Similarly, Hawthorne made the boy who could not yield to the "gentle boy's" influence a twisted cripple. Hawthorne ingeniously conceived other symbolic attributes of characters to signify their import: the gleaming smile of Minister Hooper and the perfume of Beatrice, in "Rappaccini's Daughter," to cite only two examples.

"The Artist of the Beautiful" embodies and expounds Hawthorne's critical theory. The story treats, as its author says, "the troubled life of those who strive to create the beautiful," and the opening paragraph establishes a contrast—between the artist, working in light, and the thwarters of the artist, standing in darkness—important throughout the tale.

Warland, who is given the attributes of the eternal artist, creates a butterfly whose beauty "represented the intellect, the sensibility, the soul" of the artist. Every other character, in one way or another, impedes the artist, and each is presented so as to signify one of the hostile forces which work against art. All the details, images, and happenings in the tale are richly infused with meaning, in a manner typical of the unique art which Hawthorne discovered for himself.

Melville: Symbol and Actuality

In 1850 Hawthorne and Melville, living a few miles apart but not yet acquainted, read one another's writings and admired them. What each said about the other indicates their similarities and differences. In a review, "Hawthorne and His Mosses," Melville praised Hawthorne for confronting the darker aspects of life. Hawthorne wrote:

> I have read Melville's works with progressive appreciation of the author. No writer ever put reality before the reader more unflinchingly than he does in *Redburn* and *White-Jacket. Mardi* is a rich book, with depths here and there that compel a man to swim for his life. It is so good that one scarcely pardons the writer for not having brooded long over it, so as to make it a good deal better.

Clearly there was a kinship between Melville and Hawthorne in artistry as well as in philosophy. Both thought that the theme of a fictional work was paramount. Both thought that an author should manipulate imagery, characterization, and plot to convey his ideas. But Hawthorne indicated a difference when he complained that his neighbor had not "brooded" enough over his material. Melville's fiction, if we may employ Hawthorne's terms, did not subdue "the Actual." "He felt instinctively," as William Ellery Sedgewick asserts, "that the effective use of a fact as symbol, having both inward and outward reference, depended on the preservation of its outward reality." Melville's aim—comparable with the way of writing which Hawthorne contrasted with his own in the Preface to *The Scarlet Letter*—was "to diffuse thought and imagination through the opaque substance of today, and thus to make it a bright transparency . . . to seek, resolutely, the true and indestructible value that lay hidden in the petty and wearisome incidents, and ordinary characters. . . ." Though Hawthorne admitted that he could not write thus, could not thus simultaneously convey meaning and a sense of actuality, he admired others who were able to do so, since he recognized that such writing achieved a similar end in contrasting fashion.

Billy Budd, not too representative of Melville's typical procedure, is closer to the New Englander's conception of "the Romance" than almost anything else that Melville wrote. Romance though it is, it has a factual basis and includes a few more earthy details than Hawthorne would have been apt to include.

And when one turns to other, more typical works by Melville—works in which he presents many particular and vivid details based on fact and experience and representing the everyday lives of seamen—the contrast becomes quite clear. His selection and presentation of such facts made them actual, near at hand rather than remote, and at the same time meaningful. "Benito Cereno," not only one of Melville's most typical stories but also one of his best, is a good example. Based as it is upon a first-hand account of Captain Delano's real experience, it loses little of its factuality when it is transformed into fiction. At the same time Melville's manipulation of the details and the structure of the narrative enable him to develop a significant theme.

American Humor Moves Toward Realism

It remained for the humorists of the day, though, to get the largest amount of common life into their picturings. Two sections were rich in their humor between 1829 and 1865, New England and the old Southwest—Tennessee, Georgia, Alabama, Louisiana, Mississippi, Arkansas, and Missouri. The humorists' techniques for showing scenes from ordinary life were, in important ways, the freshest of the period because humor, in a romantic era, naturally moved in the direction of realism.

American humorists were, of course, influenced by earlier literature. Eighteenth-century essayists who portrayed "characters" and eccentrics doubtless influenced comic writers in both sections, particularly those in the Southwest. Type characterizations in travel books and almanacs—of acute Yankee peddlers, slow-witted Dutchmen, rambunctious frontiersmen, haughty and hard-drinking aristocrats—helped humorists, particularly the earlier ones, individualize their characters and differentiate among those who lived in different regions. Walter Scott and other British authors who represented "low" characters by the depiction of manners, dress, and speech also served as models. And English sporting journals, which combined native characterizations with accounts of hunts and horse races, were read and imitated by Southwestern lovers of sports.

Two influences, on the other hand, did much to Americanize the humor. One was a basic, widespread, and lasting belief. The other was a popular American folk art—that of the oral tale.

The belief was defined similarly by three great observers of life in the United States—Alexis de Tocqueville from France in the 1830's, Carl Schurz from Germany in the 1850's, and James Bryce from England in the 1870's and 1880's. Bryce defined it most succinctly: "Truth is identified with common sense, the quality which the average American is most proud of possessing." Common sense, also called horse sense, native wit, and gumption, was generally considered to be that precious quality which enabled a man or woman with a keen mind and with wide experience in the world (rather than book learning), to see to the heart of any problem, solve it, and convincingly announce its solution.

Franklin's Poor Richard had revealed the quality early in the eighteenth century; the farm, the mechanic's shop, and the frontier had nurtured it over the years, and in this period its triumph in Jacksonian politics gave it enlarged prestige. Now it shaped the representation of humorous characters.

Incorrigible moralizers, New Englanders used horse-sensible characters to preach. Seba Smith showed how this might be done when in 1830 he launched his creation, rustic Jack Downing, upon a career destined to last (with some interruptions) until the eve of the Civil War. In letters which he wrote to home folk or to newspapers Jack told of his adventures in politics —in the state capital, in Washington, or on the battlefront during the Mexican War; and now and then the home folk wrote to tell Jack how things were going in Downingville. Keen eyes perceived the foibles of politicos, and sharp minds provided commentaries upon current issues.

So wide a following did Jack gain that a number of other New England humorists created similar humble commentators: Matthew F. Whittier, creator of Ethan Spike, B. P. Shillaber, whose creation was Mrs. Partington, and others. In the days of the war with Mexico, when James Russell Lowell looked for a way to convey his views to a wide public, he hit upon the idea of having an imaginary unlearned farmer, Hosea Biglow, whom he described as "common sense vivified and heated by conscience," speak for him. The resulting Biglow Papers were the most popular of all Lowell's writings. Although all the characters were invented to serve as mouthpieces, their creators tended increasingly to give them palpable and lifelike backgrounds, and to endow them with traits which made them droll, human, and persuasive. They spoke in local dialects about what their experiences had been, and what they had figured out on the basis of their experiences. So the fiction about them moved toward realism; in matter as well as in manner it was native and novel.

On the frontier, a similar respect for pawkiness flourished, along with a distrust for book learning. Davy Crockett of the Tennessee canebrakes had a meteoric rise in politics largely because his neighbors knew that he had not been unduly educated and believed that he was strong in native wit. In politics, he was exploited first by the Jacksonian Democrats and later, when he switched parties, by the Whigs, for both parties sought the support of the great masses of voters in the horse-sensible camp. Georgia humorist William Tappan Thompson invented Major Joseph Jones and, like Seba Smith before him, used his canny letter-writer to convey his political views. Other Southwestern humorists, such as George Washington Harris and T. B. Thorpe, less convinced that mother wit was a key to truth, nevertheless, in painting mountaineers, settlers, and hunters, showed a liking for its worshipers and amusement with their foibles.

In both the Northeast and the Southwest, the native humor was much influenced by a favorite ancient pastime, yarnspinning. In the homes, country stores, and taverns of New England an important diversion was the swapping of oral tales. Traveling across country, moving down or up the rivers, resting at night by campfires or household firesides, the people of the Southwest found that good stories pleasantly passed the time. Able yarnspinners were greatly admired, and masters of the art such as Davy Crockett and Abe Lincoln found that well-told anecdotes, some aptly illustrating points which they wished to make, were political assets.

The stories ranged from wild fantasy to fairly accurate accounts of everyday happenings. Playful lies comparable to their modern descendants, "fish stories" or animated cartoons, celebrated the fertility of the soil or encounters with huge beasts; an example is T. B. Thorpe's "The Big Bear of Arkansas," in which Jim Doggett describes Arkansas, "the creation state," and tells of his encounter with "the d _____ t bar that was ever grown." Or they dealt with gigantic comic demigods such as keelboatman Mike Fink or the mythical Crockett of the almanacs. Fantastic details were a product of the soaring rustic or frontier imagination. An element which did much to make the tales comic was the incongruity between the actual and the impossible. Thus, though whole sequences of events were completely impossible, happening was made to arise from happening in a seemingly logical fashion. Astonishing feats were matter-of-factly recounted in earthy dialect. Painstakingly rendered and highly authentic details gave added verisimilitude. Contrasts between the earthy and the unearthly were sometimes heightened by vulgar touches—a few lines after Jim Doggett has poetically evoked a giant bear which "looms like a black mist," for example, Jim is shamefacedly telling about losing his pants. And often, though the tale was impossible by any sane standards, the character of the teller and his motives for inventing his lie were plausibly rendered. The playfulness of tall tales was underlined, in short, by constant reminders of actuality.

Even more of actuality entered into stories of another sort told by Western firesides and eventually translated into print—comic tales about more commonplace frontier characters and happenings. Several reasons for authenticity in such narratives may be cited. There was a desire on the part of some sophisticated storytellers and writers to show that they, like eighteenth-century British humorists, could detachedly perceive and appreciate "originals." Again, there was a wish to write history—as A. B. Longstreet put it, in his seminal book, *Georgia Scenes*, ". . . to supply a chasm in history which has always been overlooked—the manners, customs, amusements, wit, dialect, as they appear in all grades of society to an eye and ear witness. . . ." Finally, of course, there was a desire for entertainment. Circuit-riding frontier lawyers, for instance, said Samuel A. Hammett in 1853, "living as they do in the thinly inhabited portion of our land, and among a class of persons generally their inferiors in point of education . . . are apt to seek for amusement in listening to the droll stories and odd things always to be heard at the country store or bar-room."

Whatever their motivation, authors who wrote such tales recorded in extraordinary detail many aspects of frontier life. Franklin J. Meine, in his excellent anthology, *Tall Tales of the Southwest*, lists a group of subjects that is strikingly inclusive—local customs, games, courtships, weddings, law circuits, political life, hunting, travel, medicine, gambling, religion, fights, and oddities in character. As Bernard DeVoto claims in *Mark Twain's America*, "No aspect of the life in the simpler America is missing from this literature." The details about backgrounds, costumes, mores, and dialect are plentiful and vivid. Regardless of their crudities and exaggerations, such authors as Crockett, Thorpe, Thompson, and G. W. Harris represent an early American achievement of what later was called "realism."

Political Oratory and Lincoln

Some humorous writing of the period 1829-1865 had affiliations with political speeches. An unsigned comic skit which went the rounds in newspapers during the 1840's purported to be a speech of one Candidate Earth, who wanted backwoods neighbors to elect him sheriff. Said he:

> Now gentlemen, don't you think they ought to make me sheriff? I say, if Bob Black has floated farther on a log, killed more Injuns, or stayed longer under water than I have, elect him; if not, I say what has he done to qualify him for the office of sheriff? Did any of you ever know him to call for a quart? I never did; I have known him to call for several half-pints in the course of a day, but I never did know him to step forward manfully and say, "Give us a quart of your best." Then I say again, what has Bob Black done to qualify him for sheriff?

In similar (though often less literate) language, Crockett and other backwoods or rural candidates regularly appealed for votes. And the very simplicity of the diction, its very freedom from adornment, recommended the speakers to constituents who preferred gumption to book learning.

A very different kind of oratory, nevertheless, was also much admired —that, say, of Daniel Webster, Wendell Phillips, Henry Clay, and of other orators not so well remembered. William Cullen Bryant, stating a general belief in 1826, noticed important likenesses between the orator and the poet: both were inspired, both deeply moved, and both were deeply moving as they appealed to "moral perceptions of listeners." The orator's voice, said Bryant, "acquires an unwonted melody, and his sentences arrange themselves in a sort of measure and harmony, and the listener is chained in involuntary and breathless attention." Some of the most admired passages in the oratory of the day, consequently, were remarkably florid, figurative, and rhythmic. Particularly admired, for instance, was the conclusion of Webster's most celebrated speech in the Senate, the "Reply to Hayne" of 1830:

> When my eyes shall be turned to behold for the last time the sun in heaven, may I not see him shining on the broken and dishonored fragments of a once glorious Union; on States dissevered, discordant, belligerent; on a land rent with civil feuds, or drenched, it may be, in fraternal blood! Let their last feeble and lingering glance rather behold the gorgeous ensign of the republic, now known and honored throughout the earth, still full high advanced, its arms and trophies streaming in their original lustre, not a stripe erased or polluted, nor a single star obscured, bearing for its motto, no such miserable interrogatory as "What is all this worth?" nor those other words of delusion and folly, "Liberty first and Union afterwards"; but everywhere, spread all over it in characters of living light, blazing on all its ample folds, as they float over the sea and the land, and in every wind under the whole heavens, that other sentiment, dear to every true American heart,— Liberty *and* Union, now and for ever, one and inseparable!

Modern appreciation for such oratorical flights is tepid; there has been a change in taste during the last century, portents of which were already beginning to appear before the Civil War.

In 1857 Edward G. Parker, in his book *The Golden Age of American Oratory*, indicated that the age was about to end. He saw two reasons for its conclusion. First, what he called "the age of chivalry" was closing and, said he, "A brazen age, anti-sentimental, succeeds. . . ." Secondly, "the growing taste of our people for reading" was bringing into prominence "accurate rhetorical composition, rather than the dashing vigor and vivacious sparkle of spontaneous oratory."

Whether for the reasons he suggested or not, Parker's prophecy was, in general, to come true. Even as he wrote, some Americans had begun to lose their liking for what Parker characterized as "oratory . . . bursting from the lips of Prophets" and to prefer "the less contagious influences of logic, and figures and facts." Addresses of Calhoun and of Webster delivered in 1850 represent, in style, the transitional period.

By 1850, Webster had developed what students call his "mature style" —a style which, compared with his earliest efforts, had greatly gained in simplicity. Edwin P. Whipple, in 1879, wrote: "The mature style of

Webster is perfect of its kind, being in words the express image of his mind and character,—plain, terse, clear, forcible; and rising to the level of lucid statement and argument into passages of superlative eloquence only when his whole nature is stirred by some grand sentiment. . . ." Modern readers, of course, shy away from the passages of "superlative eloquence" which Whipple obviously admired. But Webster does not indulge in such eloquence too often, and the bulk of his oratory is concerned with expressing thoughts clearly. Most of his famous speech of March 7, 1850, is devoted to Webster's version of history, set forth massively to be sure, but for the most part simply and moderately—at least for the time. John C. Calhoun, generally ranked below Webster at the time, may be preferred by readers today. The reason was suggested by a critic of oratory in 1849. "Mr. Calhoun," E. L. Magoon wrote, "flaunts in no gaudy rhetorical robes of scarlet and gold, but comes into the forum clothed in the simplest garb, with firm hands grasping the reins of fancy, and intent only on giving a reason for the faith that is in him." If they are not too irritated by Calhoun's preachments, readers today will admire the relatively simple dress and the tight grip upon the reins, and will find his logic and his clarity admirable.

Although modern readers can endure the reading of Webster and Calhoun, they find more moving the one speaker of the Golden Age of Oratory who, by general consent, has become a classic author—Abraham Lincoln. At least four of Lincoln's speeches—*Farewell Address at Springfield, First Inaugural Address, Gettysburg Address*, and *Second Inaugural Address*—whether one agrees or disagrees with their interpretation of history, were great utterances.

A student of Lincoln's collected speeches will find that a surprising amount of his work is far below these masterpieces in excellence. His first speech, delivered in 1832 when, as a gangling, ill-dressed youth of twenty-three, he was running for the state legislature, went this way:

> I presume you-all know who I am. I am humble Abe Lincoln. I have been solicited by many friends to become a candidate for the legislature. My politics are short and sweet like the old woman's dance. I am in favor of a national bank. I am in favor of the internal improvements system, and a high protective tariff. These are my sentiments and political principles. If elected I shall be thankful. If not it will be all the same.

The speech, to be sure, is somewhat better than that of Candidate Earth, but clearly its eloquence is in a similar style. And many of Lincoln's later speeches, among them the historic debates with Douglas, now are thought by some to have little more than a certain homespun straightforwardness, well adapted to public debate, to recommend them. At times, by contrast,

especially during his early career, Lincoln indulged in spread-eagle melodramatic oratory as tawdry as any produced at the time. An instance is a
campaign speech of 1840, in which he said:

> I know that the great volcano at Washington, aroused and directed by
> the spirit that reigns there, is belching forth the lava of political corrup-
> tion in a current broad and deep, which is sweeping with frightful ve-
> locity over the whole length and breadth of the land, bidding fair to
> leave unscathed no green spot or living thing; while on its bosom are
> riding, like demons on the wave of hell, the imps of the evil spirit, and
> fiendishly taunting all who dare to resist its destroying course with the
> hopelessness of their efforts; and knowing this, I cannot deny that all
> may be swept away. Broken by it, I, too, may be; bow to it, I never will.

Obviously the figurative language used here was meant to appeal to the
current taste. Just how Lincoln managed to steer away from both the
crude utterances of a small-town politician and the fustian elegance of the
popular orator is something of a problem. The very fact that he, unlike
many of the leaders of the day, was self-schooled probably was important.
While others among his contemporaries had studied the classical rules and
examples of oratory, Lincoln had learned his art chiefly in frontier political
debates and in clashes in law courts. Because he relied upon the teachings
of experience, he shared the democratic belief in common sense and its
direct expression, and that fact, too, was significant. Literary influences
upon Lincoln, nevertheless, were important, and fortunately some of the
most notable were those of authors who achieved forceful expression by
means of simplicity and restraint—Robert Burns, William Shakespeare, and
the translators of the Bible into the King James version. Finally, Lincoln's
own character and feeling, as they developed during the trying years of his
Presidency, were strongly reflected in his thought and the form of its expression. As Edgar Dewitt Jones remarks, somewhat flossily, in his study
of orators, *Lords of Speech*, "The graces of an orator's presence, the charm
of his voice and manner, are ephemeral; while the grandeur of his thoughts,
the magnanimity of his soul and the soundness of his reasoning live after
him. It is the substance of his speeches, together with the chaste beauty of
a style which matches the sheer beauty of his spirit, that lift Abraham
Lincoln into the small and elect company of the world's supreme masters
of public speech." Lincoln, despite the intemperance of the times in which
he lived, was a temperate and extremely sincere man. He was also something of a poet. His utterances have outlasted both the crude mouthings of
the folksy politicians and the highly ornate orations of less temperate, less
sincere, and less poetic speakers.

Poetry: A Combination of the Old and the New

Poets, like the orators of the period, employed two styles, both related to
the past as well as to their time. Makers of ballads followed an ancient tradition: their songs were composed by the people (or by an artist who felt,
spoke, and thought as they did), for the people, and were kept alive by the
people. Some popular songs of Civil War days show how both a vernacular
style and a more ornate literary style might be adapted to a single tune—
two versions of "Dixie," for instance, and "John Brown's Body" and "The
Battle Hymn of the Republic." At the time little attention was paid to
poems which used the phrasings of daily speech, but later scholars would
collect such songs and serious poets would learn much about art and life
from such earthy and vigorous songs.

Two respected poets of the period, though, showed kinship with the
popular singers. James Russell Lowell's *Biglow Papers*, as has been indicated, used diction and characterizations taken from common life. John
Greenleaf Whittier tried at times to write formidably literary verse, and
his conscious use of dialect in poetry was infrequent. Nevertheless, at his
most effective he was a writer of songs which were remarkably simple—
almost in the manner of folk songs—both in metrical form and in vocabulary. Whittier's rural upbringing, his brief schooling, and his particular
admiration for the seemingly artless songs of Robert Burns all led him to
write unpretentious poems. Never, it appears, did he give much consideration to matters of technique. His aim, as he stated it, was

> To paint, forgetful of the tricks of art,
> With pencil dipped alone in colors of the heart.

As a rule, no sign appeared of his striving for novelty. All his life, he preferred ballad measure, octosyllabics, and iambic pentameter—quite conventional forms of verse—and he used a vocabulary and figures of speech
which were far from complex. Because of their almost rustic directness and
simplicity, his poems appealed greatly to many untutored readers.

Most poets eminent in the period were less simple and immediate,
more elegant and remote. The background of the cultured New England
poets led them to think of poetry as the height of elegance. Among the
books which Holmes listed as obligatory reading for a boy of a good
Boston or Cambridge family was "Pope, original edition, 15 volumes,
London, 1717." The conviction that eighteenth-century Alexander Pope
was "the greatest poet that ever lived" was, Lowell confessed, inculcated
in him by childhood teachers; and, similarly, the other famous New
England authors, from babyhood to manhood, listened to encomiums of
the older poets. Others who had learned to like literature as youngsters in
ancestral libraries had a natural tendency to worship somewhat old-

fashioned literary gods. Bowdoin and Harvard were likely to encourage this tendency with their classical curriculums and their courses in writing based upon Blair's old-fashioned, square-toed *Rhetoric*. When Emerson was in Latin school, his favorite declamation was from the "Pleasures of Hope," a typical eighteenth-century philosophizing poem written by Thomas Campbell in heroic couplets.

But the tradition of culture, though it fostered approval of old ideas and models, also fostered the discovery and development of new ones. The new forces it put to work made certain that the prominent authors would modify, in various fashions, the ways of looking at things and the ways of voicing attitudes. In the South, Henry Timrod acknowledged the influence of seventeenth-century Milton, but he also saw that he was influenced by ninteenth-century Wordsworth and Tennyson. In poems such as "Charleston" and "Ode" he used the simple ballad stanza much liked by Wordsworth or a slight adaptation of it; in others such as "Ethnogenesis" and "The Cotton Boll" he used the irregular ode form which had been used with marked success by Wordsworth and Tennyson. Poe, who lived in England briefly during his youth, avidly read books and magazines from overseas. Literary men of Massachusetts might be sketchily informed about the nation to the West and to the South, but they were likely to travel extensively in the Old World. As V. L. Parrington has noted (in *Main Currents in American Thought*), the New England Renaissance "involved three major strands: the social Utopianism that came from revolutionary France; the idealistic metaphysics that emerged from revolutionary Germany; and the new culture that spread with the development of literary romanticism . . . these strands . . . are but different, new world phases of a comprehensive European movement. . . ." The widespread revolutionary spirit invaded not only the quiet Cambridge libraries but also the woods by Walden Pond.

From the old and new books discovered abroad and at home, American authors learned about poetic techniques. They learned procedures in writing from modern writers such as Wordsworth, Coleridge, Byron, Shelley, and Keats and from those of other times, such as the Norse epic poets, the authors of ancient Oriental works, and Plato and the Neo-Platonists. In most New England poetry, as a result, there was a combination of the old and the new—and every author's individual conception of poetry determined the nature of the combinations which he produced.

Poe: Poet of Unearthly Beauty
Poe, as Killis Campbell observed in *The Poems of Edgar Allan Poe*,

began his career as a poet by imitating Byron and Moore; he came a little later under the spell of Shelley; and both in his theorizing as to poetry and in the application of those theories to his own art he pro-

claimed himself the ardent disciple of Coleridge. In . . . 'The Raven,'
'The Haunted Palace,' and 'Annabel Lee' he followed, even though afar
off, in the footsteps of the balladists; . . . and there is an unmistakable
Gothic strain both in his earlier and some of his later verses.

Thus Poe was indebted to his immediate predecessors, and he was indebted, also, to some of his contemporaries, notably Elizabeth Barrett Browning and an American poet now pretty well forgotten, Thomas Holley
Chivers.

Despite such relationships, Poe wrote poetry which was, in some ways,
unique. This was partly because of his ability to imagine and portray
scenes of unearthly beauty—dreamlands, fairylands, cities in the sea, ghoul-
haunted woodlands, and the like. It was partly because he wrote in accordance with rather precise theories—theories about the "single effect" of
poetry, about the handling of metre and sound, and about the indirect
ways "meaning" or "truth" should be hinted, though not articulated, in
poetry.

Holmes: "Florist in Verse"

Much of Holmes' poetry had such a periwig-and-velvet-breeches quality
about it, like that of Goldsmith, Pope, Gray, Campbell, and Gay, that
Holmes appeared, as one critic put it, "less a revival of the eighteenth century than its latest survival."

Holmes' kinship with the coffee-house gentry was in part the result of
his paying them the tribute of imitation, in part the consequence of his
seeing poetry, as they often had, as a graceful social accomplishment. "I'm
a florist in verse," he sang, "and what would people say, if I came to a ban-
quet without my bouquet?" So successful was he at writing "by request of
friends" that around Boston, almost invariably, first-class celebrations,
anniversaries, banquets, receptions, and professional meetings were likely
to program an appearance of Dr. Holmes, poem in hand.

All this meant a good deal about his poems. For *vers de société* or *vers
d'occasion*, he saw as well as had the Neoclassicists, had to have certain
qualities of tone and form. In it deep emotion was as out of place as it
would be in a social group; the tone had to be light—wit and pathos were
better than deep feeling. Much depended upon exactly the right phrasing—
polished but conversational, witty, condensed. With all this in mind,
Holmes wrote some of the finest American familiar verse.

Yet Holmes himself considered his most typical poems evidences of
his talent rather than of his genius. Eventually he came to feel that his
earliest conception of poetry, that of a young man "trained after the
schools of classical English verse," had represented "simple and partial
views," since it had dealt too exclusively with "the constructive side of
the poet's function." "I should rather say," he continued, "if I were called

upon now to define that which makes a poet, it is the power of transfiguring the experience and shows of life into an aspect which comes from his
imagination and kindles that of others." His occasional poems, he told
Lowell, were "for the most part to poetry as the beating of a drum or tin-
kling of a triangle is to the harmony of a band." True poetry, he believed,
was inspired in thought and to some extent in form. Only once did he feel
sure that he had written such poetry—in "The Chambered Nautilus."

This romantic concept of the inspired poet was shared by all the
famous New England literary artists, both those of Cambridge and those
of Concord. These writers differed only in their ideas about the extent to
which a poem was inspired as compared with the extent to which it was
consciously contrived. The Brahmins rather tended, with Holmes, to emphasize the importance of careful artistry. They also joined him in allowing the older conception of poet as teacher to shape their writings.

Longfellow: Master of Words and Accents

Henry Wadsworth Longfellow in particular has been praised by many
recent scholars for his technique and scolded for his didacticism. His prosodic skill was developed most definitely, perhaps, by his achievement of
the exacting task of translating into English, without signs of painful
effort, the *chansons* of French troubadours, the *lieder* of German lyricists,
the *terza rima* and sonnets of Italians, and the sagas of Finnish bards. However he acquired his skills, as Odell Shepard says, "Together with his
thought, he had at the same moment a clear notion of the form in which it
could be expressed most effectively . . . and it is for this reason that in his
better work the thought seems to fill the form without crowding or
inflation."

Longfellow's art concealed art largely because of its simple naturalness.
He managed to get both rhyme and rhythm without using many unusual
words and, as a rule, without changing the normal order of phrases and
sentences. What Gay Wilson Allen, in his *American Prosody*, says about
the hackneyed poem "The Village Blacksmith" hints at similar compli-
ments which might be paid to more important achievements: "Its severe
simplicity of diction and regularity of rhythm is likely to make us under-
estimate the technical achievements. . . . There are only two inversions in
the whole piece: 'a mighty man is he' and 'onward through life he goes.'
The natural speech and syntax . . . was practically unique in American
versification in 1839." Longfellow regularly employed, without ostenta-
tion or evident difficulty, each of the ordinary meters (iambic, anapestic,
dactylic, and trochaic), some of them in unusual ways; he combined them
with several metrical devices which are quite extraordinary. The refrain of
"My Lost Youth," and the spacing of accented syllables in "The Skeleton
in Armor," "Jugurtha," and "The Tide Rises" offer striking examples.

This master of words and accents could make each word and each line do its job. The plots of his best narratives are developed in excellent order. His best lyrics—whatever might be said against their preachments—at least have the unity which development of a single thought or sentiment gives them. The unity of thought in such poems as "The Rainy Day," "The Arrow and the Song," and "Jugurtha" cannot be surpassed; in each the first part offers some image, and the second part suggests, usually with the aid of incremental repetition, the spiritual connotation in a detailed parallel. Similarly, even so simple a poem as "The Bridge" starts with a description of a scene, then passes to the meaning of the scene to the poet, and ends by applying the meaning to all men. In such uncomplicated structures, there is integration of the sort important in sonnets, a form Longfellow handled particularly well.

Despite such prosodic skill and such unity and coherence of thought, Longfellow is often criticized for three reasons. First, the thoughts of his lyrics too often were platitudinous. Secondly, more even than Holmes or Lowell, he was a bookish, library poet. One sees why Whitman complained that Longfellow's poetry was "reminiscent, polish'd, elegant, with the air of finest conventional library, picture-gallery or parlor, with ladies and gentlemen in them. . . ." Finally, although his poems were logically constructed, they often were badly put together emotionally or connotatively. That similes and metaphors should be more than handsome ornaments— that they should be as organic to the poem as the thought—he apparently did not conceive. Hence in many of his poems he used imagery which modern readers find incongruous, and in only a few did he avoid jarring connotations.

Lowell: Pioneer in Freedom of Verse Form

Howard Mumford Jones has noticed that "readers do not turn to Lowell as they do to Longfellow, for a body of verse; and though certain lyrics are individual favorites, they are such as two or three other poets might have written. 'To the Dandelion' is Keatsian; many readers confuse 'The First Snowfall' with Bryant's poem on the same theme, and 'The Present Crisis' inevitably suggests Whittier." This comparison can be carried further: *A Fable for Critics*, with its Pope-like critiques, suggests Holmes; and "Auspex" might well have been written by Longfellow. Lowell perhaps busied himself too much with other matters to develop a poetic style all his own.

Yet in some of Lowell's work there are merits not discoverable in Holmes or Longfellow. His *Biglow Papers* are the most effective political satire in verse yet written in America, and *A Fable for Critics* combines sharply phrased wit with shrewd literary judgments as no other poetry in this country has. In his famous "Commemoration Ode" he showed ability in shaping a long contemplative poem beyond the skill of his fellow Brahmins. He had the perception of emotional relationships that Longfellow lacked. "My notion of a true lyric," he said, "is that the meaning should float steadfast in the centre of every stanza, while the vapory emotions . . . float up to it and over it, and wreathe it with an opal halo which seems their own, but is truly its own work. The shades of emotion over, there floats the meaning, clear and sole and sharp-cut in its luminous integrity. . . ." Lowell wrote some poems in which the figurative language thus related the emotion it connoted to the meaning as a whole: "To the Dandelion," "The Courtin'," and "Auspex" are instances. Finally, Lowell did make the sort of technical contribution to American versification best suggested by his irregular "Ode Recited at the Harvard Commemoration." In Professor Allen's words, this poet's prosody "introduced into American poetry the freedom which we find in the first two or three decades of nineteenth-century English poetry. . . . This freedom includes a more varied placing of accents and the combination of different kinds of feet to produce a suggestiveness of tone and cadence. . . . Yet . . . Lowell's versification is more important for the lessons it teaches than for the poetic beauty it achieved."

Emerson and Thoreau: Rebels Against Nineteenth-Century Forms

Some free verse lines of the transcendentalist Ralph Waldo Emerson serve to set off his aims in poetry from those of the Brahmins:

> I will not read a pretty tale
> To pretty people in a nice saloon
> Borrowed from their expectation,
> But I will sing aloud and free
> From the heart of the world.

Thoreau, another transcendentalist, also stated a view of writing at variance with that of the genteel Cambridge men when he wrote: "Enough has been said in these days of the charm of fluent writing. . . . The surliness with which the woodchopper speaks of his woods, handling them as indifferently as his axe, is better than the mealy-mouthed enthusiasm of the lover of nature. Better that the primrose by the river's brim be a yellow primrose, and nothing more, than that it be something less." So far as form and substance were concerned, the most radical of the ante-bellum New England versifiers were the transcendentalists, Emerson in a few great poems and Thoreau in even fewer.

"The form [of transcendental poetry]," G. W. Cooke notes, "is often rugged, the verse is halting and defective. The metres stumble, and . . . rhymes are not correct. The poems are . . . metaphysical, subtle, and complicated in their thought. . . ." Unlike Longfellow, who acquired his free and easy ways with verse by echoing foreign metrical schemes, or Lowell, who came late enough to learn lessons from Shelley, the transcendentalists found their chief models in a seventeenth-century school of unorthodox versifiers. From the metaphysical poets—Marvell, Crashaw, Donne, and others—who had rebelled against the dulcet melodiousness of Elizabethan lyricists, these rebels against the nineteenth-century saccharinity learned the forcefulness which results from breaking up regular patterns. It may be true, as some critics claim, that the very infrequency of the Concord men's excursions into verse had something to do with the harshness of their songs. But the most important cause for their radicalism, probably, was that the nature of transcendental poetry, like that of transcendental prose, was influenced strongly by the philosophy of its creators.

According to this philosophy the matter and the expression of a poem, one and inseparable, were both spontaneously inspired. Theoretically, this would lead transcendentalists, trusting their "instincts," to set down their songs without change; actually, it did cause them to tinker with initial expressions less than other poets did. And the intuitive expression, in their opinion, would carry to others the message the poets themselves had been vouchsafed. It would do this because the poets would pass on to readers the same symbols which originally had suggested eternal verities to the poets. "Things," said Emerson, "admit of being used as symbols, because nature is a symbol, in the whole, and in every part." The whole theory of Emerson and his group has been admirably summarized by Jean Gorely:

> Emerson . . . believed that poetry . . . comes into being as the result of inspiration. In that moment the poet sees the very essence of things. . . . The poet makes the unseen visible by means of language. But he is not the conscious creator. Vision, also, shows him the symbols and the thought takes its own form in language that is rhythmical. Because of this, there is a certain indwelling beauty of poetry . . . poetry is spiritual and forms a link between the visible and invisible worlds.

Thus the symbols were important, and the ideas or deep perceptions for which the symbols stood were even more important—so significant that, as in earlier metaphysical poetry, they controlled everything else in a poem. The sentiment often cultivated by the Brahmin poets was practically crowded out from the poems of Emerson and Thoreau by the thought. Since only imagery which developed such a thought was relevant, merely ornamental imagery was avoided. And the concept being expressed determined the general structure of the poem. "It is not metres, but metre-making argument," said Emerson, "that makes a poem,—a thought so passionate and alive, that, like the spirit of a plant or an animal, it has an architecture of its own and adorns nature with a new thing." This theory suggested the four chief methods for ordering material used by Emerson and Thoreau: (1) as in "The Snow-Storm" or "Though All the Fates," the poet might give a description of an object or scene which embodied and implied meaning; (2) as in "Brahma" or "The Summer Rain," the poet might list a number of parallel phenomena; (3) as in "Each and All" or "Inspiration," the poet might record the process by which he arrived at a great truth; (4) as in "Rumors from an Æolian Harp," the poet might record a state of inspiration.

Logically, the meter in such poems should be appropriate for the emphasis of both the symbols and the truths for which the symbols stand. "There is a soberness," wrote Thoreau, "in a rough aspect, as of unhewn granite, which addresses a depth in us, but a polished surface hits only the ball of the eye." And Emerson, in "Merlin," pointed out that:

> The kingly bard
> Must strike the chords rudely and hard,
> As with hammer or with mace;
> That they may render back
> Artful thunder, which conveys
> Secrets of the solar track. . . .

In these ways, the transcendental poetry of Emerson and Thoreau looked backward to seventeenth-century metaphysical poetry, forward to the type of poetry admired most in the middle decades of the present century.

Melville: Poet in Private

Although Melville's contemporaries did not read his poetry, and in fact were largely unaware that he wrote it, the twentieth century has brought it forth from manuscripts and from his various volumes, mostly privately printed, and has discovered in it peculiarly modern qualities. Radically different from the smooth flowing verse of Longfellow or Lowell, closer in effect to the jarring dissonance of Emerson or Thoreau, Melville's poetry represents a unique personal vision—sometimes direct, sometimes angular. Though Melville's poetic voice seems occasionally to stammer, it is distinctively his own. Melville turned to the writing of poetry only after he had exhausted his fictional vein, and he chose as his first subject the Civil War, attempting to embody it in ballad and song. Disappointed in the public indifference to his poetry, he turned in his old age to his inner feelings and to the left-over scraps of his youthful experiences for poetic material. His collected poems make a surprisingly large volume, but the memorable poems are not as numerous as the exuberant poetic-prose of *Moby Dick* would lead one to expect. Robert Penn Warren has written, "Perhaps the violence, the distortions, the wrenchings in the versification of some of these poems are to be interpreted not so much as a result of mere ineptitude as the result of a conscious effort to develop a nervous, dramatic, masculine style." What struck the ears of Melville's contemporaries as awkward often strikes the modern ear as thematically harmonious. For example, in a poem like

"Housetop," one of his Civil War poems, Melville seems more akin in meaning and metaphor to, say, T. S. Eliot than to Walt Whitman, one of his contemporaries who also wrote of the Civil War *(Drum-Taps,* 1865). As in his great novels, in his poetry Melville was in advance of his time. His poems, frequently oblique, often crabbed, had to await an audience with the temperament to enjoy and the patience to ferret out their cryptic ironies and paradoxes.

Thus in the essay, in fiction, in oratory, and in poetry, the authors of the period from 1829 to 1865 combined old and new materials and techniques, giving memorable expression to the invigorating and often controversial ideas of the era. The American Renaissance was one of the richest periods in our literary history, not only in its concepts and perceptions but also in its embodiments of them.

W.B.

Chronological Table of
LITERATURE AND HISTORY

1829 ● Poe's *Al Aaraaf, Tamerlane, and Minor Poems* · Irving's *Conquest of Granada*

Andrew Jackson inaugurated seventh President

1830 ● Holmes' "Old Ironsides"

The settled frontier reached Independence, Missouri · Removal Bill, to settle eastern Indians in Oklahoma Territory, enacted by Congress

1831 ● Poe's *Poems* (second edition) · Whittier's *Legends of New England* · W. L. Garrison established the *Liberator,* an antislavery journal, at Boston

Nat Turner's slave insurrection in Virginia, in which over fifty whites were killed, and for which slaveholders blamed the *Liberator*

1832 ● Bryant's *Poems* · Irving's *Alhambra* · Kennedy's *Swallow Barn*

Jackson reelected President · Oberlin became the first coeducational college. First American clipper ship, the *Ann McKim,* launched from Baltimore

1833 ● Poe's "A MS Found in a Bottle" · Seba Smith's *Life and Writings of Major Jack Downing*

Cyrus H. McCormick's reaper · Slavery abolished in the British colonies · American Antislavery Society formed

1834 ● *Narrative of the Life of David Crockett of West Tennessee*

Indian Intercourse Act designates eastern Oklahoma as Indian Territory · Whig
Party organized in opposition to "King Andrew" Jackson

1835 ● Irving's *Tour on the Prairies* · Poe's first contribution to the *Southern Literary Messenger* in Richmond · Kennedy's *Horse-Shoe Robinson* · Simms' *Yemassee* and *Partisan* · Longstreet's *Georgia Scenes*

Seminole Indians, led by Osceola, begin war against U.S. · Samuel F. B. Morse invented the telegraph

1836 ● Irving's *Astoria* · Emerson's *Nature* · Holmes' *Poems*

Fall of the Alamo · Arkansas, the twenty-fifth state, admitted with slavery · Martin Van Buren elected eighth President

1837 ● Irving's *Adventures of Captain Bonneville, U.S.A.* · Emerson's *The American Scholar* · Hawthorne's *Twice-Told Tales*

Financial panic · Republic of Texas, with Sam Houston as president, recognized by the United States · Michigan admitted as the twenty-sixth state

1838 ● Kennedy's *Rob of the Bowl* · Emerson's "Divinity School Address" · Cooper's *American Democrat*

First Atlantic crossing by steamship took fifteen days · Cherokee Indians begin forced trek to Indian Territory

1839 ● Longfellow's *Voices of the Night*

1840 ● Poe's *Tales of the Grotesque and Arabesque* · Cooper's *The Pathfinder* · Dana's *Two Years Before the Mast*

1200 cotton factories in the United States, two thirds being in New England · United States census: population 17,000,000, including 400,000 free Negroes and 2,500,000 slaves · William Henry Harrison elected ninth President

1841 ● Cooper's *The Deerslayer* · Emerson's *Essays* (First Series) · Longfellow's *Ballads and Other Poems* · Thorpe's "Big Bear of Arkansas"

Death of Harrison; succeeded by John Tyler as tenth President · Act for preemption of public lands: settlers could preempt 160 acres at $1.25 per acre · Brook Farm Association (1841-1847) organized

1842 ● Hawthorne's *Twice-Told Tales* (second edition) · Longfellow's *Poems on Slavery* · Holmes' "The Contagiousness of Puerperal Fever"

1843 ● Thompson's *Major Jones's Courtship*

1844 ● Emerson's *Essays* (Second Series) · Lowell's *Poems*

Morse's telegraph used between Washington and Baltimore · James W. Polk elected eleventh President

1845 ● Poe's *The Raven and Other Poems*

Florida and Texas, the twenty-seventh and twenty-eighth states, annexed to the Union with slavery, making fifteen slave states, thirteen free · Seminole War ends, and most of the Indians are removed to Indian Territory

1846 ● Poe's "Literati," profiles of New York writers · Hawthorne's *Mosses from an Old Manse* · Whittier's *Voices of Freedom* · Melville's *Typee*

Great famine begins in Ireland, causing a flood of Irish immigration to the United States · Treaty with Great Britain determined the Oregon boundary line · War with Mexico begins · Wilmot Proviso, prohibiting slavery in any territory to be acquired from Mexico, passed the House but defeated in the Senate · Iowa, the twenty-ninth state, admitted as a free state

1847 ● Poe's "Ulalume" · Emerson's *Poems* · Longfellow's *Evangeline*

1848 ● Poe's *Eureka* · Lowell's *Fable for Critics; The Biglow Papers, First Series* and *Vision of Sir Launfal*

Mexican cession of what is now California, Nevada, Utah, and Arizona · Gold discovered in California · Wisconsin, the thirtieth state, admitted as a free state, restoring the balance of free and slave states · Seneca Falls woman suffrage meeting · Zachary Taylor elected twelfth President

1849 ● Thoreau's *A Week on the Concord and Merrimack Rivers* and "Civil Disobedience" · Melville's *Mardi* and *Redburn* · Parkman's *Oregon Trail*

1850 ● Emerson's *Representative Men* · Hawthorne's *The Scarlet Letter* · Whittier's *Songs of Labor and Other Poems* · Melville's *White Jacket* · John C. Calhoun's Speech on the Slavery Question · Daniel Webster's Seventh of March Speech

Death of President Taylor; succeeded by Millard Fillmore as thirteenth President · Compromise of 1850: admission of California, the thirty-first state, as a free state · A drastic Fugitive Slave Law penalized anyone aiding fugitive slaves · First act of Congress making land grants to aid in construction of railroads—in this case, the Illinois Central · United States census: population 23,000,000

1851 ● Hawthorne's *The House of the Seven Gables* · Melville's *Moby Dick* · Foster's "Old Folks at Home"

1852 ● Hawthorne's *The Blithedale Romance* and *Life of Franklin Pierce* · Melville's *Pierre* · Harriet Beecher Stowe's *Uncle Tom's Cabin*

Franklin Pierce elected fourteenth President

1853 ● Joseph G. Baldwin's *Flush Times of Alabama and Mississippi*

1854 ● Thoreau's *Walden*

Kansas-Nebraska Act established "squatter sovereignty" in those territories, leading to bloody conflicts between free-state and slave-state settlers; beginning of John Brown's abolitionist actions · Republican Party first organized as protest against the Kansas-Nebraska Act · Trade treaty with Japan

1855 ● Longfellow's *Hiawatha* · Simms' *Forayers* · Whittier's "Barefoot Boy" · Whitman's *Leaves of Grass* · Melville's "Benito Cereno"

1856 ● Emerson's *English Traits* · Simms' *Eutaw* · Whitman's *Leaves of Grass* (second edition, containing Emerson's letter)

James Buchanan elected fifteenth President · Copyright law protecting playwrights passed

1857 ● Founding of the *Atlantic Monthly* in Boston, with Lowell as editor · Founding of *Russell's Magazine* (1857-1861) in Charleston, with Paul Hamilton Hayne as editor

Supreme Court's Dred Scott decision: a Negro born of slaves was not a citizen and therefore could not bring suit in a federal court · Financial panic

1858 ● Longfellow's *The Courtship of Miles Standish* · Holmes' *The Autocrat of the Breakfast-Table*

The Lincoln-Douglas debates in Illinois on questions arising from the slavery issue · Minnesota admitted as thirty-second state

1859 ● Irving's *Life of Washington,* 5 vols. · Stowe's *The Minister's Wooing*

Oregon admitted as thirty-third state · Silver discovered in the Comstock lode, Nevada · First oil well, Oil Creek, Pennsylvania · John Brown leads raid on Harper's Ferry

1860 ● Emerson's *The Conduct of Life* · Hawthorne's *Marble Faun* · Thoreau's "Plea for John Brown" · Whitman's *Leaves of Grass* (third edition) · Howells' campaign biography of Lincoln

United States census: population 31,500,000, including 450,000 free Negroes and 4,000,000 slaves · South Carolina seceded from the Union · Abraham Lincoln elected sixteenth President

1861 ● Timrod's "Ethnogenesis" and "The Cotton Boll" · Holmes' *Elsie Venner*

Telegraphic communication opened across the continent · Kansas, the thirty-fourth state, admitted as a free state · Mississippi, Florida, Alabama, Georgia, Louisiana, and Texas seceded from the Union · Confederate States of America organized at Montgomery with Jefferson Davis as president · The Civil War began when the Confederates fired on Fort Sumter, S.C., 12 April · Virginia, Arkansas, Tennessee, and North Carolina joined the Confederacy · Great Britain and France recognized the Confederate States · The first Battle of Bull Run, a Confederate victory

1862 ● Holmes' *Songs in Many Keys* · Browne's *Artemus Ward: His Book*

Merrimac-Monitor engagement in Hampton Roads, first battle of ironclads · The Battles of Shiloh, Seven Days, second Bull Run, Antietam, Murfreesboro · Homestead Act allowed families to acquire 160 acres of public land for $1.60 per acre after living on it for 5 years

1863 ● Hawthorne's *Our Old Home* · Longfellow's *Tales of a Wayside Inn* · Whittier's "Barbara Frietchie" · Lincoln's "Emancipation Proclamation" and "Gettysburg Address"

West Virginia, formed by secession from Virginia, admitted as thirty-fifth state · Stonewall Jackson killed at Battle of Chancellorsville · Battle of Gettysburg (1-3 July) and surrender of Vicksburg (4 July), the turning point of the War

1864 ● William Cullen Bryant's *Thirty Poems* · Locke's *Nasby Papers*

Battles of the Wilderness, Spottsylvania Courthouse, Cold Harbor · Grant versus Lee in Virginia · Farragut at Mobile Bay · Sherman's March to the Sea · Nevada admitted as thirty-sixth state · Lincoln reelected President

1865 ● Lincoln's *Second Inaugural* · Lowell's "Commemoration Ode" · Whitman's *Drum-Taps* · Mark Twain's "Celebrated Jumping Frog of Calaveras County" · Shaw's *Josh Billings*

Surrender of Lee to Grant at Appomattox, 9 April · Assassination of Lincoln, 14 April; Andrew Johnson succeeded him as seventeenth President · Thirteenth Amendment officially abolished slavery

CHAPTER 4

1865-1914

The Rise of Modern America

As a strong bird on pinions free,
Joyous, the amplest spaces heavenward cleaving . . .
—Walt Whitman

Are we the eagle nation Milton saw . . . ?
—William Vaughn Moody

"Brooklyn Bridge, New York," published by the well-known American lithographers Currier & Ives in 1877

Intellectual Currents

Reunion

The Civil War left the nation disrupted. The restoration of unity—at best a difficult process—was made more difficult by the nation's failure to cope with social and economic problems, which actually the war had done nothing to solve. The Reconstruction Era was a confused period and a period of great bitterness. Ill feeling was engendered by sectional controversy, civil war, and misrule.

On the other hand, many forces worked for a restoration of national unity. The states were bound together by a common language, common traditions, and interdependent economic interests. The establishment of schools and colleges in the South by northern philanthropy and the postponement after 1883 for many decades by the national government of the attempt to control race relations in the South contributed to unity. Not the least unifying influence was postwar literature. Some writers preached the gospel of union, while others contributed less directly by writing local color stories which emphasized the virtues of common people in all regions of America.

Among those who celebrated unity and reunion, three writers stand out: Lowell in New England, Whitman in the Middle Atlantic States, and Lanier in the South. On July 3, 1875, Lowell read in Cambridge his poem "Under the Old Elm," which celebrated the hundreth anniversary of Washington's taking command of the Colonial army. After paying eloquent tribute to the greatness of Washington, the poet held out the hand of reconciliation and friendship to Virginia:

> Virginia gave us this imperial man . . .
> She gave us this unblemished gentleman:
> What shall we give her back but love and praise
> As in the dear old unestrangèd days
> Before the inevitable wrong began?
> Mother of states and undiminished men,
> Thou gavest us a country, giving him,
> And we owe alway what we owed thee then . . .
> A great man's memory is the only thing
> With influence to outlast the present whim
> And bind us as when here he knit our golden ring.

The common memory of Washington helped restore national unity after the schismatic years. Mount Vernon soon became a national shrine. The principle enunciated by Lowell was so important to the nation's well-being that in the years to follow, other great Americans, such as Jefferson, Lincoln, and Lee, irrespective of sectional differences, were to become national heroes.

Whitman's plea for reunion took the form of prophecy. The future greatness of the United States would be the achievement of states which are "varied" and "different" and at the same time united in "one identity." In the poem "As a Strong Bird on Pinions Free" (later changed to "Thou Mother with Thy Equal Brood") read at Dartmouth College in 1872, Whitman expressed unbounded confidence in the future progress of America—a progress which would be not only political and material, but also scientific, aesthetic, and moral.

> Thee in an education grown of thee, in teachers, studies, students, born
>   of thee,
> Thee in thy democratic fêtes en-masse, thy high original festivals,
>   operas, lecturers, preachers . . .
> Thee in thy pinnacles, intellect, thought, thy topmost rational joys,
>   thy love and godlike aspiration,
> In thy resplendent coming literati, thy full-lung'd orators, thy sacerdo-
>   tal bards, kosmic savans,
> These! these in thee, (certain to come,) to-day I prophesy.

It was a vision calculated to make men forget the quarrels of the past.

Although Sidney Lanier fought through the Civil War and spent several months as a federal prisoner, he did not become a Yankee-hater. He believed that the South could not attain well-being in isolation and estrangement from the North. In the centennial year of 1876, he attempted in two poems to draw the sections together in loving harmony: "The Psalm of the West" and "The Centennial Meditation of Columbia," the second of which was sung at the Philadelphia Exposition by a great chorus with orchestral accompaniment. Employing a historical approach, both of these poems glance backward over events which had brought the American nation to a new sense of pride and responsibility. In "The Psalm of the West" Lanier surveyed the early voyages to the New World (the eight sonnets on Columbus are especially notable), the settling of New England, the progress of the Revolutionary War from Lexington to Yorktown, and the Civil War between "Heart-strong South" and "Head-strong North." The "Psalm" concluded with a prophecy of America's future glory as ardent as Whitman's. The "Centennial Meditation" suggested more briefly the same historical evolution and concluded with a prophecy which was also a prayer for America's future:

Long as thy God is God above,
   Thy brother every man below,
So long, dear Land of all my love,
   Thy name shall shine, thy fame shall glow.

If the three writers just considered aided the process of reunion by emphasizing the solidarity of a new America, fictionists of the local-color school contributed to the same end with perhaps even greater effectiveness, by drawing attention to the innate virtues of Americans and by adding to their understanding of one another. During the two or three decades following the Civil War, our most popular form of literature was the regional short story. Among others, Bret Harte and Hamlin Garland in the West, George Washington Cable, Joel Chandler Harris, and Mary Noailles Murfree in the South, and Sarah Orne Jewett and Mary E. Wilkins Freeman in New England portrayed with sympathy the inhabitants of their regions. One effect of this body of literature was to assure readers that there was much natural goodness in all sections, and only the most stubborn of hard feelings could persist under such an emollient.

Consider the reputedly flinty New England character as seen in the soft light of Sarah Orne Jewett's tales. Describing a family reunion on the Maine coast, she wrote in *The Country of the Pointed Firs:* "Each heart is warm and every face shines with the ancient light. Such a day as this has transfiguring powers, and easily makes friends of those who have been cold-hearted, and gives to those who are dumb their chance to speak, and lends some beauty to the plainest face." Miss Jewett assured readers that beneath the taciturn and cold exterior of the New England character could be discovered ampleness of speech and warmth of heart. These were the points on which non-New Englanders were likely to entertain serious doubts. Miss Jewett's stories probably increased the amount of good feeling in America toward New England.

Or take the character of the Southern highlander—reputedly wild and lawless—as seen through the sympathetic eyes of Mary Noailles Murfree. She saw that friendliness, charity, the domestic virtues can be found in abundance in the hill and mountain country of the South. It is a natural goodness, produced not by schools and the higher education, but by Nature herself. "The grace of culture is, in its way, a fine thing," Miss Murfree said in a story in *In the Tennessee Mountains*, "but the best that art can do—the polish of a gentleman—is hardly equal to the best that Nature can do in her higher moods."

Or look (to mention one more example) at the Southern planter—by report brutal and tyrannical—as he is reflected in the genial pages of *Uncle Remus.* Joel Chandler Harris assured the world that mutual kindliness had existed between master and slave on the antebellum plantation and implied that not even emancipation and reconstruction could destroy the friendly relations. It was a doubtful proposition, as will be indicated later when the writings of black leaders are discussed. Grateful though they might be to Harris for faithfully recording much of their rich and imaginative folklore, Negroes were bound to doubt claims about idyllic racial relationships either before the war or after it. But whatever Negroes thought of Harris and his preachments, the infectious laughter of Uncle Remus and the pervasive good humor and kindliness expressed by him did much toward putting to flight the ill will which persisted in white partisans both North and South in the postwar years.

It is not too much to say that the writers of the period attempted to reestablish national unity. The local-color stories, in particular, were for many readers a fresh and exciting discovery of America, and the writers of this school might well have taken for their motto the words spoken by Senator Lamar of Mississippi in his eulogy of Charles Sumner: "My countrymen, know one another and you will love one another."

The remarkable extent to which division had been minimized by the end of the century was dramatically demonstrated in the war with Spain, in which northerners and southerners fought side by side and ex-Confederate generals held positions of command. World War I and World War II were to afford even more evidence of the growing solidarity of the American nation.

Social and Economic Problems

Industry and Agriculture Expand
American social and economic life changed radically and rapidly during the years between 1865 and 1914. The railroad was a typical achievement of the age, and powerful in its influence on economic and social life. In 1865 there were only thirty-five thousand miles of track in the United States; by 1900 this mileage increased to nearly two hundred thousand. The Westinghouse air brake and other inventions improved the efficiency of railroad transportation. Enormous land grants by the government financed the building of transcontinental lines: the Union Pacific, the Northern Pacific, and the Santa Fe, all of which had reached the Pacific Coast by 1884. If the cost in land grants was high, the railroads made substantial returns by peopling and developing the vast region west of the Mississippi. The roads, however, often abused their great power, and the Interstate Commerce Act of 1887 marked the beginning of federal regulation.

The railroad was only one factor in the economic revolution which followed the Civil War. A great transportation system presupposed commodities to transport, and these were supplied by an expanding industry and an expanding agriculture.

Industrial growth was stimulated by the exploitation of such resources as iron, coal, and oil; the development of improved machinery; the procurement of cheap labor through immigration; and the government's policy of protecting infant industries by high tariffs and by allowing a free hand to business. There were many marvels of scientific invention: Carnegie was using the improved Bessemer process to manufacture steel by 1875; Bell demonstrated the telephone in 1876; Edison and others made possible the dynamo, which was exhibited at the World's Columbian Exposition in Chicago in 1893 and which, as Henry Adams declared, "gave to history a new phase." Expanding industry required abundant labor; a growing stream of immigrants, at the turn of the century, came in larger proportions from the southern and eastern European countries than (as they had done previously) from the northern and western ones. They were motivated in part by hardships but even more by inducements proffered by factories and transportation lines. Immigration continued without drastic reduction until 1921.

Under these conditions, the rapidly expanding industry got out of hand, and toward the end of the century it became increasingly apparent that government regulation was necessary. Trusts and monopolies exceeded reasonable bounds. The railroads were controlled by only a half-dozen small groups of men. A disproportionate part of the wealth of the nation became concentrated in the pockets of relatively few people. Big business had formed a corrupt alliance with politics. Attempts at regulation and reform—at first ineffective—began with the Sherman Anti-Trust Act of 1890, and in response to growing social criticism became more effective after the turn of the century. Among other things, the powers of the Interstate Commerce Commission were increased, and in 1906 a Pure Food and Drugs Act heralded a new era in the responsibilities of business.

Agriculture also underwent a revolution during the post-Civil War years. Vast new lands in the West were opened to farming. New machines—reapers, binders, threshers—and new scientific devices—fertilizers, insecticides, improved strains—greatly increased the yield of the land. The methods of big business invaded the farm: the cash crop supplanted subsistence farming. But fewer people were needed to do the work, thanks to the improved machinery; the financial returns were precarious; and migration from the farms to the cities grew steadily.

Growth of Cities

Perhaps the most conspicuous change of all during these years was the rapid growth of cities, fed by immigrants from abroad and by farm and village folk from the American countryside. In 1860 one sixth of the population was urban; in 1900, one third. Between 1880 and 1900 the population of Chicago grew from a half million to a million and a half, and the number of American cities with a population of one hundred thousand or more increased from nineteen to thirty-six. City life gained in prestige while country life suffered. Thousands of young Americans supposed that a better life, somehow, could be lived in the city than in the country, and that the bigger the city, the better the life. Many novels of the time—especially those of Theodore Dreiser (1871-1945)—show the error of this supposition. The sudden growth of great urban centers created new social and economic problems, and municipal governments broke down under the strain. For the first time the evils of the slums began to loom.

Labor Organizes

The new industries exploited labor, and it was inevitable that labor should organize to combat the exploitation. A beginning was made by the Knights of Labor, founded in 1869; but the movement did not gain appreciable strength until 1886, when the American Federation of Labor was organized under the leadership of Samuel Gompers. The A. F. of L. continued to gain steadily until 1920, when it reached a peak of more than four million members. As organized labor grew in strength, industrial conflicts increased in number and intensity. The first of these was the railroad strike of 1877. Others worthy of note are the Pullman strike of 1894 and the strike in the Pennsylvania coal fields in 1902. Strikes have often been an effective weapon, and much has been accomplished to improve the lot of labor by social legislation. Since the Massachusetts "Ten Hour Act for Women and Children in Factories" in 1874, much progress has been made in the working conditions, hours, and wages of labor. Early reform legislation was often declared unconstitutional on the disingenuous principle that "a person has the right to sell his labor upon such terms as he deems proper." But after 1900, more liberal judges such as Louis D. Brandeis were instrumental in reversing many of the decisions which had blocked social reform.

The Literature of Social Criticism

St. Paul said that "the love of money is the root of all evil," and the history of America after the Civil War exhibits the truth or near-truth of that statement. Perhaps never before was a nation so engrossed in the business of making money. Perhaps never before was materialism so rampant, or so much pride taken in material achievements.

The writers of the period pointed out forcefully the evils of this crass materialism. In *Democratic Vistas* (1871) Walt Whitman warned his readers that material wealth alone would not make a nation great:

> I hail with joy the oceanic, variegated, intense practical energy, the demand for facts, even the business materialism of the current age, our States. But woe to the age or land in which these things, movements,

stopping at themselves, do not tend to ideas. As fuel to flame, and flame to the heavens, so must wealth, science, materialism—even this democracy of which we make so much—unerringly feed the highest mind, the soul.

Lanier in "The Symphony" (1875) pleaded eloquently for a Christian and chivalric code in place of the unfeeling relations between employer and employed:

'Thou Trade! thou king of the modern days!
    Change thy ways,
    Change thy ways;
Let the sweaty laborers file
    A little while,
    A little while,
Where Art and Nature sing and smile.
Trade! is thy heart all dead, all dead?
And hast thou nothing but a head?
I'm all for heart,' the flute-voice said.

In "these cold, merchantable days" the poet declared, even the love of the sexes is tainted by mercenary motives:

Now, comes a suitor with sharp prying eye—
Says *Here, you Lady, if you'll sell, I'll buy:*
Come, heart for heart—a trade? What! weeping? why?
Shame on such wooers' dapper mercery!

While these poets were voicing spiritual protests, Mark Twain (1835-1910) and C. D. Warner (1829-1900) were ridiculing the get-rich-quick schemes of their money-mad countrymen. In *The Gilded Age* (1873)—a book whose name has been given to the Grant Era (1869-1877) and by extension to the twenty or thirty years following the Civil War—the authors presented at once hilariously and devastatingly Colonel Sellers' designs for moneymaking. At one and the same time, Sellers was scheming to corner the corn and hog crops, buy up the wildcat banks, and market an "Optic Liniment" (his own concoction) throughout the world. He and his associates attempted to sell a large tract of worthless land ("the Tennessee land") to the government. Despite skillful lobbying in Washington, they failed, though by a narrow margin, and the implied moral of the book is that sober industry and contentment with a modest income honestly earned are infinitely preferable to frantic scheming to get rich quick. It was a good moral, but one which Twain himself never learned, and one which millions of Americans had not learned as late as 1929.

The Gilded Age also exposed political corruption in the national capital, where votes were bought and sold. Henry Adams (1838-1918) in his novel *Democracy* (1880) turned a censorious eye on similar political phenomena. He portrays a distinguished United States senator, the leader of his party, who accepted a bribe of $100,000. His reasons were good "political" ones, but they did not satisfy Adams' heroine, whose break with the senator parallels Adams' own withdrawal from the corrupt politics of the Gilded Age. But Adams remained a fascinated observer and refused to surrender his belief in democracy despite its current evil manifestations. "I grant it is an experiment," he has one of the characters in the novel say, "but it is the only direction society can take that is worth its taking. . . . Every other possible step is backward."

Writers were not long content with a general censure of materialism and political corruption. Growing ills awakened social consciences and called forth specific indictments, which became increasingly prominent in the literature of the late nineteenth and early twentieth centuries. Prepared by his own experience on an Iowa farm and indoctrinated in the economic theories of Henry George, Hamlin Garland in *Main-Travelled Roads* exposed the hardships and injustices suffered by the farmers in the Iowa-Wisconsin country. An angry and anger-arousing book, *Main-Travelled Roads* suggests the gathering strength of the Populist movement and helps explain the spectacular rise of William Jennings Bryan in 1896. An important phase in the history of the railroad's exploitation of the farmer is presented in Frank Norris' *The Octopus*, which powerfully portrays the struggle between the Southern Pacific Railroad (the "octopus") and the wheat farmers of California. The triumphant force is neither the railroad nor the farmers, but the wheat, which Norris represents in both *The Octopus* and *The Pit* as more powerful than any man or combination of men.

Criticisms of Industrialism

With the opening of the new century, the most popular literary subject became the exposure of injustices and abuses in American life. In politics, this was the era of Theodore Roosevelt's progressivism and "trust-busting"; in literature, the era of the "muckrakers." Literature was dedicated to the exposé, and scores of books revealed all sorts of malpractices to an indignant public. Perhaps the greatest of the muckraking books was Upton Sinclair's *The Jungle*, which dealt graphically with the life of a Lithuanian immigrant employed in the Chicago stockyards. This sturdy young man is gradually broken, and his family completely ruined, by the inhuman cruelties of the stockyards. The book's exposure of unsanitary practices in the processing of meat undoubtedly hastened the enactment of the Pure Food and Drugs Act.

The leader among the muckrakers was Lincoln Steffens, whose *The*

Shame of the Cities brought to focus the problems created by the sudden emergence of great urban communities and spurred municipal reform. Steffens' book drew attention to corruption in city government and attempted to fix the blame on certain prominent citizens. The growing problems of the big city had been noticed before, and partly as a result of the impact of this famous exposé were to be further exposed. As early as 1890 William Dean Howells (1837-1920) had exhibited the grime and squalor of New York City in *A Hazard of New Fortunes.* Less conservatively, Stephen Crane's *Maggie: A Girl of the Streets* (1893) exposed the ugly life of New York's Bowery. In *Sister Carrie* and *Jennie Gerhardt* Theodore Dreiser told affectingly of the hard lot of the underpaid working girl in cities of the Middle West. Henry Blake Fuller in *The Cliff-Dwellers* underscored the degrading effect on Chicago's social life of greed and cutthroat competition. Possibly the apogee of the literary attack on the city as a monster of corruption and vice was reached in David Graham Phillips' *Susan Lenox* (1917), whose heroine encounters nearly all the evils of our modern Babylons.

The most prominent and commanding figure in the new industrial scene was the captain of industry. The postbellum years saw the amassing of unprecedented private fortunes. Financiers like Jay Cooke, the first great American banker; John D. Rockefeller, the Oil King; Andrew Carnegie, monopolist of iron and steel; and Jay Gould, railroad magnate, became virtual rulers of America. The reputations of these entrepreneurs are now tarnished; they have been called, with a good deal of justice, the "robber barons."

The type early attracted the attention of novelists, but literary treatments for many years were comparatively gentle. In Howells' *The Rise of Silas Lapham*, a wealthy Boston paint manufacturer, crude but honest, loses his business at the crisis of his career, rather than accept for properties a price which is greater than he knows them to be worth. Howells would have defended his portrait of Lapham by saying that the great majority of American financiers were honest, that robber barons were the exception, not the rule. In *A Hazard of New Fortunes*, Dryfoos, the millionaire, is less amiable in his domestic and social relations than Lapham, and less honorable in business, though we are told that he never "wrecked a railroad" or belonged to a "swindling company or grinding monopoly."

Living abroad, Henry James (1843-1916) had the opportunity of knowing well the prosperous and emancipated Americans who took their vacations in Europe. His Christopher Newman (*The American*, 1877) and Adam Verver (*The Golden Bowl*, 1904) are men of integrity and charm who behave decently and even magnanimously. Newman is devoted to culture in a limited way; Verver has built in "American City" a museum of art which he has filled with priceless treasures. Both are men of honor as well as of cultural aspirations.

The balance has never been struck between the portraits drawn by Howells and James and the authentic careers of the robber barons. Were all successful businessmen in the Gilded Age boors and scoundrels? Some social historians have implied as much. But the modern reader—unless he is a cynic—is still free to believe that the Gilded Age produced Laphams and Newmans as well as Cookes and Goulds.

After the turn of the century, the muckrakers' emphasis on the exposé resulted in much less flattering portrayals of the American businessman. The most elaborate was made by Dreiser in two novels, *The Financier* and *The Titan*, in both of which the business career of Frank Cowperwood closely approximates the unsavory record of C. T. Yerkes. The pendulum was to swing back to a more favorable picture of the American millionaire in *Dodsworth* (1929), where Sinclair Lewis' hero, despite his wealth, is an admirable person.

The Reformers

While emphasizing the blight of materialism and the injustices of the new industrial order, the literature of social criticism was not entirely negative; there were constructive elements. Utopias were proposed. The most influential was Edward Bellamy's *Looking Backward* (1888). Believing that economic inequality was the cause of all social ills, Bellamy described a socialist utopia in which the wealth was distributed with equality among its members. A benevolent state controlled public and private economy in minute detail; it assigned members to tasks according to their aptitudes; it provided incentives through special recognition. This planned society produced sufficient wealth to permit early retirement of its members and free enjoyment of cultural pursuits. *Looking Backward* made many converts to Socialism. Other writers also proposed the socialist solution: among them, Howells in *A Traveler from Altruria* and Sinclair in *The Jungle*.

The great body of the literature dealing with social problems, however, proposed not a radical alteration of American free enterprise, but reforms and ameliorations. If men would be honest and fair, if they would be satisfied with a modest income, if they would be Christians imbued with the spirit of the Sermon on the Mount—all would be well: this is the message of many writers. Charles M. Sheldon's *In His Steps* (1896), which had a sale of more than fifteen million copies, recommended that everyone when confronted by a problem ask himself, "What would Jesus do?" Less popular and better writers also emphasized the importance of the Christian attitude. William Vaughn Moody, the first American poet to examine the new social problems with critical insight, urged in "Gloucester Moors" (1900) the necessity of a social conscience among the more fortunate members of society. The results of the Machine Age, he pointed out in "The Brute" (1900), had been disappointing: the machine had not brought

prosperity and leisure to all, but only to "the strong and cunning few."
The solution lay, Moody thought, not in the rejection of the machine, but
in better control of it and fairer distribution of the wealth which it produces. Substantial progress was to be made in the new century toward the
realization of these aims.

The Negroes' Quest

During the last decades of the nineteenth century and the early ones of
the twentieth, one group made particularly disappointing progress—the
blacks. For a while after 1865, to be sure, the Freedmen's Bureau relieved
much suffering among Negroes in the South by issuing rations, establishing
medical aid, resettling displaced persons, protecting civil rights, and setting
up schools. But black farm workers in the section continued to be victim-
ized, and when predominantly northern financiers and industrialists secured economic dominion, Negroes were doomed to continued exploitation. In the area of politics, high hopes were raised by the Emancipation
Proclamation, the 14th and the 15th amendments, and various Reconstruction laws. But soon after the war's end, whites in the South fought and
won the battle for political control. A much longer battle by blacks for
economic opportunities and civil rights began.

Until his death in 1915, the dominant figure in this conflict was
Booker T. Washington, who summarized his essential position in Atlanta
in 1895: "In all things that are purely social we can be as separate as the
fingers, yet one as the hand in all things essential to mutual progress." He
believed, in short, in accommodating black people to segregation and a
form of vocational education that would train Negroes to become servants,
farmers, and mechanics. Northern and southern whites and many blacks
hailed him as a leader, ignoring the fact that Washington advocated such
training not as an ultimate solution but as an expedient step towards complete integration. Says John Hope Franklin, "Washington's influence,
sometimes for better and sometimes for worse, was so great that there was
considerable justification in calling the period, 'The Age of Booker T.
Washington.' "

A leading critic, eventually, was W. E. B. Du Bois (1868-1963), whose
Souls of Black Folk (1903) attacked Washington in several essays. It was
wrong, Du Bois said, for the black educational leader to favor "Work and
Money to such an extent as . . . to overshadow the higher aims of life,"
and tacitly to accept the doctrine of white supremacy. Du Bois' beliefs
were memorably expressed in resolutions of the Niagara movement in
1905-1907 and of the National Association for the Advancement of
Colored People, beginning in 1910, as well as in his essays—beliefs in free
speech, voting rights, and the abolition of discrimination. Racial discrimination was not, of course, confined to the South, as blacks who went
North promptly discovered. New York City in time became a center for

activity in behalf of the Negro. Du Bois, as an officer of the NAACP and editor of the *Crisis*, lived there and for many years served as a spokesman for radicals battling to improve social and economic opportunities for Negroes. James Weldon Johnson (1871-1938), another of the many blacks who moved from the South to New York, in 1912 published *Autobiography of an Ex-Coloured Man*, in many ways a pioneer work foreshadowing Negro fiction to come in the vividness of its representation of racial prejudices. But not until after World War I would its influence—or indeed that of its author—become widely felt.

The Frontier Versus Europe: A Question of Values

The Freedom of the Frontier

"Westward the course of empire takes its way," wrote Bishop Berkeley in 1752. The westward movement in America was a fulfillment of this prophecy beyond anything which the bishop could have foreseen. Before the end of the eighteenth century, pioneers had crossed the Alleghenies; by the middle of the nineteenth century, they had settled the Mississippi Valley and had invaded California and Oregon; by the end of the century, only the Rocky Mountains and the arid tracts of Arizona and Nevada remained unsettled; and by the beginning of World War I, there was no more frontier. The "epic of America" before 1914 was the epic of the ever advancing frontier. The treatment of the frontier in literature has been of two kinds: either romantic, or realistic and critical. In the nineteenth century the romantic treatment predominated; realistic and critical treatment did not prevail until after World War I.

Whitman sounded the dominant nineteenth-century note in "Pioneers! O Pioneers!" (1865). Whitman's pioneers were heroes—"tan-faced children," "youthful and sinewy," armed with "pistols and sharp-edged axes." (A century later it was to appear that the pioneers had done too thorough a job in upheaving the soil and felling the forests.) They were "impatient" and "full of action"—a "resistless, restless race." Such was Whitman's glorification of the westward movement. Other poets of the nineteenth century echoed his praise and admiration.

The distinguished historian Frederick Jackson Turner (1861-1932) was almost as romantic in "The Significance of the Frontier in American History," written in 1893. "Stand at Cumberland Gap," he wrote, "and watch the procession of civilization, marching single file—the buffalo following the trail to the salt springs, the Indian, the fur trader and hunter, the cattle raiser, the pioneer farmer—and the frontier has passed by. Stand at South Pass in the Rockies a century later and see the same procession with wider intervals between." Turner defined the frontier as "the line of most rapid and effective Americanization." The American character was largely formed by the frontier:

To the frontier the American intellect owes its striking characteristics. That coarseness and strength combined with acuteness and inquisitiveness; that practical, inventive turn of mind, quick to find expedients; that masterful grasp of material things, lacking in the artistic but powerful to effect great ends; that restless, nervous energy, that dominant individualism, working for good and for evil, and withal that buoyancy and exuberance which comes with freedom—these are the traits of the frontier, or traits called out elsewhere because of the existence of the frontier.

Turner's sentences are almost a prose paraphrase of Whitman.

When we come to the literature written by frontiersmen, we find much that is sordid and unattractive in the life described, but the total effect is still romantic. Frontier life was vital, expansive, exuberant; it was in the full tide of growth; here was no Indian summer, no sere and yellow leaf.

The life portrayed by Mark Twain's precursors—Davy Crockett, A. B. Longstreet, W. T. Thompson, G. W. Harris—contains much that is vulgar, brutal, and unprincipled. The bloody athletic contests described by Longstreet, the rough practical jokes of Harris' Sut Lovingood may repel the delicate reader. But there is no denying the vitality, the sturdy strength and individualism, and, above all, the high spirits and love of fun. Life on the frontier must have been good to produce so much solid enjoyment; perhaps no other early settlements in the world's history have been enlivened by such hilarity.

Abraham Lincoln liked the Southwestern yarnspinners, for he was one of them; and from their writings runs a line of genealogical descent to the great works of Mark Twain: *Roughing It* (1872), in which he told tall tales of his sojourn in the Far West, and *Life on the Mississippi* (1883), *Tom Sawyer* (1876), and *Huckleberry Finn* (1884), in which he immortalized the great river. Mark Twain did not omit the seamy side of the river region —the squalor, the vulgarity, the lawlessness; but this aspect is less depressing than it might be because there was so much that was splendid and exhilarating. The splendor was symbolized by the steamboat, and "the boat *was* rather a handsome sight!" The exhilaration came as a result of freedom such as Huck and Jim achieved on their raft:

I never felt easy till the raft was two miles below there and out in the middle of the Mississippi. Then we hung up our signal lantern, and judged that we was free and safe once more. I hadn't had a bite to eat since yesterday, so Jim he got out some corn-dodgers and buttermilk, and pork and cabbage and greens—there ain't nothing in the world so good when it's cooked right—and whilst I eat my supper we talked and had a good time. I was powerful glad to get away from the feuds, and so was Jim to get away from the swamp. . . . Other places do seem so cramped up and smothery, but a raft don't.

It is important to note, however, that the freedom symbolized by Huck and his raft is social as well as individual. Despite his revolt against Miss Watson's "civilization," Huck's behavior is not irresponsible. The freedom of *Huckleberry Finn* turns out to be, paradoxically, a qualified freedom, a freedom complicated by responsibilities and social ties. As Lionel Trilling has acutely observed, "Huck is always 'in a sweat' over the predicament of someone else." It was with good reason that William Dean Howells called Mark Twain "the Lincoln of our literature."

The European Tradition

The westward movement was a powerful driving force which settled the American continent. But there has been another, a counter-force, less powerful but insistent, operating throughout our history. As Ferner Nuhn pointed out in his book *The Wind Blew from the East*, there has been in American life and literature from the beginning "the everpresent pullback toward modes of culture that lie in our past . . . the desire to retrace the racial steps . . . the nostalgic tradition." The Atlantic seaboard has felt drawn constantly to Europe; the Middle West and the Far West, to the Atlantic seaboard. In colonial times, Increase Mather and William Byrd—each in his own way—enjoyed London. In the nineteenth century, Irving and Longfellow and Lowell assimilated the culture of Europe, and Hawthorne felt acutely the ancestral ties to "our old home." Among pre-Civil War major writers, only Thoreau and Whitman never traveled abroad. In the latter half of the century, the Eastward pull began to be felt in the newly settled West: Howells and Garland were drawn to Boston by the lodestone of the East; Twain settled in Hartford. Even today some Westerners confess to a feeling of "isolation."

The counter-pull has produced two kinds of literary subjects: comparisons of the eastern and the western parts of the United States, and comparisons of Europe and America. Although the first subject may be found here and there in our literature (*A Hazard of New Fortunes* transplants several Midwesterners to the East and contrasts the regions; Moody's *The Great Divide* studies the different moralities of New England and the West), it does not attain the importance of the second: Europe versus America is one of the more significant themes in American literature.

Mark Twain treated Europe with unorthodox levity in *The Innocents Abroad* (1869). He had a frontiersman's hatred of tyranny, and Europe to him meant the twofold tyranny of church and state, of priests and kings. The best thing that had ever happened in Europe, he thought, was the French Revolution. He could not enjoy the great art of Florence when he recalled the sycophantic attitude of the artists toward the Medicis. Not only in *The Innocents Abroad* but in other works as well (*A Connecticut Yankee in King Arthur's Court, Life on the Mississippi, Huckleberry Finn*) he lashed out against feudalism and its survivals wherever he found them.

It was primarily Mark Twain's love of freedom and his sense of the dignity of the common man which blinded him to the glories of Europe.

Two contemporaries of Twain were not so blinded: Henry James spent most of his life in England because he felt that "it takes an old civilization to set a novelist in motion", Henry Adams, the historian, was drawn to medieval France as an example of "unity," against which he set the multiplicity" of the modern world.

Though James admired the "items of high civilization" which he professed to find in Europe and failed to find in America, he wrote in large part about Americans—Americans in Europe. In novel after novel *(The American, The Portrait of a Lady, The Ambassadors, The Golden Bowl)* he shows us Americans, admirable though unsophisticated, in the process of exposure to European influences. These influences make for social and aesthetic enrichment; they are, at the same time, often questionable morally. James' innocent Americans—Christopher Newman, Isabel Archer, Lambert Strether, Maggie Verver, in, respectively, the four novels just named—are shocked by the evil which they discover in Europe. But they do not succumb to the evil; indeed, they are triumphant over it. Lesser Americans in James' stories may be corrupted by Europe or may remain impervious to its culture, but his heroes and heroines, though not always happy or successful, emerge from their European experiences culturally enriched and strong of soul. Perhaps James meant to suggest that the ideal civilization would combine the freshness and moral strength of America with the rich culture of the Old World.

Adams was not interested in the richness of contemporary Europe so much as in the richness of its medieval past. In his attempt to establish historical lines of force—his "dynamic theory of history"—by which he might explain the modern world and perhaps predict its future course, Adams centered his interest in twelfth-century France and in the Cathedral of Chartres as the epitome of that time and place. In Chartres he found the perfect symbol of unity. In that distant age, the Virgin, in whose honor Chartres was built, exerted a dominating influence over all men. She was the greatest force of the age—energizing, controlling, comforting, beatifying.

If the Virgin was the symbol of medieval unity, the dynamo, Adams thought, was the symbol of modern multiplicity. The Virgin was a unifying spiritual force; the dynamo was obviously a force, but neither spiritual nor unifying. As religion decayed, enormous, incalculable forces unleashed by science—steam power, electricity, radioactivity—threatened to destroy mankind. In *The Education of Henry Adams* (1907), he posed the serious question of whether there was enough intelligence and moral character in the world to control these new forces and use them for man's welfare. The release of atomic energy makes the question an even more serious one today. *The Education* is perhaps the best statement in our literature of the background of our present problems.

In *Mont-Saint-Michel and Chartres* (1904) Adams, the disillusioned intellectual, almost surrendered to the spell of Chartres and the Virgin:

> One sees her personal presence on every side. Anyone can feel it who will only consent to feel like a child. Sitting here any Sunday afternoon, while the voices of the children are chanting in the choir—your mind held in the grasp of the strong lines and shadows of the architecture; your eyes flooded with the autumn tones of the glass; your ears drowned with the purity of the voices; one sense reacting upon another until sensation reaches the limit of its range—you, or any other lost soul, could, if you cared to look and listen, feel a sense beyond the human ready to reveal a sense divine that would make that world once more intelligible, and would bring the Virgin to life again, in all the depths of feeling which she shows here—in lines, vaults, chapels, colours, legends, chants—more eloquent than the prayerbook, more beautiful than the autumn sunlight.

Europe to Adams was a bright symbol of something eminently valuable—possibly essential to man's prosperity and happiness—which the modern world has lost.

Europe retained a good deal of prestige throughout the nineteenth century and after, despite *The Innocents Abroad* and the frontier school. But despite a growing disposition of Americans to be critical of frontier values, European prestige lost ground steadily as the twentieth century advanced.

Science and Religion

The march of science in the nineteenth century profoundly affected religious thought. Geology established the antiquity of the earth, thus discrediting the chronology of Genesis. Evolution, as set forth in Darwin's *The Origin of Species* in 1859, saw man as the result of a slow development from simpler forms of animal life, thus challenging the Christian belief in his special creation. Astronomical science seemed to point to an infinite universe, in the face of which man appeared insignificant. Before the end of the period 1865-1914, sociological, biological, and psychological investigations further reduced man's importance and autonomy. Sociologist William Graham Sumner (1840-1910) argued that human behavior was largely determined by "folkways," the mores of one's environment. Biology emphasized the determining influence of physical inheritance, of glandular secretions; psychology, the determining influence of automatic responses to stimuli. So effective was the combined onslaught of the new sciences that by the end of the period, man appeared to be—from the scientific point of view—little more than an ingenious mechanism. Scientific reasoning seemed to leave no room for the soul, or God, or the transcendental perception of truth—for those religious beliefs, in short, which had motivated most Americans for nearly three centuries and which had found eloquent expression in the writings of Edwards, Emerson, and Whitman. The inspired view of the psalmist—"What is man that thou art mindful of him? . . . For thou hast made him a little lower than the angels, and hast crowned him with glory and honor"—became little short of absurd to the scientific mind. All phenomena, we were to suppose, were naturalistic phenomena, and were explicable on purely naturalistic, as opposed to spiritual or transcendental, grounds.

Early Resistance to Science

Scientific naturalism did not capture our literature immediately, and, as one might expect, the poets offered a sturdier resistance than other writers. Although Whitman accepted the concept of evolution, it was the Emersonian (which was in turn the Lamarckian) concept of inheritance of acquired characteristics, rather than the concept of Darwin, which emphasized the struggle for survival. For Whitman, as for Emerson, the evolutionary idea exalted man by enlarging his future possibilities:

> My feet strike an apex of the apices of the stairs,
> On every step bunches of ages, and larger bunches between the steps,
> All below duly travel'd, and still I mount and mount.

As the scientific movement advanced in the post-Civil War years, Whitman became not less but more transcendental. His transcendentalism reached its highest points in the late poems, "Passage to India":

> O my brave soul!
> O farther farther sail!

and the "Prayer of Columbus" (1876):

> Shadowy vast shapes smile through the air and sky,
> And on the distant waves sail countless ships,
> And anthems in new tongues I hear saluting me.

Sidney Lanier was a spiritually minded person who had no intention of surrendering his Christian faith to the new science. But partly as a natural reaction against his strict Calvinistic upbringing in Macon, partly through the influence of his professor of science, James Woodrow, at Oglethorpe, and partly because of the liberal atmosphere at Johns Hopkins, he welcomed science with an open mind. His copy of Darwin, we are told, was copiously annotated. He made a special study of the physics of sound in connection with his investigation of prosody in *The Science of English Verse* (1880). Science, then, was an unmixed good. An intelligent man, he thought, must be, above all else, "catholic" (see, for example, "The Marshes of Glynn"): he must eschew the narrowness of creed and cultivate breadth. The ideal soul is characterized by its "loves," its points of receptivity, and, he argues in "My Springs," excludes neither science nor any other good thing:

> And home-loves and high glory-loves,
> And science-loves and story-loves.

He was aware (in "The Mocking Bird") that science might have its limitations:

> Sweet Science, this large riddle read me plain:
> How may the death of that dull insect be
> The life of yon trim Shakspere in the tree?

He admitted (in "Acknowledgement") that possibly his age was dazzled by the new science: "blinking at o'er bright science." These, however, were small reservations in Lanier's mind; no writer of the period was more hospitable to science. Lanier's eager search for truth was thoroughly admirable, but one cannot avoid a suspicion of indiscrimination and naïveté. Lanier did not recognize the contradictions involved in advocating the reconciliation of religion and science. Unlike some other reconcilers, he was apparently unaware that such a reconciliation would entail a diminution of Christian doctrine.

The breadth which Lanier extolled and exemplified was looked at more skeptically by the greatest of the New England poets of the time, Emily Dickinson. Her satire of the liberal clergyman—and she must have had in mind the pretentious "modern" preacher of the highly intellectualized and at times snobbish religion that was replacing the Calvinism of her upbringing—is a telling indictment: "He preached upon 'Breadth' till it argued him narrow—."Although she became a recluse, she continued to keep in touch with the outside world by reading; she must have been aware of the controversy surrounding "science," yet she never comments on it with more than gentle irony:

> "Faith" is a fine invention
> When Gentlemen can *see*—
> But *Microscopes* are prudent
> In an Emergency.

Ultimately, though, Emily Dickinson is a religious poet, and her religious conviction, often tested and questioned, became stronger for having been tried. For her, the things of religion still lay beyond the realm of scientific demonstration; they were still objects of faith:

I never spoke with God
Nor visited in Heaven—
Yet certain am I of the spot
As if the Checks were given—

The Spread of Mechanistic Philosophy

By the time Lanier died in 1881, Emily Dickinson in 1886, and Whitman in 1892, a religious faith untroubled by science had died in American literature. By the end of the century, poets and prose writers were feeling the full impact of the scientific movement.

Stephen Crane inferred from the biological struggle for survival and the astronomical immensity of the universe that man is unimportant:

A man said to the universe
"Sir, I exist!"
"However," replied the universe,
"The fact has not created in me
A sense of obligation."

In Crane's "The Open Boat," "a high cold star on a winter's night" becomes the symbol of the indifference of Nature and Nature's God. It seemed ironical to Crane, who found intense irony everywhere in human experience, that the discoverer of the universe should be dwarfed by his discovery, that the chief spiritual result of man's scientific achievements should be the conviction of his own insignificance.

Mark Twain, in his late forties, became a convert to scientific materialism and its denial of human free will. Partly through the influence of the new agnosticism as expounded by Robert G. Ingersoll and others, and partly, perhaps, in the attempt to stifle the deep-seated feeling that his literary performance had not been in keeping with his creative powers, he declared and attempted to prove that "man is a machine." In *What Is Man?* (1906) he summarized his argument as follows:

To me, Man is a machine, made up of many mechanisms, the moral and mental ones acting automatically in accordance with the impulses of an interior Master who is built out of born-temperament and an accumulation of multitudinous outside influences and trainings; a machine whose one function is to secure the spiritual contentment of the Master, be his desires good or be they evil; a machine whose will is absolute and must be obeyed; and always *is* obeyed.

If to Henry Adams man himself was something more than a machine, man at least seemed to be impelled along lines of force. "Modern politics," he said in the *Education*, "is a struggle not of men but of forces. The men become every year more and more creatures of force, massed about central power-houses." He began to "see lines of force all about him, where he had always seen lines of will," and thus "before knowing it," he confessed, "the mind stepped into the mechanical theory of the universe." The future which Adams envisioned for the race was not too hopeful. There was a fair possibility that man would be engulfed by the new forces: "In the earlier stages of progress, the forces to be assimilated were simple and easy to absorb, but, as the mind of man enlarged its range, it enlarged the field of complexity, and must continue to do so, even into chaos, until the reservoirs of sensuous or supersensuous energies are exhausted, or cease to affect him, or until he succumbs to their excess."

Like Adams, Theodore Dreiser believed that men were creatures of force. With the turn of the century, this idea began to appear in the naturalistic novel, which soon became its chief literary vehicle. Many naturalistic novelists felt a profound sympathy with the unfortunate members of modern society, who appeared to be the helpless and blameless victims of forces beyond their control. The mechanistic philosophy afforded a means of complete exoneration: if a person was dominated by chemical forces from within and social forces from without, he was not morally responsible for his acts or culpable for his misdeeds. In accordance with this view Dreiser wrote his great naturalistic novels: *Sister Carrie, Jennie Gerhardt*, and *An American Tragedy*. "All of us," declared Lester Kane in *Jennie Gerhardt*, "are more or less pawns. We're moved about like chessmen by circumstances over which we have no control." To Dreiser the world seemed utterly without purpose:

> In distant ages a queer thing had come to pass. There had started on its way in the form of evolution a minute cellular organism which had apparently reproduced itself by division, had early learned to combine itself with others, to organize itself into bodies, strange forms of fish, animals and birds, and had finally learned to organize itself into man. Man, on his part, composed as he was of self-organizing cells, was pushing himself forward into comfort and different aspects of existence by means of union and organization with other men. Why? Heaven only knew.

The obvious tendency in the writings of Crane, Mark Twain, Adams, and Dreiser was a growing pessimism.

Mechanistic beliefs, so prominent in the literature of the 1900's, were not unchallenged after their apparent triumph. Josiah Royce expounded at Harvard an idealism reminiscent of Emerson's. William James, another

Harvard professor, brother of the novelist and America's first great authority in the new science of psychology, emphasized in *The Varieties of Religious Experience* (1902) the energizing power of religious faith. This power could hardly be accounted for, he thought, in terms of a mechanistic universe. The creative individual need not succumb to Adams' lines of force or Dreiser's weight of circumstance. James set up the pragmatic test of truth: "The ultimate test for us of what a truth means is the conduct it dictates or inspires." And, finally, Robert Herrick among the novelists and William Vaughn Moody among the poets in the first decade of the century presented the religious view of life. But despite these dissenting voices, it appeared likely that the determinism of mechanistic science would continue to gain in popular and literary acceptance.

The New Imperialism

Throughout the nineteenth century, expansionist doctrines had been urged sporadically. Certain prominent Americans had advocated in the name of "manifest destiny" the desirability of annexing the entire North American continent. Out of this agitation had come the war with Mexico and the acquisition of large territories in the Southwest in 1845-1853 and the purchase of Alaska in 1867. But since, Alaska excepted, the new territory seemed necessary to round out our natural boundaries, this expansion could hardly be called flagrantly imperialistic.

Imperialistic sentiment came into play in the '90's, though, when the Cuban Revolution afforded an excuse for American intervention in the short war with Spain in 1898. The spectacular and exciting events of the war—Dewey's victory in Manila Bay, the crushing defeat of Cervera's squadron as it attempted to escape from Santiago, the charge of Roosevelt's Rough Riders up San Juan Hill—evoked a dubious mixture of patriotism and jingoism. After the defeat of Spain, the Filipinos resisted our rule and General Miles' army put down the insurrection. Many thoughtful Americans were alarmed at the new imperialistic policy upon which the nation seemed to be embarking. The crisis called forth protests from persons as various as William Jennings Bryan, Jane Addams, Charles W. Eliot, Finley Peter Dunne, and William Vaughn Moody.

Through the inimitable "Observations of Mr. Dooley," Dunne in 1902 satirized the whole American imperialistic policy:

"An there ye ar-re, Hinnissy. I hope this here lucid story will quite the waggin tongues iv scandal an' that people will let th' Ph'lippeens stew in their own happiness."

"But sure they might do something f'r thim," said Mr. Hennessy.

"They will," said Mr. Dooley. "They'll give thim a measure iv freedom."

"But whin?"

"Whin they'll stand still long enough to be measured. . . ."

Moody lashed out against the conquest of the Philippines in one of the
most impassioned poems of our literature, "An Ode in Time of Hesitation"
(1900):

> Are we the eagle nation Milton saw
> Mewing its mighty youth,
> Soon to possess the mountain winds of truth,
> And be a swift familiar of the sun . . .
>
> Or have we but the talons and the maw,
> And for the abject likeness of our heart
> Shall some less lordly bird be set apart?—
> Some gross-billed wader where the swamps are fat?
> Some gorger in the sun? Some prowler with the bat?

But neither the humor of Dunne nor the Miltonic fervor of Moody could
stem the tide—America took the Philippines. Still, the protests need not be
regarded as futile: they may very well have had the effect of making the
administrators more careful, for America's record in governing the Islands
has been a creditable one.

John Hay, Secretary of State under William McKinley and Theodore
Roosevelt, made partial amends to the anti-imperialists by his Chinese
policy, and Moody's tone changed from condemnation in the "Ode" to
pride in "The Quarry." Having declared the policy of the "Open Door,"
Hay backed it up by thwarting the obvious intention of the European
powers to use the Boxer Rebellion as an opportunity for the dismember-
ment of China. The American eagle—no longer a "gross-billed wader"—
now appeared in a heroic role. When China—backward, helpless, unaware
(the description of China in the poem is extraordinarily fine)—was about
to be pounced upon by the "brutes of prey," the "grand circler," uttering
a cry of warning, drove them away:

> . . . stiller-tongued, with eyes somewhat askance,
> They settled to the slot and disappeared.

A distinguished historian later declared that " 'The Quarry' is worth all of
the literature of imperialism together."

The United States emerged a world power from the war with Spain.
National pride centered in the Navy to a degree unequaled since the War
of 1812. Alfred T. Mahan's *Influence of Sea Power upon History*, whose
doctrine was espoused by Theodore Roosevelt, helped to make America

navy-minded; the victories over Spain raised naval patriotism to a high pitch; Theodore Roosevelt dramatized the role of the "big stick" by sending the fleet around the world in 1907. But the great majority of Americans were not imperialists at heart, and by 1910 pacifism seemed to be gathering strength: Bryan, thrice Democratic candidate for the Presidency, advocated disarmament; David Starr Jordan, president of Stanford, argued that war was the reversal of evolution—the survival of the unfit; William James attempted to discover "a moral equivalent of war." Not deeply affected by the flare-up of 1898-1900, the national temperament preferred peace with isolation.

R.S.
W.B.

Literary Trends

"The eight years in America from 1860 to 1868," wrote Charles Dudley Warner and his collaborator, Mark Twain, in *The Gilded Age* (1873), "uprooted institutions that were centuries old, changed the politics of a people, transformed the social life of half the country, and wrought so profoundly upon the entire national character that the influence cannot be measured short of two or three generations." Although many writers continued to follow older patterns, these changes in American life brought changes in some forms of the literature. Some changes adapted forms to the tastes of the growing middle-class reading public. Others helped express the nostalgia, puzzlement, or distress of people living in a transitional period.

Authors continued to write old-fashioned essays, but this form began to date as it was crowded from magazines by journalistic articles. By the end of the period, muckraking reports by Lincoln Steffens and others had become much more typical. A great deal of poetry—some of it weak and imitative, some of it memorable and deeply felt—was poured into prewar molds. But the period also saw the rise to prominence of much popular poetry, some created by the people for the people, some written by more literate poets who consciously tried to please the growing group of readers who enjoyed poetry in dialect. Preeminently, though, this was an age of fiction, and fiction changed more than any other type of literature. There were some developments in the drama, too, which paralleled developments in fiction and which foreshadowed some achievements of the modern period.

Older Patterns of Poetry

Much poetry—"literary" contrasted with folk poetry—showed few effects of the changing intellectual climate. Poetry lost its vitality for many readers; it awaited a rebirth, portents of which appeared in the final years of the period. This was partly because many poets whose careers had begun earlier—Bryant, Longfellow, Holmes, Lowell, Emerson, and Whittier —continued to satisfy and to determine tastes. It was partly because these established artisans and their British contemporaries were imitated in innocuous poems by hosts of inferior poets—Richard Henry Stoddard (1825-

1903), Bayard Taylor (1825-1878), Edmund Clarence Stedman (1833-1908), and Richard Watson Gilder (1844-1909), to name but a few. Even on a higher level, Edward Rowland Sill (1841-1887), Paul Hamilton Hayne (1830-1886), William Vaughn Moody (1869-1910), and Paul Laurence Dunbar (1872-1906)—all of whom had important things to say and said them with real eloquence—often utilized established verse forms. (Dunbar also wrote outstanding dialect poetry.) Stephen Crane (1871-1900) was a minor, though arresting, exception in his use of free verse. Even two major poets of the period—Emily Dickinson and Sidney Lanier—usually shaped their poetry to conform with accepted schemes. Walt Whitman, however, was an important exception.

Emily Dickinson: Meaning in Miniatures

Emily Dickinson, although only seven of her 1775 poems were published before 1890, was almost contemporaneous, as a writer, with her idol, Ralph Waldo Emerson (1803-1882): she was born in 1830 and began to write poetry, it appears, in the fifties and continued until her death in 1886. She was seemingly as innocent of theories about technique as a poet could be, as her test for poetry shows—"If I read a book and it makes my body so cold no fire can ever warm me, I know that is poetry. If I feel physically as if the top of my head were taken off, I know that is poetry." Probably when such an impressionistic critic conceived of what she was doing, she did not consider herself a rebel against established forms. Like Lanier, therefore, when she diverged from conventional procedures, she did so less because she had new theories than because, even for a poet, she was an unusual personality.

Living her isolated life in Amherst, she kept in touch with the outside world by listening to famous lecturers and reading newspapers and magazines and the books of some leading authors. An admirer gave her Emerson's *Poems* when they were still considered revolutionary; she sent a copy of Emerson's *Representative Men* to a friend; she met Emerson and heard him lecture. One belief of his which she shared and enunciated was that a task for the poet was, as Emerson put it, to "embrace the common, . . . explore and sit at the feet of the familiar, the low." "Give me," said Emerson, "insight into to-day, and you may have the antique and future worlds." Emily Dickinson saw the poet as one who distills attars "from the familiar species that perished by the door." So in stanzas ordinarily like those of Emerson and, incidentally, like those of church hymns, she tried to tell (again as Emerson phrased it) the "meaning" of "the meal in the firkin; the milk in the pan; . . . the glance of the eye . . . every trifle bristling with the polarity that ranges it instantly on an eternal law. . . ."

The common, for her, included a household group of men, women, and children; New England nature in the small range of nearby fields; and the rooms of a house as they were known to a housekeeper. She saw these with eyes focused to minute details—with intimate knowledge comparable to a nun's knowledge of each stone and lichen in her narrow cell. And when she announced what the details in her world of miniatures meant, the revelations were very personal ones—the discoveries of a mind which was both serious and playful, both mystical and whimsical. Novel imagery was the result, much of it foreshadowed by nothing else in literature so well as by the poem "Huswifery" by seventeenth-century Edward Taylor, which had told of faith by employing conceits derived from household tasks.

Poem 318 [I'll tell you how the Sun rose] is in some ways typical. Like a large share of the poems by this introspective recluse, it begins with the first personal pronoun, and goes on to record highly individual insights into a common experience. In the second line she playfully interprets the sunrise in terms of feminine fineries—"A Ribbon at a time"—a conceit paralleled, in the next lines by the image of ladylike hills that "untied their Bonnets." A comparison of the light with darting squirrels, two details of the commonplace scene—steeples that "swam" in "Amethyst" and bobolinks bursting into song—then the soft soliloquy of the watcher ("That must have been the Sun"!) give the effect of the dawn. The end of the day is impressionistically represented by figures which involve children climbing a stile and a "Dominie" putting up pasture bars and leading away his flock. All the details come from ordinary observations, and their very commonplaceness gives the interpretation a unique appeal.

Though this poem is less intense in thought and feeling than many by Miss Dickinson, its imagery is fairly representative. As Henry W. Wells remarks in *The American Way of Poetry*, "Children playing in the garret or asleep in their beds at dawn, New England customs at Thanksgiving, apples snug in the cellar through the winter, the loud ticking of the clock at night, signs on chimneys and doors, needle and thread, the little girl shut in the closet and told to be still—such images take on the most piquant and unexpected emotional meanings. . . . Her microscope requires only one clover and one bee to make a prairie; one flake of snow debating whether it will cross a rut suffices her to create at once a mood and a winter's day." The fusion of such homespun imagery with the thoughts and whimsies of a poet made Emily Dickinson's work fresh and exciting.

But Emily Dickinson's preoccupation with the homely and the familiar should not lead the reader to believe that there was no depth or pain in her poetry. Many of her poems are poems of despair, anguish, and even agony—such as "I felt a funeral, in my brain" [280], "I measure every grief I meet" [561], "I like a look of agony" [241], and "I heard a fly buzz—when I died" [465]. Her deepest concerns were modern ones: the nature of the inner self, the confrontation with death, the question of religious belief. A great number of her poems express the turbulent feelings of unfulfilled love. As her poetry has come to be more carefully read, she has appeared less a nineteenth-century poet of transcendental cheer and more a modern poet of existential despair.

Sidney Lanier: Musician and Poet

Sidney Lanier, in his conception of poetry, was much closer to prewar New England poets than he was to Walt Whitman. "Whitman," he charged, "is poetry's butcher. Huge raw collops slashed from the rump of poetry, and never mind gristle—is what Whitman feeds our souls with." In his lectures on *The English Novel* Lanier devoted a good deal of time, a bit irrelevantly, to attacks upon Whitman's heresies. And when Lanier himself wrote free verse, as he frequently did, he did not think of publishing it. Instead, he conceived of himself as writing not poems but outlines for poems which awaited more conventional artistic clothing before they were fit to appear in public. Whitman, he held, had been at his best when writing "O Captain, My Captain," his emotional and popular poem on the death of Lincoln, because in it he had "abandoned his theory of formlessness and written in form." Like the Brahmins, Lanier saw the poet achieving greatness when he used his supreme artistry to fuse beauty and truth. "Art, to be free," he wrote, "is not to be independent of form but to be master of many forms."

Lanier's departures from conventional versification came, therefore, less because he disagreed with the older poets than because he had individual tastes and talents. Even better than Emerson, he knew and loved the Elizabethans, and he tended to use many images and conceits which were Elizabethan in their daring. He was a musician and a lover of the forms of music, and in several poems, notably "The Symphony," he employed organizations analogous to those of musical compositions. Furthermore, as his *Science of English Verse* shows, he tended to think of poetic rhythms as essentially the same as musical rhythms. The result of this belief was that, though he kept within the limits which he had defined, he was a master of more complex modulations of meter, of more artful and melodic handling of vowels and consonants, than any of his predecessors save Poe.

Walt Whitman: An American Bard

In a characteristic act, Whitman favorably reviewed his own *Leaves of Grass* when it was first published in 1855. In praising his poetry, he drew this revealing self-portrait: "An American bard at last! One of the roughs, large, proud, affectionate, eating, drinking, and breeding, his costume manly and free, his face sunburnt and bearded, his posture strong and erect, his voice bringing hope and prophecy to the generous races of young and old." Whitman saw his poetry as a new poetry, himself as a new man. His break with tradition in both form and meaning was so radical that it shocked his own and later generations. His long line sweeping across the page boldly proclaimed a freedom from poetic convention at the same

time that it spoke out loudly for modern man, democracy, and science.
But though Whitman was a great innovator, blazing new trails for American literature, he was also a man of his time. Emerson's poetry, for example, obviously left its mark. Opera, with its aria and recitative, clearly was
an influence on the structure of his poems. Perhaps even more important,
the oratory and styles of the 1840's and 1850's left their imprint on his
poetry.

Whitman was like the orators of the day in that he wanted to preach
to men the ways of righteous thinking and living. In notebooks which he
filled when he was working toward the writing of *Leaves of Grass*, he
voiced his determination to "elevate, enlarge, purify, deepen and make
happy the attributes of the body and soul of man." Furthermore, as he
considered how he would deliver this message to his countrymen, he was
evidently not sure, for some time, whether his medium was to be oratory
or poetry. His considering oratory was hardly surprising, since the accepted
medium for social or religious preachments was the oration or the sermon,
and he was fascinated all his life by public speaking and public speakers.
Possibly Whitman's inability to succeed as an orator was an important
factor leading to his final decision to become a poet. In his early New
York days, so he said, he "haunted the courts to witness notable trials,
and . . . heard all the famous actors and actresses." Over the years, he listened to Webster, Garrison, Beecher, Clay, Everett, and Phillips, as well as
to less famous orators. His "Poem of Joys" contains an interesting description of the great speaker swaying his audience:

> O the orator's joys!
> To inflate the chest—to roll the thunder of the voice out from the ribs
>   and throat,
> To make the people rage, weep, hate, desire, with yourself,
> To lead America—to quell America with a great tongue.

He enjoyed the declamatory interpretations of Shakespeare by Booth and
Forrest which were then fashionable, and he himself loved to intone sonorous lines from the dramas while riding Broadway omnibuses, tramping
with friends, and strolling by the seashore. He knew and greatly admired,
too, literature which approximated the oratorical effect he wanted—the
lecture-essays of Emerson, the songs of Ossian, translations of Greek and
Latin dramas and epics, the exhortatory parts of the Bible and their adaptations and paraphrases in sermons.

In the notes that Whitman wrote for his early works, there were passages which might have done for either lectures or poems. One scrap of
paper bears the caption "Poem—Religious," and then, underneath this
title is written "or lecture on Religion"; and one note, though it was
headed "lecture," eventually was utilized as part of a poem. As a reciter of

his poetry, he attempted (though unfortunately with questionable success) to use the resonant tones, the modulations, the gesticulations of an old-school public speaker. As late as 1888, in his final Preface, he spoke of his art as a "new and national declamatory expression." There can be little question that the methods of oratory were important in shaping Whitman's style. In a note on "style" for his projected lectures he wrote: "besides direct addressing *to You* another leading trait of Lectures may well be—strong assertion—('I say') it is so?)—launched out with fire, or emphasis, or enthusiasm, or anger." This oratorical device occurs frequently in the poems, as in the line, "And I say to any man or woman, Let your soul stand cool and composed before a million universes." Other oratorical devices which are used time after time include apostrophes, rhetorical questions, aphorisms, exclamations, alliterative phrases, and parenthetical asides. Often the phrasal order is that of oratory—lines which loosely balance on both sides of a pause, or series of parallel structures all of which contribute to a periodic sentence. (See, for example, the opening stanza of "Out of the Cradle Endlessly Rocking.") In Whitman's poems, such devices regularly perform the functions of rhymes and stanzas in more conventional poems: they hold lines together and set off units of thought.

The scheme of *Leaves of Grass* as a whole and the schemes of individual poems, moreover, have noteworthy resemblances to oratory. Whitman evidently hoped that the impact of the book would be comparable to that of the dynamic presence of a great orator—that it would, as he said, "possess, more than any other known book, the magnetism of living flesh and blood, sitting near the reader, & looking & talking." Like the collected works of a great orator, it would convey, in addition to the personality of the speaker, his gospel, developed and modulated in a number of individual compositions on varied topics. There is evidence, throughout the book, that Whitman attempted to unfold his beliefs in this fashion. In quite a few of the poems, too, there are organizations typically used by orators as well as by some poets—ideas developed by analogy, by passages of narrative, by comparison and contrast, and quite a number which are developed in the style of Emerson's lectures and poems.

But although eventually Whitman's poems, in their form, thus resembled oratory, even as he conceived of them they differed from oratory. In one of his self-criticisms the poet found fault with his method of composing and delivering lectures. "The trouble," he said, "is often the endeavor (from the habit of forming the rhythmic style of *Leaves of Grass*) involuntarily to preserve a sort of rhythm in the Lecture sentences,—It seems to me this rhythm, for them, is not only not necessary, but is often dangerous to their character-requirements—which, for speaking purposes, need to be abrupt. . . ." Whitman conceived of his free-verse poems as "chants" more rhythmical than spoken discourses and corresponding, in some ways, to the arias or recitatives of operas. After starting as a quite conventional poet, he worked his way slowly toward free verse. According to Emory Holloway, in his Introduction to *The Uncollected Prose and Poetry of Walt Whitman,* "he began versifying with the simplest of forms . . . then made use of more difficult stanza forms . . . ; next he wrote a little blank verse . . . ; then he made private experiments with some of the very material he was to work over, through several years, for the 1855 edition of *Leaves of Grass.* . . ." When this first edition appeared, concludes Holloway, his verse was disciplined, "poise and sweeping rhythm were added, and a standard of line length was adopted which would fit the bold but delicate burden of his song." What he evolved was a form blending prose and poetry. This form carried still further the liberating tendencies in poetry which had been initiated by a number of his predecessors including, notably, Emerson and Thoreau. His lines, characteristically, corresponded to the grammatical-phrasings or at least the thought-phrasings of speech. His rhythms were, as he put it, "in a loose and free metre of his own, of an irregular length of lines, apparently lawless at first perusal, although on closer examination a certain regularity appears, like the recurrence of lesser and larger waves on the sea-shore, rolling in without intermission, and fitfully rising and falling." And he found, as later poets were to find, that patterns of repeated vowel and consonant sounds could do much to unify parts and wholes.

Whitman not only broke away from some of the conventions of versification; he also broke away from some of the conventions of style. He was distressed by "stock poetical touches" and by ornamentation as such in poetry. *"No ornaments,"* he sternly enjoined himself, "especially no ornamental adjectives, unless they have come molten hot, and imperiously prove themselves. No ornamental similes at all—not one: *perfect transparent clearness.* . . ." His dislike for what he called "drawing room poetry" led him, in general, to use relatively simple words and to avoid an excess of figurative language. His feelings about common speech led him to interject it into a style not then thought hospitable to it. Most orators who employed the more literary style, as we have seen, tended to disdain the use of words in the vernacular. Whitman, however, from the early days of his career, appreciated the force of humble speech, and praised such speech as growing out of human life. In his youth, he was an avid searcher after colloquial and slang phrases with life to them, and his early prose is dotted with expressions such as "loaded down to the guards," "they do say," "some pumpkins," and "a great place and *no* mistake." "Slang," he wrote, "profoundly consider'd, is the lawless germinal element, below all words and sentences, and behind all poetry, and proves a certain perennial rankness and protestantism in speech . . . an attempt of common humanity to escape from bald literalism, and express itself illimitably, which in highest walks produces poets and poems." Despite his statement in the Preface to *Leaves of Grass* on the self-sufficiency of the English language, Whitman often used foreign expressions. He reveled in nicknames for natives of different states (Kentucky Corn Crackers, Michigan Wolverines, Connecticut Wooden Nutmegs, etc.); in original place-names (Hog-eye, Lick-skillet, Rake-pocket, and Steal-easy, Texas, for instance); in the racy and imaginative phrases of bus drivers, laborers, railroad men, and boatmen. In Section 6 of "Song of Myself," for example, along with sonorous and dignified lines comparable to those of oratory, occur lines like these:

> Or I guess it [the grass] is the handkerchief of the Lord,
> A scented gift and remembrancer designedly dropt. . . .
>
>   . . . .
>
> Kanuck, Tuckahoe, Congressman, Cuff. . . .
>
>   . . . .
>
> And now it seems to me the beautiful uncut hair of graves.
>
>   . . . .
>
> The smallest sprout shows there is really no death. . . .

To mingle such homely phrasings, as Whitman typically did, with the highfalutin style of heightened oratory represented a daring experiment.

These details about the form of Whitman's poetry suggest that in numerous ways he was a culmination of several important literary tendencies of his period. They may, perhaps, also suggest how modern readers should approach his poetry. Whitman should be read differently from most poets —as a man with a message, as a chanting orator, as an experimenter with a form which blends poetry with prose and mingles the words of everyday talk with those of more formal literature. He should be read not only as a poet of his time but also as a pioneer breaking a trail toward modern poetic achievements.

Folk Songs and Folk Poetry

One of the glories of the period 1865-1914 was the discovery, by many, of one aspect in particular of our rich native folklore—the folk songs. The scholars who brought this about did not, to be sure, create the songs. The ballads had been made by humble, uneducated folk, and the scholars merely collected them and made them known. Even before the war there had been some interest in such lore, indicated by sporadic studies. Notably, young Francis James Child (1825-1896), newly appointed to the Harvard faculty, had been inspired, by study in Germany in the 1840's, to carry on research in British balladry. His lifelong work, climaxed by his five-volume collection, *English and Scottish Popular Ballads* (1882-1898), made such work "respectable" and aroused the interest of many scholars in the subject. Postwar interest in sectional life and in national history stimulated new enthusiasm. By the end of the period, therefore, knowledge about folk songs had increased tremendously.

During the Civil War and the years after it, the songs which had been chanted by soldiers were collected in such volumes as *Songs of Soldiers* (1864), *Poetry of the Civil War* (1866), and *Southern Poems of the War* (1867). At least some of the verses in these collections were of folk origin. Concurrently, several writers began to introduce the public to Negro spirituals in magazine articles such as "Negro Spirituals" (*Atlantic Monthly*, 1867) and in books such as *Slave Songs of the United States* (1867), *Jubilee Songs* (1872), and *Cabin and Plantation Songs* (1875). The last two volumes contained versions of folk songs as sung by the students of two newly founded Negro universities, Fisk and Hampton.

In the following decades, more songs of the people came slowly to light. In 1880, for example, when Joel Chandler Harris issued his first collection of Uncle Remus stories, themselves valuable as folklore, he included a number of plantation songs as he had heard them sung in Georgia. In 1883 a fine study, *Games and Songs of American Children*, was published by W. W. Newell. The American Folk-Lore Society began in 1888 the regular publication of its *Journal*, which from time to time published, along with other lore, folk songs as they were sung by the Negroes, the folk of New England, or the Southern mountaineers. Other learned journals printed occasional articles. Stedman and Hutchinson included several sections of folk songs in their anthology, *A Library of American Literature* (1889-1890). In 1894, Alfred M. Williams included in his *Studies in Folk-Song and Popular Poetry* not only the ballads of other nations but also Civil War songs and American sea-chanteys. In 1908 a new vein was discovered when N. Howard Thorp, a Southwestern cowhand and himself a maker of ballads, published a little pamphlet, *Songs of the Cowboys*. Whenever possible, he stated exactly where, when, and from whom he had picked up each song. Two years later John Lomax, who had learned at Harvard to prize the ballads he had heard as a boy and a youth in Texas, published a better-known collection, *Cowboy Songs and Other Frontier Ballads*.

During the year 1909 between the publication of these two collections, a folk song very different from cowboy ballads swept the country, carried from coast to coast by vaudeville singers and gramophone records. This was "Casey Jones," a railroad song which had been composed years before by some anonymous lyricist to celebrate "a brave engineer," and which was published in a somewhat refined version, by T. L. Siebert and E. Newton. During that year, too, a writer in the *Journal of American Folk-Lore*, Louise Rand Bascom, published the opening lines of another railroad song, as heard in North Carolina:

Johnie Henry was a hard-workin' man,
He died with his hammer in his hand.

These, she said, were all the words of the song she had heard. A few years later (1913) in "Songs and Rhymes from the South," an article in the same publication, E. C. Perrow printed fragments or complete versions of songs about this same John Henry which he had collected in east Tennessee, Indiana, Mississippi, and Kentucky. All these, as well as others to be recorded later, were apparently based upon the exploits of a giant Negro who had driven steel for the Chesapeake and Ohio Big Bend Tunnel in West Virginia in the early 1870's.

These few milestones indicate only the beginnings of the American study of folk songs which, in the modern period, was to engage the attention of both careful scholars and lovers of poetry and music. Two rather different reasons for the awakened interest in such lore may be suggested. The study of folklore, thanks largely to the efforts of Child and his students, had become both respectable and scientific. For another thing, in those days when life was beginning to show its present pace and complexity, there was an attraction in the arts and cultures of the simple, untutored folk who sang such songs. Their traditional creations, at least, were not marred by the harassing problems of a transitional period.

The makers of the songs, naturally, plied their art for reasons which had nothing to do with either the science of ballad collecting or the distress of city folk during a time of change. Their songs came directly from their own experiences, their way of living, their feelings. To express what they had to say, they fitted poetic words of the only kind they knew to music of the only sort with which they were familiar. Thus the Negroes amalgamated the old-time hymns which whites had taught them with African rhythms which had been passed along to them by their enslaved forebears; and the isolated whites of the mountains or the prairies fashioned their compositions after the example of current songs or of ballads which had been brought to America from England or Scotland by early settlers.

These folk songs had little appeal to the sizable group which thought that poetry had to be elegant, genteel, and ornamental. Appreciation of balladry was usually confined to a pair of audiences differing greatly from one another. One audience, like the makers of the songs, was, in some ways, naïve—short on book knowledge, although probably learned in the emotions and behavior of real men and women. Such an audience appreciated the songs much as had their original audiences. The other audience was highly sophisticated—one which could perceive the historical value of balladry as a cultural expression, and could appreciate simplicity of style, suggestiveness of detail, and music that, though it differed from the music currently fashionable, had a beauty of its own.

Some poets took hints about writing from the ballad makers and wrote what might be called not folk songs but "folk poetry." Some of these—John Greenleaf Whittier, for instance—used ballad verse or metrical forms resembling it, and employed language with balladlike simplicity. Others wrote poems in dialect.

In the South several poets continued a tradition started before the war, notably by Stephen Collins Foster, and wrote poetry echoing Negro melodies and dialect. Irwin Russell (1853-1879) of Mississippi, in his *Christmas Night in the Quarters* (1878), produced a sympathetic mingling of the Negroes' religion and humor in authentic dialect. Hayne and Lanier, as well as other less famous Southerners, also wrote poetry using Negro dialect. During the period, too, Paul Laurence Dunbar in *Lyrics of Lowly Life* (1896) and other books showed himself to be, as Howells held, the first writer of pure African descent "to feel the Negro life aesthetically and to express it lyrically."

The most popular dialect poetry, however, was written in the Far West and the Middle West. Outstanding were John Hay (1838-1905), author of *Pike County Ballads;* Bret Harte (1836-1902), whose most famous poem in this style was the popular "Plain Language from Truthful James"; and James Whitcomb Riley (1849-1916), whose first book was *The Old Swimmin' Hole and 'Leven More Poems* (1883). At their best, such poems caught some of the flavor of rural life and some of the tang of American speech; they had wholesome humor and sentiment. At their worst, they were maudlin in their sentimental nostalgia for the "olden times." At both their best and their worst, however, they were interesting reflections of the tastes and the expressions of the feelings of the period. The extraordinary success of such writings showed that a large class of readers had come into being who were happy to buy the writings of even "humbler poets" than those Longfellow had praised—poets whose "simple and heartfelt lays" were, indeed, extraordinarily simple.

Humor and Local Color Writing

The period 1865-1914 is noteworthy as one during which humor perceptibly contributed to the development of fiction. Mark Twain, whose works were written in this period, was praised not only for making people laugh but also for writing great fiction. His mingling, in some of his work, of the techniques of comedy with the techniques of the short story and the novel was typical: many authors found the procedures of some of the humorists useful in creating postwar fiction. Some humor, by contrast, moved further and further from fiction, in the end becoming almost divorced from it.

In the years before the Civil War, magazines and newspapers—"exchanges"—came from all over the country to the office of the little Hannibal, Missouri, newspaper run by the humorist's brother, Orion Clemens. Young Samuel Clemens, in the days when he was learning the printer's trade, read humorous writings in these publications and set some of them up in type. Some of the humor was that of New England—sketches and stories of Yankee characters like Jack Downing. More often it was the fine brand of humor then being produced in the part of the country with which he was familiar, the old Southwest.

New England's humorists told about the politicking, gossiping, and courting, of militia drills, corn huskings, quiltings—the Yankees at work and at play. Southwestern humorists wrote about similar happenings but were more concerned with such masculine matters as hunting, fishing, and yarnspinning. The humor of both areas was strongly local in its depictions of scenes and characters and in its echoings of regional speech.

This humor shaped some of the most popular fiction of the postwar era. During the decade following the end of the Civil War, Whittier and Harriet Beecher Stowe of New England, Bret Harte of the Far West, Edward Eggleston and Mark Twain of the Middle West, and George Washington Cable of the Deep South all won enthusiastic praise for their depictions of life and character in their particular corners of the country. This was the beginning of a great movement in fiction in the United States. In 1894, critic Edward E. Hale, Jr., could write, in *The Dial*, "Everybody writes 'local' stories nowadays; it is as natural as whooping cough." There was a slight exaggeration in this statement, but certainly a vast number of American authors were so engaged. Mary Noailles Murfree of Tennessee, Joel Chandler Harris of Georgia, Sarah Orne Jewett of Maine, and Mary E. Wilkins Freeman of Massachusetts are only a few of scores who wrote such fiction.

Directly or indirectly, much of this writing was influenced by the prewar humor of New England or the old Southwest. Harriet Beecher Stowe's best work took the form of fireside yarns, many of them humorous, spun by a quaint Yankee character, Sam Lawson. Mary Noailles Murfree admittedly was indebted to Sut Lovingood. Joel Chandler Harris knew American humor well, and actually wrote a good deal of it before he began to write fiction. And it is noteworthy that Bret Harte, who was so successful that many fictionists paid him the tribute of imitation, definitely believed that the humorous story of "barrooms, gatherings in the 'country store,' and . . . public meetings" was "the parent of the American 'short story.' "

Naturally, it was not so simple as that. Many influences which had shaped our fiction in the past continued to shape it. The genial essays of Irving, sentimental novels, the writings of Scott, Cooper, Dickens, and others left their imprint. Yet the prewar humorous story was influential in ways which Harte suggested when he described it: "It was concise and condensed, yet suggestive . . . delightfully extravagant—or a miracle of understatement. It voiced not only the dialect, but the habits of thought of a people or locality. . . . It went directly to the point." Many details in this formula applied to representative local color stories.

So far as the local colorists, in their narratives, lived up to this descrip-

tion, they tended to be recorders of actuality. Several thought of themselves as merely reflectors of life. Typical was Mrs. Stowe's claim that in
her New England fiction she tried to "make her mind as still and passive
as a looking-glass, or a mountain lake," in order that she might reflect
"New England life and character." "My studies for this object," she said,
"have been . . . taken from real characters, real scenes, and real incidents."
But perhaps because of the example set by romantic fictionists, perhaps,
also, because of the nostalgia which most writers felt for the past, local
colorists tended to write not of the scene of the day but of a day that was
ended. So Mrs. Stowe wrote of the New England of her childhood, Eggleston of the Indiana of frontier days, Harte of the California of the Gold
Rush, and others of happy antebellum plantations. The mists of time
blurred the mirrors somewhat, and the local colorists as a rule avoided the
sordid and the tragic in favor of geniality, sentiment, and pathos.

Some humorists of the postwar period, for instance Finley Peter
Dunne, who created Mr. Dooley, continued to write humor in the prewar
mode—the humor of localized background and character. But writings
which were generally classified as "humor" followed a new pathway—
tended in fact to become estranged from fiction. The professional humorists of the era, "Literary Comedians" or "Funny Men" as they were called,
hit upon ways of writing that appealed to enlarged audiences.

One reason for their broadened appeal may well have been precisely
the fact that they abandoned regional backgrounds, characters, happenings, and ways of talking. Characters became so generalized that it was
practically impossible for readers to tell where they lived (except vaguely
somewhere in the United States) and even—at times—whether they were
educated or unread, wise or foolish, sympathetic or unsympathetic.

The chief source of laughter came to be the humorist's style, a compound of ludicrously assembled sentences, words badly spelled, malaprop-
isms, puns, and the like. The leisurely prewar storyteller had yielded to a
jokester who tried for a laugh every few words. "Today," wrote a humorist in 1902, "the joke, or the humorous article, is funny all the way
through. In other days it was enough to write on and on, with minute and
detailed description, leading up to the comic *dénouement* in the last two
lines. Now the risibilities of the reader must be aroused with the opening
line, or the rest . . . goes unread."

Wildly comic diction, then, was the earmark of professional postwar
humorists such as Josh Billings, Artemus Ward, and a host of others.

Mark Twain: Humorist and Local Colorist

Reared on the frontier and influenced by prewar Yankee and Southwestern humorists, Samuel L. Clemens, eventually famous as Mark Twain, came

into national prominence in the postwar years when professional humorists and local colorists were flourishing. In his varied writings the student of humor may see evidence of the influences of all these schools. But since Samuel L. Clemens happened to be a genius, he frequently managed to surpass his teachers.

His most ephemeral works and passages are the creations of a "Funny Man" who was working rather too hard to get laughs. At their worst such creations were typified by the "Thomas Jefferson Snodgrass Letters," which he wrote in the late fifties, newspaper screeds soon forgotten and not reprinted until they were dug up by scholars as specimens of his youthful efforts. The style was like that of Artemus Ward and his cohorts of the postwar period—a style notable for cacography and for outlandish expressions. Later, Clemens, like other humorists of the school, refined this style somewhat—dropping bad spelling, for instance—in various sketches and in parts of his travel books. Often, in using the latter style, he was quite funny. At its best, nevertheless, this type of humor never marked his highest reaches. And now and then—as in some later chapters of *Huckleberry Finn*—burlesque and buffoonery struck discordant notes.

The artistry of the frontier oral story, by contrast, was one of Twain's most important assets. Having lived in the frontier town of Hannibal, traveled around the whole country, and worked on riverboats and in mining camps, he had, by 1865, heard as well as read a great number of humorous stories told by master storytellers. He knew, as he said in "How to Tell a Story," that ". . . the humorous story is strictly a work of art, high and delicate art—and only an artist can tell it." He knew important aspects of the technique. "The humorous story is told gravely; the teller does his best to conceal the fact that there is anything funny about it. . . ." Again, "To string incongruities and absurdities together in a wandering and sometimes purposeless way, and seem innocently unaware that they are absurdities, is the basis of the American art. . . ." Finally, he knew how the introductory framework of an enclosed narrative, as well as the language and thoughts of the yarnspinner, might be made to reveal the narrator as an appealing or amusing character. When, therefore, Clemens heard the "Jumping Frog" story unfolded by a mining-camp fireside in 1865, he was able to write it out in a masterly form. And when later, in "Baker's Blue-Jay Yarn" and other sketches, he created tall tales in the style of antebellum humorous narrative, his were even better than those earlier masterpieces.

Twain's travel books and, to some extent, his novels were combinations of similar brief narratives with longer chronological accounts. As Bernard DeVoto remarks, in *Mark Twain's America:*

> He took the humorous anecdote, combined it with autobiographical reminiscence, and so achieved the narrative form best adapted to his

mind. . . . *The Innocents Abroad* is structurally an autobiographical
narrative. Descriptive passages . . . interrupt the narrative from time to
time but its steady progress is accomplished by means of stories. Some
of them are brief, unelaborated anecdotes, in no way different from
the type out of which they proceed, but others already show Mark's
perception that this form can be utilized for more intricate effects. . . .
The same framework produces *Roughing It, A Tramp Abroad, Life on
the Mississippi,* and *Following the Equator.*

In novels such as *The Gilded Age* and *Huckleberry Finn,* Twain constructed similar mosaics made up of anecdotal units.

Just as anyone familiar with humor sees these resemblances, so anyone
familiar with local color writing notices frequent resemblances to writings
of that type. The material for all of Twain's best narratives was his boyhood home, Hannibal, and the great river which rolls before it. More accurately, the stuff of his best works was not the actuality of Hannibal, but
his memory of the scenes and of the life he had known in childhood and
youth. As a rule, his memory, somehow, had blurred away most sordid
and unlovely details, leaving an idyll to be set forth in nostalgic fiction.
The localized details and the longing for times past were completely typical of local color fiction. At times, however, he differed from many local
colorists in stressing many of the grimmer aspects of life along the river.

Two skills in particular give his best fiction, nostalgic or satirical and
long or short, much of its distinction: ability to characterize and ability to
use words in a masterly fashion. Other humorists in America before him
had managed, at best, to create only a few memorable characters. Twain
dotted his pages with them with a prodigality comparable to that of
Chaucer or Dickens. And he had such descriptive skill, such a knack for
portraying actions, such an accurate ear for speech that he could make
both characters who appeared for a few lines and characters whose stories
occupied many pages come alive. As a stylist, also, he was outstanding. He
took great pains with style; it is significant that a large share of his remarks
about literature touch knowingly upon this aspect of writing. Some of his
reasons for praising a sentence which he quotes are illuminating: "For
compactness, simplicity, and vigor of expression, I will 'back' that sentence
against any in literature." He praises a letter from his daughter Susan for
"clearness of statement, directness, felicity of expression, photographic
ability in setting forth an incident—style—good style—no barnacles on it in
the way of unnecessary, retarding words." He came close to living up to
the ideal implied by these comments. He wrote very much as he talked,
transferring the natural rhythms of speech to the printed page. His words
were simple; almost always they were distinctly American; and he used
them economically. Perhaps even more important, without any appearance
of being "literary," he was able to find words which gave full scope to his

exuberant, poetic imagination. It makes some sense, therefore, to claim, as some critics do, that Mark Twain was the first great stylist who wrote purely in the American language.

Varied Types of Realism

Even the most extravagant American humor was in some ways antiromantic; comic tall tales, by juxtaposing the workaday world with the world of fantasy, made fun of imaginative excesses. Since funny character sketches drew many details directly from actuality, they led the way toward fiction which was concerned with ordinary characters and scenes. Local color writing, which had a similar concern, also departed to some extent from the romantic fiction of the antebellum period. Scholars, therefore, see in both humorous writing and local color writing a trend toward "realism" which culminated, toward the end of the century, in numerous realistic and naturalistic fictional works.

The term "realism," like its counterpart "romanticism," is a vague term which has been variously defined. Writers pursuing it in this period differed in theory and practice. They generally agreed that realistic fiction truly presented "actuality"—"real life"—and that it was concerned with the near, rather than the distant, in time and place. Most realists, therefore, believed that the probability of happenings in novels might properly be tested, not by rules set up by the inventor of an imaginative world but by what was likely in the actions of living men and women. Alice might properly dwindle to a minute size in Wonderland, but not in a realistic novel, since there the laws of physics and of biology as well as the stern limitations of heredity and environment were constantly operative. So far there was agreement; but disagreement naturally arose when authors tried to define "actuality." Where was the "real" to be found—in the world itself, in the inductively discovered scientific truths about the nature of the world, in the impression which the world made upon the observer's mind, or in a combination of these? The methods of authors depended upon their answer to this question and upon their ability to portray what they considered to be reality.

Mark Twain clearly indicated how he thought art should portray actuality when, in a newspaper letter of 1867, he thus criticized a painting by Bierstadt: "Now, to sum up the picture's merits, those snow-peaks are correct—they look natural; the valley is correct and natural; the pine trees clinging to the bluff on the right, and the grove on the left, and the boulders, are all like nature. . . . But when I got around to the atmosphere, I was obliged to say 'This man has imported this atmosphere . . . from some foreign country, because nothing like it was ever seen in California.' " Steadfastly Twain believed that the artist in colors or in words did his work best when he was "true to nature," accurately and honestly recording what he saw. "There is nothing," he wrote in a personal letter of 1868, "that makes me prouder than to be regarded by intelligent people as 'authentic.' " So far as he could, therefore, he made his fiction an exact transcript of life. Only because his memory changed things, because his notions of propriety changed things, and because he was something of a poet did he (to use his own terms) "import" the "atmosphere" in his best narratives.

William Dean Howells, Twain's close friend, had at the start of his career a similar conception of the task of the fictionist. Fiction, Howells also thought, should be lifelike. Moreover, it should concern itself only with the most ordinary facets of life. A passage in *Their Wedding Journey* (1872) concerning the people in a railway car suggests the attitude: "It was in all respects an ordinary carful of human beings, and it was perhaps the more worthy to be studied on that account. As in literature the true artist will shun the use even of real events if they are of an improbable character, so the sincere observer of man will not desire to look upon his heroic or occasional phases, but will seek him in his habitual moods of vacancy and tiresomeness. To me, at any rate, he is at such times very precious. . . ." Howells followed this formula in his early writings, which were almost literal transcriptions of what he observed. But he recognized certain limitations which kept his literalness from being complete. It is important to recall that he first glimpsed the possibilities of realism while reading the comedies of Carlo Goldoni and that he was extremely fond of the witty novels of Jane Austen. Like these two writers, he tended to concern himself, at the start of his career, more with the comedies of human experience than with the tragedies. In addition, because he believed that typical American life was relatively pure, and because he held that, even if it were not, it was wrong for an American novelist "to deal with certain facts of life which are not usually talked of before young people and especially young ladies," he rather prudishly limited his treatment of sex.

When Hamlin Garland met Howells in Cambridge, Massachusetts, in 1885, Garland had, so Howells said later, "convictions flatteringly like mine." As Garland made clear in *Crumbling Idols* (1894), he believed in what a French critic had dubbed "veritism." The true artist, he held, "must consciously stand alone before nature and before life" and must sincerely set down "the drama of the average type of character." In two ways, however, he differed from the early Howells. In the first place, Garland was moderately frank in his consideration of sex. ("I am old-fashioned," wrote Howells of this tendency in 1912, "and I have moments when I could wish that the author had not been of such unsparing conscience.") In the second place, Garland, under the tutelage of a group of assorted nineteenth-century thinkers, acquired the belief that "to fiction is given the task of subtilely embodying the splendid creed" of improvement—social, moral, and philosophical. "It is safe to say," he prophesied in

Crumbling Idols, "that the fiction of the future will grow more democratic in outlook and more individualistic in method. . . . The higher art would seem to be the art that perceives and states the relations of things, giving atmosphere and relative values as they appear to the sight." Hence, *Main-Travelled Roads* (1891) not only pictured some of the harsher aspects of Midwestern farm life; it crusaded against them and suggested remedies.

By the time this first collection of Garland's stories appeared, Howells, too, had come to believe that fiction should have an element—one of great importance—which had been lacking in his early fiction. His first exposure, at fifty, to Tolstoy's writings had, as Howells indicated in *My Literary Passions* (1895), brought about a change in his thinking. "He," wrote Howells, "has been to me that final consciousness which he speaks of so easily in his essay on Life. I came in it to the knowledge of myself in ways that I had not dreamt before, and began at last to discern my relations to the race, without which we are nothing. The supreme art in literature had its highest effect in making me set art forever below humanity. . . ." What this meant was that Howells, in *Annie Kilburn* (1889), *A Hazard of New Fortunes* (1890), *The World of Chance* (1893), and his other mature novels, became a novelist of social purpose—selecting characters not only because they were typical but also because their characteristics and their stories taught lessons about society and economics.

Naturalism

Just as the line between some local color fiction and some realism is hard to draw, it is difficult to distinguish clearly and surely between realism and some "naturalism," another "ism" about which there was, in this period, a great deal of discussion. In general, the American naturalists—Crane, Norris, Dreiser, and others—took at least some of their cues from a group of authors, led by Émile Zola (1840-1902), who were important in France after 1880. The characteristics of the French group were admirably summarized by the late William Nitze and Edwin Dargan in their *History of French Literature:*

> Naturalism . . . is an excessive form of Realism and is usually considered as possessing the following characteristics. First, it allows a still larger variety of subjects, emphasizing the lower and coarser forms of life; it presents this material in a form which is often revolting; it rejects ideality, it minimizes heart-interest and plot interest in favor of "facts" and notations; it magnifies the study of the industries and seeks to apply to fiction the processes of the natural sciences; from these, taken in their application to heredity and environment, it draws its conception of life—deterministic, fatalistic, essentially pessimistic.

The laws of brute Nature are viewed as grimly controlling the destinies of helpless and hopeless men.

An interesting fact about this accurate description of a literary method is that it deals more with the philosophical views of novelists than with their fictional technique. The reason may well be that, for the naturalistic writers, "actuality" is located not merely in life itself but also in the philosophical interpretation of life. For Zola, art was nature, yes, but nature as it was interpreted by the artist. In a fashion theoretically comparable to that of the scientist, the naturalist exposed his sensibility to life and then "scientifically" worked with characters and actions known through his experience. But the vast difference between the artist and the scientist whom he thought he was imitating was that the artist, unable really to test his hypotheses in the laboratory, took them for granted and merely illustrated them from his experience.

American naturalists resembled their French prototypes in treating subjects barred even from realistic writings, in treating lower forms of life —thus differing from realists in their subject matter. Also each American naturalist, on the basis of his own reading and thinking, created characters and plots illustrative of his own personal "scientific" convictions. Thus Theodore Dreiser, believing that men's actions were "chemical compulsions," portrayed situations and events which made clear that characters had no control over their actions. Believing, further, that "the race was to the swift and the battle to the strong," he devised plots which showed weak characters conquered by ruthless and mighty opponents. Frank Norris, perceiving both the unconquerable forces of Nature and the relentless man-made power of the soulless railroad, devised in *The Octopus* a plot which showed Force at work:

> Men were mere nothings, mere animalculae, mere ephemerides that fluttered and fell and were forgotten between dawn and dusk. . . . Men were nought, death was nought, life was nought. Force only existed— Force that brought men into the world—Force that crowded them out to make way for the succeeding generation—Force that made the wheat grow—Force that garnered it from the soil to give place to the succeeding crop.

And Stephen Crane showed the hero of *The Red Badge of Courage* discovering naturalistic truths on the blood-drenched field of battle, and showed the correspondent in "The Open Boat" becoming aware of the complete indifference of Nature to puny men.

Dreiser, unlike some of the French naturalists, had a good deal of contempt for niceties of style. Not so Norris and Crane. Norris used a great deal of symbolism, some of it rather explicit—today's readers may feel it a bit obvious. Crane, rather more subtle as a poet, was less labored in his handling of symbolism, but much of it came into his work—usually in the form of images seen through the eyes of his characters and interpreted by their minds. The correspondent in "The Open Boat," for instance, saw a wind-tower on the tantalizing beach: "This tower was a giant, standing with its back to the plight of the ants. It represented in a degree, to the correspondent, the serenity of nature amid the struggle of the individual— nature in the wind, and nature in the vision of men. She did not seem cruel to him then, nor beneficient, nor treacherous, nor wise. But she was indifferent, flatly indifferent." Touches similar to this were to give significance, later, to settings and actions in the works of such diverse authors as Willa Cather, Ernest Hemingway, and John Steinbeck.

Henry James

To Stephen Crane, one of the most intuitive fictional artists of the period, thoughts and feelings of characters, then, were important. To Henry James, probably the most conscious artist, they were even more important. As his "The Art of Fiction" (1884) shows, James was a careful thinker about the nature of reality, the nature of art, and the relationship between the two. His belief was that "reality," as a story presented it, was twice translated, once through the author's experiencing of it, again through the artistic representation of it. Both the initial impression and the execution were important.

For him a novel "in its broadest definition" was "a personal, a direct impression of life: that, to begin with, constitutes its value, which is greater or less according to the intensity of the impression." For a person with the kind of sensitivity needed in writing great fiction, he went on, "Experience is never limited, and it is never complete; it is an immense sensibility, a kind of huge spider-web of the finest silken threads suspended in the chamber of consciousness, and catching every airborne particle in its tissue." Since "impressions were experience," James did not hesitate to advise the novice, "Try to be one of the people on whom nothing is lost!"

But having gained such a sensitive and complete impression of life, the artist, James contended, also had the problem of giving his fiction "that air of reality (solidity of specification)" which he felt was "the supreme virtue of the novel—the merit on which all its other merits . . . helplessly and submissively depend." James was aware throughout his career that to achieve this end through artistry was a highly complicated and delicate business. A brilliant series of Prefaces which he wrote, in his maturity, for the volumes of his collected works showed in detail how, during his artistic lifetime, he had struggled with problems of form to give his writings exactly the "effects" he intended.

Such a conception of fiction clearly sets James off from those practitioners who believed that the best fiction was the exact reproduction of life, as well as from those who believed that it was an embodiment of naturalistic generalizations about life. Since he saw reality—even generalizations about reality—as a series of impressions, and since he saw fiction as the artistic rendition of such impressions, his sort of realism was essentially a complicated psychological process. In his writings, therefore, one sees the impact of the new science of psychology upon which his brother, William James, was a leading authority. One sees, too, progress in the development of a technique which had been notably advanced even before James by George Eliot in England and Gustave Flaubert in France—the technique of making new psychological insights a vital part of fiction.

His 1907 Preface to *Roderick Hudson* (1876) tells in some detail how James shaped his narratives. After a "story idea" had come to him, the chief difficulty, he suggested, was to decide exactly how to limit "developments" so as to interrelate them. "Up to what point," he asked himself, "is such and such a development *indispensable* to interest? . . . When, for the complete expression of one's subject, does a particular relation stop— giving way to some other not concerned in that expression?" The complexity of experience made this problem difficult: "Really, universally, relations stop nowhere, and the exquisite problem of the artist is eternally but to draw, by a geometry of his own, the circle within which they shall happily *appear* to do so." Selection and arrangement therefore were absolutely necessary. He needed to hit upon exactly the right details of background; he needed (though later he felt he had failed, in this particular book) to devise an adequate time scheme; he needed—and this was very important—to find a "centre, the point of command of all the rest." In *Roderick Hudson*, this center was the impression of the whole action received by a secondary character:

> From this centre the subject has been treated, from this centre the interest has spread, and so, whatever else it may do or may not do, the thing has acknowledged a principle of composition and continues at least to hang together. . . . The centre of interest throughout . . . is Rowland Mallet's consciousness—which I had of course to make sufficiently acute to enable it, like a set and lighted scene, to hold the play.

James believed that what Mallet saw, felt, or guessed could, if properly rendered, be made to give the story unity and meaning. He often used this technique to give his narratives an organic unity, achieved by locating the story in the mind of some character—a consciousness, like Rowland's, "connected intimately with the general human exposure, and thereby bedimmed and befooled and bewildered, anxious, restless, fallible," in short, "not *too* acute," but endowed, nevertheless, "with such intelligence that the appearances reflected in it, constituting together there the situa-

tion and the 'story,' should become by that fact intelligible." Thus the
author created, in his story, a sensitive counterpart whose limitations and
perceptions both bounded and filled in the pattern.

James, naturally, was horrified by what he saw as the formlessness of
many fictional works written by his contemporaries. He believed, as he
said in "The Art of Fiction," that ". . . a novel is a living thing, all one and
continuous, like any other organism, and in proportion as it lives it will be
found, I think, that in each of the parts is something of the other parts."
James became a leader in calling attention to the importance of the "fictional point of view"—to the values derived from letting a narrative unfold
as it was experienced by a single character. Psychology thus became of
central importance in his fiction, and its hitherto unexploited potentialities
for fiction were suggested to a great number of writers who followed
James.

The Drama

In general, the period between the Civil War and 1914 was one of depression in the history of American drama. Hundreds of plays, to be sure, were
produced, and many were admired; but few have proved to be worthy of
memory. As Barrett Clark says of the plays of the period in *An Hour of
American Drama:* "It is not the quaintness of the language and the labored
style of these plays that has caused them to be forgotten, it is the fundamental fact that they are the products of superficial writers, of men who
could believe that 'plays are not written but rewritten,' an epigram appropriately attributed to [such popular playwrights of the period as] Bouci-
cault, Bronson Howard, Augustin Daly, Augustus Thomas, and a dozen
other able playmakers. The kind of plays these men wrote were indeed
rewritten: they had to be. But here 'rewritten' means picked apart, built
up, 'lifted,' like a dowager's face, put on a diet, painted, and rouged." During this comparatively arid period, productive chiefly of melodramas and
slick plays cunningly designed to lure cash customers, there were three
tendencies of some significance, each comparable to some contemporary
development in fiction: toward realism, toward the more intelligent consideration of serious problems, and toward symbolism.

Hamlin Garland, lecturing on "Local Color in Fiction and Drama,"
was able, so he said later, to consider quite a few playwrights who, like his
favorite fiction writers, were moving toward realism via stage representations of the life and character of certain regions. Examples—typical, though
in some ways superior—were Bronson Howard (1842-1908), who in *Shenandoah* (1888) vividly pictured the valley of the title as it had been during
the war; James A. Herne (1839-1901), who made a noteworthy effort to
draw true-to-life characters against a homely background in *Margaret*

Fleming (1890) and *Shore Acres* (1892); and Augustus Thomas (1875-1934), who dramatized the life of different regions in plays such as *Alabama* (1891), *In Mizzouri* (1893), *The Capitol* (1895), and *Arizona* (1899).

These same authors also show how the drama, like the novel, was beginning to consider serious subjects. Here, Americans were particularly influenced by the Norwegian Henrik Ibsen (1828-1906), who became world-famous during this period as an author of problem plays. Herne's *Shore Acres* was much discussed not only because it was realistic but also because it contained references to advanced scientific and social ideas, and *Margaret Fleming* dealt with family relationships in a fashion then considered quite daring. Howard's *The Henrietta* (1887) satirized the fever and the greed of financial and social life. And Thomas treated pseudo-scientific topics such as hypnotism, psychological domination, and mental healing in several of his later plays.

Toward the end of the period, many critics of the day found in Clyde Fitch (1865-1909) a man who could fuse sincerity and artistry with good theater. Fitch's creed, as he expressed it in "The Play and the Public," sounded like one of the definitions of realism then current in writings about fiction:

> In the modern play, I feel myself very strongly the particular value—a value I can't help feeling inestimable—of reflecting absolutely and truthfully the life and environment about us. Be truthful, and then nothing can be too big, nothing should be too small, so long as it is here, and there. Every class, every kind, every emotion, every motive, every occupation, every business, every idleness. . . . Apart from the question of literalism, apart from the question of art, reflect the real thing with true observation and with sincere feeling for what it is and what it represents, and that is art and literature.

Fitch tried to follow this formula in a varied group of plays, dramas which not only tried to be "true to life" but which also commented upon various problems. *The Climbers* (1901) and *The City* (1909) were serious portrayals of various aspects—political, financial, and social—of New York life. *The Girl with the Green Eyes* (1902) and *The Truth* (1907) were interesting psychological studies, the first of a character abnormally jealous, the second of a congenital liar. These plays have fine stuff in them, marred only by the need to please an audience fond of broad effects.

Two other dramatists were ranked with Fitch, or even above him: Langdon Mitchell and William Vaughn Moody. Mitchell was active contemporaneously with Fitch. His *The New York Idea* (1906) was not a conscious attempt at realism; nevertheless, since this drama, like Royall Tyler's *The Contrast* (1787) and a host of other plays, was a social comedy, it was essentially realistic in a good many of its details. And its deft construction and witty dialogue made it more memorable than many dramas of its day which were heavily serious.

Moody, a poet and a professor, started his career as a "practical dramatist" after having written poetic dramas which were profound in their ideas and impressive as poetry, but which had no chance of professional presentation. When he tried his hand at writing plays which might be produced, his very aloofness from the commercial theater helped him avoid some of its bad tendencies. As Walter Prichard Eaton remarks in *The Drama in English:* "The superficial traits of modern drama meant little to him, one way or the other. It was its deeper spirit he was after." Having such an attitude, and having, moreover, a real flair for dramatizing the psychologies of characters and for representing ideas by action, he wrote for the stage *The Great Divide*, a surprisingly successful play. This drama had in it, to be sure, elements of sensationalism and melodrama; but these were means to an end rather than ends themselves. Actually *The Great Divide* was a symbolic representation of the conflict between the Puritancial tradition of New England on the one hand and, on the other, the frontier's impulsive gusto for life. It showed the approach of a poet. "Poetry," Moody believed, "is the salvation of the stage. . . . It is the poetry in a play that makes it great." A play written in such a spirit, although in retrospect it might seem a bit crude, pointed to a better period in the American theater. As Eaton asserts, "With a play like this the modern drama in America was coming of age." It was not to come fully of age, however, until after 1914. The greatest achievements of the era between the Civil War and World War I were decidedly not in drama or (except in a few instances) in poetry, but in fiction.

W.B.

Chronological Table of
LITERATURE AND HISTORY

1866 ● Whittier's *Snow-Bound* · Charles H. Smith's *Bill Arp, So Called* · Howells' *Venetian Life*

First Civil Rights Bill passed · Ku Klux Klan organized

1867 ● Henry Timrod's "Ode" · George W. Harris' *Sut Lovingood Yarns* · Lowell's *The Biglow Papers, Second Series* · Bret Harte's *Condensed Novels* · John W. DeForest's *Miss Ravenel's Conversion*

Alaska purchased from Russia · Nebraska admitted as the thirty-seventh state · Reconstruction Act passed, providing conditions of the return of the Confederate States to the Union · Negroes granted the right of suffrage

1868 ● *The Overland Monthly* (1868-1933) established in California · Harte's "The Luck of Roaring Camp" · Louisa May Alcott's *Little Women*

Fourteenth Amendment, guaranteeing fair trial for all persons, ratified · President Johnson impeached, acquitted · Ulysses S. Grant elected eighteenth President

1869 ● Harte's "Tennessee's Partner," "The Outcasts of Poker Flat" · Mark Twain's *The Innocents Abroad* · Lowell's "The Cathedral"

Fifteenth Amendment, insuring Negro suffrage, ratified · Union Pacific Railway completed first transcontinental line, 10 May · "Black Friday" in New York, caused by gold corner, 24 September · Opening of the Suez Canal, 15 November

1870 ● Lowell's *Among My Books* · Bronson Howard's *Saratoga* · Harte's "Plain Language from Truthful James" · Joaquin Miller's *Songs of the Sierras* · Emerson's *Society and Solitude*

United States census: population 39,818,449

1871 ● Edward Eggleston's *The Hoosier Schoolmaster* · Walt Whitman's *Democratic Vistas* · Harriet Beecher Stowe's *Oldtown Fireside Stories*

Indian Appropriation Act, nullifying all Indian treaties, passed

1872 ● Mark Twain's *Roughing It* · Holmes' *The Poet at the Breakfast-Table* · William D. Howells' *Their Wedding Journey*

Grant reelected

1873 ● Mark Twain and Charles Dudley Warner's *The Gilded Age* · Howells' *A Chance Acquaintance* · Timrod's *The Cotton Boll*

Financial panic began, 19 September

1875 ● Sidney Lanier's "Corn," "The Symphony" · Howells' *A Foregone Conclusion* · Mary Baker Eddy's *Science and Health*

1876 ● Twain's *The Adventures of Tom Sawyer* · Henry James' *Roderick Hudson*

Rutherford B. Hayes elected nineteenth President · Colorado admitted as the thirty-eighth state · Southern Homestead Act repealed

1877 ● James' *The American* · Lanier's *Poems* · Sarah Orne Jewett's *Deephaven*

1878 ● James' *Daisy Miller* · Lanier's "The Marshes of Glynn," "The Revenge of Hamish"

1879 ● James' *Hawthorne* · George W. Cable's *Old Creole Days* · Howells' *The Lady of the Aroostook* · Henry George's *Progress and Poverty* · Sarah Orne Jewett's *Old Friends and New*

1880 ● Twain's *A Tramp Abroad* · Henry Adams' *Democracy* · Lew Wallace's *Ben Hur* · Lanier's *The Science of English Verse* · Joel Chandler Harris' *Uncle Remus: His Songs and Sayings* · Steele MacKaye's *Hazel Kirke*

United States census: population 50,155,783 · James A. Garfield elected twentieth President

1881 ● James' *The Portrait of a Lady*

Garfield shot, 2 July; died, 19 September; succeeded by Chester A. Arthur as twenty-first President · Tuskegee Institute founded · Federation of Organized Trades and Labor Unions, forerunner of the American Federation of Labor, founded

1882 ● Stockton's "The Lady or the Tiger?" · Twain's *The Prince and the Pauper* · Howells' *A Modern Instance*

1883 ● Edgar Watson Howe's *The Story of a Country Town* · Harris' *Nights with Uncle Remus* · Twain's *Life on the Mississippi*

1884 ● Twain's *Huckleberry Finn* · Lanier's *Poems* · Mary Noailles Murfree's *In the Tennessee Mountains* · Lowell's "Democracy" · Helen Hunt Jackson's *Ramona*

Grover Cleveland elected twenty-second President

1885 ● Murfree's *The Prophet of the Great Smoky Mountains* · Howells' *The Rise of Silas Lapham*

1886 ● James' *The Princess Casamassima*

Haymarket Riot in Chicago turned public opinion against labor organizations · American Federation of Labor organized under Samuel Gompers

1887 ● Harold Frederic's *Seth's Brother's Wife* · Joseph Kirkland's *Zury* · Mary E. Wilkins Freeman's *A Humble Romance* · Thomas Nelson Page's *In Ole Virginia*

Interstate Commerce Act marked the start of Federal regulation

1888 ● Edward Bellamy's *Looking Backward* · Howard's *Shenandoah* · Whitman's *November Boughs* and *Complete Poems and Prose* (1888-1889)

Benjamin Harrison elected twenty-third President

1889 ● Twain's *A Connecticut Yankee*

North Dakota and South Dakota admitted as thirty-ninth and fortieth states, Montana as forty-first, Washington as forty-second · Oklahoma land rush began

1890 ● Emily Dickinson's *Poems* · James' *The Tragic Muse* · Howells' *A Hazard of New Fortunes* · Jacob A. Riis' *How the Other Half Lives*

United States census: population 62,947,714 · Sherman Anti-Trust Act · Idaho admitted as forty-third state, Wyoming as forty-fourth

1891 ● Hamlin Garland's *Main-Travelled Roads* · Howells' *Criticism and Fiction* · Freeman's *A New England Nun and Other Stories* · Ambrose Bierce's *Tales of Soldiers and Civilians*

1892 ● Herne's *Shore Acres*

Grover Cleveland reelected · Bitter strike by iron and steelworkers at Homestead, Pa., broken by National Guard

1893 ● Frederick J. Turner's "The Significance of the Frontier in American History" · Stephen Crane's *Maggie: A Girl of the Streets*

1894 ● Twain's *Pudd'nhead Wilson* · James Lane Allen's *A Kentucky Cardinal* · Howells' *A Traveler from Altruria*

Pullman strike; widespread sympathetic strikes called by American Railway Union; Federal troops called out and Sherman Anti-Trust Act invoked in settlement of Pullman dispute · "Coxey's Army" of the unemployed marched on Washington

1895 ● Crane's *The Black Riders, and Other Lines* and *The Red Badge of Courage* · Garland's *Rose of Dutcher's Coolly*

1896 ● Jewett's *The Country of the Pointed Firs* · Edwin A. Robinson's *The Torrent and the Night Before* · Twain's *Joan of Arc* · Frederic's *The Damnation of Theron Ware*

William McKinley elected twenty-fifth President · Utah admitted as forty-fifth · William Jennings Bryan made famous "Cross of Gold" speech · Gold discovered in the Klondike

1897 ● Henry James' *What Maisie Knew* and *The Spoils of Poynton* · Robinson's *The Children of the Night* · William James' *The Will to Believe* · Twain's *Following the Equator*

1898 ● Crane's "The Open Boat" · Finley Peter Dunne's *Mr. Dooley in Peace and in War* · Henry James' *The Turn of the Screw*

Destruction of the battleship *Maine* precipitated Spanish-American War, which resulted in United States' acquisition of Puerto Rico, Guam, and the Philippines

1899 ● Frank Norris' *McTeague* · James' *The Awkward Age* · Crane's *War Is Kind* and *The Monster and Other Stories* · Edwin Markham's "The Man with the Hoe" · Thorstein Veblen's *The Theory of the Leisure Class*

First Hague International Peace Conference established Permanent Court of Arbitration

1900 ● Theodore Dreiser's *Sister Carrie* · Crane's *Whilomville Stories* · Howells' *Literary Friends and Acquaintance* · Ellen Glasgow's *The Voice of the People* · William V. Moody's "An Ode in Time of Hesitation"

United States census: population 75,994,575 · President McKinley reelected

1901 ● Norris' *The Octopus* · Moody's *Poems* · Clyde Fitch's *The Climbers* · Booker T. Washington's *Up from Slavery*

McKinley shot, 6 September; died, 14 September; succeeded by Theodore Roosevelt as twenty-sixth President

1902 ● Robinson's *Captain Craig* · Owen Wister's *The Virginian* · James' *The Wings of the Dove* · Fitch's *Girl with the Green Eyes* · Glasgow's *The Battleground* · Edith Wharton's *The Valley of Decision*

1903 ● Norris' *The Pit* · James' *The Ambassadors* · Jack London's *The Call of the Wild*

First flight of the Wright Brothers' airplane

1904 ● Lincoln Steffens' *The Shame of the Cities* · Ida Tarbell's *History of the Standard Oil Company* · Paul Elmer More's *Shelburne Essays* (1904-1935) · Adams' *Mont-Saint-Michel and Chartres* · O. Henry's *Cabbages and Kings* · James' *The Golden Bowl*

Theodore Roosevelt elected President

1905 ● Howells' *The Kentons* · Wharton's *The House of Mirth* · David Belasco's *The Girl of the Golden West*

1906 ● Augustus Thomas' *The Witching Hour* · Upton Sinclair's *The Jungle* · Langdon E. Mitchell's *The New York Idea* · Moody's *The Great Divide* · O. Henry's *The Four Million*

Pure Food and Drugs Act passed

1907 ● Adams' *The Education of Henry Adams*

Oklahoma admitted as forty-sixth state · "Gentlemen's Agreement" with Japan restricted immigration

1908 William Howard Taft elected twenty-seventh President

1909 ● William Allen White's *A Certain Rich Man* · Gertrude Stein's *Three Lives* · Moody's *The Faith Healer* · Percy MacKaye's *The Scarecrow*

National Association for the Advancement of Colored People founded · North Pole allegedly discovered by Robert E. Peary; his claim is still disputed

1910 ● Robinson's *The Town Down the River* · John A. Lomax' *Cowboy Songs* · Irving Babbitt's *The New Laokoön*

United States census: population 91,972,266

1911 ● Dreiser's *Jennie Gerhardt* · Wharton's *Ethan Frome*

1912 ● Dreiser's *The Financier* · Amy Lowell's *A Dome of Many-Coloured Glass* · Robinson Jeffers' *Flagons and Apples* · *Poetry: A Magazine of Verse* founded

Woodrow Wilson elected twenty-eighth President · New Mexico admitted as forty-seventh state, Arizona as forty-eighth

1913 ● Robert Frost's *A Boy's Will* · Vachel Lindsay's *General William Booth Enters into Heaven and Other Poems* · Willa Cather's *O Pioneers!*

Sixteenth (income tax) and Seventeenth (direct senatorial election) Amendments ratified

U.S.A. is the slice of a continent. . . .
U.S.A. is the world's greatest rivervalley fringed with mountains and hills. . . .
But mostly U.S.A. is the speech of the people.

—John Dos Passos

Frozen lake and cliffs, Kaweah Gap, Sierra Nevada, California, 1934; photograph by Ansel Adams

U.S.A. Between World Wars
1914–1945

Intellectual Currents

Post-War Pessimism

Thinking of the Civil War, Hawthorne spoke of the tragedy in the lives of the women whose husbands and sweethearts were killed in battle: "The girls that would have loved them," he said, "and made happy firesides for them, will pine and wither, and tread along many sour and discontented years, and at last go out of life without knowing what life is. Every shot that takes effect kills one and worse than kills the other." This aspect of war's aftermath found expression in many literary works during and after World War I. Two illustrations will suffice: Amy Lowell's poem "Patterns" (1915) and Eugene O'Neill's play *Strange Interlude* (1928). The poem is a powerful expression of sexual frustration:

> For the man who should loose me is dead,
> Fighting with the Duke of Flanders,
> In a pattern called a war.
> Christ! What are patterns for?

In the "strangled explosion" of the last line, "half-oath, half-prayer" (as Foster Damon, Miss Lowell's biographer, aptly describes it), is compressed much of war's misery. Instead of the rigid self-control described in Miss Lowell's poem, O'Neill, in a similar situation, shows breakdown. After the death of her fiancé in the war, Nina Leeds went to pieces, giving herself promiscuously to the men in an army hospital. One of the characters in the play attributed her behavior to "a desire to be kind" and "a morbid longing for martyrdom." In both instances the psychological effects of war on women are poignantly portrayed.

Other literary works deal with actual participants in World War I. John Dos Passos' *Three Soldiers* (1921) is concerned chiefly with the irksomeness of army life to a man of aesthetic temperament. John Andrews, graduate of Harvard, wants to write great music. When he is arrested for desertion at the end of the story, the wind scatters about the room the leaves of the musical score on which he had been working. War is hateful to the artist, Dos Passos said, and destructive of his art. In the minds of many men—whether artists or persons of average sensitivity—the war left memories of experiences which they tried in vain to forget. The case of the war veteran,

Stetson, in T. S. Eliot's *The Waste Land* (1922) is a classic instance. Stetson's tragic experience is likened to a corpse "planted" in a garden, which will either be dug up by "the Dog" of memory or "sprout" and "bloom" in the subconscious mind.

The tragic effects of World War I are epitomized in Ernest Hemingway's *The Sun Also Rises* (1926) and *A Farewell to Arms* (1929). In *The Sun Also Rises* we are shown the "lost generation" of expatriates who, with shattered nerves and illusions, sought amusement and forgetfulness at bullfights in Spain and in the cafés of Paris. The chief character, Jake Barnes, has been made sexually impotent by a physical injury received in the war. His condition is symbolic of the spiritual impotence of the "lost generation." In *A Farewell to Arms* the war again deprives its victims of high aims and ideals. After the "Retreat from Caporetto" (which has been justly called the finest account in all literature of the collapse of an army) Frederic Henry, the American ambulance driver, can see nothing worth living for except physical satisfactions. In the wreckage of the world about him, thought becomes a torment and a futile occupation. Hence his famous conclusion: "I was not made to think. I was made to eat. My God, yes. Eat and drink and sleep with Catherine."

America's Self-Criticism

The United States had entered World War I, as Woodrow Wilson optimistically expressed it, "to make the world safe for democracy," and the failure of that high mission produced a cynical reaction. Possibly the United States was hardly qualified to play such an exalted role. It was natural that many writers should turn a critical—sometimes a jaundiced—eye upon the American scene and that they should see more to condemn than to admire. "Debunking" became a favorite approach which after Pearl Harbor in World War II years would be called "selling America short."

Biographers of the 1920's attempted to show that our national idols had feet of clay. Historians insisted that materialistic rather than idealistic motives had determined the entire course of our history since Jamestown and Plymouth Rock. The most popular magazine of the period among the literate was the *American Mercury*, edited by H. L. Mencken, which exposed in a monthly department called "Americana" a wealth of current stupidities—at once laughable and deplorable—culled from the newspapers of the day.

The most effective and the most popular criticism of the American scene of the 1920's was written by Sinclair Lewis. His *Main Street* (1920) satirized the small town of the Middle West, where Lewis found "dullness made God." *Babbitt* (1922) ridiculed the American businessman so successfully that the words "Babbitt" and "Babbittry" were added to the dictionary. This hard-hitting satire got under the skins of many Rotarians and boosters. Among the items in Lewis' indictment were questionable business

ethics, an undeveloped literary taste, commercial criteria of success, and
ultraconservatism in social and political thinking. *Babbitt* epitomized the
unlovely aspects of the Harding era. *Arrowsmith* (1925) showed an America inimical to scholarship and pure research. Heroically devoted to medical experimentation, Dr. Martin Arrowsmith finds many stupid obstacles
in his path. *Dodsworth* (1929) satirized the American woman. Fran Dodsworth is unmercifully exposed as a pampered, selfish, superficial, pretentious snob; hers is the most damning portrait in Lewis' entire gallery. Reading between the lines today, one can see that Lewis really enjoyed many
of the people whom he ridiculed and relished much in the life which he
professed to view with contempt, and that he would not exchange his
Gopher Prairie for Utopia. But readers in the 1920's saw only the devastating satire; they hailed him as the greatest of all debunkers. His greatness
may very well lie in less obvious qualities which his contemporary readers
tended to ignore.

Though Lewis was the chief satirist of the 1920's, many other writers
presented indictments of America. Theodore Dreiser's *An American Tragedy* (1925) shows a society vitiated by perverted notions of the good life.
Though the reader might wonder if Clyde Griffiths would have amounted
to much even under ideal conditions, the mores of his materialistic and
class-conscious world are bad enough to have corrupted a stronger character. Sandburg described increasing evils of capitalism: "people living in
shanties," "$6 a week department store girls," "steel trust wops, dead
without having lived, gray and shrunken at forty years of age." Sandburg
charged that the churches were allied with big business and travestied the
teachings of Jesus. Other writers drew attention to deplorable working
conditions, and the word "proletariat" came for the first time into general
American use. O'Neill's *The Hairy Ape* (1922) presented the worker's increasing dissociation from his work, his growing feeling of not "belonging."
Carlyle had pointed out nearly a hundred years earlier the inadequacy,
from the human standpoint, of the "cash-payment nexus": a feeling of
loyalty, of belonging, is necessary to a man's satisfaction in his work. This
is still perhaps the central problem of modern industrialism. While O'Neill
expressed the problem in stirring modern terms, he offered nothing constructive: the conclusion of *The Hairy Ape* is futile and defeatist. Another
dramatist, Elmer Rice, argued in *The Adding Machine* (1923) that the
machine had a degrading effect upon the worker, that machine-tending is
the lowest of all serfdoms, and that man deteriorates as the machine im-
proves. It seemed bitterly ironical to the author that "the finest triumph
of the evolutionary process" should be a machine-tender, "operating a
super-hyper-adding machine with the great toe of his right foot."

Despite these and other searching criticisms, the general public of the
1920's was relatively complacent. During the administrations of Harding,
Coolidge, and Hoover, political conservatism was predominant. Successful

investors enjoyed a rapidly mounting "prosperity." Poor boys with ability and nerve, like F. Scott Fitzgerald's Gatsby (*The Great Gatsby*, 1925), amassed wealth quickly and spent it gaudily in the attempt to realize the dreams of their youth; Fitzgerald's novel, indeed, is a brilliant representation of this whole fabulous era. Only a few economists foresaw the crash of 1929, but their warnings were overridden by the mania for money. Irving Fisher, the eminent economist, and President Hoover both asserted that the economic structure was "fundamentally sound."

Such complacency was the prelude to bitter disillusion. After the crash came the Great Depression, during which criticism of America in literature became more serious, more bitter, and more brutal. Whether the accounts presented were of contemporary life or of life in an earlier period, many writers joined in a strident, damning chorus. With lurid, Gothic power, William Faulkner's novels told of violence and moral perversion in "Jefferson," Mississippi. These works were rich in symbolic meanings: in the words of his best early interpreter, George Marion O'Donnell, Faulkner "projected in fiction the conflict between his inherent traditional values and the modern world." Again starkly, but with human warmth, John Steinbeck's *The Grapes of Wrath* (1939)—perhaps the best single expression in our literature of the difficulties peculiar to the Depression—told of the Joad family, who lost their Oklahoma farm and traveled westward in a jalopy to California, where the family of seven workers, including women and children, were able to earn the sum total of $3.50 a day. The book gives an impression of a powerful mass movement: the "Okies" are less arresting as individuals than as representatives of the mass. With *The Grapes of Wrath*, the proletarian novel had arrived.

Negro Voices of Protest

Particularly bitter, and with good reason, were members of the most frustrated and exploited group during the period—the Negroes.

Approximately 100,000 blacks who fought during World War I enjoyed unaccustomed privileges in France and, on their return to America, were enthusiastically welcomed. On the home front, Negroes had ardently supported the war effort and had begun a mass migration to Northern cities. Increased urbanization, the employment of many in thriving industries, and greater racial cohesiveness strengthened their resistance to oppression. But many whites were determined to annul any wartime gains. In many states the Ku Klux Klan was revitalized. During the first postwar year, seventy Negroes were lynched, and between 1919 and 1921 riots flared in every part of the nation. The Great Depression hit the blacks hard: in the cities, many became unemployed; in rural areas, many had to work for starvation wages or not at all; three or four times as many Negroes as whites had to apply for relief.

Negro organizations became more and more articulate, and some radical movements (that of Marcus Garvey, for instance) prospered. Particularly effective in voicing protests were a distinguished group of black writers, participants in the "Harlem Renaissance." W. E. B. Du Bois, now a New York resident, published numerous books of his own and helped other Negroes achieve print as editor of the magazine *Crisis*. James Weldon Johnson, also living in New York, collected great spirituals in two volumes, outstanding poems in two editions of *The Book of Negro Poetry* (1922, 1931), and published outstanding works which he himself had written. His *Autobiography of an Ex-Coloured Man*, republished in 1927 as part of the Renaissance, was more widely circulated and admired than it had been in its first printing. Leading poets were Countee Cullen and Langston Hughes, and a powerful fiction writer was Jean Toomer.

Eventually the Renaissance became nationwide, spurred during the depression years by the Federal Writers Project. Richard Wright, associated with the project in Chicago, won a prize for the best work by an author in the organization with *Uncle Tom's Children* (1938, enlarged 1940), a collection of short stories. Later, as a resident of New York and then of Paris, he became the nation's foremost black writer. His *Native Son* (1940) made him the first to write authoritatively on problems of the Negro ghetto, and subsequent articles, stories, novels, and autobiographical accounts were both popular and eloquent.

During Franklin Roosevelt's administrations, Negroes, for the first time playing important advisory roles, were able to increase opportunities for the employment of blacks in government and industry and somewhat to enlarge voting rights. And Negroes, like whites, were beneficiaries of some New Deal social legislation. But the greatest efforts and the greatest gains would not come until after World War II.

The Dominance of Science and Quasi-science

Science contributed its share to a dominant mood of pessimism between the wars. Perhaps it would be more correct to say "popular science," for the reference is not to science as such, but to its embodiment in literature, where it is easily susceptible to misconstruction and falsification. In any case, the scientist is hardly to blame. It is regrettable that some of his discoveries had unfortunate results.

The new physics gave laymen the impression that the universe was somehow doomed. Historians and interpreters of science had much to say in the 1920's and 1930's about the second law of thermodynamics or the law of entropy, which seemed to mean that energy is deteriorating or becoming less available, that the universe is cooling off and running down, and that the earth will someday be unfit for human habitation. The ultimate destination of man on this planet appeared to be the "heat-death." This view of things colored the thinking of many moderns, writers and readers alike; it found its most forceful literary expression in the pessimistic poetry of Robinson Jeffers, who wrote in "To the Stone Cutters":

> . . . man will be blotted out, the blithe earth die, the brave sun
> Die blind, his heart blackening.

It was better so, the poet reasoned, for he saw in man's deepest nature a subconscious desire to return to the prenatal darkness and silence of the womb. Inspired by the new physics, Jeffers regarded life as a "blemish," and extinction as the greatest good.

Freudian psychology, too, left its mark everywhere in literature. Possibly the first fictional work in America to exemplify the deliberate use of Freudian principles was Sherwood Anderson's *Winesburg, Ohio* (1919), where almost everyone is abnormal and the abnormalities are explained in terms of sexual repression. O'Neill's *Strange Interlude* (1928) and *Mourning Becomes Electra* (1931) appear to have been constructed from Freudian blueprints. The new psychological principles were also employed in biography and literary history. Applying Freud to American literary history (*Expression in America*, 1932), Ludwig Lewisohn was able to reveal an amazing number and variety of psychological maladies among men of letters: Hawthorne's sense of guilt, for example, was "precipitated by the incest wish of infancy." By the middle 1930's many sophisticated people, through a kind of "scientific" mania for sex-analysis and sex-experimentation, had succeeded in making themselves almost as morbid on the subject as the prudish, hypocritical Victorians, whom they regarded with unmitigated horror.

Closely associated in the popular mind with Freudian psychology was the biology of glandular secretions, which, to many, seemed a new source of tyranny. Oversexed persons, like Lady Brett in Hemingway's *The Sun Also Rises*, could blame the endocrine or some other gland for their immoral behavior. Stupid, brutal persons, like Lennie in Steinbeck's *Of Mice and Men* (1937), could be explained by hypothyroidism. Little by little, the modern sciences, which had begun as a great liberating force, seemed to be imprisoning man as tightly as he had ever been imprisoned by the pseudosciences of the Middle Ages.

The new fields of economics and sociology also played enlarged roles. Charles A. Beard (*An Economic Interpretation of the Constitution*, 1913) and his successors stressed the importance of economic factors in American history. V. L. Parrington (*Main Currents in American Thought*, 1927-1930) and his disciples likewise concentrated on economic elements in American literature. It is not surprising that in much of the fiction of the period economic pressure appeared decisive or that before the end of the period man's life appeared to consist, contrary to Holy Writ, of the commodities which he possessed. Meanwhile, social pressures vied strenuously with the economic ones for the honor of being the chief determinant in human destiny. William Graham Sumner had declared that folkways were decisive, and his successors elaborated and illustrated the proposition. Many novelists were influenced by Sumner's school of sociology; in Dreiser's *An American Tragedy* (1925), for example, Clyde Griffiths is a character inescapably trapped by his environment.

The Helplessness of the Individual

Many signs seemed to point to the growing helplessness of the individual. There no longer appeared to be any such thing as an autonomous and morally responsible person: the species well-nigh disappeared from books written in the spirit of the age. This spirit found its best philosophical statement in Joseph Wood Krutch's *The Modern Temper* (1929), which pictured modern civilization as decadent since thought itself is a mark of decadence. The future belongs, as always, to the barbarians, "absorbed in the processes of life for their own sake, eating without asking if it is worthwhile to eat, begetting children without asking why they should beget them, and conquering without asking for what purpose they conquer."

The poets brilliantly expressed the mood of failure and despair. Edwin Arlington Robinson's "man against the sky" was by no means sure that he was not pursuing a

. . . blind atomic pilgrimage
Whereon by crass chance billeted we go. . . .

T. S. Eliot gave the classic picture of futility in "The Love Song of J. Alfred Prufrock": "I have measured out my life with coffee spoons. . . ." Archibald MacLeish, in *The Hamlet of A. MacLeish* (1928) echoed, with modern mutations and overtones, the despair of Shakespeare's Hamlet:

Thou wouldst not think
How ill all's here about my heart!

These three poems were characteristic. The Hamlet mood was congenial to all of them, but they exemplified Hamlet's confusion and indecision rather than his capacity for heroic action. Submerged in endless debate, the man against the sky or Prufrock or MacLeish's Hamlet could never have killed the king.

While these poets were portraying the helplessness of the intellectual, entangled in the toils of thought, novelists were discovering another kind of helplessness in the masses—a helplessness not explicable by intellectualism, but by biological and social determinism. Novels such as *An American Tragedy* and *The Grapes of Wrath* abundantly illustrate the tyranny of social and economic pressure and the impotence of the individual in the face of overwhelming circumstance. The most complete illustration of modern determinism in American fiction is Dos Passos' trilogy *U.S.A.* (published in one volume in 1937), which is at once—in the apt description of Alfred Kazin—"the dominant social novel of the thirties" and "the coldest and most mechanical of tragic novels," indeed our largest and most comprehensive fictional gallery of human automatons. The reader finds it difficult, if not impossible, to take an interest in its people as persons: it has been justly said that Dos Passos did not create character. The twenty-odd people in *U.S.A.* exhibit the mechanical behavior, the unawareness, the moral irresponsibility of robots, as they are pushed about over the continent by irrational force.

Counter-Attitudes

American literature between the wars was thus predominantly pessimistic. It would be a mistake, however, to suppose that all literature in this period was negative and despairing. Positive forces did not die; they were rooted too deeply in human nature. Of course, few writers were entirely negative or completely pessimistic.

First among the positive forces was what Browning called "our manhood's prime vigor": "How good is man's life, the mere living!" exclaimed that now unfashionable Victorian poet. One would not expect to find an entire generation of American writers silent on this theme. In fact, it appears frequently in the literature of the period. The most notable examples of *élan vital* are found in the writings of those incorrigible romanticists, Ernest Hemingway and Thomas Wolfe. Whatever the state of the world at large, these writers were able to enjoy living. No author has ever shown a greater spirit of youth than Wolfe. In this respect he stands at the opposite pole from Jeffers. No author has ever celebrated friendship and love with greater ardor and tenderness than Hemingway. At the end, tragic though it is, of *For Whom the Bell Tolls* (1940), Robert Jordan "told himself," "You had a lot of luck to have had such a good life."

Other instinctive forces which were not extinguished, no matter how pessimistic the age, were love of the earth, love of humanity, love of country—they appeared separately and combined in a variety of patterns. The good earth was never better than in the poems of Robert Frost, and was never exhibited with greater tang or economic urgency than in the essays of the Southern Agrarians (*I'll Take My Stand*, 1930), who argued for the way of life of Thomas Jefferson. Love of humanity, ranging from individuals to the mass, from personal kindness to faith in the common man, still manifested itself. Sandburg was devoted to "the people" with an ardor as warm as Whitman's. Steinbeck's characters had a friendly warmth: human kindness could hardly go further than in the concluding scene of *The Grapes of Wrath*. Love of country still flourished, ranging between a lively sense of the past and its historic glories and a passionate, instinctive attachment to the place of one's birth. Wolfe's devotion to America was more instinctive. To him, it was the "fabulous country—the place where miracles not only happen, but where they happen all the time" (*Of Time and the River*, 1935). Like Whitman, he tried to take in all of America equally, though neither quite succeeded; for just as Whitman's affection was intensely localized in Manhattan and the Brooklyn Ferry, so Wolfe's was rooted deepest in "old Catawba, there in the hills of home," the hills of North Carolina.

There were also positive intellectual and moral forces at work in the literature of the 1920's and 1930's. In the midst of a world which appeared given over to naturalism and moral chaos, the "neohumanists"—Paul Elmer More, Irving Babbitt, and Norman Foerster—argued for the necessity of discipline, of standards of excellence, and of traditional values. Control must come from within, they reasoned; the "inner check" is the only saving virtue, and the most available sources of that virtue are the classic disciplines (see *Humanism and America*, 1930, by Foerster and others). Less "humanistic" but more human and genuinely fortifying was the note sounded with charm and firmness by two novelists—Ellen Glasgow and Willa Cather. While most of the male novelists were advertising failure, Glasgow and Cather preferred to show the possibility of success. In *Barren Ground* (1925), Glasgow reversed two stock pictures of failure. It had been generally supposed that success of any sort on a farm was no longer possible, but Dorinda Oakley actually reclaimed the barren ground. It had been generally supposed, too—especially in the South—that a girl could scarcely survive disappointment in love, but Dorinda survived. Willa Cather also showed the triumph of fortitude. Beautiful and heart-warming, *My Ántonia* (1918) portrays a pioneer immigrant woman, passionately devoted to her family and to her life on the Nebraska prairie, triumphant over difficulties which would have defeated a less robust soul. *Death Comes for the Archbishop* (1927) is likewise a story of heroism—the heroism of two Catholic missionaries in the Spanish Southwest. The building of the cathedral in Santa Fé is a splendid culmination of their efforts to succeed in a strange environment. Even in the pessimistic gloom of the years between the wars, Cather and Glasgow were able to say: "Success is the reward of the stronghearted. This is the meaning of America, and of life."

One other positive force must be mentioned: religious faith. In the literature of no other period in our history had the note of religious faith been so nearly absent. Its rare occurrence seemed anachronistic to many readers, though later generations may judge otherwise of—to mention two commanding examples—*Death Comes for the Archbishop* and T. S. Eliot's *Ash-Wednesday* (1930). "Where there is great love," Cather's Father Latour says, "there are always miracles. The miracles of the Church seem to me to rest not so much upon faces or voices or healing power coming suddenly near to us from afar off, but upon our perceptions being made finer, so that for a moment our eyes can see and our ears can hear what there is about us always." If Cather's case for religion was chiefly emotional and aesthetic, Eliot's was chiefly intellectual. After the futility of "The Love Song of J. Alfred Prufrock" (1917) and the despair of *The Waste Land*—the most powerful single statement of the aridity of the world between the wars and the most influential poem of the century—Eliot moved on to the firmly religious position of *Ash-Wednesday*. The poem does not record an easy victory. There is no disposition to nurse the illusion that the modern person can recover the spontaneous, unquestioning faith of an earlier age: the poet does not "hope to know again the infirm glory of the positive hour." The road to belief is tortuous. Final attainment is possible only through realizing the necessity of surrendering the individual will to the divine will.

The Political Struggle

The years between the wars seem to fall into a series of periods, each of which profoundly affected the lives of all Americans: World War I, reluctantly entered by the United States in 1917; the period of peacemaking, which ended with general disillusionment about the value of the war; the boom-time era, which ended with the stock market crash of 1929; the period of depression, followed by slow recovery; then the period during which the world drifted toward another war.

Each of these eras was marked by political disputes, some of them unusually bitter. Looking back, we may see that the domestic conflict centered upon the role of the state versus the role of the individual, while the conflict concerning foreign relations set isolationism against participation in world affairs.

The domestic policies of the Democrats under President Woodrow Wilson were thus summarized by the party in 1916: "We found our country hampered by special privilege, a vicious tariff, obsolete banking laws and an inelastic currency. . . . Under our administration, under a leadership that has never faltered, these abuses have been corrected and our people freed therefrom." Such was the work of Wilson's "New Freedom," as seen by his followers. The Republican presidents who came into office after the war, by contrast, tended to give business a freer hand and to increase tariffs. Harding, Coolidge, and Hoover emphasized free enterprise and minimized governmental control. Hoover wrote in 1922: "Salvation will not come to us out of the wreckage of individualism. What we need today is steady devotion to a better, brighter, broader individualism—an individualism that carries increasing responsibility and service to our fellows." Those who took an opposing point of view, championed by Franklin D. Roose-

velt, came into power after Hoover's policies failed to end the Depression
which had begun in 1929. Their position was that the federal government
had to assume a greater responsibility in curbing a ruthless economic individualism and in assisting its victims. Many measures of the "New Deal,"
therefore, limited the scope of free enterprise.

There was more general agreement concerning international affairs. At
the end of World War I, the public was in favor of the League of Nations
and the participation of the United States in world affairs. After the disillusionment of the peace, however, public opinion tended toward pacifism
and isolationism. As Fascism and Nazism developed in the 1930's, and as
the inevitability of war became increasingly apparent, a growing and soon
dominant group became convinced that the United States could no longer
separate itself, either in war or in peace, from the rest of the world.

R.S.
W.B.

Literary Trends

Twentieth-century American literature, like twentieth-century American life, divides into three periods, with the two World Wars marking the transitions. Between 1910 and 1917, modern American drama and poetry came of age, in an idyllic moment wherein innocence and maturity blended. The second decade of the century was a time of rebellion and experiment which produced writers with extraordinary literary talent. Many of the writers of that awakening have left marks upon subsequent literature in the United States. World War I marked a hiatus, but it was followed by a similar awakening in fiction which, particularly after the stock market crash of 1929, became strongly social in flavor. With the appearance of Fitzgerald, Hemingway, and Faulkner, the American novel commanded a new respect around the world. Drama and poetry developed steadily between the wars, and there arose what amounted to a revolution in criticism.

The "Little" Movement

If names meant anything, the literary movement which began shortly after 1910 was at first a "little" movement. In cities and towns all over the nation, and after World War I in Paris and London, "little groups" devoted themselves to the modest project of revolutionizing literature. They produced plays in "little theaters" and published poems and stories in "little magazines." The oft-repeated word "little" proclaimed hostility to "big" theatrical producers and "big" national magazines and publishing houses which catered to masses of people.

The word "little" also implied rebellion against the alleged conservatism and shallowness of writers for large audiences. Such writers, the rebels contended, prolonged the thoughtless optimism, the prudishness, and the simple and unlifelike depictions of "the Victorians." Like literary rebels who had started movements in previous ages, the new young writers looked to other times and other lands for models which met their peculiar needs. Dramatists turned to the experimental playwrights of Europe. Poets turned to radical American poets of the past (such as Emily Dickinson, Walt Whitman, and Stephen Crane) and to the poets of France and Great Britain. Novelists looked back to American realists and naturalists or looked abroad for contemporary models. Adapting the methods of a host of un-Victorian authors, American writers between World Wars I and II produced highly experimental works which they believed represented life more truly than older writings had.

And, though the movement, at the start, was "little," in the end it tended to dominate the national literature. Group theaters developed leading playwrights; and several poets and fiction writers who had started as contributors to *Poetry, The Little Review, transition, Story,* or other little magazines eventually won national and even international recognition.

The experiences of 1910–1940 show how crucial to the health of American literature were the relatively uncommercial outlets for the work of new writers. The situation against which the writers of those decades were rebelling intensified with the development of new mass media—the movies, radio, and television. All of these were too big, cost too much for the luxury of experimenting with the innovations of inexperienced writers, and tended to aim their offerings at the lower levels of popular taste. Indeed, it is possible to say that without the "little" movement there would have been almost no twentieth-century American literature worth studying.

Experiments in Drama

Although the theater was popular in America from colonial times (there were probably more theaters in the country in the nineteenth century than there are now), and although many Americans wrote plays which were produced, American drama of a quality to command respect abroad is the product of the twentieth century. It began in rebellion.

By 1915 the movies had all but killed the legitimate theater everywhere except in the largest cities. "Road shows" were becoming a thing of the past, and New York theatrical producers were too concerned with receipts to give art much of a chance. In Europe, however, the drama was flourishing, with a lively experimental theater centering around the Théâtre-Libre of Paris (founded in 1887), the Abbey Theater of Dublin (1894), the Moscow Art Theater (1897), and the Kleines Theater of Berlin (1902). Americans traveling abroad observed these vigorous groups and came home to ask why the United States could not have something like them.

Finding others who were sympathetic, they helped to establish numerous community playhouses or workshops—"little theaters"—all over the country, from Boston, where the Toy Theater operated, to Palo Alto, California, where the Stanford University Theater was active. Simultaneously, a number of colleges offered work in playwriting and production under such teachers as George Pierce Baker of Harvard, Thomas Wood Stevens of Carnegie Institute of Technology, A. M. Drummond of Cornell, E. C. Mabie of Iowa, and Frederick Henry Koch of North Carolina. In the little theaters (some of them most active in the summer months near popular resort areas) and in the college workshops, amateur authors, actors, and producers carried on experiments more radical than any which commercial theaters were likely to attempt. Both the little theater movement and the college theater gained momentum almost year by year, some of them branching out into productions especially for children or with touring companies to play in school auditoriums. The summer theaters flourished and in a few cases elaborate regional theaters were established, with generous support from local drama-lovers or even from foundations. In these essentially noncommercial theaters amateurs and apprentices often acted with professionals or under their direction.

In time, the results of the grass-roots drama experiments were very considerable. Most influential were three little theater groups which later became leading commercial producers. The Washington Square Players, founded in Greenwich Village in 1915, became the Theatre Guild in 1919; the Provincetown Players, also founded in 1915, left their fishing-shack playhouse on Cape Cod to go to New York City in 1917; and the Group Theatre, founded by some insurgent Theatre Guild members, became professionally active in 1931. These organizations, successful both commercially and artistically, were responsible for initial productions of plays by such outstanding authors as Paul Green, Eugene O'Neill, and Clifford Odets.

Imagination and Realism

Authors writing for the new theater not only tried to avoid the clichés of plot, characterization, dialog, acting, and staging which had stultified the older drama, but they experimented imaginatively in numerous ways. Even after being highly successful with one type of play, many authors turned to completely different types.

For instance, S. N. Behrman, trained by Professor Baker of Harvard, alternated between writing highly successful social comedies and fantasies: after making a hit with *The Second Man* (1927), he offered a comic version of a classic legend in *Amphitryon 38* (1937). Marc Connelly, who began his career as a collaborator with George S. Kaufman in writing satirical comedies such as *To the Ladies* (1922), turned, with Kaufman, to the writing of the expressionistic play *Beggar on Horseback* (1924) and later wrote, solo, the prize-winning folk Biblical play, *The Green Pastures* (1930), based upon Roark Bradford's Negro Sunday-school stories. Elmer Rice, trained by the Morningside Players, a little theater group, succeeded equally well in writing his expressionistic *Adding Machine* (1923) and his realistic *Street Scene* (1929).

Clearly, the writers and the public of the period before World War II saw values in both realistic modes of writing and the more imaginative. Such hospitality led to one development, evident in some dramas, which was more or less peculiar to the period—the mingling of the realistic with the romantic or the fanciful. An instance is the work of Thornton Wilder, sharply focused on the problems of everyday American life but staged with little or no scenery. Wilder deliberately invited greater audience involvement than more traditional forms of drama permitted, in the hope of transcending time and space. *The Happy Journey to Trenton and Camden* (1931), *Our Town* (1938), and *The Skin of Our Teeth* (1942) were popular with little theater and college groups. Such combinations of fantasy and reality foreshadowed the theater of the absurd, which flourished after World War II.

Expressionism

The mingling of the realistic and the fantastic or symbolic is called expressionism, and is generally ascribed to the influence of August Strindberg (1849–1912), an enormously productive Swedish dramatist whose work ranges from such studies of abnormal psychology as *The Father* (1887) to masterpieces of symbolism such as *The Dream Play* (1902). What expressionism means can be seen, though, from some American examples.

Connelly and Kaufman's *Beggar on Horseback* (1924), for instance, starts with a scene in the apartment of the hero, Neil, a penniless composer. The settings are realistic. The characters are introduced as true-to-life figures—the workingwoman with whom the hero is in love, the rich Gladys Cady, whom he is tempted to marry, and Gladys' money-grubbing family. Then the hero takes a sedative and has a dream forecasting the life he is to have if he marries the rich girl. The dream, thereafter, is presented objectively on the stage, with the distortion, the stylization, the symbolism of some dreams, set forth in dialog which often has the repetitious quality, the rhythmic cadences, and the vocabulary of poetry. The costumes and settings are not realistic but are like those in dreams. A few lines of the stage directions at the time the dream starts suggest the technique:

> . . . it begins to grow light again—but it is no longer Neil's room. It is a railway station, with the arch of Track 37 prominently visible, and other arches flanking it at the side. A muddled train schedule is printed on the station walls, with strange towns that never existed. Neil's piano, however, has remained where it was, and so has his easy chair. Then, down the aisles of the lighted theater, there comes suddenly a double wedding procession. One section is headed by Mr. Cady and Gladys— Mr. Cady in golf knickers and sox, knitted vest, and frock coat, with a silk hat prominently on his arm. Gladys is the gorgeously attired bride, bearing proudly a bouquet that consists entirely of banknotes. Behind them stream four ushers—spats, frock coats, and high hats, to say nothing of huge bridal veils, draped over their heads.

When the dream has concluded, the scene again becomes the composer's apartment, and the action returns to the realm of the everyday world.

Experiments of this kind abound in the work of Eugene O'Neill, the outstanding dramatist of the period. He studied playwriting in Professor Baker's class at Harvard, and his first plays were produced by the Provincetown Players, his later ones by the Theatre Guild. Starting with realistic writing in such plays as *Beyond the Horizon* (1920) and *Anna Christie* (1922), he shifted to expressionistic writing in *The Emperor Jones* (1921), wherein the uneasy conscience of a fleeing Negro dictator is dramatized by symbolic scenes showing his mental return to earlier black history—a slave auction block, a slave ship, the ministrations of a Congo witch doctor. In *The Hairy Ape* (1922) some of the scenery and much of the dialog and action are realistic. In some scenes, however, masked characters, marionette-like processions, monologs, and choric effects lift the action into the realm of fantasy. The primitive Yank, despite his tough vocabulary, has an articulateness which is more in character for O'Neill than for the battered stoker. The rhythms of much of the dialog are much more poetic than those of ordinary speech.

In other plays O'Neill experimented with devices which are now familiar, but which were relatively new at the time. *Desire Under the Elms* (1925) uses a set showing four rooms of a farmhouse, two downstairs and two above, together with an exterior dominated by the symbolic trees which give the play its name. The action weaves in and out, sometimes in one room, sometimes in another, sometimes in two at once, and sometimes in connection with what is going on outside. *The Great God Brown* (1926) employs a Greek device, the portrayal of its characters in masks, to which O'Neill resorted in a few other plays. *Strange Interlude* (1928) seeks to extend the bounds of drama by portraying, in addition to the speech of its characters, their inner thoughts, by means of lengthy soliloquies spoken as the other onstage characters "freeze" into the background—a device which some theatergoers found more ridiculous than rewarding. O'Neill continued to be fond of symbolism, which he nowhere handled more effectively than in *Mourning Becomes Electra* (1931), a trilogy of plays retelling in an American setting the Greek myth of Orestes and his sister's vengeance on their faithless mother, Clytemnestra. Yet he could on occasion return to realism, as in *Ah, Wilderness!* (1933), or try his hand at mystical poetry, as in *Lazarus Laughed* (1927). His great ingenuity, supported by steady advances in theater technology, particularly in lighting, together with his philosophical turn of mind, make him the dominant figure thus far in twentieth-century American drama. His shadow lingered long after his death in 1953, for among his manuscripts were *Long Day's Journey into Night* (produced in 1956), which won for him posthumously his fourth Pulitzer Prize, and *A Touch of the Poet* (1957), both of which had considerable success.

The Drama As Social Criticism

The new drama was marked not only by its experimentation but also by its greater concern with social problems. Many of the plays already mentioned testify to this fact. O'Neill's *The Hairy Ape* deals forcefully with the need for a man to believe that his work is meaningful—a need which in an industrial society is seldom easily satisfied. *What Price Glory?* (1924) by Maxwell Anderson and Laurence Stallings was only one of many plays showing the American disillusionment with a war which was supposed to make the world safe for democracy. The manifestations of American materialism, as exemplified by the *nouveaux riches* and the code of big business, were the object in satire in *Beggar on Horseback* and in numerous other plays, among them O'Neill's *Marco Millions* (1927).

The heyday of the social drama, however, was the 1930's. From the hardships which followed the breakdown of the vaunted American economic system came innumerable plays which glorified the common man at the expense of his leaders or which were thinly veiled socialistic tracts. Some of them came out of the WPA Theatre (officially the Federal Theatre Project of the Works Progress Administration), a New Deal agency which lasted from 1935 to 1939. At its height the WPA Theatre was operating in forty states and employing 10,000 persons. Other social dramas were the contributions of the little theater groups, notably the Group Theatre, which introduced the work of Clifford Odets. *Waiting for Lefty* (1935), a depiction of a taxicab drivers' strike employing such devices as action in the auditorium as well as on the stage, the unfolding of the story in blackouts, and the employment of declamatory speeches, remains the best known of the so-called proletarian plays. Strong social overtones are also audible in Odets' *Awake and Sing* (1935) and *Golden Boy* (1937), other Group Theatre productions.

Lillian Hellman's strike play, *Days to Come* (1936), failed, but *The Little Foxes* (1939) is among the most memorable Broadway plays of social protest. Taking her title from the Song of Solomon (2:15: "Take us the foxes, the little foxes, that spoil the vines: for our vines have tender grapes"), Hellman created a Southern family, the Hubbards, whose love of money and the power it brings has smothered all humane values. She returned to the Hubbards, somewhat less successfully, in *Another Part of the Forest* (1946). Another of Hellman's socially oriented plays was her prophetic *Watch on the Rhine* (1941), in which she indicated that Americans soon would have to deal with Fascism.

The Poetic Renaissance

Although various dates have been mentioned as marking the beginning of the poetic renaissance, the date most widely accepted is 1912, the year of the founding of *Poetry, A Magazine of Verse* by Harriet Monroe (1860–1936) and a group of subscribers. The motive of this publication, as the first issue stated it, was "to give to poetry her own place, her own voice." "The popular magazines," explained the editors, "can afford her but scant courtesy—a Cinderella corner in the ashes—because they seek a large public which is not hers, a public which buys them not for their verse but for their stories, pictures, journalism, rarely for their literature even in prose. ... We believe that there is a public for poetry, that it will grow, and that as it becomes more numerous and more appreciative the work produced in this art will grow in power, in beauty, in significance."

The magazine, from its founding down to the present, has admirably fulfilled its function, and in time its prophecy was justified. *Poetry* has introduced many new poets to the public. Additional interest in poetry was excited by the books of some poets, notably Masters' *Spoon River Anthology* (1915), which was extraordinarily popular. Poets who read their own poetry to the public—Frost, Sandburg, and Lindsay, in particular—won a wider audience. Then various little magazines followed the lead of *Poetry*, devoting much space to poems and to critical discussion: *Contemporary Verse* (1916–1929), *The Double Dealer* (1921–1926), *The Fugitive* (1922–1925), *Palms* (1923–1940), and others. Books on the new poetry by persuasive critics (Amy Lowell, John Crowe Ransom, Elizabeth Drew, George Williamson, and M. L. Rosenthal, to name but a few) helped cultivate understanding and appreciation. The result was the creation of a sizable public which bought books of contemporary poetry and read it with enthusiasm.

Critics of modern poetry, many of whom advocated detailed analysis of individual poems, found that a common attitude among the new poets was one of rebellion against Victorian poetry. Sometimes, as in the works of E. A. Robinson, this rebellion was visible chiefly in *what* the poet said—the voicing of un-Victorian philosophical attitudes. More often, however, the poets rebelled against conventional poetic techniques—a rebellion indicated by *how* the poet expressed himself.

In poetry, as in the drama, there were innumerable experiments. As Frost observed humorously, "Poetry ... was tried without punctuation. It was tried without capital letters. It was tried without any image but those to the eye. ... It was tried without content under the name of poesie pure. It was tried without phrase, epigram, coherence, logic, and consistency. It was tried without ability. ... It was tried without feeling or sentiment. ..." The sources of these experimental techniques were also numerous—the English metaphysical poets of the seventeenth century, the symbolists of France, the "radical" American poets of the nineteenth century, and others. A complete consideration of the period, therefore, would deal with innovations and influences by the score. Our more limited consideration will deal with three of the chief rebellions against older techniques: (1) against the older ideas about the "seriousness" proper to poetry, (2) against conventional versification, and (3) against conventional "poetic" diction.

"Serious Humor"

During the last decades of the nineteenth century and the early years of the twentieth century, poets in general lagged behind fiction writers in adapting their methods to changing views of life in the United States. The more advanced novelists, dissatisfied with what they had thought were romantic oversimplifications, had turned to realism and naturalism partly because they believed that these modes made possible more inclusive—and truer—representations of life. But most poets had continued to write romantic poetry. Love or hate or sorrow had continued to be an "all out" business with them, completely disconnected from workaday concerns such as digging ditches, say, or sipping coffee, or selecting neckties. The attitude of the best poetry, in accordance with the urgings of Matthew Arnold and other leading critics, was one of "high seriousness." Poets had values about which they had no doubts, and though their poems might show vacillations, they moved forward steadily to firm conclusions.

There had been some exceptions: Walt Whitman had fused "fleshly" and "spiritual" viewpoints; Emily Dickinson had been simultaneously playful and serious while writing of love, nature, religion, or even death; William Vaughn Moody had assumed the comic role of "a little man in trousers, slightly jagged," to discuss the serious problem of evolution; Stephen Crane had written with ironic humor of man's sense of self-importance in the face of the indifferent universe. These poets, it now developed, foreshadowed the concept of "seriousness" combined with humor which was to shape interwar poetry. Cleanth Brooks, in *Modern Poetry and the Tradition*, contrasts the new conception with the older:

> The two conceptions are almost diametrically opposed. Arnold's sincerity expresses itself as a vigilance which keeps out of the poem all those extraneous and distracting elements which might seem to contradict what the poet wishes to communicate to his audience. It is the sincerity of the conscientious expositor who makes his point, even at the expense of suppressions and exclusions. . . . The second conception of poetry, on the other hand, reveals itself as an unwillingness to ignore the complexity of experience. The poet attempts to fuse the conflicting elements in a harmonious whole.

Modern poets, in other words, feeling that life is more complicated than most romantic poets have admitted, reveal its conflicting aspects, its colliding values. Inevitably, therefore, their poems—excepting those of Jeffers and others who view life as completely tragic—deal with incongruities;

and humor, wit, or irony of varied shades become important even in very serious poems.

The incongruity in many of the best poems of Vachel Lindsay, for instance, is akin to that in American folklore. In such poems, one may hear echoes of the fireside talk of frontier yarnspinners. Lindsay is a myth-maker, and though his myths stop short of the most inventive tall tales, they achieve comparable fusings of the real and the imagined. His Andrew Jackson "was eight feet tall. . . . His sword was so long he dragged it on the ground." In "General William Booth Enters into Heaven" (1912) the paradise that Booth enters is part supernatural, part Illinois country town. His Simon Legree is the legendary creation of a Negro preacher. Even his Lincoln, in "Abraham Lincoln Walks at Midnight" (1919), stalking through Springfield at night, assumes the guise of a folk creation.

Sandburg, likewise, embodies playful myths and imaginative tall tales in serious poems. His "Chicago" (1916) is a giant personification comparable to the frontier demigods; in *Lincoln: The Prairie Years* (1926), he re-creates a half-mythical Lincoln by giving folk pictures of him; in *The People, Yes* (1935), he praises the people by telling of their folklore. In addition to frontier or rural humor, he makes use of the wry humor of the dispossessed as it is voiced in hobo ballads which he has reproduced in his *American Songbag* (1927): hate, bitter contempt, and tenderness are mingled in "To a Contemporary Bunkshooter" and also in "A.E.F." (1920).

The humor of two New England poets, Robinson and Frost, as Constance Rourke has remarked in *American Humor*, also prolongs an older tradition:

> For companions in the legendary village of Tilbury Town Robinson has chosen types recurrent throughout early American comedy, ne'er-do-wells, liars, the quirky, the large-hearted and lost, spendthrifts of time and money and love. Robinson is master of that unobtrusive irony that has belonged to the Yankee; like the older Yankee he turns constantly to a dry metaphor—"an old vanity that is half as rich in salvage as old ashes." . . . A reticent humor runs through much of Robinson's poetry, so quietly as to pass unnoticed by many readers, yet producing a constant lighting and relief and change, with a balancing of forces against the impending tragedy. . . . Frost [too] has kept the native humor, often deepened to a bitter irony, but delicately infused; most of his humor, like that of the early Yankee tradition, is so deeply interwoven with his further speech as to be almost inseparable from it.

The humor of these New England poets, then, is related to the Yankee humor of the *Farmer's Almanacs* and of pre-Civil War rural humorists.

In summary, four modern poets—Lindsay, Sandburg, Robinson, and

Frost—re-create in serious poetry the extravagant humor of the old West or the dry humor of New England. Another group—claiming T. S. Eliot, Wallace Stevens, Ezra Pound, E. E. Cummings, William Carlos Williams, and many others as part of its membership—embodies more subtle (albeit ironic) incongruities in its poetry. Cleanth Brooks sees "wit" as the instrument used by these poets in fusing disparates; and his definition of wit shows how it may be used for serious purposes:

> Wit is not only an acute perception of analogies; it is a lively awareness of the fact that the obvious attitude toward a given situation is not the only possible attitude. Because wit, for us, is still associated with levity, it may be well to state it in its most serious terms. The witty poet's glancing at other attitudes is not merely "play"—an attempt to puzzle or show off his acuteness of perception; it is possible to describe it as merely his refusal to blind himself to a multiplicity which exists.

The perception of such multiplicity has frequently caused poets in this group to discard or greatly modify older ways of organizing poems in favor of "witty" organizations which emphasize ironic incongruities. Contrasting aspects or values are placed side by side, and their disparate qualities are emphasized by the omission of most transitions. What Eliot calls " 'links in the chain,' of explanatory and connecting matter" are left out. Though such arrangements may, for a time, puzzle readers used to Victorian poetry, they are inevitable considering the poets' assumptions about reality. As Eliot has pointed out, "Such selection of sequences of images and ideas has nothing chaotic about it. There is a logic of imagination as well as a logic of concepts." Eliot and others of his group in their poems seek to arrange details in accordance with "the logic of imagination."

A hypothetical poem held together by what Eliot calls "the logic of concepts" might begin with a poetic statement of the idea that modern man is less romantic than man was in the past. "Look upon modern man," it might continue, and thereupon it might describe modern man in unromantic terms. The description might be followed by a transition—"It was not so with man in other days"—and the transition might introduce a description of a romantic character of the past. Possibly the poet might thereafter summarize the whole idea of the poem, and then lament the departure of romance. In such a structure no "links in the chain" would be missing and the meaning would be explicitly formulated. In a terse passage in *The Waste Land* (1922), by contrast, Eliot's "logic of imagination" enabled him to omit transitions, generalizations, or statements of attitudes— he simply juxtaposed images, with those of the opening two lines providing a meaningful ironic contrast with those of the last four:

At the violet hour, the evening hour that strives
Homeward, and brings the sailor home from sea,
The typist home at teatime, clears her breakfast, lights
Her stove, and lays out food in tins.
Out of the window perilously spread
Her drying combinations touched by the sun's last rays. . . .

The opening two lines here connote the romance of purple twilight for ad-
venturous sailors turning homeward; the remaining lines show the drab
office worker clearing up dirty breakfast dishes, dining on canned food,
and then washing and hanging out her underwear.

Comparable ironic contrasts or ironic parallelisms—or, more often,
parallelisms and contrasts combined—are implied in the order of the images
in many modern poems. In Eliot's "The Love Song of J. Alfred Prufrock"
(1917), "The Hippopotamus" (1920), and "Gerontion" (1920) the images
are much more complex, but the juxtaposition is the essential thing. Thus
"the logic of imagination" which shapes these poems expresses irony, and
in its "serious humor" Eliot's poetry shows its kinship to that of even such
a broadly humorous poet as Vachel Lindsay. Similar juxtapositions involv-
ing irony are used by Pound, Stevens, Cummings, and Williams, often for a
purpose somewhat similar to that of the early Eliot—to underline the tawdriness of modern life. And later poets employed the device in ways of
their own.

New Rhythms

During the early years of the poetic renaissance, one great battle was
for the recognition of free verse—verse which, though rhythmic, does not
use regular meters or rhymes. Keith Preston, a Chicago newspaper column-
ist, implied what was a widespread belief when he wrote that one of the
saddest of the literary scenes was the graves of "little magazines" that had
"died to make verse free." Casual readers, for a long time, thought that
"the new poetry" and "free verse" were synonymous. Many leaders in the
movement did for a time write much free verse—Amy Lowell, Carl Sandburg, William Carlos Williams, Wallace Stevens, and others obviously in the
tradition of Walt Whitman.

By degrees, free verse came to be accepted by the public. Poets were
aided by the growth of Whitman's reputation during this period, by the
popularity of Edgar Lee Masters' *Spoon River Anthology*, and by critics,
poets, and teachers who championed vers libre. By 1940, radio plays written in free verse appealed to wide audiences, and many an amateur poet
who mailed his early efforts to the home-town newspaper wrote in free
verse.

By then, however, many leading poets considered free verse rather old-
fashioned. Having won all the freedom they wanted, many poets eventually

decided that they could do with less than vers libre allowed. Nevertheless, free verse had the important effect of revealing possible variations in verse forms. Such poets as E. A. Robinson, Countee Cullen, and Langston Hughes—poets who were in some ways highly conventional in their prosody—diverged from regularity rather more than they probably would have done in an earlier period—and were less criticized for their divergences.

Even so "classical" a poet as Robert Frost was not untouched by the new tendency toward freedom. His theory of prosody, as Lawrance Thompson explains in *Fire and Ice*, attempted to reconcile "three separate planes of sound" which affect rhythms:

> The first of these is the basic and theoretically rigid meter, which Frost is willing to reduce "virtually" to "strict iambic" and "loose iambic." These basic accents, fitted to the variable structure of the line and of the stanza, offer an underlying foundation of words and phrases. The second plane of sound is derived from the words and phrases as they might be pronounced without regard to meaning, without regard to context. The third plane of sound is derived from the tones of voice which give particularly intended shades of meaning to the words when they are spoken as units in their contexts of phrases and sentences.

For example, in the opening lines of Frost's "Mending Wall" (1914) the "basic pattern" is iambic pentameter (e.g., "Something there is that doesn't love a wall"). However, normal accentuation, regardless of contexts, in such words as "something," "ground-swell," and "makes gaps" causes deviations from the regular iambic pattern. A proper reading of the poem, also, will suggest the character of the speaker and the quizzical, teasing tone of his remarks: such a character, probably, in the line "And spills the upper boulders in the sun," would maliciously emphasize and caress with his tongue the word "spills"—a word which embodies the whole playful destruction of walls by nature which so distresses the orderly neighbor. And later, in line 15, "And keep the wall between us as we go," the word "between," important as it is in the concept being developed, may properly be given a stress—be set off by significant pause—suggestive of its contextual importance. The sense Frost revealed, here and in other poems, of these three different planes of sound doubtless does much to account for a quality which many critics have seen in his poems: for poetry, they are often extraordinarily close in their rhythms to the everyday talk of New England farmers.

Vachel Lindsay, as his remarks here and there about metrics indicate, learned a great deal about versification from three poets: Dryden (1631–1700), Poe (1809–1849), and Swinburne (1837–1909). Each of these achieved noteworthy effects by varying established rhythms and by exploiting, to the full, the possibilities of tone-color—vowel and consonant arrangements. Dryden's "A Song for St. Cecilia's Day" brilliantly utilizes variations possible in an irregular ode to contrast the sounds of musical instruments, and it is not difficult to imagine Lindsay writing a gloss for Dryden comparable to that he provided for his own "The Congo" or "General William Booth Enters into Heaven," offering instructions for the reading of the lines. So glossed, Dryden's lines would show clearly the source of some of Lindsay's practices.

But Lindsay's rhythms also had more immediate sources. During his boyhood in Springfield, he came to know the rhythms of church oratory, both white and Negro, and those of open-air political oratory. At Hiram College, he was trained in the florid public speaking fashionable during his youth. Rhythms of the Gregorian Chant were also, he acknowledged, influential. "From Boston to Los Angeles," he wrote, "we American versifiers, democratic poets, face the problem of our potential audiences of one million or one hundred million that we have never conquered, but which the Chautauqua orator like [William Jennings] Bryan . . . may reach any day. From this standpoint, Bryan is the one living American poet till we make a few songs sturdy enough to endure the confusion of the Chautauqua tent. . . ." To capture such audiences, Lindsay wrote poems such as "General William Booth Enters into Heaven"—an experiment in what he called "The Higher Vaudeville"—designed to attract popular attention. Recited as this poet recited such poems, this and others proved attractive to unsophisticated high-school students and even to tired businessmen. Beginning with Lindsay, poets began to record readings, and this medium had considerable effect.

It is not surprising that Vachel Lindsay, cramped by wholly traditional rhythms, and an adapter of folk and jazz rhythms, was enthusiastic about the poetry of Langston Hughes. Hughes, like James Weldon Johnson, but to an even greater extent than Lindsay, adapted the rhythms of Negro sermons in many poems.

Although T. S. Eliot, Wallace Stevens, Hart Crane, Allen Tate, and others of their "school" probably were not overfond of Lindsay and may or may not have read Hughes or Johnson, they adapted rhythms to materials in a comparable fashion. Eliot, who wrote a few poems close to free verse in form early in his career, eventually used rhyme and fairly conventional meters. Like Lindsay, however, he found contrasts in rhythms useful to express contrasting moods, attitudes, or materials.

Jeffers started his career as a conventional versifier, but his later poetry —that most admired by his critics—follows a metrical scheme which, as he said, is a "compromise" avoiding both "arbitrary form and capricious lack of disruption of form." Jeffers says of his meter:

I want it rhythmic and not rhymed—moulded more closely to the subject than in older English poetry—but as formed as alcaics if that were

> possible too. The event is of course a compromise. . . . My feeling is for the number of beats to the line. There is a quantitative element too in which the unstressed syllables have part.

Taking this statement as a clue, Herbert Klein made a study reported in *The Prosody of Robinson Jeffers* (1930). His finding was that, considered carefully, the rhythms of this poet are much less chaotic than, at first glance, they appear to be. The reason is that Jeffers was aware not only of the patterns of English verse but also of the quantitative patterns common to classical poetry. Says Klein:

> Briefly, my conclusion is that Jeffers uses stress to define and limit the line; quantity to regulate it. That is to say, the sheer possible syllabic length of the line is set (within exceptionally broad limits) by the number of stresses which the beat pattern of the poem permits. But the tempo of the lines, the contrast of breathless haste in one line (or joyful skipping) with sonorous deliberation (or hard wrenching plodding) in another is due to quantity.

Because he had a better knowledge of ancient poetry and a greater liking for it than most modern American poets have, Jeffers achieved metrical effects which are new, individual, and arresting.

The effect, in the end, of all this experimentation was to give modern poets a very wide range indeed in their handling of rhythms. Patterns of emphasis could be adjusted in many ways to the thoughts and emotions being expressed, and readers accustomed to the new poetry readily accepted any metrical patterns, no matter how bizarre, which justified themselves by their achievements. And the flexible rhythms were highly appropriate to the expression of the contrasts and incongruities so important in many modern poems.

The Language of Modern Poetry

After 1914 there was about as much variety in the kinds of language used as there was in the kinds of rhythms. Robinson, in general, used the same sort of diction as had been used in the Victorian period, though shorn of clichés and many of its ornaments, and so did some other poets. However, at the start of the period, other poets—like Dryden, Wordsworth, and Whitman before them—consciously rebelled against what they believed to be "unnatural" or ineffective ways of saying things, characteristic of older poetry. The rebellion was justified, so writers said, by several convictions: that a new language was needed to cope in a real way with the modern world, that many "poetic" expressions had been worn threadbare, that concrete rather than abstract words were best for stating truth, and that modern poets did well to draw upon the common speech, which still was a great source of poetry.

The ways of rebelling, however, differed. They differed, quite often, in accordance with the poets' ideas about the ways "common speech" should be translated into poetry. For in this period when various classes expressed themselves in contrasting ways, it was possible to disagree about the class of men whose talk should be imitated. Should it be the speech of the factory worker, say, of the farmer, or of the learned scholar? Even after deciding upon the kind of speech to be used in poetry, poets differed about the selection, the intensification necessary if ordinary talk was to be transmuted.

Robert Frost conceived of himself as a user of the talk of New Hampshire farmers. He approvingly quoted R. W. Emerson's lines about Down East talk in "Monadnock," lines which point out that country folk, with their paltry vocabularies of a hundred words or so, are "the masters who can teach" the poet our "ancient speech," and he admired the dialogs in Shakespeare, made up as they are of "lean sharp sentences, with the give and take, the thread of thought and action quick, nor lost in a maze of metaphor and adjective." Frost usually lived up to his implied ideal. He used an extraordinarily large proportion of monosyllables, forty in a row, for instance, at one point in "The Death of the Hired Man" (1914), and very few long words; he often employed provincialisms. His lines, whether they serve as dialog or as first-person voicings of the poet's thought, often have a sparse epigrammatic quality like that of folk speech (lines 1, 27, 32–33 in "Mending Wall," for example). Since Frost deliberately used such simple, undecorated diction, very close to ordinary speech, he perforce suggested poetic meanings in subtle and delicate ways; and the unwary reader is likely to miss complexities firmly embodied in his laconic poems.

Lindsay and Sandburg employ words in a fashion in some ways comparable to Frost: some of their poems are couched in the Midwestern counterpart of New England farm language. Both of these poets, in addition, following the example of Whitman (whom both admired), mingle poetic words with more vernacular expressions. And each experiments with somewhat different elements in our national speech. The language which Lindsay calls "really American" is the pure and simple English of the Elizabethan period, still spoken in unspoiled rural districts: he cites as an example the language of Mark Twain's *Roughing It* (1872). But he conceives of this speech as potentially "eloquent" since its users "are all orators and preserve in eloquent periods the United States language." Such are the elements which Lindsay tries to utilize in his poetry—"the Grand Style," but employed with earthiness and native humor. Sandburg draws upon the talk of common men for the epigrams and sayings in some of his poems. He draws, in addition, upon the language of the factory or of the city sidewalk for such expressions as "where do you get that stuff"; "the . . . bunch backing you"; "a good four flusher"; and "he starts people puking" (all in "To a Contemporary Bunkshooter")—language highly appropriate to express the proletarian sentiments of the speaker.

Jeffers varied his diction over the years. His earlier poems are, on the whole, pretty conventional: their styles are like those of older writers and often embody inversions—orderings of words which are not found in conversation. Later poems are couched in a larger vocabulary which draws upon science—physics, biochemistry, geology, botany—for many words. But mingled with these are colloquial phrases and contractions. And the style also is richly figurative.

Jeffers, at times, wrote moderately obscure lines—one may cite these in "Roan Stallion" (1925):

> The atom bounds-breaking,
> Nucleus to sun, electrons to planets, with recognition
> Not praying, self-equaling, the whole to the whole, the microcosm
> Not entering nor accepting entrance, more equally, more utterly, more
>   incredibly conjugate
> With the other extreme and greatness; passionately perceptive of
>   identity. . . .

But he is not alone in being obscure. Even such an old-fashioned poet as Robinson is hard to understand now and then, and so are such ordinarily forthright poets as Lindsay and Sandburg. Modern poetry, as a matter of fact, has been much criticized for the obscurity of its language.

Such obscurity is not, as some have thought, the result of a deliberate attempt to blur meaning: actually it attempts to express meaning which is hard to decipher chiefly because it is complicated. T. S. Eliot, like several of his contemporaries, wrote poetry not immediately clear even to sophisticated readers, but he amply justifies his diction, and that of other poets, in outstanding critical essays.

In these he indicates that he shares the belief that poets should write verse after the manner of the actual talk of men. He praises Donne, the seventeenth-century English metaphysical poet, for "managing to maintain a tone of direct and informal address"; he commends Dryden for having a talent which is "exactly the same" as Donne's; he holds that "no serious critic" will disapprove of Wordsworth's avowed attempt "to imitate, and as far as possible, to adopt, the very language of men." In general, carrying out his own theories, Eliot does achieve a conversational tone in his poems. But Eliot sees that certain demands of poetry may make conversational language unsatisfactory. "There is," he says, "no conversational or other form which can be applied indiscriminately": some ideas and feelings may be best expressed in other styles. Moreover, he feels that the poet cannot "talk like *any* class of society," since he has to talk "like himself—rather better, we hope, than any actual class; though when any class of society happens to have the best word, phrase, or expletive for anything, then the poet is entitled to it."

And indeed the poet who achieves all that Eliot sees him doing must be an artist in manipulating language. The language important to the poet, Eliot feels, "is that which is struggling to digest and express new objects, new groups of objects, new feelings, new aspects. . . ." Such living language, this poet holds, in "Tradition and the Individual Talent," combines traditional with novel meanings: "whatever words a writer employs, he benefits by knowing as much as possible of the history of those words, of the uses to which they have already been applied. . . . The essential of tradition is this: in getting as much as possible the whole weight of the history of the language behind his word." Hence a sense of the traditional is valuable. The essential of novelty, by contrast, is the expression of that which is characteristic not only of the age but also of the individual poet. The modern poet, aware of the complexity of his period and of his reactions to it, must "become more and more comprehensive, more allusive, more indirect, in order to force, to dislocate if necessary, language into his meaning." In addition to thus expressing what is traditional and what is unique, the language of today's poetry, Eliot thinks, fuses two other elements—feeling and thought. Poets of today will be condemned if, like Tennyson and Browning, they do not feel their thought as immediately as the odour of the rose." Instead each should reveal in his words "a direct sensuous apprehension of thought, or re-creation of thought into feeling, which is exactly what we find in Donne," greatly admired by Eliot as well as other modern poets.

The title of Eliot's "The Love Song of J. Alfred Prufrock" offers an example of these fusings in diction. The words "love song" in the title have *traditional* signification: in past periods, they stood for an expression of affection which was direct and passionate. This *individual* love song, by contrast, represents our peculiar era by not expressing affection and by being indirect and unimpassioned. Similarly, the word "song," which in the past stood for simple singing, in this poem stands for complex thinking. Again, in "J. Alfred Prufrock" (one of those names "parted on the side," today typical of some pretentious people), "Alfred" has been *traditionally* associated with the man of action, Alfred the Great; but in this *individual* poem, it applies to a "hero" who is exactly the opposite of a man of action. Fusion of *thought* and *feeling* is illustrated by line 51, in which Prufrock thinks "I have measured out my life with coffee spoons." Prufrock's thought is that he has wasted his life in meaningless social rituals; but this is expressed in sensory terms—terms of feeling—in the image of annoyed frustration: the delicate handling of ineffectual little spoons from which coffee cannot be savored but must be sipped.

Some modern poets, then, for all their approval of the use of conversational language, often depart from the simplicities of social talk in order to express complex meanings. Their choice of language, together with the varied rhythms they employ and the tone of "serious humor" they frequently adopt, expresses the ideas and feelings poets have about the modern world.

The New Criticism

Possibly the outstanding new trend in literature between wars was the development of the so-called New Criticism. For the first time in our literary history, there seemed to be more practicing critics than poets or novelists or dramatists. Such literary quarterlies as *Kenyon Review, Sewanee Review,* and *Hudson Review*—and many others of a similar kind—were so largely devoted to criticism that some midcentury observers said that our age had become more critical than creative.

The New Criticism was, in its inception, primarily a protest against the historical approach emphasized by professors and graduate schools. The new critics rightly insisted that a literary work—whether poem, play, story, or novel—is a work of art, that it has a uniqueness, an independent life of its own, that it is its own excuse for being. They deplored the historical emphasis, which substituted for the close analysis of a literary work a biographical and historical commentary on the author's life and his age, the circumstances of composition, textual variants, and other matters which the new critics maintained were irrelevant to the aesthetic question. Allen Tate threw down the gauntlet in his "Miss Emily and the Bibliographers" (1940). For a good many years there were lively skirmishes between "historians" and "critics."

The most valuable product of the movement was a considerable body of important critical writing, writing which subjected literature—particularly individual works of literature—to a new kind of scrutiny. Critics had not often before examined literary texts so closely and so perceptively. T. S. Eliot and I. A. Richards were early leaders. They were soon followed by such expert practitioners as R. P. Blackmur, Allen Tate, John Crowe Ransom, Kenneth Burke, Cleanth Brooks, Philip Rahv, and Lionel Trilling, to name only a few. These critics differ a good deal among themselves: Brooks, for example, has been concerned largely with the tensions and paradoxes of the individual poem; Burke, with semantic suggestiveness; Trilling, with symbolic overtones; and so on. But they all agree in placing the individual work at the center and in focusing our attention upon that.

The new critical movement for a time seemed in danger of carrying its principles too far when it tended to divorce the literary work from its milieu. A later trend recognized the fact that history as well as analysis had its place in literary study, and there was something of a rapprochement between the warring schools. But the contribution of the New Criticism was a solid one. Thanks to its practitioners, the literary work itself has regained its rightful primacy.

The New Fiction

During the period 1912 to 1920, then, "the new drama" and "the new poetry" reached notable heights. "The new fiction," by contrast—at least that which people bought and talked about a great—lagged behind. Consistent authors of best sellers included Gene Stratton Porter, Harold Bell Wright, and Zane Grey. The most popular novels left out the less savory aspects of American life, and their optimistic plots showed virtuous characters triumphant, after a struggle, over vicious villains. Obviously this fiction, although written in the twentieth century, prolonged the tradition of nineteenth-century sentimentalism.

Early in the 1920's, though, the beginnings of a change became apparent. On the best-seller list for 1920 appeared F. Scott Fitzgerald's *This Side of Paradise*, Edith Wharton's *The Age of Innocence*, and Sinclair Lewis' *Main Street*, books in sharp contrast with previous best sellers. The last of these shortly became sensationally successful. In an article in *Bookman* (September 1921), a British novelist, Archibald Marshall, discussed "half a dozen novels said to represent a new development in American fiction, all of which are now being widely read." There was, indeed, "a new development." During the years that followed, pre-1920 novelists tended slowly to recede in importance while very different writers such as Lewis, Hemingway, Faulkner, Dos Passos, Steinbeck, and Wolfe replaced them not only in critical esteem but also—at least at times—in general popularity.

Probably the huge audience which fictionists had was in large measure responsible for the late burgeoning of the new fiction. More numerous than the readers of either poetry or drama, fiction readers for a long time were still content with old-fashioned narratives. They preferred "pure" and "sweet" stories to the more rugged works of Stephen Crane and Theodore Dreiser. But after many readers had been disillusioned by the outcome of World War I or had been converted by preachers of disillusionment such as Henry Adams and H. L. Mencken, a part of the older audience began to demand fictional works of a different sort. These were joined by a large share of the younger readers. Increasing numbers approved of the tendency which Archibald Marshall saw in best sellers "to portray the meanness of life in a particular [American] community." Attacks made by older neglected novelists, voiced anew, were considered with respect. Interest in E. W. Howe, Joseph Kirkland, and Crane was reawakened and redoubled. Dreiser's reputation prospered, and in 1925, when Dreiser published *An American Tragedy*, he found to his pleased surprise that the new audience was large enough to make that book for a time a best seller. By the 1930's, many books as stern as Dreiser's managed to win wide and appreciative audiences—not such wide ones, to be sure, as escapist novels like *Anthony Adverse* and *Gone with the Wind*, but very respectable audiences nevertheless.

Readers, then, who turned to fiction writers of the newer sort did so less because of their manner than because of their matter. But the authors of the new fiction, like the interwar poets, rebelled against older techniques, and they naturally needed new techniques appropriate to their preachments. Looking back to their most sympathetic predecessors, the realists and naturalists of the period 1880–1920, they found useful hints. And considering their new views of life, they hit upon methods of unfolding narratives which served their purposes.

Regardless of the sources of their techniques, fiction writers tended to drop the old argument concerning the relative merits of romanticism, realism, naturalism, expressionism, and other "isms," and to agree with Percy Lubbock, an influential critic of fiction, when he wrote: "The best form is that which makes the most of its subject—there is no other definition of the meaning of form in fiction." Authors and critics admired equally the novels of Dreiser and Farrell, cast in the form of naturalism; those of James Branch Cabell, written after the pattern of romances; and those of Robert Nathan, in the form of fantasy. What mattered most was that the fiction, as the phrase constantly had it, should "tell the real truth about life as it was." Detail, plot, and characterization were manipulated chiefly to achieve the end Mencken had in mind when he spoke of the "fundamental purpose" as being "to make the novel true."

Detail in Modern Fiction

Two ways of handling detail, perhaps, are outstanding in modern fiction—the "documentary" and the "poetic." The documentary method, discoverable in Fitzgerald's *This Side of Paradise* and in the writings of Sinclair Lewis, John Dos Passos, Richard Wright, and many other modern novelists, amasses detail. Probably Dreiser, as much as any previous author, is its parent, and its ideal is something like scientific accuracy and completeness. An example of this method in an extreme form is the chapter in *Main Street* wherein Lewis tells of Carol Kennicott's stroll down the street after which the novel is named. A grocery is thus described:

Howland & Gould's Grocery. In the display window, black, overripe bananas and lettuce on which a cat was sleeping. Shelves lined with red crêpe paper which was now faded and torn and concentrically spotted. Flat against the wall of the second story the signs of lodges—the Knights of Pythias, the Maccabees, the Woodmen, the Masons.

In similar detail, for several pages, Lewis tells about building after building along the street—a total of twenty-five of them. The method is almost photographic in the multiplicity of descriptive touches used. The intention behind it, apparently, is to give such overwhelming documentation that the reader feels that the picture must be accurate.

Similarly, when Lewis records conversations, he sets down something close to a complete transcript: the repetitions of phrase and the peculiarities of expression seem to be mimicked to perfection. Consider this snatch of conversation between Babbitt and Littlefield, after Babbitt has brought up the subject of politics:

> "In my opinion, what the country needs, first and foremost, is a good, sound, business-like conduct of its affairs. What we need is—a business administration!" said Littlefield.
>
> "I'm glad to hear you say that! [said Babbitt] I certainly am glad to hear you say that! I didn't know how you'd feel about it with all your associations with colleges and so on, and I'm glad you feel that way. What the country needs—just at this present juncture—is neither a college president nor a lot of monkeying with foreign affairs, but a good—sound—economical—business—administration, that will give us a chance to have something like a decent turnover."

These monotonously repeated phrases and "thoughts" seem almost stenographic in their accuracy and their completeness.

Of course, there is selection even in such passages as these, and other authors who use this method are likely to be somewhat more selective than Lewis. The basis of the selection is the author's view of the scene or speech he is presenting. Lewis, for instance, gives an impression of the tawdriness, the dullness of Main Street in the first passage, and an impression of the unintellectual, standardized attitudes of Americans in the second. The abundant details are so chosen as to document amply each interpretation.

"Poetic" handling of detail, by contrast, is very highly selective, and although the details are likely to be literally accurate, they are also symbolically, i.e., poetically, significant—reminiscent not so much of Dreiser as of Stephen Crane and Frank Norris.

Willa Cather discusses the problem of detail in "The Novel Démeublé" (the unfurnished novel). She quotes approvingly Mérimée's dictum to the effect that the art of choosing from innumerable details is more important than attentive observation or exact rendition, and scoffs at the "popular superstition that 'realism' asserts itself in the cataloguing of a great number of material objects . . . and in minutely and unsparingly describing physical sensations." Balzac, she holds, failed as an artist insofar as he "tried out the value of literalness . . . to the uttermost." Tolstoy, by contrast, succeeded because he made the physical details "so much a part of the emotions of the people that they are perfectly synthesized." Hawthorne, too, used details sparsely but made all he used unobtrusively valuable to the mood of the story. Cather concludes:

> Whatever is felt upon the page without being specifically named there—

that, one might say, is created. It is the inexplicable presence of the thing not named, of the overtone divined by the ear but not heard by it, the verbal mood, the emotional aura of the fact or the thing or the deed, that gives high quality to the novel or the drama, as well as to poetry itself.

The implication, of course, is that the details in Willa Cather's novels should have an "emotional aura," an implicit value, comparable to that of the images in poetry.

Ernest Hemingway, although quite different from Cather in many respects, had similar theories about the handling of details. In all save one of his books (*To Have and Have Not*, 1937, in which he tried, with dubious success, to write like Dos Passos), Hemingway reduced descriptive detail to the minimum. His problem—the problem of all writers—as he saw it, consisted of "knowing what you truly felt, rather than what you were supposed to feel," and then setting down "the real thing, the sequence of motion and fact which made the emotion." Details, in other words, are primarily valuable to suggest the experiencing of feelings, and Hemingway believed that if these are stated "purely enough," they will be "valid . . . always." "All good books are alike," he has said, "in that they are truer than if they had really happened and after you are finished reading one you will feel that all that happened to you and afterwards it all belongs to you: the good and the bad, the ecstasy, the remorse and the sorrow, the people and the places and how the weather was. If you can get so you can give that to people, then you are a writer." Details, selected with the lyric skill necessary for such an achievement, ideally create what this author called "a fourth and a fifth dimension"—perhaps the prototype of Cather's "whatever is felt upon the page without being specifically named." The fact or the detail becomes a symbol, and Hemingway, like his master, the Mark Twain of *Huckleberry Finn*, achieved poetry in what appears to be matter-of-fact prose.

This may be seen in the opening paragraph of "In Another Country" (1927):

> In the fall the war was always there, but we did not go to it any more. It was cold in the fall in Milan and the dark came very early. Then the electric lights came on, and it was pleasant along the streets looking in the windows. There was much game hanging outside the shops, and the snow powdered in the fur of the foxes and wind blew their tails. The deer hung stiff and heavy and empty, and small birds blew in the wind and the wind turned their feathers. It was a cold fall and the wind came down from the mountains.

The paragraph is factual, but it differs from Lewis' description of Main Street in the nature of its details. Hemingway's sparse details are more than literal: they are symbolic. Poetically they stand for the "other countries" which lonely characters of the story sense but do not enter—that of battle from which their wounds have removed them, that of peace glimpsed through lighted windows from dark streets, that of nature symbolized by the game, and the country, finally, of death—connoted by the cold, the dark, and by the wind which blows from the mountains.

Poetic details comparable to those in the passage just quoted occur, as one would expect, in the writings of Willa Cather. They are to be found in Steinbeck and Wolfe (although both of these writers often employ the literal method characteristic of Lewis), in the packed long stories of Katherine Anne Porter, and in the poetic prose—at times interspersed with lyrics—of Jean Toomer. In fact, if a trend in the handling of detail is to be discovered in the modern period, it is a trend toward selectivity and poetic suggestion rather than exhaustive documentation. F. Scott Fitzgerald interestingly illustrates this trend: it can be seen very clearly when *This Side of Paradise* (1920), which is exhaustive in its handling of detail, is compared with *The Great Gatsby* (1925), which is more selective and lyrical. This change in method indicates the direction followed by many writers of the period.

Plot Patterns

Accepting the Nobel Prize in December 1930, Sinclair Lewis delivered an address, "The American Fear of Literature," in which he catalogued conservative criticisms of contemporaneous writers. Eugene O'Neill, for instance, who had transformed American drama "from a false world of neat and complete trickery to a world of splendor and fear and greatness," was criticized because "he has seen life as not to be neatly arranged in the study of a scholar but as a terrifying, magnificent, and often quite horrible thing akin to the tornado, the earthquake, the devastating fire." The description applies not only to this dramatist but also to a number of fiction writers. They, too, refused to arrange happenings in neat and complete patterns comparable to those in older fiction. It was this fact, probably, that Archibald Marshall had in mind when he accused the new fictionists of failing to tell a story. "There is no progress," he complained.

Like Marshall, readers accustomed to Victorian plots found that many modern novels, especially those of the twenties, bewilderingly departed from established narrative forms. Often novelists like Dreiser, whom many of the new novelists admired, were satisfied to write simply biographies of characters—sometimes from birth to death, sometimes from day to day over a shorter but not particularly exciting period. Such biographies often tell of characters who do not change: like picaresque figures they merely do various things and meet a series of people. Marshall used as an example Carol Kennicott in *Main Street*, who, he said, "remains at the end much as she was at the beginning." "And her successive revolts," he added, "have little dramatic quality in them." Similarly, in *Babbitt, Arrowsmith, Elmer*

Gantry, Dodsworth, and other novels, as Carl Van Doren notices, Lewis "employs an easy arrangement nearer chronicle than drama." James T. Farrell and Thomas Wolfe also use such arrangements as are supplied by apparently unmanipulated biography, continuing their biographies through several volumes. In *All the King's Men* by Robert Penn Warren, the narrative thread is the biography of the demagogic chief character, Willie Stark.

John Dos Passos used a similar technique in *Three Soldiers,* but he complicated his story element by unfolding, simultaneously, several biographical chronicles—moving briskly and without transitions from one to the other. His *Manhattan Transfer,* as Professor J. W. Beach remarks in *American Fiction, 1920–1940,* "is a picture of chaos, moral and social; and the narrative technique corresponds to the theme. Each chapter is a loose bundle of incidents from the lives of many different persons or groups, anywhere from four or sixteen in number, completely unrelated save in time and their common involvement in the chaos of Manhattan." *U.S.A.* does much the same thing with a broader picture screen, the entire nation, as a background. The biographies of twelve people, scattered from the East to the West Coast, are presented in fragmentary parts. These people encounter many characters who move into and out of their lives. In addition, at intervals, "Newsreels," "The Camera Eye," and biographies of leading public figures are interspersed. The "Newsreels" present impressionistic pictures of the nation of the day. The "Camera Eye" passages offer stream-of-consciousness interpretations. The brief biographies show, with selected details, the lives of leaders in ways which emphasize the trends of the times. These thumbnail biographical accounts are comparable, as a result, to the biographies of major characters, although their parts are drawn together—are not separated by stretches of narrative.

But there are many modern narratives, nevertheless, which do show developments, developments which occur when the characters learn something—discover something. Faulkner's narratives often show a discovery of the terrible in human existence. "A Rose for Emily" (1930), although comparatively uncomplicated, shows the method in miniature, for it tells how the villagers learn, detail by detail, of the horror of Miss Emily Grierson's life. Sometimes it is not the characters so much as the readers who make the discovery. *The Sound and the Fury* (1929), for example, one of Faulkner's best works, follows a jumbled plan, even as to time, which is justifiable largely because it makes such an unfolding possible. The order and relationships of happenings are further obscured because the story is told as it is seen not by one character but by three characters, in turn, and then by the author. But the result of the whole procedure is a parading of various fragments which finally cease to be disconnected and become, instead, interrelated parts of a terrible picture. The discovery, therefore, takes place in the mind of the reader rather than in that of anyone in the story. Faulkner uses similar schemes—in eventual effect, at any rate—in other narratives.

The plot of discovery may be useful, of course, for affirmative as well as negative fictional works. Willa Cather often shows characters seeking and finding satisfactory self-fulfillment—the artist in *Song of the Lark*, the pioneer in *My Ántonia*, the soldier in *One of Ours*, the intellectual in *The Professor's House*, religious men in *Death Comes for the Archbishop*. When, in the latter part of the 1930's, fiction writers (like writers in other fields) began to forsake critical attacks in favor of positive preachments, this pattern tended to be prevalent.

Hemingway marks this transition. His story "The Killers" (1927) shows the youthful Nick apprehending some of the terror of the world—apprehending ruthlessness and violence, not through books and motion pictures but through first-hand experiences. Hemingway's earlier novels (*The Sun Also Rises*, 1926, and *A Farewell to Arms*, 1929) and various short stories show characters making discoveries, usually of such a primitive sort that they indicate not the rehabilitation of human values so much as their disintegration. The chief characters in *To Have and Have Not* and *For Whom the Bell Tolls* (1940) find a social faith. The simple fisherman in *The Old Man and the Sea* (1952) finds fulfillment even in defeat. Increasingly, as the United States moved toward World War II, and affirmations became more important for some novelists than attacks, fictional narratives tended to show similar discoveries—in Lewis' *Work of Art* (1934) and *It Can't Happen Here* (1935), in Steinbeck's *The Grapes of Wrath* (1939), and in Wolfe's *You Can't Go Home Again* (1940). In the later part of the period, nevertheless, as in the earlier, the plots of discovery served admirably for the development of the authors' ideas.

Characterization and Psychology

From the beginning, authors of fiction have had certain limited ways of characterizing—showing the characteristics of the people about whose lives they wrote: they could comment upon them, describe their physical backgrounds and their outward appearance, tell of their actions or of their thoughts, set forth their conversations or the conversations of others about them. During the interwar period, fictionists did not manage to hit upon any new devices, but in various ways they manipulated and modified the older ones. One older device tended to disappear altogether: the comment of the author upon the characters. Fearful of appearing to moralize, and dubious, as a matter of fact, about their ability to state positive values, the authors in these years tended to drop out of their stories and to become relatively dramatic—objective—in their characterization. Description, too, was used less frequently as a characterizing device, although some authors (as has been suggested) continued to rely upon detailed description of background and physical appearance. For the most part, however, modern fiction writers depended for characterization upon the presentation of the words, deeds, and thoughts of their characters.

The handling of these characters was shaped largely by the science of psychology, which, as has been stated, was of great importance in modern fiction. Seemingly, like Henry James before them, modern authors found central to their writing problem the selection of a fictional point of view—the kind of insight or insights they as authors were to have into the minds of their characters. And, of course, the statement of the insights was determined by the authors' concepts of psychology. Sherwood Anderson, for instance, was strongly influenced by the Freudian concept of human behavior, and stories in *Winesburg, Ohio,* his most famous collection, almost all dealt with complexes or phobias.

Hemingway, in some of his writings, seemed to follow the lead suggested by behavioristic psychologists when they scoffed at the scientific value of studying "consciousness" and urged, instead, the observation of human behavior. Often, Hemingway merely set down remarks and actions of the characters, or, as he put it, "what really happens in action"—but he left to be inferred what the characters were feeling or thinking. "The Killers" is a perfect example, set forth as it is without a single glimpse into its characters' thoughts: it has the dramatic objectivity of a play. "In Another Country," though a first-person narrative, holds to a minimum the unfolding of the narrator's thoughts. When such a technique is used, whether Hemingway's characters are sophisticates or prizefighters, the subtle nuances of their thoughts and feelings—exactly the things with which Henry James was chiefly concerned—are not and cannot be presented. When he wrote these stories Hemingway's belief, apparently, was that such subtleties are relatively unimportant—that the primitive and universal emotions related to physical pleasure or pain are those most significant both in life and in art. Hence Hemingway, at times, has been classified as a "primitivist."

Steinbeck, too, was often a primitivist in his psychology. He tended, as Edmund Wilson noticed in *The Boys in the Back Room* (1941), "to present life in animal terms," to deal "either with the lower animals or with human beings so rudimentary that they are almost on the animal level." In consequence, as Wilson says, "The chief subject of Mr. Steinbeck's fiction has been . . . not those aspects of humanity in which it is most thoughtful, imaginative, constructive, nor even those aspects of animals that seem most attractive to humans, but rather the processes of life itself. . . . And it is only, as a rule, on this primitive level that Mr. Steinbeck deals with moral questions: the virtues like the crimes for Mr. Steinbeck are still a part of . . . planless and almost aimless, of . . . almost unconscious, processes of life." Even the psychology of labor movements, as this author saw it, was animallike. Striking fruitpickers became "groupmen," and a character describes them: "It was like all of them disappeared, and it was just one big animal, going down the road. Just all one animal. . . ."

The somewhat similar psychological technique employed by Dos Passos

also might well have stemmed from the psychological theories of the be-
haviorists, which tend to reduce action to two elements, stimuli and
responses. His vast collection of human beings, though varied, seems (as Professor Beach suggests) to be capable of only a few responses to basic stimuli. "The presence of a given organism within the field of vision provokes the
response of 'love'; discomfort drives one to a more comfortable attitude; a
feeling of emptiness provokes boredom and sets one on the track of entertainment and novelty; a business opportunity releases effort and ambition."
Dos Passos' human beings are comparable to laboratory mice which react
one way when a bell rings, another way when a light flashes.

This brand of psychology tends to make characterization less subtle in
interwar fiction than it had been in the older fiction. In some instances, by
contrast, twentieth-century psychological concepts tend to make characterization rather more complex. Freud and his various followers made authors
aware of the complexity of human motives and of the strangely illogical
processes of the subconscious. Some writers tried to reproduce these complicated mental processes by the stream-of-consciousness technique—
recording the strange digressions and the random associations taking place
in the minds of their characters. In *The Sound and the Fury*, Faulkner, using the "floating point of view" described earlier, records different happenings as they occur in the thoughts—both conscious and unconscious—of a
series of characters. Katherine Anne Porter, in a number of outstanding
stories—for example, "Flowering Judas" (1930)—has focused upon the
happenings by showing the thoughts a leading character has about them.
Hemingway, in some of the most important passages of *A Farewell to
Arms*, *To Have and Have Not*, and *For Whom the Bell Tolls*, momentarily
departs from his characteristic dramatic method when he uses the stream-
of-consciousness technique to tell what thoughts and fragments of thoughts
are running through his characters' minds. And Wolfe, when he tells what a
leading character is thinking, often employs poetic prose suggestive of both
thought and emotion.

Such are some of the varied methods of characterization which were
suggested to interwar fictionists by psychology. Psychological insights
characteristic of the period have had, as we have seen, profound effects
upon the form of drama (notably expressionistic drama), upon the form of
poetry, and upon the forms of novels and stories.

W.B.

Chronological Table of
LITERATURE AND HISTORY

1914 ● Theodore Dreiser's *The Titan* · Robert Frost's *North of Boston* · Vachel
Lindsay's *The Congo and Other Poems* · Amy Lowell's *Sword Blades and
Poppy Seed* · Eugene O'Neill's *Thirst and Other One Act Plays*

World War I began in Europe, 1 August · Panama Canal opened · Federal Trade
Commission established

1915 ● Willa Cather's *The Song of the Lark* · Dreiser's *The "Genius"* · Edgar Lee
Masters' *Spoon River Anthology*

The Provincetown Players, Washington Square Players, and The Playhouse
established · *Lusitania* sunk by German submarine, 7 May, with loss of American lives

1916 ● Sherwood Anderson's *Windy McPherson's Son* · Frost's *Mountain Interval* ·
Robinson Jeffers' *Californians* · Lindsay's *A Handy Guide for Beggars* ·
O'Neill's *Bound East for Cardiff* · Edwin Arlington Robinson's *The Man
Against the Sky* · Carl Sandburg's *Chicago Poems* · Mark Twain's *The Mysteri-
ous Stranger*

Woodrow Wilson reelected President

1917 ● Anderson's *Marching Men* · T. S. Eliot's *Prufrock and Other Observations* ·
Hamlin Garland's *A Son of the Middle Border* · Lindsay's *The Chinese Nightingale and Other Poems* · Robinson's *Merlin*

Germany began unrestricted submarine warfare, 1 February · United States
severed diplomatic relations with Germany, 2 February; declared war, 6 April ·
Czar Nicholas of Russia abdicated, 15 March, and Bolshevists under Lenin
assumed power

1918 ● Stephen Vincent Benét's *Young Adventure* · Cather's *My Ántonia* · Sandburg's *Cornhuskers* · *The Education of Henry Adams,* privately printed in 1907,
made available to public and became a best seller

Wilson outlined Fourteen Points for peace, 8 January · Russia made separate
peace with Central Powers in treaty of Brest-Litovsk, 3 March · Kaiser Wilhelm
abdicated, German Republic proclaimed, 9 November · Armistice signed, 11
November

1919 ● Anderson's *Winesburg, Ohio* · Irving Babbitt's *Rousseau and Romanticism* ·
H. L. Mencken's *Prejudices* (first series) and *The American Language* · O'Neill's
The Moon of the Caribbees, and Six Other Plays

Communist International (Comintern) organized in Russia · Benito Mussolini
organized Italian Fascist movement · Treaty of Versailles signed but rejected
by United States Senate · Eighteenth amendment, prohibiting liquor traffic,
ratified

1920 ● Anderson's *Poor White* · Benét's *Heavens and Earth* · Clarence Day's *This Simian World* · John Dos Passos' *One Man's Initiation—1917* · Eliot's *The Sacred Wood* · F. Scott Fitzgerald's *This Side of Paradise* · Sinclair Lewis' *Main Street* · O'Neill's *Beyond the Horizon* · Robinson's *Lancelot* · Sandburg's *Smoke and Steel*

League of Nations established at Geneva, Switzerland · Warren G. Harding elected twenty-ninth President · Transcontinental airmail service and commercial radio broadcasting initiated · United States census: population 105,710,620

1921 ● Anderson's *The Triumph of the Egg* · Dos Passos' *Three Soldiers* · O'Neill's *The Emperor Jones*

Washington Conference for the Limitation of Armament opened · First restrictive immigration act initiated the quota system

1922 ● Benét's *Young People's Pride* · Eliot's *The Waste Land* · Fitzgerald's *The Beautiful and Damned* · Lewis' *Babbitt* · O'Neill's *Anna Christie* and *The Hairy Ape*

Mussolini and the Fascist Party took over the government of Italy · Russian government organized as the Union of Socialist Soviet Republics · Nineteenth amendment, guaranteeing women suffrage, declared constitutional

1923 ● Anderson's *Many Marriages* and *Horses and Men* · Cather's *A Lost Lady* · Frost's *New Hampshire* · Robinson's *Roman Bartholow* · Wallace Stevens' *Harmonium*

President Harding died, 2 August; Calvin Coolidge became thirtieth President

1924 ● Kenneth Burke's *The White Oxen* · Eliot's *Homage to John Dryden* · Ernest Hemingway's *In Our Time: Stories* · Jeffers' *Tamar and Other Poems* · Herman Melville's *Billy Budd, Foretopman* first published

Coolidge elected to full term as President

1925 ● Anderson's *Dark Laughter* · Cather's *The Professor's House* · Dos Passos' *Manhattan Transfer* · Dreiser's *An American Tragedy* · Fitzgerald's *The Great Gatsby* · Jeffers' *Roan Stallion* · Lewis' *Arrowsmith*

John T. Scopes found guilty of violating Tennessee state law forbidding teaching the theory of evolution

1926 ● Cather's *My Mortal Enemy* · Hart Crane's *White Buildings* · William Faulkner's *Soldiers' Pay* · Hemingway's *The Sun Also Rises* and *The Torrents of Spring* · O'Neill's *The Great God Brown* · Sandburg's *Abraham Lincoln: The Prairie Years*

Germany admitted to League of Nations

1927 ● Cather's *Death Comes for the Archbishop* · Faulkner's *Mosquitoes* · Hemingway's *Men Without Women* · Jeffers' *The Women at Point Sur* · Lewis' *Elmer Gantry* · O'Neill's *Marco Millions* and *Lazarus Laughed* · Robinson's *Tristram* · Sandburg's *The American Songbag*

Charles A. Lindbergh made first solo nonstop flight from New York to Paris

1928 ● Benét's *John Brown's Body* · Eliot's *For Lancelot Andrewes* · Frost's *West-Running Brook* · Jeffers' *Cawdor and Other Poems* · O'Neill's *Strange Interlude* · Sandburg's *Good Morning, America* · Allen Tate's *Mr. Pope and Other Poems*

Herbert Hoover elected thirty-first President · Kellogg-Briand Peace Pact to outlaw wars signed by fifteen nations in Paris; eventually sixty-two nations signed · Amelia Earhart became first woman to fly the Atlantic

1929 ● Faulkner's *Sartoris* and *The Sound and the Fury* · Hemingway's *A Farewell to Arms* · Jeffers' *Dear Judas and Other Poems* · Lewis' *Dodsworth* · Robinson's *Cavender's House* · James Thurber and E. B. White's *Is Sex Necessary?* · Thomas Wolfe's *Look Homeward, Angel: A Story of the Buried Life*

Postwar prosperity ended with stock-market crash, 29 October, the beginning of the Great Depression

1930 ● Crane's *The Bridge* · Dos Passos' *The 42nd Parallel* · Eliot's *Ash-Wednesday* · Faulkner's *As I Lay Dying* · Twelve Authors (the Southern Agrarians), *I'll Take My Stand: The South and the Agrarian Tradition*

Sinclair Lewis became the first American to win the Nobel Prize in Literature · United States census: population 122,775,046

1931 ● Anderson's *Perhaps Women* · Burke's *Counter-Statement* · Cather's *Shadows on the Rock* · Faulkner's *Sanctuary* · O'Neill's *Mourning Becomes Electra* · Lincoln Steffens' *Autobiography* · Thurber's *The Owl in the Attic* · Edmund Wilson's *Axel's Castle*

King Alfonso XIII forced to leave Spain; a republic was proclaimed

1932 ● Anderson's *Beyond Desire* · Day's *God and My Father* · Dos Passos' *1919* · Faulkner's *Light in August* · Lillian Hellman's *The Children's Hour* · Hemingway's *Death in the Afternoon* · Jeffers' *Thurso's Landing and Other Poems*

Congress authorized establishment of Reconstruction Finance Corporation (RFC) to aid railroads and financial institutions affected by the depression · Franklin Delano Roosevelt elected thirty-second President

1933 ● Hemingway's *Winner Take Nothing* · Jeffers' *Give Your Heart to the Hawks and Other Poems* · Lewis' *Ann Vickers* · O'Neill's *Ah, Wilderness!* · Robinson's *Talifer*

Hitler became Chancellor of Germany · Roosevelt inaugurated numerous measures to relieve severe economic distress: National Industrial Recovery Act (NRA), Agricultural Adjustment Act (AAA), Civilian Conservation Corps (CCC), Tennessee Valley Authority (TVA) · Japan signified intent to withdraw from the League of Nations · Prohibition amendment repealed

1934 ● Lewis' *Work of Art* · O'Neill's *Days Without End*

Securities Exchange Act (establishing SEC), Home Owners' Loan Act (HOLC) enacted for recovery from depression · Hitler combined presidency and chancellorship of Germany and assumed title of "Der Fuehrer"

1935 ● Burke's *Permanence and Change—Anatomy of Purpose* · Cather's *Lucy Gay-heart* · Day's *Life with Father* · Eliot's *Murder in the Cathedral* · Jeffers' *Solstice and Other Poems* · Lewis' *It Can't Happen Here* · Robinson's *King Jasper* · John Steinbeck's *Tortilla Flat* · Stevens' *Ideas of Order* · Wolfe's *Of Time and the River*

Works Projects Administration (WPA), National Youth Administration (NYA) set up to provide "work relief" · NRA declared unconstitutional · Social Security Act passed · Committee for Industrial Organization (CIO) founded · Italian forces invaded Ethiopia · German rearmament begun

1936 ● Faulkner's *Absalom, Absalom!* · Frost's *A Further Range* · Sandburg's *The People, Yes* · Steinbeck's *In Dubious Battle* · Stevens' *Owl's Clover* · Robert Penn Warren's *Thirty-six Poems*

AAA declared unconstitutional · King George V of England died; his eldest son, Edward VIII, succeeded, but abdicated, and was in turn succeeded by George VI · German troops began to occupy the Rhineland, defying treaty agreement · Revolt against Spanish Republican Government began; many Americans supported the anti-Franco Loyalists · Roosevelt reelected President

1937 ● Benét's *The Devil and Daniel Webster* · Dos Passos' *The Big Money* · Heming-way's *To Have and Have Not* · Jeffers' *Such Counsels You Gave to Me and Other Poems* · Steinbeck's *Of Mice and Men* · Stevens' *The Man with the Blue Guitar and Other Poems* · Thurber's *Let Your Mind Alone*

Japan invaded China and occupied both Peiping and Shanghai · Roosevelt signed Neutrality Act prohibiting export of arms to belligerent nations

1938 ● Benét's *Johnny Pye and the Fool-Killer* · Faulkner's *The Unvanquished* · Hemingway's *The Fifth Column and the First Forty-nine Stories* · Lewis' *The Prodigal Parents* · Steinbeck's *The Long Valley* · Wilson's *The Triple Thinkers* · Richard Wright's *Uncle Tom's Children*

Hitler invaded Austria, 11 March; German-Austrian union (Anschluss) pro-claimed two days later · Prime Minister Neville Chamberlain of Britain signed a "Peace Declaration" with Hitler at Munich, yielding to Nazi demands that Czechoslovakia cede the Sudetenland to Germany; Czechoslovakia subsequent-ly partitioned among Germany, Hungary, and Poland · House Committee to Investigate Un-American Activities formed

1939 ● Dos Passos' *Adventures of a Young Man* · Eliot's *The Idea of a Christian So-ciety* · Faulkner's *The Wild Palms* · Katherine Anne Porter's *Pale Horse, Pale Rider* · Sandburg's *Abraham Lincoln: The War Years* · Steinbeck's *The Grapes of Wrath* · Warren's *Night Rider* · Wolfe's *The Web and the Rock*

Franco completed conquest of Spain · Germany and Italy announced military and political alliance · Germany and Soviet Russia signed ten-year nonaggres-sion pact · Germany attacked Poland, 1 September · Britain and France declared war on Germany, 3 September · Prohibition of arms export repealed in special session of Congress, 4 November · Russia invaded Finland, 30 November

1940 ● Cather's *Sapphira and the Slave Girl* · Faulkner's *The Hamlet* · Hemingway's *For Whom the Bell Tolls* · Lewis' *Bethel Merriday* · Carson McCullers' *The Heart is a Lonely Hunter* · Mencken's *Happy Days, 1880-1892* · Thurber's *The*

Male Animal (with Elliott Nugent) · Wolfe's *You Can't Go Home Again*
German armies swept across Europe, conquering Holland, Belgium, and France
· Winston Churchill replaced Chamberlain as Prime Minister of Britain · Italy
and Germany invaded Greece · First peacetime conscription inaugurated in the
United States, 29 October · Roosevelt elected President for third term · United
States pledged aid to Britain "short of war" · United States census: population
131,669,275

1941 ● Burke's *The Philosophy of Literary Form* · Dos Passos' *The Ground We
Stand On* · Fitzgerald's *The Last Tycoon* · McCullers' *Reflections in a Golden
Eye* · Mencken's *Newspaper Days, 1899-1906* · Steinbeck's *Sea of Cortez*
(with E. F. Ricketts) · Wilson's *The Boys in the Back Room* and *The Wound
and the Bow*

Congress passed the Lend-Lease Act by which U.S. could lend goods to democratic countries in return for services · Russia and Japan signed a five-year
neutrality treaty, 13 April · German troops invaded Russia, 22 June · Atlantic
Charter announced, 14 August · Pearl Harbor attacked by Japan, 7 December;
Japanese troops simultaneously occupied Guam and Wake Island and landed
in the Philippines · United States declared war on Japan, 8 December · Germany and Italy declared war on the United States, 11 December · United
States declared war on Germany and Italy, 13 December

1942 ● Frost's *A Witness Tree* · Marion Hargrove's *See Here, Private Hargrove* ·
Randall Jarrell's *Blood for a Stranger* · Karl Shapiro's *Person, Place, and Thing*
· Steinbeck's *The Moon is Down* and *Bombs Away* · Stevens' *Parts of a World*
Thurber's *My World—and Welcome to It* · Eudora Welty's *The Robber Bride-
groom*

Declaration of the United Nations issued, 1 January · Last American troops
defeated in the Philippines, 6 May · Japanese invasion fleet turned back at Midway Island, 4-7 June, an important American victory · American and Australi-
an troops began offensive, establishing bases in New Guinea and on Guadalcanal
in the Solomon Islands · Women's Army, Naval, and Coast Guard units formed

1943 ● Dos Passos' *Number One* · Eliot's *Four Quartets* · Lewis' *Gideon Planish* ·
Mencken's *Heathen Days, 1890-1936* · Ernie Pyle's *Here Is Your War* ·
Thurber's *Men, Women, and Dogs* · Wendell Willkie's *One World*

Dwight D. Eisenhower chosen as supreme commander for attack on Italy ·
Russia announced destruction of German army of 300,000, encircled at Stalin-
grad since November · Allies occupied Tunis and Bizerte, last Axis positions in
North Africa, and from there conquered Sicily · Mussolini resigned and Pietro
Badoglio, his successor, signed armistice, 3 September; Allies landed on Italian
mainland · Roosevelt, Churchill, and Chiang Kai-shek conferred at Cairo,
Egypt, 21-26 November, agreeing that postwar Korea should be independent ·
Roosevelt, Churchill, and Stalin conferred at Teheran, Iran, 22 November-2
December, where they agreed upon future war operations

1944 ● Dos Passos' *State of the Nation* · John Hersey's *A Bell for Adano* · Robert
Lowell's *Land of Unlikeness* · Porter's *The Leaning Tower* · Shapiro's *V-Letter
and Other Poems* · Jean Stafford's *Boston Adventure*

Allied invasion of Western Europe began, 6 June (D-Day), with landings in Normandy; Eisenhower was supreme commander · American troops returned to Guam, 20 July · Paris liberated, 29 August · Germany invaded from the west, 12 September · American troops returned to the Philippines, landing on Leyte, 19 October · Roosevelt elected for fourth term as President

1945 ● Benét's *Western Star* · Gwendolyn Brooks' *A Street in Bronzeville* · Burke's *A Grammar of Motives* · Frost's *A Masque of Reason* · Jarrell's *Little Friend, Little Friend* · Mencken's *The American Language, Supplement One* · Shapiro's *Essay on Rime* · Steinbeck's *Cannery Row* · Wright's *Black Boy*

Roosevelt, Churchill, and Stalin conferred at Yalta, in the Crimea, discussing postwar policies, 4-11 February · Roosevelt died, 12 April; Harry S Truman became thirty-third President · Death of Hitler announced, 1 May · Germany surrendered unconditionally, 7 May (V-E Day) · Truman, Churchill, and Stalin, with their foreign ministers, conferred at Potsdam, 17 July-2 August, providing for occupation of Germany, reparations, and procedure for peace treaties · Charter of the United Nations issued by the San Francisco conference · Atomic bomb dropped on Hiroshima, Japan, 6 August · Unconditional surrender of Japan announced by President Truman, 14 August (V-J Day)

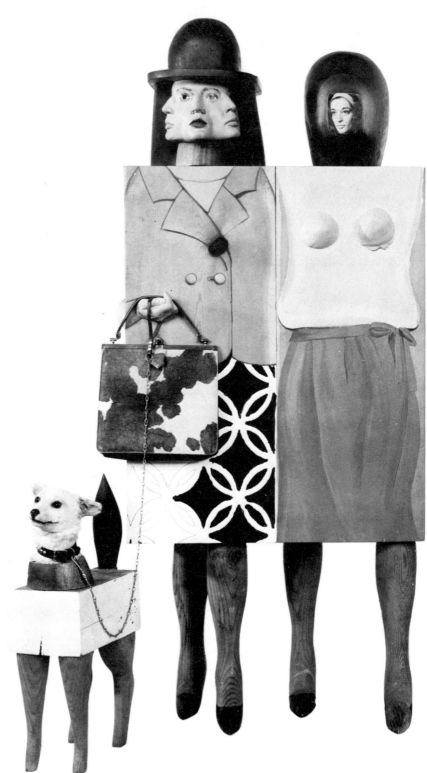

"Women and Dog," sculpture by Marisol of wood, plaster, synthetic polymer paint and miscellaneous items.

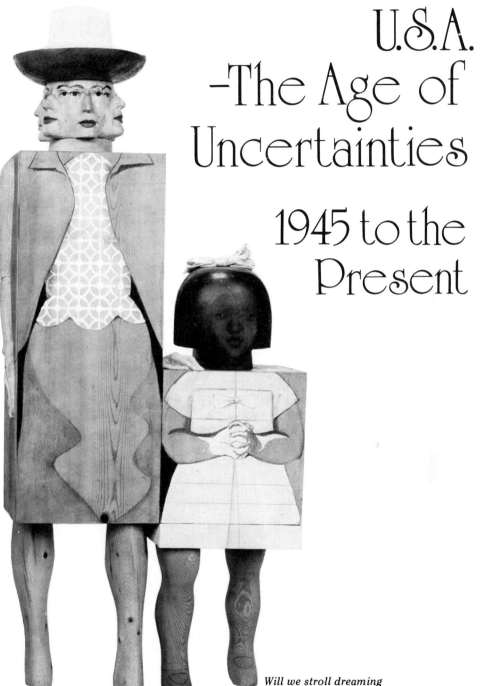

CHAPTER 6

U.S.A.
-The Age of
Uncertainties

1945 to the
Present

Will we stroll dreaming
  past the lost America of love
  past blue automobiles in driveways,
  home to our silent cottage?
                    —Allen Ginsberg

Intellectual Currents

The Impact of World War II

The outbreak of war in Europe in 1939, our Lend-Lease to Britain and to Russia, and our own entrance into the war following Japan's surprise attack on Pearl Harbor in December 1941 had the effect of stepping up American production. In what turned out to be a war for survival, criticism of capitalism, so common in the depression years, all but disappeared. American technological know-how was applied to the logistic problems of global war. Out of American factories rolled the airplanes, the tanks, the guns and ammunition necessary to wage war in remote corners of the world; from American farms, which were becoming more and more mechanized, came much of the food which supplied the Allied armies. Eventually the power of the Nazis, who had occupied the greater part of Western Europe, was broken, and the Japanese were pushed back from the islands of the western and southern Pacific, the Philippines, and Malaya. The fighting ended in Europe on May 8, 1945, and in the Pacific, except for scattered pockets of resistance, on August 14, 1945.

Like most wars, World War II settled some issues but raised others in their place. The Nazi concept of a Europe ruled by a superior race, with its horrifying anti-Semitism and its bland assumption that the end justified any means, was effectually destroyed, as was the Japanese dream of a vast Asian and Pacific empire. It soon became evident, however, that the United States was going to have to worry for a long time over four questions, which may be stated as follows:

(1) What is to be done with "The Bomb," as we have come to call the vast complex of possibilities, most of them frightening, which were opened up by the splitting of the atom?

(2) What is the best way to preserve constitutional or representative democracy in a world which has proven easy prey for dictators and which is in large part dominated by Marxist and collectivist convictions?

(3) What is to be the machinery for preserving peace among nations, in a world wherein time and space, thanks to incredibly swift transportation and communication, mean less than they ever have before?

(4) What, if the United States is to maintain its leadership and influence among those who believe in an open and free society, is to be done about its internal imperfections, those failures to square its practices with its theories which have persisted for generations?

These have been the major problems since World War II: the use of atomic energy, the cold war, the role and adequacy of the United Nations, and the persistence of racial strife. One needs only to read a newspaper to see that they are still with us, and that they are all still unsolved. Since these problems are probably responsible for most of the tensions observable in contemporary literature, their origins are worth recalling.

"The Bomb"

The first atomic bomb, a fission bomb, was exploded at Alamogordo, New Mexico, on July 14, 1945. Scientists of many nations other than the United States participated in the development of theoretical physics which lay behind nuclear fission, and there is every reason to believe that other nations would have built the Bomb (as Russia did later), no matter what happened in America. Americans, however, bear the responsibility for its first use in warfare. At Hiroshima on August 8, 1945, 79,000 persons died, and over 73,000 were killed at Nagasaki on the day following. Thousands more were horribly injured by the accompanying effects of radiation. President Truman, who made the decision, has said that the American use of the Bomb saved as many lives as it destroyed, for it brought an abrupt end to a war which might otherwise have dragged on for years. No historical event, however, has made the world at large more critical of the United States than this demonstration of what would almost certainly happen to civilian populations in the event of a third World War.

Nor is the Bomb, now the far more powerful fusion type, the only instrument which terrifies men and women today. New sources of power and ingenious electronic devices have made possible the construction of guided missiles, some with a range of thousands of miles and capable of delivering multiple atomic warheads anywhere on the earth. Others can be fired from beneath the surface of the ocean. The major nations now have arsenals and missile delivery systems that are able to reduce any great city on any continent to rubble within a short time.

The official American position has been that this arsenal is the chief deterrent against attack from Russia or any other possible enemy, and for ten years the superiority of American arms inspired widespread confidence. On October 4, 1957, however, the Russians launched into orbit the first earth satellite, Sputnik I. A painful reexamination of the American situation immediately followed. The American educational system came under scrutiny, especially as the Russians continued to score "firsts" in the developing space race. But some of the country's uneasiness was dispelled when, on July 20, 1969, America was the first country to land men on the moon and to bring back samples of the moon's crust.

Progress has been made in the use of the atom for peaceful aims and of space vehicles for weather prediction and communication. The development of technology in the last few decades, however, has unquestionably added to world-wide anxiety about the future. Can the instruments of death be destroyed or banned? Can the vast new sources of power be used to improve the human condition rather than to set the stage for a world-wide holocaust? These are questions which all Americans, and all thoughtful and informed men everywhere, continue to ask. Their effect upon the American psyche is well summed up by the central character in Steinbeck's *The Winter of Our Discontent* (1961):

> When a condition or a problem becomes too great, humans have the protection of not thinking about it. But it goes inward and minces up with a lot of other things already there and what comes out is discontent and uneasiness, guilt and a compulsion to get something—anything —before it is all gone. Maybe the assembly-line psychoanalysts aren't dealing with complexes at all but with those warheads that may one day be mushroom clouds.

Fear of the Bomb and distrust of a society which could allow its production are seen everywhere in contemporary literature, most conspicuously perhaps in the work of the "beats," the "hippies," and the "yippies," whose rejection of all values but those of sensation displays anti-intellectualism in a strength new to the American experience.

The Cold War

The rivalry between democracy and closed societies, such as that of Communism, is as old as political theory. In 1945, however, it took new shape. During the first week of February, Stalin, Churchill, and Roosevelt met in Yalta, in the Crimea. As a result of their conference, Russia entered the final phase of the war against Japan, with the promise of the strategic Kurile Islands and the restoration of the southern half of Sakhalin, lost to her at the end of the Russo-Japanese War of 1904–1905. The Yalta meeting immensely strengthened Stalin's hand in postwar settlements. The crucial decision, however, was made at Potsdam between July 17 and August 8. Stalin, Churchill, and Truman (Roosevelt had died on April 12) agreed to divide the occupation of Germany among Russia, Great Britain, France, and the United States. Russia was understandably anxious to protect herself by extending her sphere of influence to the west, and the democracies were determined to demilitarize a nation which twice in twenty-five years had destroyed the peace of the world. Before long, however, the one-time allies were battling over ideological issues.

The Russian plan unfolded as the extension of the Communist system by political methods, including infiltration and subversion. Communists took over the governments of Hungary, Rumania, and Poland in 1947, that of Czechoslovakia in 1948, and by 1949 were in control of the East German Democratic Republic and the People's Republic of China.

To this rapid spread of Communist influence the United States opposed an enormous foreign aid program, the pros and cons of which continue to be incessantly debated. Foreign aid began with the Truman Doctrine of 1947, under which military aid was sent to Greece and Turkey. In the same year the massive economic assistance of the Marshall Plan, which in a period of four years amounted to approximately twelve billion dollars, was offered to the free nations of Western Europe. In addition, the United States entered into elaborate military alliances in several parts of the world, most importantly under NATO (North Atlantic Treaty Organization, 1949) and SEATO (Southeast Asia Treaty Organization, 1954). By the 1970's, these alliances seemed to create as many problems as they solved.

As American military assistance was extended to various countries, and as American military bases multiplied around the world, America became more and more deeply involved in military actions. In the 1950's, the focus of action was Korea, in the 1960's, Vietnam. Both of these countries were torn into North and South, communist and anti-communist sectors. And in both countries America became more complexly enmeshed than it first imagined possible. Domestic critics began to refer to a "military-industrial complex" (a term first used by President Eisenhower in his farewell address) in the country that waxed fat on conflicts and brush-fire wars.

And complicating international relations even more was the growing antagonism between Russia and Red China. As the decade of the 70's arrived, the world appeared divided not into two but three armed and hostile camps, each nuclear armed—America, Russia, and China. The nightmare prophecy in 1948 by Englishman George Orwell's apocalyptic, anti-utopian novel, *1984*, seemed prematurely fulfilled. The possibility of a warmer international climate occurred in the early 1970's, however, when the United States and China resumed diplomatic relations after twenty-five years, and trade and nuclear ban treaties were made with the U.S.S.R.

The Instruments of Peace

From the early days of the Republic, scattered Americans have displayed an interest in the elimination of war through international cooperation. In 1799, for example, Dr. Benjamin Rush devised *A Plan of a Peace-Office for the United States*, one of whose purposes was to "subdue that passion for war, which education, added to human depravity, have made universal." In the nineteenth century, Elihu Burritt, a self-educated blacksmith, devoted his life to pacifist activities, proposing in *Olive Leaves* (1848) both a world congress and a world court for settling international disputes. The only alternative to these organizations that he saw was a world-wide strike of workingmen against any war—an idea he may have derived from the *Communist Manifesto*. Burritt organized a long series of world peace conferences; his example led Czar Nicholas II of Russia to call the Hague International Peace Conference. From that meeting came the International Court of Justice at The Hague, eventually housed in a building for which Andrew Carnegie donated $1,500,000. It provided a place for the arbitration of disputes among those nations which subscribed to the Hague Convention of 1899.

With these precedents, the League of Nations was conceived in 1920 as a part of the Treaty of Versailles. It incorporated the world court at The Hague as a part of its structure and, despite Woodrow Wilson's failure to convince the Senate that the United States should join, was a significant instrument of peace for nearly twenty years.

World War II appreciably lessened the isolationist sentiment among Americans, so that one of the chief war aims of the United States became the establishment of more effective international communication and control. The scheme for the United Nations was devised at the Dumbarton Oaks Conference in 1944, and the charter was adopted at San Francisco in June of 1945, with fifty nations participating. The organization began its work in the following October and in 1952 occupied its permanent headquarters on the East River in New York City. It has since been a major forum for the discussion of international problems. Its power has been enhanced by distinguished executive officers, notably Trygve Lie, Dag Hammarskjöld, and U Thant, and has on occasion deployed its own military forces. The Cuban blockade of 1962 and the later involvement in Vietnam showed that the United States was not willing to relinquish its right to unilateral action, but America has continued to support the fledgling organization in its quest for peace.

Many Americans are still critical of the form, the expense, and the possible effects of the United Nations, but a majority appears to believe that its work has been on the whole beneficial and that American participation is a necessary part of peaceful existence in the atomic age. Under United Nations auspices, the United States is at least taking its part in the effort to minimize international friction. The problems of a population explosion, in part the result of advances in medical science, and of the dislocation attendant upon technological change are world problems in which Americans are deeply involved.

A new sense of international responsibility is reflected in much contemporary literature and will continue to be: One of its results has been to arouse an intense interest in the United States and its literature throughout the free world. Programs of exchange of teachers and students, such as that devised by Senator Fulbright, have taken hundreds of Americans abroad to lecture and have interested thousands of young people, from West Germany to Japan and India, in American literature. The image of America is being conveyed by the nation's literary art more than ever before.

Internal Problems

The new internationalism, with its concern for the good opinion of the peoples of the less fortunate countries, has led Americans to an agonizing appraisal of their own internal problems. The greatest of these continues to be that of finding the best means of eliminating racial and economic oppression in a nation which prides itself on its democracy. Liberation movements have been launched for many minority groups, including the Indians, the Mexican-Americans (Chicanos), and women (though they are not a minority). But the most dramatic struggle for basic human rights has been waged by the blacks.

The generation following the Civil War thought it had settled the Negro question by the abolition of slavery and the adoption of the Fifteenth Amendment to the Constitution (1870), which asserted that "The right of citizens of the United States to vote shall not be denied or abridged by the United States or any State on account of race, color, or previous condition of servitude." The underlying conviction was that the right of suffrage would enable the Negroes to secure the fairness of treatment and equality of opportunity to which all citizens in a democracy are theoretically entitled.

The American Negroes made remarkable economic progress in the last decades of the nineteenth century. The Fifteenth Amendment, however, was circumvented in some states by literacy tests and poll taxes, and in cities where blacks voted they were often the victims of "machine" politics and unscrupulous political bosses. In time it became clear that suffrage was not the only civil right which the Negroes had been denied. As the social responsibility of government broadened, "Jim Crowism" or the segregation of the races in humiliating ways did not disappear. As Wallace Stegner has said in *One Nation*, Jim Crowism made the function of the Negro

> to do the dirtiest job, get the least pay, live in the poorest shacks, receive an inferior education, have the least protection from the law, and serve as a whipping boy when white men need one.

In the aftermath of World War II strong feelings about this situation stirred both whites and blacks. The white Americans were sensitive to the accusation that, while they roundly condemned the apartheid policy of the Union of South Africa, they permitted similar discriminatory practices in their own land. Blacks, on the other hand, felt more keenly the discrepancy between the official pronouncements of democratic society and the hard facts of discrimination—and they began to do more about it. They may, indeed, have gained a new sense of destiny from the upsurge of black nationalism in Africa, where since World War II a large number of the former colonies of France, Great Britain, and Belgium have become Negro republics.

The identification of the vast majority of American Negroes with the Christian church and with the aims and ambitions of democracy is probably an adequate safeguard against actual insurrection, but the unrest of recent times is the most remarkable feature of American social conflict. This unrest became apparent in the thirties when the pressure for municipal, state, and federal "fair employment" legislation began to be felt. Laws passed since then are meant to make sure that citizens are not discriminated against because of their race or religion. They forbid advertising that jobs are open to whites or Gentiles only, or that rental housing is not available to just anyone who is capable of paying for it, or that an employer requires an applicant for a position to provide a photograph of himself. The intent is to see that a man be judged on his merits, not on the color of his skin or on his faith. After World War II the National Association for the Advancement of Colored People, an organization founded in 1909, began to take a more militant position, particularly on the matter of educational segregation. Its legal battle for equal and unsegregated educational opportunities culminated in a unanimous decision of the Supreme Court in 1954, which declared racial segregation in American public schools unconstitutional. The persistence of Jim Crowism in bus terminals, lunch counters, and rest rooms was the prime concern of another organization, CORE (Congress of Racial Equality), a biracial group committed to improving the condition of Negroes by the technique of passive resistance. Protest against discrimination reached a climax in the summer of 1963, when all of the civil rights organizations joined to sponsor a national demonstration in the form of a march on Washington, D.C.

As discrimination continued and black poverty deepened in an increasingly affluent society, nonviolent protest gave way to aggressive militancy and eruptions of violence. Riots broke out in the long, hot summers—in 1965 in Watts (Los Angeles), in 1966 in Chicago and Cleveland, in 1967 in Cincinnati, Newark, and Detroit. In 1968, after the tragic assassination of the black apostle of nonviolence, Nobel Prize winner Rev. Martin Luther King, Jr., cities all over America witnessed rioting, burning, looting, and shooting.

Although the Civil Rights Bills of 1964 and 1965 were the strongest in the nation's history, they were not sufficient to ease the tensions. Racism is such a deep social sickness in America that more than laws are required for remedy. Black writers who "tell it like it is" will perhaps help find the cure. Ralph Ellison's *Invisible Man* (1952), James Baldwin's *The Fire Next Time* (1963), Malcolm X's *Autobiography* (1965), and Eldridge Cleaver's *Soul on Ice* (1968) are examples of works that have had wide social impact.

T.H.
J.M.

The Political Scene

Franklin D. Roosevelt's death on April 12, 1945, stunned the world, and elevated to the presidency of the United States, in the midst of World War II, a man relatively unknown—Harry S Truman. But though as vice-president he had been kept uninformed on the momentous secret and semi-secret war-time developments requiring executive decision, he quickly informed himself and began immediately a confrontation of some of the most vital events the country had ever faced—victory in Europe in May 1945, the formation of the United Nations in June, the dropping of the atomic bomb on Hiroshima in August, the surrender of Japan in September.

By comparison with these stirring events, the remainder of the Truman administration (1945–1952) seemed tame and uneventful. But there were some surprises from the unpredictable Missourian, most notably his election victory in 1948 over Thomas E. Dewey—the candidate, once defeated by Roosevelt, who seemed assured of victory by all the signs except the counted ballots. During the Truman era the United States became inextricably committed to global responsibilities, in many places, such as Greece and Turkey, taking over the role once assumed by the British. These responsibilities entailed the outlay of vast sums of money for economic and military aid, and in some cases the commitment of American troops. Such a case was South Korea, invaded by the North Koreans in 1950. Through the United Nations, the United States participated in this "brush fire" war until an uneasy armistice was signed in 1953.

The political campaign of 1952 was the first in twenty years that did not pit an incumbent Democrat against an out-of-office Republican. The Republican party deliberately and somewhat painfully passed over its favorite conservative spokesman, Senator Robert Taft, to nominate the popular General of the Armies, Dwight D. Eisenhower, as its candidate. The Democrats themselves had hoped that the General might turn out to be one of them. When he proved not to be, the Democratic convention nominated Adlai Stevenson, Governor of Illinois. The country's election of Eisenhower might have expressed its weariness of the Korean War, its objection to the petty scandals of the Truman administration, its distaste for the intellectual image of Adlai Stevenson, or its desire to relax under the leadership of the comforting father-image of Dwight Eisenhower.

Whatever the cause, the country settled back during the Eisenhower administration into a relaxed self-assurance that things were in good hands and that the status quo would prevail—at least for the time being. As during the war, when he brilliantly discharged his delicate responsibility of finding the area of agreement among the many and frequently conflicting allied forces, Eisenhower looked upon himself as a great moderator or compromiser. But he discovered that it was a role he could not always play—as, for example, in the McCarthy affair. No other incident so well characterizes the tone and temper of the early 1950's. Senator Joseph McCarthy, from Wisconsin, had early in his career discovered the political capital to be made out of attacking domestic communism everywhere, whether it really existed or not. His indiscriminate and reckless charges, hurtled forth from his safe senatorial immunity, created a kind of intellectual reign of terror that lasted until McCarthy over-extended himself in 1954 and took on in public combat (on television) the United States Army. Eisenhower remained aloof, the Senate censured McCarthy, and the problem finally went away. But the McCarthy era left many deep scars in American intellectual life.

Eisenhower's second term, which he won by repeating his victory over Adlai Stevenson, saw the launching of the space age—by the Russians. When the Soviet's first sputnik sailed into the sky in October, 1957, Americans, jolted out of their complacency and apathy, began in earnest to question their own capacities—their educational system, their industrial ingenuity, their government bureaus, their moral vitality. Although this self-reappraisal was agonizing, the atmosphere was far healthier than that of the McCarthy era, charged as it was with suspicion and fear.

Like the election of 1952, that of 1960 found neither candidate occupying the White House. But Richard Nixon, the Republican candidate, had been Eisenhower's vice-president for eight years. The Democratic candidate, John F. Kennedy, was the first Catholic to run for the presidency since the defeat of Al Smith by Herbert Hoover in 1928. Kennedy won the election by an extremely slender margin, and thus became not only the first Catholic President but also the first American President born in the twentieth century. There was nothing of nostalgia in the Kennedy style, but there was vigorous engagement with the present and a strong pull to the future. His most notable and characteristic achievement was the signing of the nuclear test ban treaty with Russia in 1963. Kennedy's assassination in Dallas, Texas, on November 22, 1963, shocked people everywhere. His youth and unfulfilled promise, and the meaninglessness of the act, committed by an unstable youth named Lee Harvey Oswald, deepened America's grief and sense of loss.

Lyndon B. Johnson had been chosen by Kennedy as his running mate in part because he was a Texan who might help hold the South for the Democrats. Kennedy's death thus brought the first Southerner to the White House since before the Civil War. On assuming office, Johnson pledged continuation of Kennedy's policies, including his support for the important Civil Rights program. His long experience in Congress and as Senate majority leader served him well in securing the passage of legislation for this and other Democratic programs. Unopposed in his own party as the presidential candidate in the 1964 election, he faced Barry Goldwater, the conservative Republican candidate, who had won his nomination over more liberal Republican opposition. Goldwater's electoral defeat was the greatest since that suffered by Alfred M. Landon in 1936.

As rioting became commonplace in cities and on campuses, partly in protest against discrimination and poverty, but also in rebellion against the increasing involvement in Vietnam, Johnson was obliged to renounce a second term. The scramble for the Democratic nomination saw the sensational, if temporary, success of Eugene McCarthy, who campaigned vigorously against American involvement in Vietnam; and the tragic assassination of New York Senator Robert Kennedy, brother of the slain President. The election pitted Vice-President Hubert Humphrey against former Vice-President Richard Nixon, with Alabaman George Wallace running as a third-party candidate. In one of the greatest comebacks in political history, Richard Nixon became President of a disturbed, divided, and uncertain country in 1969.

The Social Scene

Life off the political stage, far removed from the daily headlines, had its own distinctive flavor, notably different from the life of the pre-World War II period. The world-shaking events that took place on center stage and crowded the headlines had a way of sinking deeply into the modern consciousness and abiding there as a kind of imprisoned spectre, haunting the imagination and chilling the conscience, deforming the perspective and paralyzing the will. Some of these numbing events were the creation and use of the atomic bomb in 1945, the explosion of the hydrogen bomb in 1953, and the launching of the first man-made satellite in 1957. In effect these events were made possible by man's penetration into both the micro- and macrocosmic worlds, areas previously visited only by the poet's vivid imagination. But the scientist's penetration released powers undreamed of by the poet, powers with potential destructiveness that seemed Godlike— or Satanic.

The events themselves were rarely the direct subject of literature, perhaps because of their unbelievable, even melodramatic quality. There were exceptions, of course, such as John Hersey's *Hiroshima* (1946) or Karl Shapiro's "The Progress of Faust" (1947), in which Faustus turned up in his latest manifestation

to pose
In an American desert at war's end
Where, at his back, a dome of atoms rose.

But the cataclysmic events were more usually reflected in literature indirectly, in their subtle effects on human feeling and human behavior. After World War II, in the Atomic Age, in the Hydrogen Age, in the Space Age— in the Age of Anxiety, Absurdity, or Anguish—man's sense of identification with the future was undermined, his belief in the richness of his possibilities diminished. Perhaps his plight can best be summed up by his loss of identity. Sometime in his past, within memory, he had known who he was; but his doubts had multiplied, until now, in the second half of the twentieth century, his uncertainty had become acute.

All of the forces in the culture seemed joined in a conspiracy to deprive man of his humanity, to shrivel into insignificance the vital *selfhood* of the individual. There were immense pressures enforcing *conformity* to a mass society, there were glacial pressures that seemed gradually to *dehumanize* the individual, and there were invisible pressures which *alienated* man from his own kind, setting him off apart and alone. *Conformity, dehumanization, alienation*—these terms suggested some of the most alarming aspects of life in the United States in the 1950's, '60's, and '70's. For what consolation it might afford, the resulting moral paralysis was not solely the dilemma of the United States but the concern of modern man everywhere.

Conformity

In the years since 1900, America had ceased to be a society divided into rural and urban elements and had become in essence a vast suburban society, in which all the empty space between cities was gradually being filled with development or "project" houses on interminable stretches of occupied, usually deforested land in which the keynote was *sameness*— sameness in homes, incomes, dress, interests, and ideas. In the homes lived organization men who had long since signed away their primary emotional loyalty to the company or corporation or institution or bureau into which they fitted and to which they offered their daily devotion, and for which they expended all of their vital energy. Clearly the age was an age of affluence, in which wealth went to the man who best became a cog in the well-oiled, smoothly purring machine. Organization men lived comfortable lives surrounded by all the endless satisfactions of suburbia. But strange though it was, the fuller the life appeared, the emptier it seemed to become—especially to the man of thought and perception.

Dehumanization

As man explored more deeply the nature of the minutest particle of matter, and at the same time began sorties out into space to discover the nature of the planets and the solar system, he found himself tracing the lineaments of a creation in which he appeared a kind of cosmic irrelevancy. Every new advance in science and technology seemed to subtract an invisible sum from the stature of man. In an age of automation, machines took over the complex jobs of running themselves, leaving countless numbers of "mere" humans jobless. Even human intelligence seemed about to be replaced by the speedier, more efficient, errorless computers. Science knew no bounds in controlling and manipulating environment. Special poisons sought the elimination of ugly weeds to create luxuriously deep lawns for all the project houses in all the developments. Other poisons eliminated annoying insects, and still others were designed for other pests. And in a kind of cosmic joke, all of the poisons dumped and poured and sprayed by man onto nature seemed to rise up in invisible wrath and turn on their creators— on the land, in the oceans, and through the air. In poisoning his environment, man may have been most efficient in poisoning himself. But however much modern man may have felt diminished by the various forces that pressed him, he was by no means diminished in numbers. In fact, as he multiplied endlessly he seemed bent on extinction through self-suffocation. At current rates of increase, the three billion men of mid-twentieth century would, by the twenty-first century, be doubled to six billion. In this great swarm of people, the amount of control over individual lives for the sake of the society would have to expand enormously. As he increased in numbers, man in his essence—in his individuality and humanity—seemed gradually to shrink and to shrivel.

Alienation

After the battlefields abroad during World War I, the lost generation of the 1920's had seen the American dream evaporate; the stunned generation of the 1940's and after saw the dream transfigured into a nightmare that would not go away. If the end of the world was a vivid metaphor to the one generation, it had become a shocking probability to the other. Democratic ideals, individual goals and purposes, religious beliefs and institutions —all seemed somehow suddenly irrelevant to the fateful questions of sheer existence that daily confronted the human race. Man's situation, indeed, seemed absurd; his behavior had no meaningful relation to his destiny. He was not, as the lost generation conceived him, a tragic figure—tragedy assumed some kind of purposeful action in a meaningful universe; he was, instead, a comic figure performing inconsequential acts in a meaningless universe. The old values seemed no longer to apply. On one level this loss of values manifested itself in the debasement of the old ideal of individualism: root, hog, or die; every man for himself. On another level this loss was manifested in a kind of agonized despair sustained to the point of dull-eyed apathy. If there was a characteristic vision, it was a vision arising not from dream or ideal, but from startling and shocking incongruities, from absurd and ridiculous juxtapositions. Cut off from the past and deprived of the future, unable to communicate with his fellows, modern man found himself alone and abandoned, his essential plight defined by his isolation and alienation.

This description of contemporary man may seem a bit exaggerated, and no doubt it is. Nevertheless there is truth in it, and it suggests the image projected by much contemporary literature—the plays *Camino Real* (1953) by Tennessee Williams and *The American Dream* (1960) by Edward Albee, the novels *Catcher in the Rye* (1951) by J. D. Salinger and *Catch-22* (1961) by Joseph Heller, the poems "Skunk Hour" (1959) by Robert Lowell and *The Bourgeois Poet* (1964) by Karl Shapiro. All these disparate works have in common their image of man alienated. They share too a kind of wildly comic tone in the description of his plight. Frequently the reader has difficulty locating the madness that flashes forth: is it in the alienated character? is it in the world he inhabits? is it in the man or in the fabric of the culture? Moreover, these works echo questions that run through much of modern literature—the question of identity: whom am I? what is man? All these characteristics tend to set these works apart from the earlier literature. It is difficult, perhaps impossible, to imagine any one of them being written before World War II.

It would, of course, be quite misleading to imply that contemporary life had nothing of joy or affirmation in it, or that these elements were not reflected in contemporary writing. But unquestioning affirmation was a phenomenon of the second- and third-rate literature, whereas joy tended to go underground, out of the public eye, into the sanctuary of interior being. Joy was, then, a mood especially appropriate for poetry, and could be found, for example, in the poems of Theodore Roethke and Richard Wilbur. But wherever found, the joy seemed apologetic when it did not appear subversive. It was like a joke enjoyed at a wake, a feeling of well-being curiously experienced at a funeral. Serious writers in their serious work could find little to celebrate in a world teetering erratically on the edge of an abyss.

J.M.

Literary Trends

Fiction: The Quest Absurd

From all appearances, there was a strong continuity in American fiction running through World War II and into the years beyond. American naturalism survived the war, as John Dos Passos and John Steinbeck were joined by younger writers such as Norman Mailer and Nelson Algren. American Gothic romance continued to flourish as a peculiarly Southern transplant, with Erskine Caldwell and William Faulkner joined by Truman Capote and Carson McCullers. Realism similar to that of Hemingway turned up in the novels of Bernard Malamud and Saul Bellow, a poetic style similar to that of Fitzgerald in the rhythmic prose of J. D. Salinger and John Updike.

But in spite of all this apparent continuity, most critics felt that the war represented a disjuncture that cut deep into the fictional psyche of the country. After the war, the old fictional gods—Fitzgerald, Hemingway, Faulkner—seemed no longer centrally relevant to the times: they were like slightly faded photographs, vivid reminders of a bygone era, tokens of a rapidly receding past. Dos Passos and Steinbeck were identified with social problems that had been so completely transfigured as to appear frighteningly strange and incredibly complex. The new times were alien times, the new problems mercurial and opaque. It was a time for a new art, for new novelists. And the new fabulists did appear, sometimes quietly, sometimes heralded by trumpets sounding alarums.

Generalizations tend to distort, especially those about an era so overwhelmingly close to the contemporary, but some might be tentatively ventured for the fiction of the '50's, '60's, and '70's. This fiction seemed to exhibit three main characteristics:

1. The new novels were largely novels of noncommitment. The authors appeared freed from belief in any political philosophy, social ideal, religious dogma, or moral system—and frequently uneasy in their freedom. Their characters went off on endless quests in flight from what was, in search of—they knew not what. The novel of restless movement almost became a genre in its own right, and the most remarkable example, though not the finest artistic achievement, was Jack Kerouac's *On the Road* (1957).

2. In modern fiction, humor took on new dimensions. The world and all its problems assumed grotesque, incongruous shapes, and man confronting the world saw that his own position was impossibly ridiculous. In some

cases modern fictional humor seemed to be a sustained, almost hysterical, hilarity. It was as though serious confrontation of the world would be unbearable if not unbelievable. Reality was so painful that it could be approached only by a kind of outraged irony. The modern quest was the quest absurd. The hero was crazy, maladjusted, the society was insane. Two of the most brilliant examples of this new humor were J. D. Salinger's *Catcher in the Rye* (1951) and Joseph Heller's *Catch-22* (1961).

3. Although the question of identity ran deep in earlier American literature, it took on a new poignancy in the modern novel. The new hero had his literal identity, an address and a name, but in spirit he was Ishmael still, searching for a strayed self. The farther he traveled the less he discovered. He became an alien in his own country—or rather, the country turned alien before his very eyes. The familiar landscape became foreign and simple language an enigma. The quest for identity—the search for the self's spiritual reality—seemed a distinctively modern obsession. It was, for example, dramatized with brilliance in Ralph Ellison's *The Invisible Man* (1952) and Wright Morris' *The Field of Vision* (1956).

If these were the traits that seemed to set modern fiction apart, they did not make themselves immediately visible after World War II. Instead, they gradually emerged as the years turned into decades, and as the old patterns of thinking and seeing gradually loosed their grasp on the imagination. A closer look at the literature of these years suggests some of the complexity of literary history as it continuously mingles old with new, the familiar with the strange.

J.M.

Novelists of the Past

Hemingway died in 1961, Faulkner in 1962. Nobel Prize winners both, they were the outstanding figures among the many competent novelists who appeared in the interwar era. Their high reputations overshadowed all the others, although their actual production after 1945 was not great. In *Across the River and into the Trees* (1950) Hemingway described the reflections of a fighting man on war and on many other matters. For the setting he chose Italy and the landscape of *A Farewell to Arms. The Old Man and the Sea* (1952), a parable of man's relation to nature and "luck," a favorite word of his, explored the emotions of a brave fisherman in deadly danger, thus linking it to his accounts of bullfighting and big-game hunting. Faulkner added materially to his Yoknapatawpha County series with *Intruder in the Dust* (1948), *Knight's Gambit* (1949), *The Town* (1957), and *The Reivers* (1962). He also returned to the characters of *Sanctuary* in *Requiem for a Nun* (1951) and added a new dimension to his work with *A Fable* (1954), his fullest treatment of religion. Judging by the extent of critical interest in his work, Faulkner was easily the most significant novelist of the era.

Other novelists of the 1920's and 1930's were still active. Dos Passos (who died in 1970), although turning more and more to interpretations of American history, continued his studies of political and economic strife in a number of books, of which *Midcentury* (1961) is the most interesting because of its use of "Documentary" inserts, which recall the "Newsreels" and "Camera Eye" of *U.S.A.* Steinbeck (who died in 1968) maintained his popularity, although most critics found his work after *The Grapes of Wrath* inferior and uneven. Some surprise was expressed when he was awarded the Nobel Prize in 1962. The public, however, followed him faithfully through *East of Eden* (1952), *Sweet Thursday* (1954), *The Winter of Our Discontent* (1961), and a number of lesser pieces, widely circulated in paperback.

The Novels of World War II

Predictably, novels of World War II were numerous and popular, many being made into movies. Some were by new writers, others by experienced storytellers.

The first to attract wide attention was *A Bell for Adano* (1944) by John Hersey, who as correspondent for *Time* covered both the Pacific and the European theaters of the war. Its portrait of a well-intentioned officer dealing with the civilians of a small Italian town may have strengthened his American readers' new sense of international destiny. Hersey's account of the effects of the Bomb, *Hiroshima* (1946), is a classic of factual reporting. His later novels have not won much critical admiration.

In 1948 came the first two large-scale war novels. One, *The Young Lions*, was the work of Irwin Shaw, who had previously written a number of plays and short stories. His use of a multiple point of view enabled him to study the mentality of some Nazi participants as well as that of several American soldiers; it is perhaps the most original of World War II novels. Later, Shaw published *The Troubled Air* (1950), a study of the fear of Communist influence in the radio world, and *Two Weeks in Another Town* (1960), which portrays Americans in postwar Europe. The second 1948 sensation among war novels was Norman Mailer's *The Naked and the Dead*, a description of a minor but typical military operation on a Pacific island. It employs some of the unconventional devices pioneered by Dos Passos and, like *The Young Lions*, has a multiple point of view. Its concern centers on the hierarchical structure of the army. *The Naked and the Dead* was Mailer's first book, and the only one which can be called a story in the conventional sense. In *Barbary Shore* (1951), *The Deer Park* (1955), *The White Negro* (1958), *Advertisements for Myself* (1959), and *An American Dream* (1965), he is largely on the side of the beats and hippies, with whom, indeed, he has been closely associated. His reportorial writing, especially *Armies of the Night*, an account of the 1967 march on the Pentagon in protest against the Vietnam war, won a Pulitzer award in 1969 and somewhat restored his earlier reputation.

Herman Wouk's *The Caine Mutiny* and James Jones' *From Here to Eternity* were both published in 1951. Wouk was no novice. He had graduated from Columbia in 1934 and had done some radio writing before the war. In *Aurora Dawn* (1947) and *The City Boy* (1948), moreover, he had shown promise of comic talent in his handling of the advertising business and summer camp life, respectively. *The Caine Mutiny*, however, was a lengthy study of men on a small naval vessel in the Pacific, in which the theme of discipline versus individual responsibility was studied meticulously. Wouk's tendency toward prolixity was not curbed in *Marjorie Morningstar* (1955), one of the longest seduction tales in literature.

Jones was largely self-taught, and *From Here to Eternity* was the result of his determination to tell the truth about army life, recording even its rough vocabulary. Of all the war stories, it probably catches best the monotony and unbearable boredom of barracks life, with its callowness and disregard for individual dignity. It has been followed by *Some Came Running* (1957), *The Pistol* (1959), and *The Thin Red Line* (1962). Jones has continued to be interested in the psychology of the military cadre, and his blunt honesty is generally acknowledged as rare in contemporary writing.

The final World War II novel worth special mention is Joseph Heller's *Catch-22* (1961), an air force story which alternates widely between sheer horror and grim, fantastic comedy. Combat airmen's slim chances of survival gave them a devil-may-care attitude and led to much off-duty recklessness, a fact of which Heller makes good use. His narrative has surrealistic touches resembling those in Albee's plays.

The World War II novels form an interesting contrast to the World War I stories by Hemingway, Dos Passos, E. E. Cummings *(The Enormous Room)*, and others. The irksomeness of army life ("Hurry up, hurry up—and wait" as its tempo has been called) is portrayed in much the same terms at both periods, and there are stupid officers in both, but the second group lacks the tinge of self-pity which World War I writers tended to have. War was still horrible, but it was less so than the ovens of the German concentration camps.

The Fiction of the South

A conspicuous feature of the interwar period, and of that since 1945, is the Southern Renaissance. It has had important consequences in poetry and criticism, through the work of John Crowe Ransom, Donald Davidson, Allen Tate, Cleanth Brooks, Robert Penn Warren, and Randall Jarrell. Its contribution to fiction, especially in the short story, has been equally significant.

Faulkner, of course, leads the list, but also important are (in the order of their birth) Katherine Anne Porter, Caroline Gordon, Robert Penn Warren, Eudora Welty, Carson McCullers, Truman Capote, William Styron, and Flannery O'Connor.

Porter, Gordon, Welty, and O'Connor, primarily short-story writers—
and exceptionally admirable ones—also all wrote at least one novel. The
novels of McCullers *(The Heart Is a Lonely Hunter*, 1940; *Reflections in a
Golden Eye*, 1941; *The Member of the Wedding*, 1946; and *Clock Without
Hands*, 1961) are among the most widely admired works of fiction of our
time, with much the same sense of the tragic beauty of life that one finds
in the best work of Sherwood Anderson.

Capote's work *(Other Voices, Other Rooms*, 1948; *Tree of Night*, 1949;
The Grass Harp, 1951; and *Breakfast at Tiffany's*, 1958) does not go beyond the *novella* in length; he turned to what he calls the "non-fiction
novel," exemplified by *In Cold Blood* (1965), a true narrative of an actual
Kansas murder told with all the skill of a novelist. Warren and Styron, however, have worked on a larger scale. Both are highly literate and self-
conscious novelists, and it is likely that readers will continue to return to
Warren's major works *(All the King's Men*, 1946; *World Enough and Time*,
1950; *Brother to Dragons*, 1953; *Band of Angels*, 1955; and *The Cave*,
1959) as well as to Styron's *(Lie Down in Darkness*, 1951; *The Long
March*, 1952; *Set This House on Fire*, 1960; and *The Confessions of Nat
Turner*, 1967).
                                                          T.H.
                                                            J.M.

The New Black Fiction

After World War II, new black writers appeared upon the scene, commanding the attention that Richard Wright had attracted before them.
Ralph Ellison won the National Book Award in 1952 for *Invisible Man*, his
first novel. As the narrator traces through the labyrinth of his life, from his
expulsion from a small Southern Negro college to his nightmarish experiences trying to survive in New York, he tries to find the pattern that will
yield meaning and revelation for himself. But the incidents of his life remain
stubbornly enigmatic, his own identity a mystery to the last. Yet in telling
his tale he achieves a kind of purge that will ultimately enable him to
emerge from his Dostoyevskian underground to undertake a new role, a
new definition of self.

James Baldwin, some ten years younger than Ellison, possibly has been
more widely heralded because of his active participation in the Civil Rights
movement of the early '60's. His books of essays, such as *The Fire Next
Time* (1963), are eloquent, impassioned ultimatums to his white countrymen to understand the complexity of their own guilt, the erosion of their
own identity in the "white man's problem"—his benighted treatment of
the Negro. But Baldwin's reputation rests in large part on a series of novels
he has written. The first, *Go Tell It on the Mountain* (1953), is a vivid portrayal of the evangelistic environment he knew as a boy in New York, in
which transplanted Southern Negroes attempted to adapt their rural culture
to a violent urban setting. *Giovanni's Room* (1956) does not touch on the
problem of race relations, but exploits a Paris setting to represent a strange

love story in which the protagonist awakens to the reality of his own inverted sexuality. *Another Country* (1962) and *Tell Me How Long the Train's Been Gone* (1968) combine the themes of the previous two novels in less successful explorations of the twin themes of racial mingling and sexual inversion. But, like Ellison, Baldwin must be credited with major achievements not only in black fiction, but also in American fiction.

The Search for Identity

The 1950's, finally, were distinguished by a number of serious efforts to answer the question of how a man should live in the fragmented and fractured society of our times. What is the individual, after all, and how does he stand in relation to his family, his friends, and the innumerable complexes to which he at one time or another is related, briefly or at length? A major theme of recent fiction has been this search for identity.

Of many authors who might be chosen to represent this theme, five are outstanding, for somewhat different reasons. In the order of their birth dates they are Wright Morris (1910), Bernard Malamud (1914), Saul Bellow (1915), J. D. Salinger (1919), and John Updike (1932).

Wright Morris was born in Central City, Nebraska. Although he left the state at an early age, the place haunts his work in the way that it did Willa Cather's. Morris has been a prolific writer ever since publication of his first book, *My Uncle Dudley*, in 1942. Novels which might be singled out as typical and among his best are *Man and Boy* (1951), *The Huge Season* (1955), *The Field of Vision* (1956), *Love among the Cannibals* (1957), and *Ceremony in Lone Tree* (1960). Whereas Willa Cather discovered her values in the pioneering past, Wright Morris probes deeply into the present and ends up with a question mark. Things seem to have gone wrong in the present, and the past remains inscrutable and unyielding in its mystery. In *The Field of Vision* Morris assembles his Nebraskans in a bullfight arena in Mexico, and as he rotates his point of view the reader becomes gradually aware of the absolute isolation of each character, one from another. Each has an interpretation of the past they all shared years ago in Nebraska, but all is distortion. The truth remains buried, inaccessible. The most perceptive of all the characters, Gordon Boyd, the only one who has in a sense (and only in a sense) escaped Nebraska, remains the most uncertain of his own and his friends' identity: the key period of his youth was the time he tried to walk on water—and failed, in the presence of his friend. His entire life, it seems, is some kind of crazy attempt to walk on water. The same characters turn up in *Ceremony in Lone Tree*, at a celebration in the abandoned plains town for the ancient Scanlon, the surviving pioneer. Again a rotating point of view reveals the immense barriers that separate these intimately related people, and the broad comedy is pervaded by an acute sense of loss. The quest for self goes on, doomed to failure in the isolation that none seems able to escape.

Malamud grew up in Brooklyn. In short stories (collected as *The Magic Barrel*, 1958, and *Idiots First*, 1963) and in an impressive novel (*The Assistant*, 1957), he has depicted the Jews and Italians of New York City's slums. Bruised in spirit by their hopeless struggle with circumstances and unscrupulous neighbors, they attain human dignity in Malamud's presentation, which is marked by severe clarity and unsentimental compassion. *The Assistant* is the story of Frank Alpine, a young Italian who moves into the home and failing grocery store of Morris Bober, a Jew. Although Alpine cannot keep his hands off Bober's daughter or out of Bober's till, he undergoes a degree of moral illumination and at the end of the book is converted to Judaism. Malamud's other novels are *The Natural* (1952), *A New Life* (1961), *The Fixer* (1966), and *The Tenants* (1971). The first describes the downfall of a baseball player; the second follows a Jewish teacher from New York through an eventful year in the English department of a small university on the west coast; the third fictionalizes an actual instance of brutal anti-Semitism; *The Tenants* explores the interrelations of two writers, one Jewish, one black, living in a condemned building. These books contain episodes which are more sensational, and also more predictable, than anything in *The Assistant*. Their strength lies in characterization. Malamud's fiction as a whole seems to say that the individual's best chance of accommodation to the world is to abide by his dreams and his faith, his religion in the broad sense of the word.

Although Bellow was born in Canada, he has spent much of his life in Chicago. To his credit are six substantial novels: *Dangling Man* (1944), *The Victim* (1947), *The Adventures of Augie March* (1953), *Henderson the Rain King* (1959), *Herzog* (1964), and *Mr. Sammler's Planet* (1970). In addition he has published a brilliant novella, *Seize the Day* (1956). "Dangling man" tells his story in a journal which extends from December 12, 1942, through April 9, 1943. He is awaiting a call for induction. Separated by his condition from his former world, and not yet caught up in that of the army, he can look at himself, his friends and relatives, and the whole matter of human life with thoughtful detachment. One of his central questions—and Bellow is full of questions—is "How should a good man live; what ought he to do?" *The Victim* pursues the same theme in a New York setting, and on a somewhat smaller scale. Asa Leventhal, the protagonist, is the busy editor of a trade magazine, puzzled about his relations to his family and to his associates. In *The Adventures of Augie March*, undoubtedly one of the finest novels ever written about Chicago, many persons and factors are posed in their relation to the hero, and his reactions and judgments are analyzed. In *Henderson the Rain King*, Bellow sends his hero to Africa where he becomes involved in a fantastic series of events designed to get him thoroughly acquainted with himself. *Herzog* is the story of an intellectual seeking to preserve his sanity. In Bellow's latest novel, Mr. Sammler is an old man whose cogitations concern not only the world's acute problems but also his own. In combination with Bellow's exploration of the theme of identity is a good measure of the comic spirit; he sees a great deal of what George Meredith called the "overblown, affected, pretentious, bombastic, hypocritical, pedantic, fantastically delicate" in human life.

For Meredith's adjectives, Holden Caulfield, the teen-age hero of Salinger's *The Catcher in the Rye* (1951), has a single synonym—*phony*. Ever since Holden Caulfield emerged as the twentieth-century rival of Huck Finn, to avoid the phony has been the goal of Salinger's young readers. Holden tells his story in his own terms, which are so ritualistically vulgar that students continue to regard them as the height of honesty. The closest approach to a second novel by Salinger is an unfinished chronicle of the Glasses, a New York family of Irish-Jewish descent. The parents were once vaudeville actors; each of their seven children is a genius or close to it; the family *esprit de corps* is high but edgy. Eight stories or character studies relating to the Glasses have been published, in *Franny and Zooey* (1961) and *Raise High the Roof Beam, Carpenters*, and *Seymour: An Introduction* (1962). Salinger's only other book is a collection of his early work, *Nine Stories* (1953). Many of Salinger's characters are a little off balance, and some of them are way off. They are, however, highly intelligent, sensitive, and perceptive, and they seek to understand their rather complicated selves. The Glasses, for example, are students of Zen Buddhism. Salinger is evidently fascinated by braininess and family affinities. He is, one should add, almost the only contemporary who has specialized successfully in short fiction rather than the novel.

Updike has thus far published poems (*The Carpentered Hen*, 1958, and *Telephone Poles*, 1963), short stories (*The Same Door*, 1959, and *Pigeon Feathers*, 1962), and novels (*The Poorhouse Fair*, 1959, *Rabbit, Run*, 1960, *The Centaur*, 1963, *Couples*, 1968, *Bech: A Book*, 1970, and *Rabbit Redux*, 1971). He most often approaches the problem of personal identity by describing elderly people and their relationship to others, although in *Rabbit, Run* the hero is a young man. Updike is rather more of an experimentalist than the older writers so far discussed; one of his favorite devices is a tightly controlled time line. *The Poorhouse Fair*, in which the action covers a single day, winds up with a series of flashes of poetic intensity. *The Centaur* is a curiously contrived overlay of a contemporary story upon a mythological base. *Couples* is a panoramic drama of sexual obsession and promiscuity in suburbia. With Updike, as with the other four seekers for identity, the hope is that the best is yet to come.

Cultural Commentaries

A phenomenon of modern literature is the amount of commentary on U.S. society and culture that pours from the presses. Americans appear obsessed with self-examination and self-explanation. Typical examples abound: the beat novelist Jack Kerouac, whose *On the Road* (1957) was the "Beat Bible," frequently turned to nonfiction to explain the beat movement. Norman Podhoretz, editor of *Commentary*, felt moved to confess and tell all about the literary establishment in an autobiographical volume, *Making It* (1967). Susan Sontag followed all the zigs, zags, and gyrations of modern art in books like *Against Interpretation* (1966). Truman Capote, Norman Mailer, and Tom Wolfe were proponents of the "New Journalism," a subjective form of reporting that sought to go beneath the surface of events as well as to relate the writer's own involvement, especially emotional involvement.

For black writers, the straight, unfictionalized account appeared the most effective way of telling their story of oppression and agony. Even James Baldwin, famed as a fictionist, seemed at his best as a writer in such essay volumes as *Nobody Knows My Name* (1961). Martin Luther King, Jr., wrote in the evangelistic tradition in such eloquent volumes as *Why We Can't Wait* (1964). Malcolm X seemed to speak with a tongue of fire in his *Autobiography* (1965). And Eldridge Cleaver told it "like it is" from his perspective in prison in *Soul on Ice* (1968). From the number and nature of books such as these, one might conclude that the modern experience was too fantastic for fiction, too explosive for mere fabrication: truth, straight, transcended imagination.

T.H.
J.M.

Poetry: The Quiet Revolution

Is there a new poetry? The fact that the question can even be posed suggests something of a paradox on the literary scene. The rebirth of poetry in the earlier part of the century was an event worthy of prolonged celebration. But there was something strange in a revival that, as it grew in strength, declined in intelligibility and popularity. As poetry developed into a palpable presence, even an establishment, it lost its audience. Since the audience for poetry in America is so miniscule, it is possible that there could have been a revolution without anyone much noticing. And moreover, a few immense figures out of the past—Frost, Eliot, Williams, Stevens—have so dominated the contemporary poetic landscape that they have tended to cast in shadow the new poets who have tried to emerge.

In 1955, Donald Hall concluded an essay entitled "The New Poetry" *(Anchor Review)* with the conjecture: "Maybe we are only at the beginning, and not at the end, of a poetic golden age." In 1962, when Mr. Hall undertook to identify the new American poets in an anthology entitled *Contemporary American Poetry*, he spoke more boldly: "For thirty years an orthodoxy ruled American poetry. It derived from the authority of T. S. Eliot and the new critics; it exerted itself through the literary quarterlies and the universities. It asked for a poetry of symmetry, intellect, irony, and wit. The last few years have broken the control of this orthodoxy. The change has come slowly and not as a rebellion of young turks against old tories."

Perhaps there has been an invisible rebellion going on, and perhaps there is, already on the scene, a new poetry. If the outlines of that new poetry appear a little blurred, perhaps the blur is in the eye of the beholder too long accustomed to the twilight of the past and too little accustomed to the more intense daylight of the present. The contemporary situation may be analogous to that in the nineteenth century, when the Victorian poets sought to find their own identity, to emerge from under the shadow of the Romantics who had fought and won a poetic revolution. Finally Tennyson and Browning found their own voices, quite distinct in accent and tone from the voices of Wordsworth and Coleridge.

And it is surely no distortion to compare the radical literary innovations of Pound and Eliot with those of Wordsworth and Coleridge, the founding of *Poetry* magazine in 1912 with the publication of the *Lyrical Ballads* in 1798. Just as the Romantic revolution was most vigorous in its early years, so the American poetic renaissance flourished at first—and then the blood began to thin. For some ten years—from the establishment of *Poetry* in 1912 to the publication of *The Waste Land* in 1922—there was all the excitement of free and fruitful creativity, experimentation, innovation, discovery, achievement. But after 1922, an invisible dogma seemed to settle gradually over the literary landscape, a pall over creative experimentation. Rebellious manifestos turned into pious pronouncements of orthodoxy: Shelly was out, Donne was in; Whitman wouldn't do, Dickinson would do very nicely. Major reputations soared and cast their long shadows into the future, over the '40's, '50's, and into the '60's. Wallace Stevens lived into 1955, E. E. Cummings into 1962, Robert Frost and William Carlos Williams into 1963, and T. S. Eliot lived into 1965. Only the other guiding father of the new poetry, Ezra Pound, survived into the '70's.

But as the past receded, times changed. After World War II, the literary battles appeared not only won, but perhaps won too well. In part the battles had been with the conservative academic establishment, but by mid-century this bastion had been captured and placed in the service of the rebels—who in turn were rapidly becoming an establishment in their own right. Such is the fated course of all revolutions. The storming of the universities by the poets turned ultimately into the flight of the poets to the universities. The conquered soon became the conqueror—because of the simple matter of the budget control. As the twentieth-century patron of poets, the universities did not assign themes and exact poems as tribute—but they insinuated themselves in subtle ways into the poetry.

Whereas Eliot went into publishing, Stevens into insurance, Williams into medicine, after the war Shapiro went to the University of Nebraska.

Lowell turned up at Harvard, Roethke went to the University of Washington, Wilbur was on the staff at Wesleyan (Conn.), and Snodgrass taught at Wayne State in Detroit. Indeed, it is difficult to find a poet today without an academic connection. This major fact in the story of modern poetry explains much about its nature. And still more is explained by another remarkable difference in the status of the poet. If a campus could not have a poet in residence, it tried to bring one in for lectures or readings. The stock in well-known contemporary poets soared. They were in demand to be exhibited and lionized. Probably more people heard poets than read them. And certain it is that a poet could make more money lecturing or reading than he could writing a new poem. And there was real irony, perhaps academic, in the fact that an established poet was frequently offered higher sums for the holograph of his poem than for the right to print the poem itself.

Whereas in 1912 Harriet Monroe found that poetry had no real outlet, and she established her magazine of verse to fill this gap, a half-century later there was a plethora of outlets for poetry, including not only *Poetry* itself and a number of imitators, but also innumerable little magazines and journals. But whereas the little magazines of the earlier part of the century were rebels against the establishment, most of the little magazines of mid-century were subsidized by the academies themselves. There was no lack of space to publish poems. Almost any poet could find a publication to accept his poems. And moreover, poets no longer found it hard to publish volumes of verse. They found their books more and more welcomed by the university presses, which prided themselves on publishing a distinguished series of poets.

One might imagine, from this situation, that America would be a land of smiling, contented poets. Poets seemed to have everything, and they did —that is, everything except an audience. Many of the poets blamed the audience's absence on the audience. But others were haunted by a sense of guilt, by a feeling that the poets themselves might bear some responsibility for the apathy of the audience. Indeed, there was an undercurrent of resentment against the unbelievably generous academy. And there was the occasional remembrance of those university poets of the nineteenth century (Longfellow and Lowell, for example) and their mediocre verse, and of the unorthodox, anti-establishment poets (like Whitman and Dickinson) and their brilliant and lasting poetry. Was the situation, perhaps, too comfortable for poetry in mid-twentieth century?

The question, however irrelevant, was an inevitable one in an affluent society. And it was also inevitable that the academy's domination of modern poetry should be challenged. Extremes beget extremes. Against the well-made, well-mannered poem arose the wild, ill-tempered howl of the so-called beat generation.

The movement sometimes called the "New Bohemianism," but more often referred to as the "beat" or "beatnik" complex, first developed in the early 1950's in San Francisco with some encouragement from Kenneth Rexroth, San Francisco correspondent for *The Nation* and an old-time radical. Housed in such places as the City Lights Bookstore and in the small jazz night clubs, it spread to Greenwich Village and elsewhere. For the thoroughgoing beat there was not much point in writing anything, since he held that he might better be employed in scrutinizing his own emotions. Yet the beats, like other rebel groups, felt the need to communicate their protest, at least to their fellow spirits. They wrote more fiction than poetry, but two of them became well known for their verse. Lawrence Ferlinghetti was the author of *A Coney Island of the Mind* (1958), a curious piece meant to be recited, full of parody and jazz lingo. It is a more interesting poem than Allen Ginsberg's *Howl* (1956), of which the first line is "I saw the best minds of my generation destroyed by madness, starving hysterical naked." It is of some significance that Ginsberg at first planned to use Whitman's word *Yawp* ("I sound my barbaric yawp") as his title. The beats became somewhat less conspicuous after 1960, but the movement, however much exaggerated and exploited by the mass media, made its point of protest against the academic establishment—and shook some people out of their lethargy.

But to divide contemporary poetry into academic verse and "beat bleats" is to emphasize its major weaknesses. There were also major strengths. The first important break with the orthodoxies of Eliot and Pound came with World War II, when poets discovered that their situation demanded something more than the standardized intellectual, ironic, impersonal approaches of the past. In trying to capture the essence of their experience, the war poets rediscovered the emotional and the personal. In short, these poets turned from a poetry of the mind and tradition to a poetry of feeling and experience, as can be seen in Karl Shapiro's "Troop Train" ("And on through crummy continents and days,/ Deliberate, grimy, slightly drunk we crawl. . ."), or in W. D. Snodgrass' "Returned to Frisco, 1956" ("We shouldered like pigs along the rail to try/ And catch that first gray outline of the shore/ Of our first life").

Black poets, too, mined their own emotions and their own harrowing experiences in such volumes as Gwendolyn Brooks' *The Bean Eaters* (1950) and LeRoi Jones' *Preface to a Twenty Volume Suicide Note* (1961). Gwendolyn Brooks, who won the Pulitzer Prize for poetry in 1950 for *Annie Allen*, dominated the field of black poetry for a decade, and is recognized as a leading American poet. LeRoi Jones had the same value for the '60's, both in poetry and drama. Just as Brooks dominated the field of black poetry in the '50's, Jones dominated it in the '60's.

The orthodox New Critic, schooled in Eliot's dogma of an impersonal poetry as escape from emotion, might well cry out in the face of this poetry—"But where is your objective correlative?" These new poets didn't seem to have one, and, moreover, didn't seem to care. They insisted on confronting experience not with the eyes of a previous generation, but with their own eyes, and to find its meaning with their own voices.

Beginning with World War II, then, poetry seemed to have a new accent, however quiet and unpronounced. Gradually other new elements emerged as the war poets developed and new poets appeared. To simplify and abbreviate, these new elements may be best indicated by a series of descriptive, even contradictory terms, meant only to be suggestive: a poetry of colloquial idiom, a poetry of radical alienation, a poetry of suburbia, a poetry of momentary joy, a poetry of small experience.

Poetry of Colloquial Idiom

The war between the British and the American language goes back into the nineteenth century, and was central in the split between such traditionalists as Longfellow and Lowell on the one hand and such linguistic innovators as Whitman and Dickinson on the other. During the 1920's, it was the traditionalists led by T. S. Eliot who won the day. William Carlos Williams wrote in his *Autobiography: "The Waste Land* wiped out our world . . . Eliot returned us to the classrooms." After World War II, Williams' reputation returned, especially with the publication of his long poem *Paterson* (1946-58), and the influence of his American idiom felt. But the pull to colloquial speech did not have to be learned. Observe Shapiro's "crummy" or Snodgrass' "like pigs," delivered not in dramatic but in their own voices. Compare the language of Pound's *Cantos* and Eliot's *Waste Land* with the language of Williams' *Paterson* and Shapiro's *The Bourgeois Poet* to find the gulf between the two tongues of American poetry. It is not merely a matter of slang, though slang is an important element in the new poetry. It is, primarily, a matter of linguistic attitude toward experience—a way of perceiving not with eyesight but with tongue.

Poetry of Radical Alienation

Very little of the first-rate poetry of the twentieth century could be described as yea-saying and affirmative, but there were many ways of being negative. Eliot's poetry set one pattern of images for his own and later generations: a waste land haunted by hollow men. His was a vision that went primarily outward. After World War II, the vision turned inward, towards a self-sickness frequently inexplicable and mysterious in origin. This radical alienation was less social and more personal than that of the orthodoxy. It was an agonizing reappraisal of the self in its most sordid moments. Robert Lowell's "Waking in the Blue," concluding with the chilling line, "each of us holds a locked razor," is an example of this theme in contemporary poetry. W. D. Snodgrass' "The Men's Room in the College Chapel" ("This is the last cave, where the soul/ turns in its corner like a beast") is of this genre, suggesting a world in which every man hides deep within his being a savage self clawing to escape.

Poetry of Suburbia

If poetry once divided between country and city, as for example between Robert Frost and T. S. Eliot, in mid-twentieth century the two divisions coalesced in suburbia, with its combination of subdued country (parks) and modified city (shopping centers). What this merge meant is difficult to assess. But as the city was the place of terror (as in Eliot) and the country a place for renewal (as in Frost), so one might assume that the suburb might be the place of quiet despair. For Richard Wilbur, an incident during the mowing of the lawn can become the subject of a poem—"The Death of a Toad." In such a comfortable domestic scene there sounds an undercurrent of horror, as the dead toad's "antique eyes . . . still appear/ To watch, across the castrate lawn,/ The haggard daylight steer." The image of the "castrate lawn" might serve to symbolize the substitute waste land of the post-World War II poets. For other examples of such poems see Snodgrass' "April Inventory" or Lowell's "Skunk Hour" or Theodore Roethke's "Root Cellar."

Poetry of Momentary Joy

It may at first seem inconsistent to find both alienation and joy characteristic of the poetry of the mid-twentieth century. But when it is seen that the poetry is an inward, personal poetry, and that both alienation and joy are genuine moods of the contemporary man of sensitivity, particularly the poet, the presence of the two conflicting themes in the same poetry should be no surprise. Something of both these themes, intricately intertwined, is sounded in Theodore Roethke's "The Waking"—"This shaking keeps me steady. I should know./ What falls away is always. And is near." But more clearly a poem of celebration is Roethke's "Four for Sir John Davies," in which he says, "I tried to fling my shadow at the moon./ The while my blood leaped with a wordless song."

Poetry of the Small Experience

There seem to be no sweeping or magniloquent gestures in contemporary poetry. It is primarily a poetry of the small, severely prescribed, intensely personal experience. And the experience is more likely to be an ordinary, everyday involvement of some kind, rather than some unusual occurrence or encounter. If the experience appears strange, it is probably a matter of the poet's perception and penetration into its depths. For example, Richard Wilbur reconstructs the romantic dream of a commuter in "In the Smoking-Car." And his "Potato" probably does as much for that unlikely subject as is poetically possible. Roethke goes back to his boyhood to write about the time his drunken father danced with him in his arms in "My Papa's Waltz." W. D. Snodgrass, in "These Trees Stand . . . ," writes simply about a walk he took but the poem achieves an unexpected dimension in the refrain: "Snodgrass is walking through the universe."

Clearly all these themes are important in contemporary poetry, but they are not the whole story by any means. In a literature which is still evolving, as all contemporary literature is, the critic can report only what he thinks he has discovered. The literature itself may veer off in other directions tomorrow, or it may have deep undercurrents that will not surge to the surface until some time in the future. One of the pleasures of reading contemporary poetry is in exploring its depth and in weighing its permanence—largely without benefit of guides or directions.

J.M.

Drama in Transition

The State of the Theater

With new experiments ventured in American fiction and with new accents sounding in American poetry, it would seem natural to expect new developments in American drama. But any high expectation is doomed to disappointment. Frederick Lumley, in *Trends in Twentieth Century Drama* (Revised Edition, 1960), wrote: "The brightest prospect for the American theatre is that the stage is set, and, as showmanship would put it, the potentialities are tremendous. Eyes look not on the achievements of the past— for there are few worth looking at—but on the future, the period in which the new 100 per cent American drama will grow to maturity. . . . The American dramatist has not equalled the standard of the novelists in modern American literature, but in the long run the theatre would seem to offer to-day more promise than the novel."

The word *promise* seemed to be the term most frequently applied to the American theater. But *change* seemed to be the keynote. Probably the most important development after World War II was the introduction and fantastic growth of television. Just as the motion pictures had, earlier in the century, radically diminished the scope and changed the nature of the legitimate theater, so television wrought another revolution, affecting both stage and movies. Just what the results of that revolution may have been is not yet clearly seen, but it would seem that, like the movies before (and the theater before that), television has taken over the basic role in mass entertainment. Motion pictures have taken themselves more seriously, and may come to rival the stage as a primary medium for serious dramatists. And even television, with its insatiable appetite for material, may prove the breeding grounds for important dramatists: there are, for example, the cases of playwright Paddy Chayefsky, who first won critical attention for a TV script, *Marty* (1955), and of Neil Simon, trained in the same school.

Although Broadway continued to be the center of the American theater, the two lost their synonymity some time after World War II. The reasons for this were no doubt complex, but of primary importance was the shifting population density in the country, together with a rising interest in developing local culture made possible by the affluence of the society. As the costs of production soared after the war, Broadway became commercial with a vengeance, more and more reluctant to gamble on serious critical successes that might prove costly failures—leaving debts counted in the hundreds of thousands of dollars. As a result, Off-Broadway theaters sprang up, primarily around Greenwich Village, to accommodate the experimental dramatists, to import the new foreign playwrights, and to attempt revival of the important drama of the past. As time passed, the line of demarcation between Broadway and Off-Broadway inevitably blurred, with commercialization motivating some of the Off-Broadway productions, and with Broadway taking over some of the serious and important Off-Broadway plays. The importance of Off-Broadway may be gauged, for example, by its nurturing the talent during the late 1950's of the important new playwright, Edward Albee.

Whereas little new seemed to be developing in touring companies or summer stock, past means of moving the theater into and across the country, there were important new developments in the growth of resident professional companies. Such companies were first established Off-Broadway (Living Theatre, Circle-in-the-Square), and the ambitious Lincoln Center Repertory Company launched its first season in 1963-64 in New York with a new play by Arthur Miller (*After the Fall*). But what was most exciting was the appearance of resident companies outside New York—the Actors Workshop in San Francisco, the Dallas Theatre Center, the Guthrie Theater in Minneapolis. Together with proliferating community and university theaters, the resident companies seemed to indicate a nationwide vitality of interest in drama that Broadway did not fill. It remains to be seen whether the repertory companies will spark new creativity in American dramatists, but the possibility is open.

Continuations from the Past

With the remarkable exception of Eugene O'Neill, the dramatists of the 1920's and 1930's seemed to have spent their force by the time of World War II. Robert Sherwood's *There Shall Be No Night* (1940) did not survive the war which was its theme. Maxwell Anderson continued to write historical plays, such as *Anne of the Thousand Days* (1948) and *Barefoot in Athens* (1952), and in *The Bad Seed* (1954) he returned to the contemporary scene, but his new plays tended to diminish his reputation. William Saroyan's *Get Away Old Man* (1944) apparently marked the end of his impact on the theater, strongly felt in the preceding decade. Thornton Wilder, out of all these dramatists, probably stands alone in adding to his reputation with a remarkable play, *The Skin of Our Teeth* (1940), a comic allegory of man's endurance through the ages against overwhelming odds.

But the most impressive force in the American theater after World War II continued to be Eugene O'Neill—a force that extended considerably beyond his death in 1953. After remaining silent for so many years that he was almost forgotten (his last play was *Days Without End*, 1934), his long play about man and his illusions, *The Iceman Cometh*, appeared in 1946. O'Neill had long been suffering with Parkinson's disease, but he had continued to write and lay aside his plays. *A Moon for the Misbegotten* appeared in 1952, followed by *Long Day's Journey into Night* in 1956 and *A Touch of the Poet* in 1957. One of the best of all O'Neill's plays, *Long Day's Journey into Night* was painfully frank in its treatment of autobiographical material, as well as emotionally exhausting in its probing beneath the surface of conventional family relationships.

In competition with the professional playwrights, the poets took up their pens to write drama. T. S. Eliot had published *Murder in the Cathedral* in 1935, but few saw him as a force in the theater. There followed *The Family Reunion* in 1939, which, like its predecessor, was an experiment in poetic drama. A decade later, in 1949, Eliot produced *The Cocktail Party*, a serious comedy of high sophistication, exploring the religious theme of salvation. This was followed, in 1953, by *The Confidential Clerk*, another comedy with the serious theme of the search for a father. Another poet, Archibald MacLeish, surprised the theatrical world by writing one of the most widely discussed plays of its season—*J.B.* (1958). Like the Eliot plays, *J.B.* was a poetic drama placed within a mythic frame to explore a religious theme. Though these poetic dramas helped to keep serious theater alive during lean times, they did not in themselves seem to contain the seeds of the future American theater.

One of the liveliest elements in the postwar theater was the musical comedy. In many respects the rage for musical comedy was one of the sicknesses of the theater, especially as it filled the stages with costly but tasteless, talentless spectacles that dazzled audiences made up largely of businessmen traveling to New York on lush expense accounts. But the genre occasionally achieved an extra dimension beyond mere entertainment which appeared to make it a uniquely American art form. The production which, in 1943, set a standard of excellence in its ingenious fusion of plot, music, lyrics, and ballet to bring life to American folk themes and materials was Richard Rodgers' and Oscar Hammerstein's *Oklahoma!*; another notable example of the genre is Leonard Bernstein's *West Side Story* (1957), a New York slum version of the Romeo and Juliet theme.

The New Playwrights

But in spite of the renewed interest in Eugene O'Neill and the high achievement of some of the poetic dramas and musical comedies, the real excitement in drama after World War II was generated by the appearance during the 1940's of some new gifted playwrights, among them Tennessee

Williams, Arthur Miller, and William Inge. In a sense, Williams' *A Streetcar Named Desire* (1947) was a continuation of the psychological explorations of Eugene O'Neill, and Miller's *Death of a Salesman* (1949) was an extension of the social probing of the depression dramas of the 1930's. But these plays and others by these playwrights also added new dimensions and pointed to new possibilities in the American theater, both in technique and theme.

An unhappy childhood and a good deal of knocking about at odd jobs in the lower Mississippi valley underlie the remarkable creative work of Tennessee Williams. He also had some training in the academic world of theater, first at Iowa and later with Theresa Helburn and John Gassner at the New School for Social Research. Since the success of *The Glass Menagerie* (1945), which many critics still consider his best effort, scarcely a season has lacked a new Williams play, and two of them, *A Streetcar Named Desire* (1947) and *Cat on a Hot Tin Roof* (1955), have been Pulitzer Prize winners. All of Williams' plays are marked by his concern for warped personalities, many of them regarded by his audiences as physically or psychically abnormal, so that he has accustomed the public to relatively unpleasant experiences in the theater. Like Theodore Dreiser's, however, Williams' preoccupation with the sordid and the sickly is combined with considerable tenderness for the victims of life, and his gallery of queer people, looked at as a whole, is a commentary on the fragility of happiness in a hostile world. Along with undertones of social criticism, a strong strain of violence has added to Williams' shock value in the theater.

Arthur Miller, a New Yorker by birth, studied playwriting under Professor Kenneth E. Rowe at the University of Michigan, where two years in succession he won Hopwood Awards. He got out of college in 1938, just in time to join in the last months of the WPA Theatre. He worked during the war in the Brooklyn Navy Yard, continuing his writing. His first play was *The Man Who Had All the Luck* (1944), but his first success was *All My Sons* (1947), a study of the results of failure in family and social responsibility. Remarkable for its tightness of structure and its honest facing of the problem of how a man should act in the complicated modern world, this play established Miller as the dramatist with the most to say in the post-Bomb era. He quickly followed it with *Death of a Salesman* (1949), generally considered one of the strongest plays of the last few decades. Although a family play with a depression background, it is a remarkably subtle utilization of the facility with which the modern stage can create the illusion of blending past and present, and it ends with a moving statement of the theme that "There, but for the grace of God, go I." Man's search for identity and honesty and integrity in family and social relations is the theme, also, of *The Crucible* (1953), in which Miller went back to the Salem witchcraft episode of the seventeenth century to say what badly needed to be said about the Communist-hunting hysteria of 1954, which ended with the censure of Joseph R. McCarthy of Wisconsin by the United States Senate for his abuse of witnesses in the course of his widely publicized investigation of subversive activities. In *A View from the Bridge* (1955), enlarging what was originally a one-act play, Miller developed his favorite theme, "I want my name," in a more universal context, even though the setting was the Brooklyn waterfront. It was a measure of Miller's contemporary reputation that he was chosen by the New York Lincoln Center Repertory Company to write its inaugural play, *After the Fall*, produced in 1964. Other plays—*Incident at Vichy* (1964), *The Price* (1968)—have demonstrated Miller's versatility in working with a variety of themes and techniques. Although Miller's total product has not been great, *Death of a Salesman*, *The Crucible*, and *A View from the Bridge* are read and performed all over the world. Of all our contemporaries, he comes closest, perhaps, to rivaling Eugene O'Neill.

William Inge, a playwright frequently associated with Williams' psychological themes, is an interesting product of the college theater movement. A graduate of the University of Kansas, he was associated in play production at Stephens College with Maude Adams, the famous actress, and just after the war he taught a playwriting course at Washington University in St. Louis. His first play, *Farther Off from Heaven*, was produced at Margo Jones' little theater in Dallas in 1947. His second effort, *Come Back, Little Sheba* (1949), had a highly successful Broadway production by the Theatre Guild and was followed by *Picnic* (1952), *Bus Stop* (1955), and *The Dark at the Top of the Stairs* (1957). More recent plays have quickly failed. Inge's specialty is the study of the personal adjustment of frustrated "little" people, and he has tended to write to a popular but not very profound formula. Doc, the alcoholic in *Come Back, Little Sheba*, is perhaps his best character thus far. There is a good deal of sex and symbolism in Inge's work which makes good theater, but most critics have complained about a lack of depth.

Theater of the Absurd

Of all literary genres, drama seems in the twentieth century to be the most persistently international. After World War II, a new kind of drama began to appear, related, of course, to prewar expressionism and various other special cults of the arts—cubism, surrealism, abstract expressionism. This new drama first appeared abroad, in such plays as Eugene Ionesco's *The Bald Soprano* (1950), Samuel Beckett's *Waiting for Godot* (1952), Jean Genet's *The Balcony* (1956). These plays and others tended to defy traditional theatrical and dramatic conventions and held in common a point of view which seemed almost baldly nihilistic. The production of such plays, and interest in them, had gathered enough momentum and force that by the end of the 1950's, Martin Esslin could publish a full-scale assessment of the movement in *The Theatre of the Absurd* (1961).

Esslin's definition is worth noting: "The hallmark of this attitude [in the theatre of the absurd] is its sense that the certitudes and unshakable basic assumptions of former ages have been swept away, that they have been tested and found wanting, that they have been discredited as cheap and somewhat childish illusions. The decline of religious faith was masked until the end of the Second World War by the substitute religions of faith in progress, nationalism, and various totalitarian fallacies. All this was shattered by the war. . . . In an essay on Kafka, Ionesco defined his understanding of the term [absurd] as follows: 'Absurd is that which is devoid of purpose. . . . Cut off from his religious, metaphysical, and transcendental roots, man is lost; all his actions become senseless, absurd, useless.' "

The delay in the coming of the theater of the absurd to the United States has been attributed to two factors. First, America did not suffer from World War II either physically or spiritually to the degree that Europe suffered. And second, there has always been a strong streak of idealism and optimism in American thinking, which runs back as far as the old original hope of establishing a new Eden in the American frontier wilderness. But whatever the causes of the delay, American playwrights began in the late 1950's to show the influence of the European avant-garde drama. Jack Gelber's *The Connection* (1959) portrayed a group of hopeless dope addicts waiting for their fix—killing time with jazz and inane conversation. Arthur L. Kopit's *Oh Dad, Poor Dad, Mamma's Hung You in the Closet and I'm Feeling So Sad* (1960) presented the trials of a lady, perhaps insane, traveling about the world (also probably insane) with her languid son and the preserved body of her deceased spouse.

But these plays, however advanced in conception, showed the marks of immaturity in execution. The most talented American playwright writing in the vein of the theater of the absurd was Edward Albee. However his work might ultimately be classified—and his most recent dramas do not seem "absurd"—Albee was the strongest new talent to turn up for some years in the American theater.

Like the boyhood of Holden Caulfield in J. D. Salinger's novel *The Catcher in the Rye*, Albee's boyhood left him at odds with his family and with most of the schools he attended, including Trinity College, where he resided for only a year and a half. He began to write poetry as a schoolboy and, although he had ample private means, continued to write after settling down, in a fashion, in Greenwich Village in 1949. He was then twenty. In 1958 he showed his first short play, *The Zoo Story*, to a friend, who sent it to an acquaintance in Germany, where it was produced and published the following year. It and three other brief plays were produced in off-Broadway theaters in New York in 1960 and 1961.

Albee's *The American Dream* (1961) is typical of his technique and theme. The characters have only such names as "Mommy," "Daddy," "Grandma," and "Young Man." The dialogue is filled with delightful nonsense and charming non sequiturs, but there runs beneath the surface a serious element which emerges periodically. When, near the end of the play, the Young Man appears at the door and tells the story of his past, the audience learns that he is the twin of the baby that Mommy and Daddy had once mangled and emasculated. As the twin, feeling a strong empathy with his brother's wounds, the Young Man's emotions—his humanity—have atrophied. He says: ". . . since then I have not been able to *love* anyone with my body. And even my hands . . . I cannot touch another person and feel love. And there is more . . . there are more losses, but it all comes down to this: I no longer have the capacity to feel anything. I have no emotions. I have been drained, torn asunder . . . disemboweled. I have, now, only my person . . . my body, my face." This hollow shell, a zombie with a handsome exterior, is, Albee seems to be saying, the end of the American dream.

The feeling of personal isolation in Albee's plays is characteristic of the age; but he heightens his effects by exaggeration and violence—at times something not unlike surrealism—which his audiences have found remarkably compelling. Of his work he said in 1963:

> What happens in my plays is, I think, an accurate mirror of reality.
> There's always a certain amount of selection and hyperbole in art, but
> not so much that what I say is less than true. What people object to in
> my plays is a certain objectivity. I suffer for my subjects of course, but
> I do not slip over into sentimentality. Everything must be measured
> against something else, I feel, to be understood. One enlarges the can-
> vas to see what the separate elements are. I have a faculty for objectiv-
> ity even in my own life. Half the time I find my own rages and anxieties
> quite funny. Maybe . . . I don't exist at all.

The search for identity in a confusing—and absurd—age, which Albee's statement suggests as his main concern, is a primary theme in the full-length plays that enabled Albee to move from Off-Broadway to Broadway, first in 1962 with *Who's Afraid of Virginia Woolf?* in 1963 with an adaptation of Carson McCullers' novel, *The Ballad of the Sad Café,* in 1964 with *Tiny Alice,* in 1966 with *A Delicate Balance,* in 1967 with *Everything in the Garden,* and in 1971 with *All Over.* But in addition these plays are explorations in depth of the whimsical ways of love, in all its bewildering variety and agonizing intensity.

Much of the promise of the American theater is in reality the promise of Albee and other such bold and talented dramatists who might succeed in revitalizing an art form that seems periodically to be gasping its last breath.

J.M.

T.H.

Chronological Table of
LITERATURE AND HISTORY

1946 ● Dos Passos' *Tour of Duty* · Dreiser's *The Bulwark* · Hersey's *Hiroshima* · Jeffers' *Medea* · Lowell's *Lord Weary's Castle* · McCullers' *The Member of the Wedding* · O'Neill's *The Iceman Cometh* · Warren's *All the King's Men* and *Blackberry Winter* · Welty's *Delta Wedding*

First Assembly of the United Nations met at London, 10 January · League of Nations dissolved itself, 18 April, turning over its assets to the United Nations · First convictions of high-ranking Nazis for war crimes announced by International Military Tribunal at Nuremberg

1947 ● Dreiser's *The Stoic* · Frost's *A Steeple Bush* and *A Masque of Mercy* · A. B. Guthrie's *The Big Sky* · Lewis' *Kingsblood Royal* · James Michener's *Tales of the South Pacific* · Shapiro's *Trial of a Poet and Other Poems* · Steinbeck's *The Pearl* and *The Wayward Bus* · Stevens' *Transport to Summer* · Warren's *The Circus in the Attic and Other Stories*

"Truman Doctrine" inaugurated by Congressional appropriations for economic and military aid to Greece and Turkey, where Communist coups were feared · "Marshall Plan" of aid to free nations announced by Secretary of State George C. Marshall

1948 ● Cather's *The Old Beauty and Others* · Faulkner's *Intruder in the Dust* · Jeffers' *The Double Axe and Other Poems* · *Literary History of the United States,* ed. R. E. Spiller and others · Norman Mailer's *The Naked and the Dead* · William Van O'Connor's *Sense and Sensibility in Modern Poetry*

Economic Cooperation Administration (ECA) organized to supervise aid to free nations · Korea partitioned into northern People's Democratic Republic (Communist) and southern Republic of Korea · Truman elected to full term as President

1949 ● Nelson Algren's *The Man With the Golden Arm* · Gwendolyn Brooks' *Annie Allen* · Faulkner's *Knight's Gambit* · René Wellek and Austin Warren's *Theory of Literature* · Welty's *The Golden Apples*

North Atlantic Defense Treaty (NATO) signed by twelve nations, including U.S. · Federal Republic of West Germany and German Democratic Republic (Communist) proclaimed · People's Republic of China (Communist) set up; Chinese Nationalist government fled to Formosa

1950 ● Burke's *A Rhetoric of Motives* · Hersey's *The Wall* · Steinbeck's *Burning Bright* · Stevens' *The Auroras of Autumn* · Viereck's *Strike Through the Mask!*

North Korean troops invaded South Korea; Security Council called upon all U.N. members to aid in enforcing its order for withdrawal of North Koreans to the 38th parallel; Truman ordered U.S. to assist South Koreans · U.S. census: population 150,697,361

1951 ● Truman Capote's *The Grass Harp* · Faulkner's *Requiem for a Nun* · James Jones' *From Here to Eternity* · Lewis' *World So Wide* · J. D. Salinger's *The Catcher in the Rye* · Richard Wilbur's *Ceremony and Other Poems* · Herman Wouk's *The Caine Mutiny*

Twenty-second amendment, limiting presidential terms, ratified

1952 ● Ralph Ellison's *Invisible Man* · Hemingway's *The Old Man and the Sea* · William Inge's *Picnic* · MacLeish's *Collected Poems, 1917-1952* · O'Connor's *An Age of Criticism* · O'Neill's *A Moon for the Misbegotten* · Steinbeck's *East of Eden*

Dwight D. Eisenhower elected thirty-fourth President of the U.S.

1953 ● Aiken's *Collected Poems* · Saul Bellow's *The Adventures of Augie March* · Roethke's *The Waking: Poems 1933-1953* · Sandburg's *Always the Young Strangers* · Shapiro's *Poems, 1940-1953*

First hydrogen bomb exploded · All price controls remaining from war years ended · Korean armistice signed, 27 July

1954 ● Louise Bogan's *Collected Poems, 1922-1953* · Cummings' *Poems: 1923-1954* · Faulkner's *A Fable* · Stevens' *Collected Poems* · Welty's *The Ponder Heart*

First nuclear submarine, *Nautilus,* launched · Army-McCarthy hearings held, April-June · U.S. Supreme Court outlawed school segregation · Southeast Asia Treaty Organization (SEATO) formed

1955 ● Auden's *The Shield of Achilles* · Elizabeth Bishop's *Poems: North and South* · Jarrell's *Selected Poems* · John O'Hara's *Ten North Frederick* · Warren's *Band of Angels* · Sloan Wilson's *The Man in the Gray Flannel Suit* · Wouk's *Marjorie Morningstar*

1956 ● John Berryman's *Homage to Mistress Bradstreet* · John F. Kennedy's *Profiles in Courage* · Marianne Moore's *Like a Bulwark* · Wright Morris' *The Field of Vision* · O'Neill's *Long Day's Journey into Night*

Eisenhower reelected · Salk antipolio vaccine put on the open market

1957 ● James Agee's *A Death in the Family* · John Cheever's *The Wapshot Chronicle* · James Gould Cozzens' *By Love Possessed* · Faulkner's *The Town* · Jack Kerouac's *On the Road* · Kenneth Rexroth's *In Defense of Earth*

Soviet Sputnik sent into orbit—space age begins

1958 ● Capote's *Breakfast at Tiffany's* · Stanley Kunitz's *Selected Poems, 1928-1958* · MacLeish's *J. B.* · Bernard Malamud's *The Magic Barrel* · Mark Van Doren's *Autobiography*

U.S. satellite Explorer I sent into orbit · Boris Pasternak refused Nobel Prize

1959 ● Jacques Barzun's *The House of Intellect* · Bellow's *Henderson the Rain King* · Faulkner's *The Mansion* · Leslie A. Fiedler's *Love and Death in the American Novel* · Lorraine Hansberry's *A Raisin in the Sun* · Delmore Schwartz's *Summer Knowledge* · Warren's *The Cave*

Alaska and Hawaii became 49th and 50th states of the Union · Big Four met in Geneva to discuss reunification of Germany

1960 ● Flannery O'Connor's *The Violent Bear It Away* · Sandburg's *Harvest Poems, 1910-1960* · Shapiro's *In Defense of Ignorance* · Irwin Shaw's *Two Weeks in Another Town* · William Styron's *Set This House on Fire* · Updike's *Rabbit, Run*

John F. Kennedy elected thirty-fifth President of the U.S. · U.S. census: population 179,323,175

1961 ● John Cheever's *Some People, Places, and Things That Will Not Appear in My Next Novel* · Dos Passos' *Midcentury* · Ginsberg's *Kaddish* · McCullers' *Clock Without Hands* · Phyllis McGinley's *Times Three* · Malamud's *A New Life* · Salinger's *Franny and Zooey* · John Steinbeck's *The Winter of Our Discontent*

U.S. broke diplomatic relations with Cuba · Berlin Wall built · First American astronaut in suborbital flight · Twenty-third amendment ratified, permitting citizens in Washington, D.C., to vote in presidential elections

1962 ● Albee's *Who's Afraid of Virginia Woolf?* · Baldwin's *Another Country* · Allan Dugan's *Poems* · Faulkner's *The Reivers* · Frost's *In the Clearing* · James Jones' *The Thin Red Line* · Mailer's *Death for the Ladies* · Katherine Anne Porter's *Ship of Fools* · Salinger's *Raise High the Roof Beam, Carpenters; and Seymour: An Introduction* · Updike's *Pigeon Feathers*

Telestar, communications satellite, sends live TV picture from the U.S. to Europe · First American manned orbital flight · Supreme Court decision that the reading of an official prayer in schools is unconstitutional

1963 ● Edward Albee's *The Ballad of the Sad Café* · James Baldwin's *Blues for Mister Charlie* · LeRoi Jones' *The Dutchman* · Arthur Miller's *After the Fall* · Howard Nemerov's *The Next Room of the Dream* · Anne Sexton's *All My Pretty Ones* · John Updike's *The Centaur* · Kurt Vonnegut's *Cat's Cradle*

The White House stated that aid to South Vietnam would be continued but predicted that the war would end by 1965 · Two hundred thousand people participated in a Freedom March on Washington, demanding immediate civil rights for blacks · President John F. Kennedy assassinated November 22 in Dallas, and Vice-President Lyndon B. Johnson became thirty-sixth President of the U.S.

1964 ● Edward Albee's *Tiny Alice* · Saul Bellow's *Herzog* · John Berryman's *77 Dream Songs* · Hemingway's *A Moveable Feast* · LeRoi Jones' *The Slave* and *The Toilet* · Robert Lowell's *Benito Cereno* and *For the Union Dead* · Arthur Miller's *Incident at Vichy* · Theodore Roethke's *The Far Field* · Karl Shapiro's *The Bourgeois Poet*

Martin Luther King, Jr., awarded Nobel Peace Prize · President Johnson elected to full presidential term · Civil Rights Act of 1964 signed into law · Economic Opportunity Act authorizing youth and community antipoverty programs passed

1965 ● *The Autobiography of Malcolm X* · James Baldwin's *Going to Meet the Man* and *The Amen Corner* · Claude Brown's *Manchild in the Promised Land* · Randall Jarrell's *The Lost World* · Jerzy Kosinski's *The Painted Bird* · Norman Mailer's *An American Dream* · Flannery O'Connor's *Everything that Rises Must Converge*

Gemini 5, with two astronauts aboard, orbited the world for eight days and achieved the first space rendezvous · U.S. troops in Vietnam exceeded 125,000; demonstrations against the war became vociferous · Massive power failure blacked out much of the East for as long as thirteen hours

1966 ● Edward Albee's *Malcolm* and *A Delicate Balance* · John Barth's *Giles Goat-Boy* · Truman Capote's *In Cold Blood* · Bernard Malamud's *The Fixer* · Sylvia Plath's *Ariel* · William Stafford's *The Rescued Year* · Jean-Claude van Itallie's *America Hurrah!*

War in Vietnam gradually escalated; U.S. had 190,000 troops there

1967 ● Edward Albee's *Everything in the Garden* · Arthur Miller's *The Price* · Marianne Moore's *Complete Poems* · William Styron's *The Confessions of Nat Turner* · Thornton Wilder's *The Eighth Day*

U.S. government predicted victory in Vietnam as the war escalated · Stalin's daughter, Svetlana Alliluyeva, came to U.S. as an exile · Israel and the Arabs fought a war won by Israel in six days

1968 ● Gwendolyn Brooks' *In the Mecca* · Jerzy Kosinski's *Steps* · Norman Mailer's *Armies of the Night* and *Miami and the Siege of Chicago* · N. Scott Momaday's *House Made of Dawn* · John Updike's *Couples*

U.S.S. *Pueblo* captured by North Korea · Robert F. Kennedy and Martin Luther King, Jr., assassinated · Russia invaded Czechoslovakia, overturning the liberal regime of Alexander Dubcek · Antiwar riots in Chicago marred the Democratic National Convention · Richard M. Nixon elected thirty-seventh President of the U.S.

1969 ● John Berryman's *His Toy, His Dream, His Rest* · Lonne Elder's *Ceremonies in Dark Old Men* · Jules Feiffer's *Little Murders* · Charles Gordone's *No Place to Be Somebody* · Philip Roth's *Portnoy's Complaint* · Kurt Vonnegut's *Slaughter-House Five* · Paul Zindel's *The Effect of Gamma Rays on Man-in-the-Moon Marigolds*

U.S. astronauts were the first men to walk on the moon, July 20 · Nixon activated his policy of withdrawal of troops from Vietnam and "Vietnamization" of the war · Widespread student dissatisfaction with U.S. war policy leads to revolts at San Francisco State, Harvard, Cornell, Howard, CUNY, Berkeley, and elsewhere

1970 ● Saul Bellow's *Mr. Sammler's Planet* · Elizabeth Bishop's *The Complete Poems* · Philip Booth's *Margins: A Sequence of New and Selected Poems* · James Dickey's *Deliverance* and *The Eye-Beaters, Blood, Victory, Madness, Buckhead and Mercy* · Ernest Hemingway's *Islands in the Stream* · Joyce Carol Oates' *Them* · Eudora Welty's *Losing Battles*

Postal workers in New York City staged first postal strike · First Earth Day, April 22, focused attention on environmental problems · Four students killed by National Guardsmen during a demonstration at Kent State University, Ohio · U.S. census: population 203,184,772

1971 ● Jerzy Kosinski's *Being There* · Bernard Malamud's *The Tenants* · Carson McCullers' *The Mortaged Heart* and *The Previously Uncollected Writings* · Wright Morris' *Fire Sermon* and *War Games* · Flannery O'Connor's *The Complete Stories*

U.S. supported South Vietnam's invasion of Laos, but President Nixon asserted that troop withdrawal would continue · The dollar was allowed to "float," freed from its tie to gold, in a move to devalue and thus correct the trade imbalance

1972 ● John Berryman's *Delusions, Etc.* · Archibald MacLeish's *The Human Season: Selected Poems, 1926-1972* · Joyce Carol Oates' *Marriages and Infidelities* · Ishmael Reed's *Mumbo Jumbo* · Louis Simpson's *Adventures of the Letter I* · Eudora Welty's *The Optimist's Daughter*

President Nixon visits China, thawing a relation frozen for twenty-five years · President Nixon visits Moscow and signs agreements on arms limitation, space exploration, environment, and health · President Nixon wins reelection, overwhelmingly defeating Democratic candidate George McGovern · Olympic games in Munich terrorized by eight Arab "Black Septembrists" who killed eleven Israelis · Peace agreement made with North Vietnam, effectively ending U.S. role in Vietnam War · Watergate scandals (wiretapping and burglary perpetrated by Republican campaign workers on Democratic headquarters) diminish Nixon's power and threaten to destroy his presidency

Biographies
and Bibliographies

HENRY ADAMS 1838–1918

Henry Adams, born in Boston of very wealthy parents, inherited from his illustrious family not only a brilliant mind but also the cherished tradition of culture and useful service. It was not surprising that, after he had been trained in a Boston private school, then in Harvard, and finally—for some years—in centers of European culture, he showed real talents for several different kinds of endeavor. During the Civil War period he efficiently acted as secretary to his father, who served for a time as United States congressman and later as minister to England. Between 1868 and 1870 he was a journalistic commentator, of much promise, upon domestic and foreign affairs. Between 1870 and 1876 he was the competent editor of a long-established and distinguished magazine, the *North American Review*. Simultaneously he was a highly successful teacher of medieval history at Harvard, where, among other important innovations, he introduced the graduate seminar.

Adams is noteworthy as a social theorist and as a historian whose philosophy of history was based on a deterministic outlook. His *Education of Henry Adams* is significant not primarily as an autobiography but as a record of his search for a satisfactory world view. Though it describes the scepticism of a man living in a chaotic age, the book is not without order; subtlety and sureness make it an outstanding masterpiece among American works of its genre.

Novels: *Democracy* (1880) · *Esther* (1884)

Nonfiction: *Life of Albert Gallatin* (1879) · *John Randolph* (1882) · *History of the United States During the Administrations of Jefferson and Madison* (1889-1891) · *Mont-Saint-Michel and Chartres* (1904, revised in 1913)

Autobiography: *The Education of Henry Adams* (1907; publicly printed, 1918)

EDWARD ALBEE 1928–

Edward Albee was born in Washington, D.C. Abandoned by his parents, he was adopted when two weeks old by Reed and Frances Albee, the millionaire owners of a chain of theaters. He spent some time at Trinity College but at twenty-one left school and went to live in New York City, where he drifted from one odd job to another while he tried to find himself as a writer. He wrote much poetry and worked on a novel and, when he was almost thirty, turned to playwriting. With *The Zoo Story*, his first play, and the four that immediately followed it, Albee achieved recognition and was held by some to be a new Tennessee Williams.

Many feel that Albee's plays are characteristic of the theater of the absurd. Yet much of their excellence lies in the author's ability to render

dialog precisely and to create believable and interesting characters.
The Zoo Story (1958) · *The Sandbox* (1959) · *The American Dream*
(1961) · *Who's Afraid of Virginia Woolf?* (1962) · *The Ballad of the Sad
Café* (1963) · *Tiny Alice* (1964) · *Malcolm* (1965) · *A Delicate Balance*
(1966) · *Everything in the Garden* (1967) · *All Over* (1971)

SHERWOOD ANDERSON 1876–1941

Sherwood Anderson was born in Camden, Ohio, and much of his boyhood
was spent in Clyde, another small Ohio town. The poverty of his family
was perhaps the chief reason why he quit school at the age of fourteen and
got a job. Thereafter, for a good many years, he worked at a great variety
of jobs (all requiring manual labor), first in Clyde and then in Chicago. In
1898 he joined the National Guard, and his company was sent to Cuba for
patrol duty after the defeat of the Spanish forces. Upon his return from
Cuba in 1899, he enrolled (somewhat belatedly—he was twenty-three) in
Wittenberg Academy, a preparatory school in Springfield, Ohio, and was
graduated the following year. Soon thereafter, he became a writer of advertising copy. He was so successful in this line that he organized, in 1907, in
Elyria, Ohio, the Anderson Manufacturing Company, which specialized in
roof paint. In 1912 Anderson—though married and the father of three children, and eminently successful in the manufacture and sale of roof paint—
left his factory and did not return. Anderson went at once to Chicago,
where he soon became a member (though he perforce continued for a good
many years to write advertising copy for a living) of the circle of writers
who were making the "Chicago Renaissance."

Though the Midwest was his rightful milieu, and Chicago his proper
cosmopolitan center, Anderson moved restlessly to this place and that, always seeking a fulfillment which he could never achieve: to New York,
which he mistakenly regarded as a better place for him than Chicago, and
where he sought the guidance of Waldo Frank and Van Wyck Brooks; to
Paris, where he met Ernest Hemingway and Gertrude Stein; to New Orleans,
where his association with William Faulkner probably contributed little to
his literary career. After 1927 he lived (with his fourth wife) on a farm
near Marion, Virginia, and, having bought the two newspapers in the town,
gave much of his time to journalism. Even here, in a handsome house of
native stone built into the Virginia hillside, he was unhappy, presumably
because of the failure of his creative powers and the decline of his literary
reputation. During his later years he espoused with noble (if sometimes
ingenuous and misguided) fervor the cause of the Southern textile workers.

In *Winesburg, Ohio* and in the two collections *(The Triumph of the
Egg* and *Horses and Men)* which followed it, Anderson created stories
which, because of their intensity and unconventionality, are his special
contributions to American literature.

Short Stories: *Winesburg, Ohio* (1919) · *The Triumph of the Egg* (1921) ·
Horses and Men (1923)

Novels: *Poor White* (1920) · *Many Marriages* (1923) · *Dark Laughter*
(1925)

Autobiography: *A Story Teller's Story* (1924) · *Tar: A Midwest Childhood* (1926)

Nonfiction: *Perhaps Women* (1931) · *Puzzled America* (1935)

JAMES BALDWIN   1924–
Alongside Richard Wright and Ralph Ellison, James Baldwin ranks as one
of the major black writers of the twentieth century. Born in New York in
1924, he grew up in Harlem and graduated from high school in 1942. After
a time of drifting from one small job to another, he left at the age of
twenty-four for Europe, where he remained for about ten years. The cause
for this self-exile is plain. Baldwin has written: "In America, the color of
my skin has stood between myself and me; in Europe, that barrier was
down. . . . The question of who I was had at last become a personal question, and the answer was to be found in me." Baldwin found the answer,
in part, at least, in his identity as a novelist. His own experiences, his life in
Harlem and in Europe, and questions of homosexuality and race are the
materials from which he writes.
   Baldwin has also written plays, but he has become most celebrated for
his volumes of essays, and it is possible, when all the returns are in, that he
will rank higher as an essayist than as a novelist.
Novels: *Go Tell It on the Mountain* (1953) · *Giovanni's Room* (1956) ·
Another Country (1962) · *Tell Me How Long the Train's Been Gone*
(1968)
Drama: *Blues for Mr. Charley* (1964)
Essays: *Notes of a Native Son* (1955) · *Nobody Knows My Name* (1961) ·
The Fire Next Time (1963)

IMAMU AMIRI BARAKA: see LeRoi Jones

JOHN BARTH   1930–
Born in 1930 in Cambridge, Maryland, John Barth attended the public
schools there and Johns Hopkins University in Baltimore. Beginning in
1953, he combined an academic with a writing career as he began teaching
in the English department of Pennsylvania State University, moving later
to the State University of New York at Buffalo. His first novel, *The Floating Opera* (1956), won praise from the critics, as have most of his subsequent works. His 1972 novel *Chimera* shared the National Book Award for
Fiction (1973).
   John Barth's name usually turns up in the category of Black Humorists,
those writers who seem to say that we live in a time of domesticated horror
and familiar agony, and we might as well thumb our noses in hilarity at an
absurd and insane world. He certainly is, in any case, one of the most
gifted and widely experimental novelists writing in America today.
Novels: *The Floating Opera* (1956) · *End of the Road* (1958) · *The
Sotweed Factor* (1960) · *Giles Goat-Boy* (1966) · *Chimera* (1972)
Short Stories: *Lost in the Funhouse: Fiction for Print, Tape, Live Voice*
(1968)

DONALD BARTHELME   1931–
Donald Barthelme was born April 7, 1931, in Philadelphia, grew up in
Houston, and now resides in New York. He is extremely reticent about his
personal life, and little more is known about him beyond the fact that he
represents an important new talent in American fiction. He has published
stories in many periodicals, but has appeared most frequently in *The New
Yorker.*
   Barthelme appears to be a master of the miniature shock and the small
surprise. His is a pop fiction to match the pop art of our time, and it is in

harmony with the happening and psychedelic experience. The world in Barthelme's fiction is the real world—but the real world as it is reflected by the curved and distorting amusement-house mirror.

Novel: *Snow White* (1967)
Short Stories: *Come Back, Dr. Caligari* (1964) · *Unspeakable Practices, Unnatural Acts* (1968)

EDWARD BELLAMY 1850–1898

Edward Bellamy was born in Chicopee Falls, Massachusetts. At eighteen he spent the better part of a year in Europe, where, as he wrote later, "my eyes were first fully opened to the extent and consequences of man's inhumanity to man." After two years of study he was admitted to the bar, but he gave up law almost at once in favor of journalism. In 1875 Bellamy began to contribute short stories to the national magazines and by 1880 had published nine times in *Scribner's Monthly, Lippincott's,* and *Appleton's.* Then, late in 1886, the year of the Haymarket affair, he began to compose *Looking Backward,* which convinced thousands of Americans that the society it described was just what they wanted. Bellamy soon became the leading force in the Nationalist movement which followed. In January 1891 he founded his own weekly, *The New Nation,* and it is probable that his followers lent their influence to the formation of the People's Party, founded in May 1891. There is scarcely an aspect of present-day social planning with which Bellamy did not deal in some detail in his novels. Like Henry George, he had a "call" to reaffirm the philosophy of the rights of man and a "vision" of a society in which there would no longer be economic injustice.

Six to One: A Nantucket Idyl (1878) · *Dr. Heidenhoff's Progress* (1880) · *Miss Ludington's Sister: A Romance of Immortality* (1884) · *Looking Backward: 2000-1887* (1888) · *Equality* (1897) · *The Duke of Stockbridge: A Romance of Shays' Rebellion* (mostly written before 1880; completed and published, 1900)

SAUL BELLOW 1915–

Saul Bellow, one of the most admired of the contemporary American writers of fiction, was born in Lachine, Quebec, in 1915. Since his family moved to Chicago soon after and he was reared and educated in and near that city, he considers himself a Chicagoan. He studied at the University of Chicago and Northwestern University, where he received his B.S. in 1937. He taught in Pestalozzi-Froebel Teachers College, Chicago, between 1938 and 1942 and during these years began publishing his writings. Later he taught at the University of Minnesota and at the University of Chicago; he is still teaching at the latter school. He has received a number of grants and awards, including a Guggenheim Fellowship (1955–1956) and the National Book Award for Fiction in 1971 for *Mr. Sammler's Planet.*

Bellow discourages formal criticism of his work, holding that his writings should be regarded as "entertainment." Nevertheless, one of his appeals is his unabashed and mature confrontation of some of today's most pressing problems.

Novels: *Dangling Man* (1944) · *The Victim* (1947) · *The Adventures of Augie March* (1953) · *Henderson the Rain King* (1959) · *Herzog* (1964) · *Mr. Sammler's Planet* (1970)
Short Stories: *Seize the Day* (1956) · *Mosby's Memoirs and Other Stories* (1968)
Drama: *The Last Analysis* (1965)

HUGH HENRY BRACKENRIDGE 1748–1816
Hugh Henry Brackenridge, "our first back-country writer," was born in Scotland in 1748 and came to York County, Pennsylvania, then a frontier region, when he was five. At fifteen he was teaching school in Maryland; at the age of twenty he entered the College of New Jersey (now Princeton), where he was a classmate of James Madison and Philip Freneau. Before his graduation in 1771, he had dabbled in satirical verse and fiction.

Brackenridge had a number of different careers during his lifetime: schoolmaster, chaplain, magazine publisher, lawyer, and political leader. He moved from Philadelphia to Pittsburgh in 1785, but the move did not bring him tranquillity. Rather, it deposited a thoughtful democrat with literary tastes in a turbulent center of frontier democracy. The result was the picaresque novel *Modern Chivalry*, of which the first volume appeared in 1792, and the whole in finally revised form in 1815. There is no better record of the society which rebelled against Alexander Hamilton's internal revenue measures in the so-called Whiskey Insurrection of 1791-1794.
Modern Chivalry (1792, 1815)

WILLIAM BRADFORD 1590–1657
William Bradford sailed on the *Mayflower* in 1620. Following the landing at Plymouth in December of that year, Bradford, as his *History of Plymouth Plantation* (1620-1647) records, took a leading part in the affairs of the colony. He was chosen governor in the annual elections no less than thirty times, serving continuously from 1622 to 1656, except for five years when he was relieved at his own urgent request. Whether his art was conscious or not, Bradford's prose is worthy of a distinguished place in the English tradition of his century.
Mourt's Relation (with Edward Winslow, 1622) · *History of Plymouth Plantation, 1620-1647* (published, 1856)

ANNE BRADSTREET 1612–1672
Anne Bradstreet and her husband, Simon, a graduate of Cambridge, came to Massachusetts with John Winthrop and other prominent first settlers of the Massachusetts Bay Colony. Her husband became a noted leader in the affairs of the Massachusetts Bay Colony. Anne Bradstreet had eight children; hers was the busy, heroic life of a wife and mother in a pioneer community. She found time, nevertheless, for the writing of verse, a considerable quantity of which was published in London in 1650 with the title, *The Tenth Muse Lately Sprung up in America*. Mrs. Bradstreet's most original poems, and some may think her best, are her private domestic pieces, unpublished until after her death, in which she reveals her religious difficulties and her wifely and maternal devotion.
The Tenth Muse Lately Sprung up in America (1650) · *The Works of Anne Bradstreet*, ed. J. H. Ellis (1867; reprinted, 1932)

GWENDOLYN BROOKS 1917–
Gwendolyn Brooks was born in Kansas but taken only a month later to Chicago. There she grew up, went to college, worked, married, lived through World War II. She never lost an early pleasure in poetry, and in 1944 some of her writing was printed in *Poetry, A Magazine of Verse*. A year later *A Street in Bronzeville* was published, bringing her a number of fellowships and grants-in-aid which were amply rewarded by *Annie Allen*, the story of a black girl's life from childhood to maturity. In 1949 it won the Pulitzer Prize for Poetry.

Technically Brooks' poetry is impressive for range and variety of form. She delicately combines direct and vivid sense impressions with the somewhat elliptical style characteristic of T. S. Eliot and his admirers.

Poetry: *A Street in Bronzeville* (1945) · *Annie Allen* (1949) · *The Bean Eaters* (1960) · *Selected Poems* (1963) · *In the Mecca* (1968)

Novel: *Maud Martha* (1953)

CHARLES FARRAR BROWNE (Artemus Ward) 1834–1867

Born in Waterford, Maine, Charles Farrar Browne started out as a printer's devil and in time moved from his printer's case to the editorial desks of various newspapers. He was an editor of the Cleveland, Ohio, *Plain Dealer* in 1858 when some playful letters he composed started him on his way to fame. Artemus Ward, the purported author of the letters, introduced himself as the illiterate, humorless owner of an itinerant waxworks and menagerie. After these pieces had won a large following for him, Browne went to New York to work on the comic magazine *Vanity Fair,* and in 1861 he embarked on a highly remunerative career as a comic lecturer. Browne was typical of a majority of the humorists of his day—professional funnymen, literary comedians who exploited the humor of diction rather than the humor of character. Their writings are interesting as social documents and as works foreshadowing much of the "free association humor" of such authors as Benchley, Thurber, and Perelman.

Artemus Ward: His Book (1862) · *Artemus Ward: His Travels* (1865) · *Artemus Ward in London* (1867)

WILLIAM CULLEN BRYANT 1794–1878

William Cullen Bryant was born at Cummington, in western Massachusetts. Brought up in a Calvinistic and Federalist environment, he took himself and the world very seriously as soon as he knew anything about them. His first verses appeared in a newspaper when he was ten, and he saw his first book in print five years later, when his father arranged for the publication of *The Embargo,* an attack on Jefferson's methods of avoiding entanglement in the Napoleonic conflict. He had only one year of college, at Williams, and then, because there was no livelihood in poetry, he turned to the study of law. Admitted to the bar in 1814, he practiced in several Massachusetts towns with moderate success, occasionally using his leisure for composing poems. After 1817, when his father sent some of his poems to a Boston friend and "Thanatopsis" came out in the *North American Review,* he became known as poet and reviewer for that periodical and others. In 1821 he married Fanny Fairchild, the "fairest of the rural maids"; theirs was an unusually happy marriage.

In 1825 Bryant had the courage to give up the law for the uncertainties of a literary life and deserted Massachusetts for New York City. Within a few months he formed a connection with the *Evening Post,* a daily newspaper which had been founded by Alexander Hamilton; in 1829 he became the editor-in-chief and held the position until his death in 1878. As a part owner of the paper, he grew wealthy and was able to afford much European travel for himself and his family, as well as to establish a comfortable home at Roslyn on Long Island.

Bryant's poetry, although apparently simple, does, in fact, defy categorization. Although his concern for form and clarity, harmony and serenity is typically "classical," his poetic theories and his themes—the past, death, freedom, nature—have much in them that is ordinarily called "romantic."

The Embargo (1808) · *The White Footed Deer and Other Poems* (1844) ·
Poems (1821, 1832, 1836, 1847, 1854, 1871, 1876)

WILLIAM BYRD   1647–1744

Although William Byrd's birthplace was a tidewater plantation, he was educated in England and on the Continent. He was trained not only in business
and law but also in the social graces and in classical and Neoclassical
literature. Shortly after his return from England to America in 1692, Byrd
assumed his place as a member of the ruling circle in Virginia. He served
several times as a representative in the House of Burgesses; on various occasions he represented the colony in England: he was also appointed a
member of the Supreme Council and held that dignified position for the
remainder of his life. His journal writings, in which his witty perceptions
are recorded in well-turned phrases, reveal not only his admiration of Neoclassical literature but also the complexity of a Virginian who was not only
an aristocrat but also a businessman and a man of the world.

The History of the Dividing Line (1728) · *The Secret History of the Line*
(1728) · *A Progress to the Mines* (1732) · *A Journey to the Land of Eden*
(1733)

GEORGE WASHINGTON CABLE   1844–1925

George Washington Cable's father came from an old slaveholding family in
Virginia; his mother was a native of New England and a strict Puritan.
Cable himself was born in New Orleans, where he spent much of his life.
For more than ten years after the Civil War, in which he had served and
had been wounded, he was clerk and bookkeeper for a cotton firm. During
these years, however, he read much, delved into the old French and
Spanish records of New Orleans, and began to write. His first story ap-
peared in *Scribner's Monthly* in 1873 and was followed by other stories of
New Orleans in the early nineteenth century, a colorful mélange of races.
Despite the success of his early local color stories, Cable turned reformer,
and in *The Silent South* (1885) he zealously advocated reforms in racial
relations. The book made him so unpopular in the South that he moved to
Massachusetts.

Like many other writers of local color fiction, Cable was a romantic
realist and was inclined to play up the moral ending and the picturesque.
But if his edification is sometimes a little forced, his exoticism is at least
based on fact. He deserves to be remembered as the literary discoverer of
romantic New Orleans and as the facile recorder of his discoveries.

Short Stories: *Old Creole Days* (1879) · *"Posson Jane" and Père Raphael*
(1909)
Novels: *The Grandissimes* (1880) · *Madame Delphine* (1881) · *Dr. Sevier*
(1885) · *John March, Southerner* (1894)
Essays: *The Silent South* (1885) · *The Negro Question* (1890)

WILLA SIBERT CATHER   1873–1947

Willa Cather was born near Winchester, in the northern tip of Virginia, but
from her ninth to her nineteenth year she was a Nebraskan, growing up in
what was then a pioneer rural community, settled largely by Norwegian
and Bohemian immigrants. After some tutoring at home she went to high
school at Red Cloud and then to the University of Nebraska, where she
graduated in 1895. By that time she had acquired a deep interest in good
music, an enthusiasm for the work of Henry James, and a desire to write,

heightened by some experience with newspaper work and a few appearances in the college magazine.

Only gradually did she find her power as a writer. Her first published
stories and poems appeared in 1900. She had then worked for five years on
the Pittsburgh *Daily Leader.* Her first book, *April Twilights* (1903), a
volume of poems, came out while she was teaching English in Allegheny
High School. In 1906 she moved to New York City to work on *McClure's
Magazine,* of which she was managing editor from 1908 until 1911. It
seems likely that the most important event of Cather's years as editor was
her connection with Sarah Orne Jewett, who advised her late in 1908 to
find time and quiet to perfect her work if she wished her gifts to mature.
Following this advice, she resigned her editorship to write. With the novels
that soon followed, *My Ántonia* among them, her reputation as a writer
was firmly established.

The secure position of Willa Cather among present-day American writers is the result of her allegiance to the belief that fiction is a form of art
worth practicing with the utmost seriousness. The effects which she chiefly sought were in the realm of subtleties of character and situation. But
she was, nevertheless, aware of the importance of setting and physical
action. She stood for tradition and refinement of art in life and in fiction.
Novels: *O Pioneers!* (1913) · *The Song of the Lark* (1915) · *My Ántonia*
(1918) · *One of Ours* (1922) · *The Professor's House* (1925) · *My Mortal
Enemy* (1926) · *Death Comes for the Archbishop* (1927) · *Shadows on the
Rock* (1931)
Poetry: *April Twilights* (1903)
Short Stories: *The Troll Garden* (1905) · *Youth and the Bright Medusa*
(1920) · *Obscure Destinies* (1932) · *The Old Beauty and Others* (1948) ·
Collected Short Fiction, 1892-1912 (1965)
Essays: *Not Under Forty* (1936)

KATE CHOPIN   1851–1904

Kate Chopin was born Katherine O'Flaherty in St. Louis of Irish and
French parents. She graduated from a convent and was active in St. Louis
society until her marriage at 19 to Oscar Chopin, a Louisiana Creole. The
couple lived with their six children on a Louisiana cotton plantation until
Oscar's death, when Kate Chopin returned to St. Louis. There, at the age
of 39, she produced her first novel, *At Fault* (1890). She was active as a
short story writer; about half her stories were collected in two volumes,
Bayou Folk (1894) and *A Night in Acadie* (1897). These portrayed Acadians in mid-Louisiana whom she had come to know when living on the
plantation before her husband's death, but they are more than simply local
color stories: they are written with an economy, polish, and proportion
reminiscent of one of her main influences, De Maupassant. Her most
famous work is a novel, *The Awakening* (1899), which pioneered as a
psychological novel and was much criticized for its frankness in treating
sex and portraying adultery.
The Complete Works of Kate Chopin, ed. Per Seyersted (1969)

ELDRIDGE CLEAVER   1935–

Eldridge Cleaver was born in Wabbaseka, Arkansas, near Little Rock. His
first job was as a shoe-shine boy, but he turned to dealing in marijuana, was
caught, and served his first of two prison terms. During his second term, in
California's Folsom State Prison, he underwent a religious conversion and

joined the Black Muslims, becoming a follower of Malcolm X. It was also
during this time that he discovered his interest in books and his talents as a
writer: his first book, *Soul on Ice* (originally titled *Letters from Prison*),
has become a handbook for many black youths. Upon his release from
prison he became active in the Black Panthers and was ultimately involved
in confrontations with the police: after a gunfight in which he was
wounded, Cleaver refused to surrender to the authorities for parole viola-
tion, and fled with his wife and child to Cuba and eventually to Algeria,
where he continues to live in exile.

Essays: *Soul on Ice* (1968) · *Post-Prison Writings and Speeches* (1969)

SAMUEL L. CLEMENS (Mark Twain) 1835–1910

Samuel Langhorne Clemens spent his boyhood years in Hannibal, Missouri,
where he became a printer's apprentice. Having learned to set type, he
wandered eastward as far as New York, picking up printing jobs in one city
after another. Then, back in the Middle West in the 1850's, he learned the
pilot's trade and spent some of his happiest years steering boats up and
down the Mississippi. Later, he adopted the pseudonym "Mark Twain," an
expression used by steamboatmen when testing the depth of the channel.
The job of piloting lasted until the boom days of river trade were cut off
by the Civil War. In 1861, after brief service in the Confederate Army, he
went out to the Far West. There, he took some fliers in mining stock, did
some prospecting, and finally got into journalism of the masculine humorous sort which flourished in the Far West.

The journalistic work, in Nevada and in California, launched him on
his career as a humorist. Having invested some of his royalties from his
first popular book in a Buffalo newspaper, Clemens was an editor for a
time. He financed many inventions and get-rich schemes and eventually set
up as a large-scale publisher of books—his own as well as those by other
authors. In 1894, when the author-businessman was fifty-nine, some important financial investments proved unwise, his publishing house failed,
and he faced financial ruin. Refusing to accept bankruptcy, he paid off his
debts dollar for dollar, earning enough to do so by publishing and by making a lecture trip around the world.

After he had hit upon his mature technique, two methods—that of the
old Southwestern humorists and that of the funnymen—were intermingled
in most of his writings. Whenever in his fiction (for example *Huckleberry
Finn*), his training as a professional humorist caused him to add buffoonery
and burlesque to materials inhospitable to the broadest comedy, his writings tended to suffer from unevenness of tone. However, he had the happy
ability of always finding the best word, and more than any other classic
fictionist, he captured the American language in print. In addition, he had
a genius for creating living, memorable characters.

Travel Narratives: *The Innocents Abroad* (1869) · *Roughing It* (1872) ·
A Tramp Abroad (1880) · *Following the Equator* (1897)

Novels: *The Gilded Age* (with Charles Dudley Warner, 1873) · *The Adven-
tures of Tom Sawyer* (1876) · *The Prince and the Pauper* (1882) · *The
Adventures of Huckleberry Finn* (1884) · *A Connecticut Yankee in King
Arthur's Court* (1889) · *Puddn'head Wilson* (1894) · *The Mysterious
Stranger* (1916)

Autobiography: *Life on the Mississippi* (1883) · *Autobiography* (1924,
1940)

JAMES FENIMORE COOPER   1789–1851

James Fenimore Cooper was born in New Jersey and soon moved to the town which his father had laid out—Cooperstown, New York. He was brought up in a community in which the Coopers were by far the most important personages; his future was from the first defined as that of a landowner and estate manager. He had the education of a gentleman, first under a private tutor in Albany and then in Yale College, which expelled him in 1806 for too much pleasure-seeking. After spending three years in the United States Navy, he married Susan Augusta De Lancey, daughter of a wealthy family in Westchester County. Both he and his wife had money of their own, and there was more in prospect. Thus, in 1819 at the age of thirty, Cooper was a gentleman farmer and a small capitalist, with neither the ambition nor the necessity for authorship.

Seldom, perhaps, has a novelist developed more casually. The tradition is that, reading aloud to his wife a story of English country life, he remarked that he could do as well himself and set out to do so. The result was the novel *Precaution* (1820), abounding with moral sentiment on marriage and picturing English society. It was published in 1820, and, although not especially successful, it led directly to *The Spy* (1821), which was enormously so. The course of Cooper's life was changed abruptly, and he began to produce a stream of books which, at the time of his death in 1851, consisted of thirty-three novels and numerous volumes of social comment, naval history, and travel.

Cooper's right to be called the first great American novelist can scarcely be challenged. The recognition of his greatness came as early as when his friend Bryant referred to him as the American Hesiod or Theocritus, a poet of the youth of a nation.

Essays: *The American Democrat* (1838)
Novels: *Precaution* (1820) · *The Spy* (1821) · *The Pioneers* (1823) · *The Pilot* (1823) · *Lionel Lincoln* (1825) · *The Last of the Mohicans* (1826) · *The Prairie* (1827) · *The Bravo* (1831) · *The Heidenmauer* (1832) · *The Headsman* (1833) · *Home as Found* (1838) · *The Pathfinder* (1840) · *The Deerslayer* (1841) · *Satanstoe* (1845) · *The Chainbearer* (1845) · *The Redskins* (1846)

CHARLES EGBERT CRADDOCK: see Mary Noailles Murfree

HART CRANE   1899–1932

Hart Crane was born in Garrettsville, Ohio, and later lived in Cleveland, where he attended a public high school for three years. He did not go to college but while still in his teens dedicated himself to a poetic career. For a livelihood, Crane did various jobs in his father's candy business, working as clerk in a candy store, traveling salesman, warehouse manager, and the like, but he later found less uncongenial employment as a writer for advertising agencies, first in Cleveland and then in New York. Like Sherwood Anderson, whom he admired, he gravitated to New York and its literary coteries. Here Crane profited by his associations with Gorham Munson, Waldo Frank, Allen Tate, Malcolm Cowley, and others. Otto Kahn, the philanthropist, gave him a thousand dollars (and offered more) so that he might have leisure for his poetry. His magnum opus, *The Bridge*, was published in 1930 and met with a mixed reception. Neurotically unhappy for a long while, Crane sought peace of mind, without success, in the Adirondacks, Europe, Cuba, Mexico. En route to the United States from Mexico,

April 27, 1932, he committed suicide by jumping from the deck of a
steamship into the Caribbean Sea.

Crane's fame, it now appears, rests securely upon *The Bridge*, perhaps
the most ambitious poem in English since *The Waste Land*, to which it is in
some ways similar, though it is neither as well unified nor as firmly sustained as Eliot's masterpiece.

White Buildings (1926) · *The Bridge* (1930) · *Collected Poems* (1933)

STEPHEN CRANE   1871–1900

Stephen Crane was born in Newark, New Jersey, the son of a Methodist
preacher. He spent a semester at Lafayette College, where he shocked his
English professor by declaring that Tennyson's poetry was "swill"; and a
semester at Syracuse University, where he played shortstop on the varsity
nine. Believing earnestly that he must devote his life to "the business of
writing," he began with journalism. His brief career as a newspaper writer
gave him rich and varied opportunities for observation: in the New York
Bowery, in Texas and Mexico, and—under war conditions—in Greece and
in Cuba. After 1897 he lived in England with Cora Taylor, a woman he had
met in Florida; one of his close friends there was Joseph Conrad. Crane
died in the Black Forest, in Germany, where he had gone with the hope of
improving his health.

As a poet, Crane is an interesting link between Emily Dickinson and
the Imagists of the 1910's. As a writer of fiction, he is important both as
an early naturalist and as an expert craftsman.

Novels: *Maggie: A Girl of the Streets* (1893) · *The Red Badge of Courage*
(1895)

Short Stories: *The Open Boat and Other Tales of Adventure* (1898) · *The
Monster and Other Stories* (1899) · *Whilomville Stories* (1900)

Poetry: *The Black Rider and Other Lines* (1895) · *War Is Kind and Other
Lines* (1899)

MICHEL GUILLAUME ST. JEAN DE CRÈVECOEUR   1735–1813

Michel Guillaume St. Jean de Crèvecoeur was born in France. Educated in
a Jesuit school and in England, he sailed for Canada before he was twenty
and there enlisted in the army. About 1759 Crèvecoeur drifted down
through the English colonies and in 1764 applied for naturalization in New
York. He married and for approximately fifteen years lived as a gentleman
farmer in a well-established and prosperous rural community. Soon after
his marriage, he appears to have begun setting down his impressions of the
country; and by 1780 he was forced to leave America because his moderate
opinions had made both Whigs and Tories suspicious of him. For a time he
was a protégé of Madame d'Houdetot, whom Rousseau had loved. Partly
through her influence, he was sent back to New York as consul-general,
and for seven years he did his best to keep alive American friendship with
France. The last twenty-three years of his life were spent in Europe.

Crèvecoeur wrote well, though unevenly. The fashion of his day
compelled him to shape his best-known book into a series of letters, but
within these he displayed a considerable command for three different
forms: the prose essay, the short story, and the dramatic dialog.

Letters from an American Farmer (1782) · *Sketches of Eighteenth Century
America* (pub. 1925) · *Travels in Pennsylvania and New York*, ed. P. E.
Adams (1962)

DAVID CROCKETT 1786-1836
Although he was born and reared in a Tennessee frontier log cabin and had little formal education, David Crockett became a United States Congressman and a hero of the folk. His accomplishments had become legendary even before his heroic death in the Alamo in 1836. In 1834 he had published his autobiography, *A Narrative of the Life of David Crockett of West Tennessee.* This and others of his accounts did much to bring in the fireside yarn, with its authentic rendering of Western ways of living, thinking, talking, and narrating, as an eventual literary influence upon authors such as Harte and Clemens.
Narrative of the Life of David Crockett of West Tennessee (1834) · *A Tour to the North and Down East* (1835)

COUNTEE CULLEN 1903-1946
Countee Cullen grew up in Harlem with foster parents, attended De Witt Clinton High School, and began to publish poetry before his graduation from New York University in 1925. After earning an M.A. at Harvard, where he studied under the poet Robert Hillyer, he became for a time assistant editor of *Opportunity*, a little magazine important in the publishing of Negro writing during the Harlem Renaissance.

Cullen published a number of volumes in quick succession, the first, *Color*, in 1925. He admired such poets as John Keats, which led to his use of more conventional poetic forms than those used by Langston Hughes. But Cullen's material was mined from his own experience. In a sense he never ceased to marvel at God's seeming caprice: "To make a poet black, and bid him sing!"

Something of the diversity of Cullen's talents is indicated by his translation of *Medea* and by his novel of Negro life in Harlem, *One Way to Heaven.* He also collaborated with Arna Bontemps in converting Bontemps' novel *God Sends Sunday* into a successful Broadway musical, *St. Louis Woman.*
Poetry: *Color* (1925) · *Copper Sun* (1927) · *The Ballad of the Brown Girl: An Old Ballad Retold* (1927) · *The Black Christ and Other Poems* (1929) · *On These I Stand* (1947)
Novel: *One Way to Heaven* (1932)

E. E. CUMMINGS 1894-1962
Edward Estlin Cummings, the son of a minister, was born and educated in Cambridge, Massachusetts; in 1915 and 1916 he received his B.A. and M.A. from Harvard. During World War I he served with the ambulance corps, and through the error of a military censor he spent some time in a French detention camp. His book, *The Enormous Room*, details his experiences there. After studying art for a time in Paris, he began to experiment with new techniques of writing such as unconventional typographical arrangements, oddities of spelling and punctuation, and the abolition of capital letters. Magazines such as *Vanity Fair, The Dial,* and others accepted his poems, and he published many individual volumes of poetry and novels.
Poetry: *Tulips & Chimneys* (1923) · *Collected Poems* (1938) · *Poems: 1923-1954* (1954) · *One Hundred Selected Poems* (1959)
Novel: *The Enormous Room* (1922)

CLARENCE SHEPARD DAY, JR.   1874–1935
Clarence Day was born in New York City, the grandson of the founder of
a great metropolitan newspaper and the son of a Wall Street broker. He
attended Yale, graduating in 1896, then began to work in the stock exchange. Having found that he had little enthusiasm for finance, Day joined
the Navy during the Spanish-American War. A severe attack of arthritis
ended his period of service and left him partially crippled throughout the
rest of his life. Despite his crippled hands, Day became a cartoonist of some
repute: his deft impressionistic line drawings in some ways foreshadowed
those of such imaginative moderns as William Steig and James Thurber.
Day also became a journalist and a writer of essays, sketches, and books.
    Day's first book, *This Simian World* (1920), is a somewhat Swiftean
satire in which man is compared, usually to his disadvantage, to other animals, and his faults are ascribed to his simian ancestry. After publishing
some books of cartoons and essays, he found and worked his best vein, the
comic family reminiscence, of which *Life with Father* is one of the best-
loved examples.
God and My Father (1932) · *In the Green Mountain Country* (1934) · *Life
with Father* (1935) · *Life with Mother* (1937)

JAMES DICKEY   1923–
James Dickey was born in Atlanta, Georgia. He was educated at Vanderbilt
University and has taught at Rice University and the University of Florida,
and has worked in advertising. He was awarded the National Book Award
for Poetry in 1966, and the same year was appointed Consultant in Poetry
at the Library of Congress.
    A prolific writer, Dickey is unique in his use of language, falling some-
where between the tightly constructed spareness of a disciplined academic
poet and the casually dribbled spontaneities of an undisciplined beat poet.
Dickey is unusual as a modern poet because he is nearly always readable
and almost always understandable. His poetic voice speaks with a distinctly
Southern accent, easy and relaxed, and it often speaks of his boyhood
experiences and legends of the South.
Poetry: *Into the Stone* (1960) · *Drowning with Others* (1962) · *Helmets*
(1964) · *Buckdancer's Choice* (1965) · *Poems 1957-1967* (1967) · *The
Eye-Beaters, Blood, Victory, Madness, Buckhead and Mercy* (1970)
Essays: *The Suspect in Poetry* (1964) · *Babel to Byzantium* (1968) · *The
Self as Agent* (1970)
Novel: *Deliverance* (1970)

EMILY DICKINSON   1830–1886
Emily Dickinson was the daughter of lawyer Edward Dickinson of
Amherst, Massachusetts, a rather stern Calvinist. Despite her repressive sur-
roundings she was a vivacious, fun-loving girl and was well educated in the
Amherst Academy and Mount Holyoke. In time, something happened to
her which caused her to become a recluse in her house at Amherst, where
she wrote much verse but refused to publish it during her lifetime. Books
of her poems were published starting in 1890. These were greatly edited.
Her complete works are now available in an excellent three-volume edition,
The Poems of Emily Dickinson, edited by Thomas H. Johnson (1955).
Johnson also has edited her delightful letters.
    Beginning in the 1920's many critics have praised Dickinson, along

with Whitman, for pioneering in modern poetry. The use she made of imperfect rhyme, or eye-rhyme, and, in particular, her habit of packing her lines with cryptic meanings have endeared her to present-day readers. Her vivid imagination and her playful spirit also made her as fond of poetic conceits as had been John Donne, idol of the moderns.

The Poems of Emily Dickinson, ed. Thomas H. Johnson (3 vols., 1955) · *The Letters of Emily Dickinson*, ed. Thomas H. Johnson (3 vols., 1958)

MR. DOOLEY: see Finley Peter Dunne

JOHN DOS PASSOS 1896–1970
John Dos Passos' father was a New York lawyer, the son of a Portuguese immigrant; his mother's family lived in Maryland and Virginia. Born in Chicago, Dos Passos was (as he has put it) "carted around a good deal as a child"—to Mexico, England, Europe, Washington City, tidewater Virginia. He prepared for college at Choate School in Wallingford, Connecticut, and was graduated from Harvard, *cum laude*, in 1916. During World War I he served first with a French ambulance unit and later in the United States Medical Corps as a private. After the war, he went to various parts of Europe and America as a newspaper correspondent.

Dos Passos' trilogy, *U.S.A.*, is the most impressive "social" novel which has been written thus far in America. The style, which Kazin well calls "a hard, lean, mocking prose," is an efficient instrument for the portrayal of the modern machine age. The books which followed *U.S.A.* indicate that Dos Passos moved steadily away from his earlier position at the extreme left. The later Dos Passos was less obviously doctrinaire and mechanical, and more human and humanistic.

Three Soldiers (1921) · *Manhattan Transfer* (1925) · *U.S.A.* (1937) · *Adventures of a Young Man* (1939) · *The Grand Design* (1949) · *Chosen Country* (1951) · *Midcentury* (1961)

FREDERICK DOUGLASS 1817?–1895
Frederick Bailey, as he was first named, or Frederick Douglass, as he later called himself, was born in Tuckahoe, Maryland, probably in February 1817, the son of a Negro slave and a white man. Hired out in 1834, he was driven by a slave-breaking master's brutality to rebel. "This battle," he said, "was the turning-point in my career as a slave. . . . From this time I was never again . . . whipped." After an abortive attempt to escape in 1836, he succeeded in 1838.

Douglass' eloquent speech at an abolitionist meeting in Nantucket in 1841 led to his being employed as an antislavery lecturer. His *Narrative of the Life of Frederick Douglass An American Slave Written by Himself*— first published in 1845 and later revised and republished—is, according to Benjamin Quarles, "one of the most arresting autobiographical statements in the entire catalogue of American reform." Douglass' eloquence as both a writer and an orator enabled him until his death to continue to be one of the most influential battlers for the black revolution.

Autobiography: *Narrative of the Life of Frederick Douglass An American Slave Written by Himself* (1845) · *My Bondage and My Freedom* (1855) · *Life and Times of Frederick Douglass* (1892)

JACK DOWNING: see Seba Smith

THEODORE DREISER 1871–1945

The twelfth in a family of thirteen children, Theodore Dreiser was born in Terre Haute, Indiana, where his father, a German immigrant, was proprietor of a woolen mill. The burning of the mill, which was not insured, left the family in extreme poverty. Dreiser's formal schooling was received in an Indiana high school and at Indiana University, where he stayed only one year because he felt that the curriculum "did not concern ordinary life at all." More useful than college to Dreiser were various odd jobs in Chicago— washing dishes in a restaurant, shoveling coal in a railroad yard, working in a hardware factory, collecting bills for a furniture store. Valuable also to the future novelist were his experiences as a reporter on the Chicago *Globe* and on other newspapers in St. Louis, Cleveland, Pittsburgh, and New York. His newspaper career extended until about 1905. For a while he was con- nected with certain "pulp" magazines, and from 1907 to 1910 he was editor of *The Delineator*. Jobs like these were necessary to pay expenses; his novels brought him little money for many years. In the meantime, he had married but did not find marriage to his liking and was divorced. In time he married actress Helen Patgas and lived in the California movie colony for three years before moving to New York State in 1924. After a visit to Russia in 1927 he became an enthusiastic supporter of socialism, but towards the end of his life he had developed a serious interest in orien- tal mysticism.

No other American novelist has documented his stories quite so care- fully or has written a social record of American life so convincingly authen- tic. Though Dreiser's work is often dull and sometimes reveals the author's lack of a sense of humor, it is important as the first entirely "naturalistic" American fiction.

Novels: *Sister Carrie* (1900) · *Jennie Gerhardt* (1911) · *The Financier* (1912) · *The Titan* (1914) · *The "Genius"* (1915) · *An American Tragedy* (1925) · *The Bulwark* (1946) · *The Stoic* (1947)

Short Stories: *Free and Other Stories* (1918) · *Chains* (1927) · *A Gallery of Women* (1929)

W. E. B. DU BOIS 1868–1963

William Edward Burghardt Du Bois, author, scholar, teacher, sociologist, and black leader, was in an important sense the progenitor of today's black militancy and cultural development. Born in Great Barrington, Massachu- setts, on February 23, 1868, he graduated from Fisk University, won a second B.A. and a Ph.D. from Harvard, and carried on graduate study in Berlin. Between 1897 and 1910, he taught economics and history in Atlan- ta University. In 1905 he helped found the Niagara Movement, which in 1908 evolved into the National Association for the Advancement of Colored People, and from 1910 to 1932 he edited the organ of that asso- ciation, *Crisis*. A leader of the movement to bring about the liberation of African colonies from 1900 on, at the age of ninety-four he became a citi- zen of Ghana. The next year, on August 27, 1963, he died in Accra.

A prolific writer, Du Bois published articles and books in the fields of sociology, history, education, and religion and, in addition, a book of poems and five novels: listing them all would take pages. His *The Philadel- phia Negro: A Social Study* (1899) pioneered in a vast area previously unexplored. A series of studies ranged over Afro-American and African his- tory, and nearly a score of additional sociological books dealt with a host of aspects of the lives of black people.

The Souls of Black Folk: Essays and Sketches (1903) · *Darkwater: Voices from Within the Veil* (1920) · *Black Folk, Then and Now* (1939) · *Dusk of Dawn: An Essay Toward an Autobiography of a Race Concept* (1940) · *The World and Africa* (1947) · *An ABC of Color: Selections from Over a Half Century of the Writings of W. E. B. Du Bois* (1963) · *The Autobiography of W. E. B. Du Bois* (1968)

PAUL LAURENCE DUNBAR 1872–1906

Paul Laurence Dunbar was born on June 27, 1872, in Dayton, Ohio; he was the son of former slaves. In the high school which he attended—he was the only black in his class—he was editor of the school paper and class poet. Shortly after his graduation he was an elevator boy when his first book, *Oak and Ivy*, appeared in 1893. He did not win wide recognition, however, until after *Majors and Minors* appeared in 1895 and was favorably reviewed by William Dean Howells. Dunbar's reputation was enhanced when he gave a number of platform readings and published *Lyrics of Lowly Life*, with an introduction by Howells, in 1896; in fact, this was his best-known book. Beginning in 1898, the author gave his full time to writing and platform appearances, but in 1899 his health failed and he succumbed to tuberculosis on February 8, 1906. In addition to three more books of poetry, he published a number of less noteworthy fictional works.

Poetry: *The Complete Poems of Paul Laurence Dunbar* (1913, 1968; includes all earlier books of poetry)
Short Stories: *Best Stories* (1938)

FINLEY PETER DUNNE (Mr. Dooley) 1867–1936

In Chicago, which had been his birthplace, Finley Peter Dunne attended high school and worked his way up from office boy on a newspaper to a job as a reporter. When in 1892 he chanced to put a piece commenting on current affairs into the dialect of an Irish saloonkeeper, he hit upon a way of writing destined to make him famous. After some experiments and changes, the saloonkeeper became Martin Dooley, whose unlearned but vivid diction and common-sensible philosophy showed his relationship with the long line of horse-sense humorists admired by Americans. Dunne's essays do more than amusingly illuminate the times which produced them: because they are rich in commentary upon the human foibles of all periods, they have enduring merit.

Mr. Dooley in Peace and in War (1898) · *Mr. Dooley in the Hearts of His Countrymen* (1899) · *Mr. Dooley's Philosophy* (1900) · *Mr. Dooley's Opinions* (1901) · *Observations of Mr. Dooley* (1902) · *Dissertations by Mr. Dooley* (1906) · *Mr. Dooley Says* (1910) · *New Dooley Book* (1911) · *Mr. Dooley on Making a Will* (1919)

JONATHAN EDWARDS 1703–1758

Jonathan Edwards was born in East Windsor, Connecticut, where his father was minister. He received his early education at home and was graduated from Yale College before he was seventeen. He spent two additional years at Yale in the study of theology, and, after eight months of preaching in a Presbyterian church in New York City, he spent three more years as a tutor. Early in 1727 he joined his grandfather, the Reverend Solomon Stoddard, in the church at Northampton, Massachusetts, married, and became full minister at Stoddard's death in 1729.

As a clergyman Edwards developed an absorbing interest in what we would now call the psychology of religion. He welcomed the "awakenings" which came periodically in his church and eventually announced that he could not conscientiously admit to communion those persons who had made no public relation of religious experience. His congregation was unwilling to accept this return to the stricter ways of the first generation in New England, and in 1750 Edwards was dismissed. From 1751 until 1757 he was pastor at Stockbridge, Massachusetts, at that time an Indian mission village on the frontier. He then accepted a call to the presidency of the College of New Jersey (now Princeton University), where he died of smallpox three months after his installation. To many, Edwards is the greatest theologian that America has yet produced and unquestionably one of the most original minds in our country's history.

A Divine and Supernatural Light (1734) · *A Faithful Narrative* (1737) · *Sinners in the Hands of an Angry God* (1741) · *Some Thoughts Concerning the Present Revival of Religion in New England* (1742) · *A Treatise Concerning Religious Affections* (1746) · *Freedom of the Will* [short title] (1754) · *Original Sin Defended* [short title] (1758) · *Two Dissertations, I. Concerning the End for Which God Created the World. II. The Nature of True Virtue* (1765)

THOMAS STEARNS ELIOT 1888–1965

Born in St. Louis, where his grandfather had founded Washington University and where his father was president of a local industry, T. S. Eliot attended Smith Academy in St. Louis and then Milton Academy in Massachusetts in preparation for entering Harvard in 1906. Influenced by Irving Babbitt and George Santayana, he chose philosophy as his main course of study. Although he studied in Europe and completed a doctoral dissertation on the philosophy of F. H. Bradley, he never returned to Harvard for formal acceptance of the degree. He resided in England from 1914 until his death and became a British subject in 1927.

After his marriage to Vivienne Haigh Haigh-Wood in 1915, Eliot taught and for a time worked at Lloyds Bank in London. He then turned to editorial work on such publications as *The Egoist* and *The Criterion*, and became a director of Faber and Faber, a British publishing firm. He returned to the United States in 1932-1933 to give a series of Charles Eliot Norton lectures at Harvard. In 1948, a year after his first wife died, he was awarded the British Order of Merit and the Nobel Prize for Literature. In January 1957 Eliot married Miss Valerie Fletcher, who had been his private secretary.

Eliot's essays altered the current of literary criticism. Owing to his influence, the "metaphysical" became a mark of excellence, and English and American poets were reappraised in the light of this new standard. This metaphysical revolution also produced a style of criticism which is remarkable for its close analysis of the relation of structure and style to content. Because Eliot was preeminently a poet, he ultimately transcended the political and religious questions to which he sometimes turned his attention. Even the excellence of his literary theories must take second place to the excellence of his verse in which he strove for, and achieved, the utmost in condensation.

Poetry: *Poems* (1917, 1919, 1920) · *The Waste Land* (1922) · *Ash-Wednesday* (1930) · *Four Quartets* (1943)

Drama: *The Rock, A Pageant Play* (1934) · *Murder in the Cathedral*

(1935) · *The Cocktail Party* (1950) · *The Confidential Clerk* (1954) · *The Elder Statesman* (1958)
Criticism: *The Sacred Wood* (1920) · *For Lancelot Andrewes* (1928) · *The Use of Poetry and the Use of Criticism* (1933) · *The Three Voices of Poetry* (1953) · *The Frontiers of Criticism* (1956) · *On Poetry and Poets* (1957)

RALPH ELLISON   1914–

Ralph Ellison was born in Oklahoma City in 1914, and early developed an interest in music, especially jazz. He majored in music at Tuskegee Institute, and went to New York in 1936 intending to become a composer. However, he struck up a friendship with Richard Wright and became interested in writing fiction. He began to publish stories in the little magazines, but put a major effort into the writing of *Invisible Man*, which won the National Book Award for 1952 and which is considered the most brilliant novel of the American black experience. After the publication of his novel, Ellison continued to publish in the magazines, and some of the fictional pieces have been announced as passages from a novel in progress.
Novel: *Invisible Man* (1952)
Essays: *Shadow and Act* (1964)

RALPH WALDO EMERSON   1803–1882

Ralph Waldo Emerson was descended from nine successive generations of ministers. His father, who was minister of the First Church, Unitarian, in Boston, Ralph Waldo's birthplace, died when Emerson was eight years old, leaving a widow and four sons in difficult financial circumstances. Nevertheless, with the assistance of their Aunt Mary Moody Emerson, all four sons went through Harvard, Ralph Waldo graduating in 1821. He taught school for a while, attended the Harvard Divinity School, spent a winter in Florida for his health, and, in 1829, became pastor of the Second Church of Boston and married Miss Ellen Tucker. In 1831 his wife died. A year later he resigned his pastorate because of his unwillingness to administer the Lord's Supper.

In 1833 Emerson went abroad and visited Landor in Italy, Coleridge and Wordsworth in England, and (most important of all, because the meeting was the beginning of a lifelong friendship) Carlyle in Scotland. Upon his return to America, he bought a house and two acres of land in Concord, married Miss Lydia Jackson, and in 1836 published his first volume, *Nature*. Except among the Transcendentalists, it met with a mild reception; but the two challenging addresses which followed soon after, *The American Scholar* in 1837 and *The Divinity School Address* in 1838, made Emerson famous. From 1840 to 1842 he assisted Margaret Fuller in editing *The Dial* and from 1842 to 1844 was himself editor. He lectured extensively and successfully in England in 1847-1848. In the 1840's and 1850's Emerson's energies were rigorously tested by the ever increasing demand for his time as a lecturer in New England, the middle Atlantic states, and the "Northwest."

Emerson kept aloof from the slavery controversy in the 1830's and 1840's, but later events drove him inexorably into the ranks of the radical abolitionists. In 1859 he took his stand publicly as champion of John Brown. From 1861 to 1865 he was caught in the general hysteria of war; "Emerson," Hawthorne said in 1861, "is breathing slaughter like the rest of us." On January 1, 1863, he read the "Boston Hymn" in the Boston

Music Hall, and in April 1865 he objected in his journal that Grant's terms of surrender were "a little too easy."

In 1871 Emerson was beginning to show definite signs of decline. His writings were becoming less coherent, and his memory was slipping. In 1872, with part of a fund that his friends had collected for him, he made his last visit to Carlyle and, upon his return from Europe, settled into a quiet retirement. In 1882 he died of pneumonia and was buried, appropriately, near Thoreau.

Emerson's ability as a lecturer to convince his audience of the individual's personal worth qualifies him to be judged and appreciated not primarily as a metaphysical philosopher but as a moral teacher. His poetry, influenced as it was by seventeenth-century poets, has become increasingly appreciated.

Essays: *Nature* (1836) · *The American Scholar* (1837) · *The Divinity School Address* (1838) · *Essays, First Series* (1841) · *Essays, Second Series* (1844) · *Representative Men* (1850) · *English Traits* (1856) · *The Conduct of Life* (1860)

Poetry: *Poems* (1847)

WILLIAM FAULKNER 1897–1962

William Faulkner was born in New Albany, Mississippi, and lived for most of his life in the neighboring county seat, Oxford, where the University of Mississippi is situated. The Faulkner (or Falkner) family has long been prominent in politics, railroad building, and planting; one great-grandfather of William's was the author of a popular antebellum romance, *The White Rose of Memphis*. The Sartoris family, prominent in a number of Faulkner's novels, appears to be in part a projection of his own clan.

Early in World War I, Faulkner, just out of high school, ran off to Canada to join the British air force. He was sent to England for training and saw about one year of service in France before he was wounded in a crash. Back in Mississippi, he was for a time a student in the university; he then worked at such odd jobs as clerking in the college postal station and house painting. Encouragement for his writing apparently came from various friends, among them Phil Stone, an Oxford lawyer; Stark Young, then teaching at Amherst; and Sherwood Anderson, with whom he lived in New Orleans in 1922.

In 1929 he married Estelle Oldham and by that time had already decided on writing as his career. After 1936 he occasionally went to Hollywood to write for various motion pictures, and made some visits abroad for the State Department. However, in spite of these trips and occasional visits to New York, Faulkner spent much of his time in Oxford, Mississippi. Even after he became a writer in residence at the University of Virginia, he continued to return to Oxford until 1959 when he announced his intention to settle in Charlottesville, Virginia. He held an honorary post at the University until his death in 1962. He received among other awards the Pulitzer Prize for both *A Fable* (1954) and *The Town* (1957) and, in 1950, the Nobel Prize for Literature.

The fiction of William Faulkner has as many different planes of interest as that of any contemporary American writer. On one level much of it is sheer horror, a twentieth-century throwback to the Gothic romance. On another it is Hawthornesque in its exploration of the methods and effects of symbolism and allegory. On still another it is a vast and intricate legend of the disintegration of the Old South, epiclike in conception and not unworthy of comparison with James Joyce's portrayal of Dublin in *Ulysses*. To

the student of technique it is notable for its bold experimentation with narrative point of view, while the reader with an eye for style finds it full of some of the lushest rhetoric of our time. All in all, Faulkner's stories are almost incredibly subtle. They make such great demands of their readers that the surprising thing is that they have been as popular as they have.
Novels: *Soldier's Pay* (1926) · *Mosquitoes* (1927) · *Sartoris* (1929) · *The Sound and the Fury* (1929) · *As I Lay Dying* (1930) · *Sanctuary* (1931) · *Light in August* (1932) · *Pylon* (1935) · *Absalom, Absalom!* (1936) · *The Wild Palms* (1939) · *The Hamlet* (1940) · *Intruder in the Dust* (1948) · *Requiem for a Nun* (1951) · *A Fable* (1954) · *The Town* (1957) · *The Mansion* (1959) · *The Reivers* (1962)
Short Stories: *These 13* (1931) · *Doctor Martino and Other Stories* (1934) · *The Unvanquished* (1938) · *Go Down, Moses* (1942) · *Knight's Gambit* (1949) · *Big Woods* (1955)
Poetry: *The Marble Faun* (1924)

LAWRENCE FERLINGHETTI   1919–

Born in 1919 in Yonkers, New York, Lawrence Ferlinghetti served in France during World War II. He took an M.A. at Columbia University in 1947 and a Doctorat de l'Université de Paris in 1950. In the early 1950's he found his way to San Francisco, where he established the City Lights Bookstore, a project combining bookselling and publishing. This enterprise became the literary center of the Beat Generation: in the polarization of modern poetry between academic and antiacademic, Ferlinghetti has played an important role in promoting the antiacademic beat poets. Among many notable publications appeared Allen Ginsburg's *Howl* in 1956. Ferlinghetti's own publications have been various and numerous, and include volumes of all genres.

   If nothing else, Ferlinghetti and the other City Lights poets have, through their irreverent blasts, exuberant affirmations, and verbal anarchy, forced modern criticism to reconsider its established positions and dogmas.
Poetry: *Pictures of the Gone World* (1955) · *A Coney Island of the Mind* (1958) · *Starting from San Francisco* (1961, 1967) · *The Secret Meaning of Things* (1968)
Novel: *Her* (1960)
Plays: *Unfair Arguments with Existence* (1963) · *Routines* (1964)

F. SCOTT FITZGERALD   1896–1940

F. Scott Fitzgerald was born in St. Paul, Minnesota, and educated in the public schools of St. Paul, at the Newman School of Hackensack, New Jersey, and at Princeton University. In college he formed a friendship with Edmund Wilson and contributed poems and stories to the *Nassau Literary Magazine*. He left Princeton in 1917 to join the army, soon after the United States entered World War I. He was commissioned a lieutenant in the infantry but was not sent overseas. In 1920 he married Zelda Sayre of Montgomery, Alabama. That same year he published *This Side of Paradise*, a novel about the flaming youth of the postwar era, which made him famous. Thereafter, Fitzgerald devoted himself to the writing of prose fiction. He often lived abroad—in Paris, in Italy, and on the French Riviera. His last years were spent in Hollywood, where he died of a heart attack.

   Fitzgerald is admired particularly for capturing the spirit of the 1920's —both the recklessness and the fear and cynicism that colored its gaiety. During the late 1940's and early 1950's there was a notable Fitzgerald revival to which many distinguished writers and critics contributed, and Fitzgerald achieved, suddenly, a critical importance. Most students are now inclined to agree with Arthur Mizner's judgment that "Fitzgerald's reputation as a serious novelist is secure."

Novels: *This Side of Paradise* (1920) · *The Beautiful and Damned* (1922) · *The Great Gatsby* (1925) · *Tender Is the Night* (1934) · *The Last Tycoon* (1941)

Short Stories: *Flappers and Philosophers* (1920) · *Tales of the Jazz Age* (1922) · *All the Sad Young Men* (1926) · *Taps at Reveille* (1935)

BENJAMIN FRANKLIN 1706–1790

The details of Benjamin Franklin's early life are familiar through his autobiography. There he tells of his ancestry and birth in Boston, of his early apprenticeship to his printer brother, of the circumstances which led to his running off to Philadelphia when he was seventeen, of his disillusion there and in London concerning easy roads to wealth. In 1728 he founded his own printing firm, determined to make his fortune by hard work and thrift. Only men with financial security could afford to indulge themselves in the public service which he had in the back of his mind.

It took just twenty years for him to make enough money so that he could retire. He then turned first to science, long one of his enthusiasms, and within a few years was internationally famous for his *Experiments & Observations on Electricity*, first published in London in 1751. Already, however, he was busy with public projects and political affairs, notable among them the founding of the Library Company of Philadelphia (1731), the organization of the American Philosophical Society (1743), the proposal for the Academy of Philadelphia, later the University of Pennsylvania (1749), and his service as clerk of the colonial legislature (1736-1751).

There was scarcely a stage in the process of binding disparate colonies into a great nation wherein the calm counsel of Benjamin Franklin had no part. He was probably the first American to assert the principle of "no taxation without representation"; between 1757 and 1775 he was the chief representative of the colonial point of view in England; in 1775-1776 he was a key member of the Second Continental Congress, where he was one of the drafting committee for the Declaration of Independence; between 1777 and 1785 he was in France, where he was largely responsible for the alliance without which the Revolution could hardly have been successful and where he helped to negotiate the treaty of peace; and in 1787, back in Philadelphia, he ended his good works by acting as a balance wheel in the stormy Constitutional Convention.

In an age which tended to like ornate Latinate prose Franklin cultivated simplicity in style and structure. He felt that his literary purposes were utilitarian and did not think of himself as an author in the belletristic sense, although all his life he had a critical eye for style both in prose and in poetry.

"The Dogood Papers" (1721) · *A Dissertation on Liberty and Necessity, Pleasure and Pain* (1725) · *Poor Richard's Almanac* (1732-1764) · *Plain Truth* (1747) · *Experiments and Observations on Electricity* (1751; 2nd ed., 1754; 4th ed., 1769) · *Autobiography* (first part written 1759; first published 1868) · *The Interest of Great Britain Considered with Regard to Her Colonies* (1760) · *The Ephemera* [in French] (1778) · *Dialogue Between Franklin and the Gout* [in French] (1780)

MARY E. WILKINS FREEMAN   1852–1930

The most realistic of the New England local colorists, Mary E. Wilkins was born in Randolph, a village in eastern Massachusetts. She attended the schools of Randolph and of Brattleboro, Vermont, where her family lived for a while and her father kept a store, and she spent one year (1870-1871) at Mount Holyoke Female Seminary. After the death of her parents in 1883, she returned to her native village to live; the village and the country around it furnished the material for her early stories. After her marriage in 1902 to Dr. Charles M. Freeman of Metuchen, New Jersey, Mrs. Freeman attempted, with indifferent success, to enlarge the scope of her writing.

Despite a voluminous and varied output, her reputation and importance still rest upon the early stories of village and rural life in Massachusetts. Because the style of these stories is as spare and angular as the characters it is used to describe, Mrs. Freeman is, with justification, considered a realistic writer of New England.

A Humble Romance and Other Stories (1887) · *A New England Nun and Other Stories* (1891)

PHILIP FRENEAU   1752–1832

As a young man of sixteen, Philip Freneau entered Princeton, where he became a close friend of James Madison and H. H. Brackenridge and was graduated in 1771. He tried teaching and the study of theology, with no enthusiasm, and by 1775 he was in New York writing satires. The next year he went to the West Indies. In 1778 when he was returning to New Jersey, his ship was captured by the British, but he was permitted to land near his home and promptly enlisted in the militia. He became both a propagandist and a blockade runner for the cause of the Revolution. On one of his voyages in 1780 he was captured and held for six weeks on a prison ship.

The war over, Freneau turned again to the sea to make a living. In 1790, after six years of shipping, Freneau married and settled down to a literary career. In 1791 in Philadelphia he founded the *National Gazette* to provide a focal point for the opposition to the policies of Hamilton. But Freneau's enthusiasm for the French Revolution and Citizen Genêt lost him support and the *National Gazette* expired in 1793. During the last thirty-nine years of his life, Freneau was in almost constant financial difficulty. His literary ventures were of little assistance, and in 1803 he was forced once more to return to the sea. Between 1795 and 1815 five volumes of his poems were collected. Although he was obviously imitative in his forms and themes, he has historic interest as a precursor of Bryant, Emerson, Poe, Whittier, and Longfellow.

The Rising Glory of America (with H. H. Brackenridge, 1772) · *The American Village* (1772) · *The British Prison-Ship* (1781) · *The Poems of Philip Freneau* (1786) · *The Miscellaneous Works of Mr. Philip Freneau Containing His Essays and Additional Poems* (1788)

ROBERT FROST   1874–1963

Despite the fact that he was born in San Francisco, California, Robert Frost's forebears for nine generations had been New Englanders, and most of his life, from 1885 to his death, he lived in New England. Frost's father died in San Francisco when the boy was ten, and the widow went East to Lawrence, Massachusetts, with her children, to live with their grandfather. Frost attended school in Lawrence and did such good work that, at graduation, he was high-school valedictorian. In the autumn of 1892 Frost entered Dartmouth, but, finding college life unattractive, he shortly withdrew. During the next few years, he worked in a mill for a time, took a tramping trip through the South, did some teaching, some newspaper work, and married Elinor White, who in high school had been his only rival for class valedictorian. In 1897 he tried college again, this time Harvard, where he enjoyed the study of Latin, Greek, and philosophy. At the end of two years, however, he again left college and moved to a farm near Derry, New Hampshire, which had been given to him by his grandfather. Because farming proved rather unprofitable, Frost turned to teaching at nearby Pinkerton Academy (1905-1911) and then at New Hampshire State Normal (1911-1912).

Meanwhile, he had made a rather discouraging start as a poet. From early boyhood he had been an enthusiastic reader and writer of poetry. In his teens he had begun to publish a few of his poems in magazines. His poetry, however, did not seem very attractive to most buyers: in twenty years, he earned about two hundred dollars, in all, from his verses. In 1911, at thirty-six, he decided to sell his farm and to spend a few years in concentrated poetic work, to determine once and for all whether he could succeed in literature. Attracted by the relatively low cost of living in England, he went abroad with his family in 1912. By 1913 he managed to find a British publisher for his first book of verse, *A Boy's Will*. This, as well as his second book, *North of Boston* (1914), was very favorably received by English readers and critics.

When, in 1915, Frost returned to America, he learned that his two books, upon republication in this country, had won appreciation of a sort to make him rub his eyes. Regardless, he resumed his old vocations of farming—in New Hampshire and Vermont—and of teaching; but now he gave more time to composition. After 1915 he taught at Amherst College, the University of Michigan, the University of Vermont, and the Bread Loaf School of English at Middlebury College, and he also published numerous books of verse. Frost received the Pulitzer Prize for American Poetry four times: in 1924, 1931, 1937, and 1943. A careful study of his poetry will show that, for all his appearance of rustic simplicity, Frost has more of significance to say than many of his contemporaries among whom he holds a high position.

A Boy's Will (1913) · *North of Boston* (1914) · *Mountain Interval* (1916) · *Selected Poems* (1923, 1931, 1934) · *New Hampshire* (1923) · *West-Running Brook* (1928) · *A Further Range* (1936) · *A Witness Tree* (1942) · *Come In* (1943) · *A Masque of Reason* (1945) · *Steeple Bush* (1947) · *A Masque of Mercy* (1947) · *The Road Not Taken* (1951) · *Hard Not to be King* (1951) · *In the Clearing* (1962)

HAMLIN GARLAND 1860–1940

Born on a farm in Wisconsin, Hamlin Garland moved with his family to Iowa and then to South Dakota. As a boy he learned the endless routine of the dirt farmer but still found time for the world of books. At an early age, encouraged by his mother, he determined to make himself a teacher, yet he was twenty-four before he really broke with farming. He chose to study in Boston, and there he quickly educated himself in the theaters, in the homes of writers, actors, and artists, and most of all in the Boston Public Library. Gradually he found modest employment as a lecturer, teacher, and reviewer. In 1887, when he returned to South Dakota to visit his parents, he had acquired enough perspective to see that farm life was far from idyllic. When he returned to Boston he wrote the tales collected in *Main-Travelled Roads.* After 1916, when he moved to New York, Garland attained a new popularity by turning to autobiography. In 1922.*A Daughter of the Middle Border* won the Pulitzer Prize for Biography.

Garland was interested in many things, perhaps too many for his artistic salvation. To him, veritism was only one cause among many, and although he tried to present life truthfully he never had an irrepressible passion to say something important supremely well.

Short Stories: *Main-Travelled Roads* (1891)
Novels: *Rose of Dutcher's Coolly* (1895) · *The Captain of the Gray-Horse Troop* (1902)
Essays: *Crumbling Idols* (1894)
Autobiography: *A Son of the Middle Border* (1917) · *A Daughter of the Middle Border* (1921)

ALLEN GINSBERG   1926-

Allen Ginsberg was born in Newark, New Jersey; he attended Columbia University, where in 1949 he received his B.A. The most significant poet of the beat generation, he has read his poetry not only in coffeehouses but in major universities both in the United States and in England. His poetry, though neither disciplined nor startlingly original in its statements, is significant as an accurate expression of a truly free imagination.

Howl (1956) · *Kaddish* (1961) · *Empty Mirror* (1961) · *Reality Sandwiches* (1963) · *Planet News 1961-1967* (1968)

ALEXANDER HAMILTON   1757-1804

Alexander Hamilton was born in the West Indies. At an early age he displayed an amazing talent for business and was sent to New York to finish his education. In 1774, when he was an undergraduate at King's College (now Columbia University), he joined the Whig opposition to the British and soon distinguished himself as a speaker and pamphleteer. In 1776 he served in the Continental Army and became Washington's aide-de-camp. Despite a temporary break with his commander he served brilliantly to the end of the war and thereafter was a nationally known lawyer and public servant. His most important contributions to government were his draft of the call for the Constitutional Convention, his success in obtaining the ratification of the new form of government by New York, his term as first secretary of the treasury in 1789-1795, and his influence as Washington's most trusted adviser. Hamilton's opposition to Aaron Burr, first in the Presidential election of 1800 and later in the contest of 1804 for the governorship of New York, resulted in the famous duel in which Hamilton was killed.

On political questions Hamilton was always well informed, and he wrote clearly and effectively for the audience to which he addressed himself. There are few better practitioners of argument in American literature.

A Full Vindication of the Measures of the Congress from the Calumnies of Their Enemies (1774) · *The Farmer Refuted* (1775) · *The Federalist* (with Jay and Madison, 1787-1788)

THOMAS HARIOT   1560-1621

In 1585 Thomas Hariot, a twenty-five-year-old Englishman already known in Oxford as a talented mathematician, landed on Roanoke Island, off the coast of what is now North Carolina, with the hundred-odd men involved in Sir Walter Raleigh's most ambitious attempt to establish a colony in North America. He stayed in Virginia (as all the territory claimed by the British had been named) for a little over a year, surveying its resources with scientific care. On his return to England he found it necessary to defend Raleigh's projects against slander from those members of the company who had been miserable in America because "there were not to bee found any English cities, nor such faire houses, nor at their owne wish any of their olde accustomed daintie food, nor any soft beds of downe or fethers." Hariot's defense of Raleigh and Virginia took the form of a forty-six-page pamphlet, *A Briefe and True Report of the New Found Land of Virginia* (London, 1588). Hariot knew that a living was to be had in America, and easily, but he knew also that men would have to learn to use the commodities which the country provided. His book, therefore, was one of the first "promotion tracts," designed to inform prospective emigrants of the opportunities the New World could offer to ambitious men.

After the tract was published, he was pensioned by the Earl of Northumberland so that he could devote himself to mathematics and astronomy, and in his later years he was famous for his work in algebra. He is remembered today chiefly as a scientist.

GEORGE WASHINGTON HARRIS 1814–1869
Though he spent most of his life in Knoxville, Tennessee, George Washington Harris was forced to leave that sleepy town to try his hand at various jobs in order to make a living. As a writer for the New York *Spirit of the Times,* he won fame as a writer of wildly comic stories couched in the quaint language of his Tennessee mountain character, Sut Lovingood, who used both great and little men as victims of his humor. A climactic figure in the development of the Southwestern humor much enjoyed by Mark Twain, G. W. Harris is particularly admired for his ability to capture in print the comic movement and the poetry of the oral tale.
Sut Lovingood Yarns (1867)

JOEL CHANDLER HARRIS 1848–1908
Joel Chandler Harris was born near Eatonton, Georgia. His mother, deserted by his father, took in sewing for a living. Between the ages of thirteen and seventeen (the Civil War years), Harris lived on the nearby plantation of Joseph Addison Turner and helped Turner print a weekly paper. At this time he got an education by working on the paper and by reading in Turner's excellent library; he also became intimately acquainted with the life of the Southern plantation and especially with the speech and folklore of the Negroes. After the war he worked for brief periods on newspapers in Macon, New Orleans, and Savannah. In 1876 he joined the staff of the Atlanta *Constitution,* and for twenty-four years, through editorials, book reviews, feature articles, and especially the Uncle Remus stories, he helped mightily to make the *Constitution* the most influential newspaper ever published in the South. Without esteeming his tales the less as comic masterpieces of their kind, or enjoying them the less for their unalloyed humor, one can be glad that these stories contributed to some reconciliation between the North and the South.
Short Stories: *Uncle Remus: His Songs and His Sayings* (1880) · *Nights with Uncle Remus* (1883) · *Mingo. and Other Sketches in Black and White*

(1884) · *Uncle Remus and His Friends* (1892) · *Told by Uncle Remus* (1905)
Novels: *Sister Jane* (1896) · *Gabriel Tolliver* (1902)

BRET HARTE 1836 –1902

Bret Harte was born in Albany, New York, and had a rather sketchy education. After his widowed mother moved the family to San Francisco, he joined them—in 1854—on the Pacific Coast. There he taught school, worked in the mines for a short time, served as a Wells Fargo Express messenger, and eventually became a printer. Developing his skill as a writer, he in time worked into various editorial jobs on some of the California magazines.

In 1868 he published "The Luck of Roaring Camp" in the newly founded *Overland Monthly*, of which he was editor. When the issue containing "The Luck" reached the East, the story was an immediate success, and other stories in the same vein augmented Harte's popularity. In 1871, with an impressive contract from the *Atlantic Monthly* in his pocket, Harte started East, leaving the Far West permanently. His journey across the continent was a triumphant progress, and he was hailed in the East as a new genius.

The part of his life which came after this journey was largely an anticlimax. A few more stories and some of his many poems were up to the early standard, but his work became repetitious and, in the end, not much more than the working out of a formula. In 1878 he went abroad on a consular appointment to Germany. From 1888 until his death in 1902 he lived in England.

Harte's great success is important in American literary history because of the impetus it gave to local color writing. The unconventional morality—for the time—of his fiction prepared the way for characterization and scenes in later fiction which increasingly departed from prudish standards.
Short Stories: *The Luck of Roaring Camp and Other Sketches* (1870) · *Tales of the Argonauts* (1875) · *Colonel Starbottle's Client* (1892)
Novel: *Gabriel Conroy* (1876)
Poetry: *The Lost Galleon* (1867) · "Plain Language from Truthful James" (1870)

NATHANIEL HAWTHORNE 1804–1864

Although Hawthorne's seventeenth-century ancestors were important men in Massachusetts, the family declined in prominence during the century which followed. When Hawthorne's father died in 1808, he left a widow and three children in reduced circumstances.

In 1825 Hawthorne was graduated from Bowdoin College, where Longfellow was his classmate. After graduation he returned to his mother's house in Salem and lived there in comparative seclusion for twelve years. During those years he read and wrote but destroyed much of what he had written. After anonymous publication in magazines, his tales were first collected in *Twice-Told Tales*.

Soon after Hawthorne discontinued his life of solitude, he became, for about a year, a weigher and gauger in the Boston Custom House; for several months in 1841 he was at Brook Farm, the Utopian community headed by George Ripley. In 1842 he married Sophia Peabody, a follower of the Concord Transcendentalists.

Hawthorne returned to Salem in 1845, and in 1846 there appeared a second collection of his tales, *Mosses from an Old Manse.* This volume attracted few readers, so, because of his financial needs, in 1846 Hawthorne accepted an appointment as surveyor in the Salem Custom House. Inasmuch as he held the appointment as a loyal Democrat, he was dismissed in 1849, after three years' service, to make room for a Whig incumbent. The three years following his dismissal were his most productive: in 1850 *The Scarlet Letter* appeared; in 1851, *The House of the Seven Gables;* and in 1852, *The Blithedale Romance. The House of the Seven Gables* was written at Lenox, in the Berkshires, where Hawthorne met and became the close friend of Herman Melville.

From 1853 to 1857 Hawthorne was consul at Liverpool, having been appointed by his old college friend, Franklin Pierce, then President of the United States. Hawthorne returned in 1860 to "The Wayside" in Concord, which he had purchased a short time before going abroad. His last novel was *The Marble Faun* (1860). At his death he left many uncompleted works of fiction.

Of all the writers of the New England flowering, Hawthorne, justifiably, seems the most certain to endure. Many have noted that he reflects the New England spirit in his consciousness of sin and anticipates in his symbolism a now common manner of literary expression.

Short Stories: *Twice-Told Tales* (1837; enlarged, 1842) · *Mosses from an Old Manse* (1846) · *The Snow Image and Other Twice-Told Tales* (1851)
Novels: *The Scarlet Letter* (1850) · *The House of the Seven Gables* (1851) · *The Blithedale Romance* (1852) · *The Marble Faun* (1860)
Autobiography: *Our Old Home* (1863) · *The American Notebooks* (1868, 1932) · *The English Notebooks* (1870, 1941) · *Passages from the French and Italian Notebooks* (1871)

PAUL HAMILTON HAYNE   1830–1886

A native of Charleston, and the nephew of Robert Y. Hayne, to whom Webster made his famous reply in the year of the poet's birth, Paul Hamilton Hayne was educated at the Coates School, where his lifelong friendship with Henry Timrod began, and at the College of Charleston. He was a member of the Charleston literary group, presided over by William Gilmore Simms, which founded *Russell's Magazine* in 1857, and during its short life of four years Hayne was the editor of that notable literary journal. His house and library were destroyed when Sherman took Charleston in 1865. After the war, he lived at "Copse Hill" in the pine barrens near Augusta, Georgia, where he managed to support himself and his wife by his writing.

Hayne's best poems describe emotionally and pictorially the aspects of nature which he knew most intimately—the mockingbird, for example, and the pine forest. His effects are vivid and delicate, though even his happiest work is marred by trite phrasing and there is no great power of thought. Hayne is worthy of study, nevertheless, as a minor poet whose work is representative of much of the romantic verse of the Old South.

The Complete Poems of Hayne (1882)

ERNEST HEMINGWAY   1899–1961

Ernest Hemingway was born in Oak Park, Illinois. He went through high school, winning some fame in boxing and football, and then became a reporter on the Kansas City *Star.* During World War I, he served on the Italian front. In postwar days, as a newspaper correspondent, he was one of the expatriates who inhabited the Left Bank in Paris. There he began to write fiction and was "discovered" by the critics in the United States. He returned to his homeland to write, going abroad now and then for travel in Europe or for big game hunting in Africa. During the Spanish Revolution and World War II he was a correspondent abroad. After the war, he lived in Cuba until he was forced to leave because of the Castro revolution. After some traveling he settled in Idaho and, following hospitalization, died of a gun-shot wound—perhaps by his own hand.

Hemingway was influenced by Mark Twain's style, which, though like oral speech, was notable for its poetic overtones. Sherwood Anderson and Gertrude Stein, whom he knew in Paris, probably encouraged him to cultivate this apparently naïve colloquial style. From them, too, he may have received instruction in emphasizing basic emotions which led Oscar Cargill to classify him, as well as these two teachers of his, as "Primitivists." From Stephen Crane, by contrast, Hemingway perhaps learned something about handling symbolic or connotative details to give prose what he calls "a fourth or fifth dimension." As a result, in Hemingway's best narratives, there is a unique combination of strength—even at times brutality—with poetic subtlety and depth of sympathy which appeals to modern readers.

Short Stories: *In Our Time* (1924) · *Men Without Women* (1927)
Novels: *The Sun Also Rises* (1926) · *A Farewell to Arms* (1929) · *To Have and Have Not* (1937) · *For Whom the Bell Tolls* (1940) · *Across the River and into the Trees* (1950) · *The Old Man and the Sea* (1952) · *Islands in the Stream* (1970)
Autobiography: *Death in the Afternoon* (1932) · *The Green Hills of Africa* (1935) · *A Moveable Feast* (1964)

OLIVER WENDELL HOLMES 1809–1894

The birth and rearing of Oliver Wendell Holmes were in the tradition of the Brahmin class to which he belonged. He was born in an old house which had historical associations with important battles of the Revolution. He was what he called "a man of family"—one "who inherits family traditions and the cumulative humanities of at least five generations." He was educated at a leading private school, at Harvard, and abroad. In his profession, medicine, he won honors first as a scholar and later (1847-1882) as a noted professor at Harvard. At the request of his friend, James Russell Lowell, then editor of the *Atlantic Monthly,* Holmes made a contribution to the new magazine. It took the form of a series of papers entitled *The Autocrat of the Breakfast-Table* which lasted from 1857 to 1858 and which brought fame not only to its author but to the magazine as well. In books like his *Autocrat,* rather than in novels such as *Elsie Venner,* Holmes excelled. And his verse, like his prose, is at its best when it is most informal.

Nonfiction: *The Autocrat of the Breakfast-Table* (1858) · *The Professor at the Breakfast-Table* (1860) · "Mechanism in Thought and Morals" (1870) · *The Poet at the Breakfast-Table* (1872)
Poetry: *Poems* (1836, 1852, 1862, 1865, 1877) · *Before the Curfew and Other Poems* (1888)
Novels: *Elsie Venner* (1861) · *The Guardian Angel* (1867) · *A Mortal Antipathy* (1885)

WILLIAM DEAN HOWELLS 1837–1920

William Dean Howells was born at Martin's Ferry, Ohio. His father was a printer and journalist in several Ohio towns, and the boy learned early to help. He received little formal education, but he had a passion for languages and literature. From 1856 to 1861 Howells was a reporter and an editorial writer on the *Ohio State Journal* of Columbus. He wrote in 1860 a campaign biography of Lincoln and was rewarded by an appointment as consul at Venice. In the meantime, he had been trying his hand at poetry. When three of his poems appeared in the *Atlantic* in 1860, Howells paid his first visit to New England. James T. Fields, editor of the *Atlantic*, Lowell, and Holmes received him most cordially. Hawthorne, after talking with Howells, wrote on his card as an introduction to Emerson, "I find this young man worthy."

Howells was in Venice from 1861 to 1865. In 1862 he married Eleanor Mead, of Brattleboro, Vermont. When he returned to America, he was made an assistant editor of the *Atlantic* and settled in Cambridge. In 1872 he became editor-in-chief and continued in that position until 1881. Howells moved in 1888 to New York, where he lived—allowing for excursions back to New England and to Europe—the rest of his life. From 1900 on he wrote the "Easy Chair" department of *Harper's Monthly*, which brought him increasing influence and prestige. He received honorary degrees from Harvard, Yale, Columbia, and Oxford and for many years was president of the American Academy of Arts and Letters.

Howells was strong in the belief that realism in fiction should portray the typical rather than the exceptional and that the typical was comparatively decent. Consequently, Howells has been much criticized by Naturalists, Freudians, and Socialists. But he wrote well, and during the last two decades of the nineteenth century he was our chief recorder in prose fiction of the domestic life of middle-class America.

Autobiography: *Venetian Life* (1866) · *Literary Friends and Acquaintance* (1900)
Criticism: *Modern Italian Poets* (1887) · *Criticism and Fiction* (1891)
Novels: *Their Wedding Journey* (1872) · *A Modern Instance* (1882) · *The Rise of Silas Lapham* (1885) · *A Hazard of New Fortunes* (1890) · *A Traveler from Altruria* (1894)

LANGSTON HUGHES 1902–1967

"The poet laureate of Harlem," Langston Hughes was born in Joplin, Missouri, in 1902. He lived for a time with his grandmother in Lawrence, Kansas—she was the last surviving widow of John Brown's raid. After her death, he went at the age of thirteen to live with his mother in Lincoln, Illinois, and later to Cleveland, where he graduated from high school. After spending some time with his father in Mexico, he attended Columbia for a year in 1921. He went as a seaman to Africa and Europe, and in 1924 worked in nightclubs in Paris. After a period in Italy, Hughes worked his way on a tramp steamer to New York and went to work in Washington, D.C., as a busboy in a hotel. It was in Washington that Vachel Lindsay read his poems and praised him.

Hughes published his first volume of verse in 1926: *The Weary Blues*. His bibliography lists thirteen volumes of verse, as well as many volumes of fiction. A series of popular books portrays the life, hard times, and penetrating opinions (especially about the attitudes of white people toward black people) of an average Harlem man by the name of Simple (*Simple Speaks His Mind*, 1950, and others). But though talented as a prose writer, Langston Hughes is more likely to be remembered for his poetry, especially the poetry of anguish and prophecy describing promises unkept and dreams deferred.

Poetry: *The Weary Blues* (1926) · *Fine Clothes to the Jew* (1927) · *Dear Lovely Death* (1931) · *The Dream-Keeper* (1932) · *Scottsboro Limited* (1932) · *New Song* (1938) · *Shakespeare in Harlem* (1942) · *Fields of Wonder* (1947) · *One-Way Ticket* (1949) · *Montage of a Dream Deferred* (1951) · *Ask Your Mama; 12 Moods for Jazz* (1961) · *Selected Poems* (1965) · *The Panther and the Lash* (1967)

Novel: *Not Without Laughter* (1930)

Short Stories: *The Ways of White Folks* (1934) · *Simple Speaks His Mind* (1950) · *Laughing to Keep from Crying* (1952) · *The Best of Simple* (1961)

WILLIAM INGE   1913–1973

Born in Independence, Kansas, William Inge was educated in his own state and, upon receiving his M.A. in 1938, joined the staff of Stephens College for Women where he taught until 1943. He gave up teaching to become the drama-music critic for the St. Louis *Star-Times*, but in 1946 he returned to academic life and became an instructor in English at Washington University, to remain there until 1949. In 1944 he was much impressed with Tennessee Williams' *Glass Menagerie* and decided that he would attempt playwriting. His first play, *Farther Off from Heaven*, was produced in 1947 in the experimental theater run by the late Margo Jones in Dallas. Ten years later, this was rewritten as *The Dark at the Top of the Stairs.*

"The average play of the fifties," observes Gerald Weales, "concerns itself with the problems of adjustment, of acceptance." In achieving such adjustment, the characters are likely to solve important psychological problems. Because he fit this pattern, Inge was "probably the most representative playwright of the fifties."

Farther Off from Heaven (1947) · *Come Back, Little Sheba* (1949) · *Picnic* (1952) · *Bus Stop* (1955) · *The Dark at the Top of the Stairs* (1957) · *A Loss of Roses* (1959) · *Splendor in the Grass* (1961) · *Natural Affection* (1963) · *Out on the Outskirts of Town* (1964) · *Where's Daddy?* (1966)

WASHINGTON IRVING   1783–1859

Washington Irving was born in New York City, the eleventh and last son of Scotch-English parents. A delicate boy, he found his chief pleasures in light literature, the theater, art, travel, and, most particularly, good company. At nineteen, while reading law, he contributed a series of essays dealing largely with the theater to his brother Peter's newspaper, the *Morning Chronicle*, signing them in the eighteenth-century manner as "Jonathan Oldstyle." Between 1804 and 1806 he traveled in Europe, unconcerned about the political turmoil in Napoleon's empire, but much impressed with such new friends as Washington Allston, the painter.

Back in New York and admitted to the bar, he joined his brother and James Kirke Paulding in the *New Yorker*-like series, *Salmagundi*, which ran for twenty numbers in 1807-1808. A more extended burlesque, begun with Peter Irving, resulted in *A History of New York . . . By Diedrich Knickerbocker* (1809). In 1815 he went to Liverpool on business and found that family affairs there were in great disorder because of a brother's illness. Three years later the Irving firm was bankrupt, and his great decision—to make his living by authorship—was more or less forced upon him.

Various governmental appointments were urged upon him in his later years. He wisely refused offers of nominations to a seat in Congress, to the post of mayor of New York, to the secretaryship of the Navy. In 1841, however, he accepted the appointment of minister to Spain and was in Madrid from 1842 until 1845, when he resigned. Except for this period, much of his time after 1835 was spent in the rambling, stepped-gabled cottage at Sunnyside, near Tarrytown and Sleepy Hollow on the Hudson, where he died on November 28, 1859.

Irving's historical work exemplifies the antiquarian spirit which he shared with Scott and other romanticists, but he is most significant for bringing American fiction into the main stream of world literature. Though he owes much to many of his immediate predecessors and contemporaries, there is much in Irving that is his own.

Short Stories: *The Sketch Book* (with many essays, 1819-1820) · *Bracebridge Hall* (1822) · *Tales of a Traveller* (1824) · *The Alhambra* (1832) **Nonfiction:** *Salmagundi* (with others, 1807-1808) · *A History of New York . . . By Diedrich Knickerbocker* (1809) · *The Crayon Miscellany* (1835) · *Astoria* (with nephew Pierre, 1836) · *Adventures of Captain Bonneville, U.S.A.* (1837) · *Life of Oliver Goldsmith* (1840) · *Life of Washington* (5 vols., 1855-1859)

HENRY JAMES 1843–1916

Born in New York City and for a number of years a resident of Boston, Cambridge, and Newport, Henry James eventually became an expatriate. In his early life, the frequent removals of his family from place to place prevented him from taking root anywhere. There were long and repeated visits to Europe—to England, Germany, France, Switzerland, Italy—and intermittent sojourns in America. By the time he had reached maturity, periodic migrations had become a habit—especially migrations to Europe.

After an important year in Paris (1875-1876), where he came under the influence, in varying degrees, of Turgenev, Maupassant, Flaubert, Daudet, and Zola, he began in England a residence which proved to be permanent. For some twenty years (1877-1897) he lived principally in London, and for almost another twenty years (1897-1916) he lived principally at Rye. During these years, however, he continued his frequent excursions to the Continent, and three or four times he revisited the United States. As early as 1880 he could report that he felt himself to be "a thoroughly naturalized Londoner." But it was not until 1915, when he was seventy-two, that James, apparently in protest against American isolationism during the early years of the first World War, became a British subject.

Despite the excellence of his large output of criticism and short fiction, James is important chiefly for his novels. He began as a writer of the international novel and even in his later work continued to employ international characters and comparisons. In his later work the center of his interest shifted increasingly to psychological processes and "method." James was perhaps the first novelist to recognize fully the complexities which may grow out of the relationship of one sensitive person to another, and to record them with fine discrimination and microscopic detail.

Novels: *Roderick Hudson* (1876) · *The American* (1877) · *Daisy Miller* (1878) · *The Portrait of a Lady* (1881) · *The Bostonians* (1886) · *The Tragic Muse* (1890) · *The Spoils of Poynton* (1897) · *What Maisie Knew* (1897) · *The Wings of the Dove* (1902) · *The Ambassadors* (1903) · *The Golden Bowl* (1904)
Short Stories: *Terminations* (1895)
Criticism: *Hawthorne* (1879) · *Partial Portraits* (1888) · *Notes on Novelists* (1914)

RANDALL JARRELL   1914–1965

Born in Nashville, Tennessee, and a graduate of Vanderbilt University, Randall Jarrell taught at various colleges and universities from 1937 until his death, with a four-year interruption for service in the Army Air Force. Jarrell's writings inspired by his service experiences established him as a poet. From 1956 to 1958 he was poetry consultant to the Library of Congress.

Jarrell's poetry is characteristically stark and violent. Although some critics feel that he often fails to justify the source of the emotions which he presents, his seeming lack of control may be justified as a demonstration of his scorn for polished art as opposed to sincere and immediate statement. He also wrote some perceptive criticism and one novel, *Pictures from an Institution* (1954).

Poetry: *Blood for a Stranger* (1942) · *Little Friend, Little Friend* (1945) · *Losses* (1948) · *The Seven-League Crutches* (1951) · *Selected Poems* (1955) · *The Woman at the Washington Zoo* (1960) · *Selected Poems* (1964) · *The Lost World* (1965)

Essays: *Poetry and the Age* (1953) · *A Sad Heart at the Supermarket* (1962)

ROBINSON JEFFERS   1887–1962

Robinson Jeffers was born in Pittsburgh, the son of a classical scholar and a theologian. At the age of five he was reading Greek; at fifteen he had some mastery of Italian, French, and German, together with a love of mountains and of poetry. After a year at the University of Western Pennsylvania (now Pittsburgh), he entered Occidental College as a junior, and in 1905, aged eighteen, he took his B.A. Precocious, shy, but blessed with a rugged physique and a love for the outdoor life, he would probably have found any of the workaday vocations difficult. Graduate work in England gave way to preparation for medicine, medical school to a determination to write, although it was accompanied by courses in forestry, zoology, and law in the University of Washington. Finally, in 1912, he attained independence with a small income from the legacy of a distant relative, and late in the following year he was married, after many tribulations. A plan to live abroad was spoiled by the outbreak of war in Europe, and late in 1914 Jeffers and his wife settled at Carmel, California. There they lived until his death, and there Jeffers built a house with his own hands and found the materials for most of his distinctive poetry.

As the most blackly pessimistic of contemporary American poets, Jeffers has often been compared with Eugene O'Neill, and it is true that they share a temperamental melancholy which critics like to call Celtic, as well as a great debt to the themes and methods of Greek tragedy. Jeffers, however, is more clearly the product of an age in which the modern sciences have destroyed most of the basic assumptions of the past.

Flagons and Apples (1912) · *Californians* (1916) · *Tamar and Other Poems* (1924) · "Roan Stallion" (1925) · *The Women at Point Sur* (1927) · *Cawdor, and Other Poems* (1928) · *Dear Judas, and Other Poems* (1929) · *Thurso's Landing, and Other Poems* (1932) · *Give Your Heart to the Hawks, and Other Poems* (1933) · *Solstice, and Other Poems* (1935) · *Such Counsels You Gave to Me, and Other Poems* (1937) · *Be Angry at the Sun* (1941) · *Medea* (1946)

THOMAS JEFFERSON 1743-1826

Thomas Jefferson was born near Charlottesville, Virginia, the son of a planter who had married into the famous Randolph family. At fourteen he inherited nearly three thousand acres of land and a considerable number of slaves. He studied hard at William and Mary during 1760-1762. He then read law, was admitted to the bar in 1767, and succeeded in combining his profession with the management of large estates. On New Year's Day, 1772, he married Martha Wayles Skelton, an attractive widow with whom he was deeply in love.

Member of the Virginia House of Burgesses, 1769-1774; member of the Virginia Conventions of 1774 and 1775; Virginia delegate to the Second Continental Congress, 1775-1776; member of the legislature of the new state of Virginia, 1776-1779; governor of Virginia, 1779-1781; member of Congress under the Articles of Confederation, 1783-1784; American minister to France, 1784-1789; Secretary of State, 1790-1793; vice-president, 1797-1801; President of the United States, 1801-1809—the list by itself is a thumbnail sketch of the birth and youth of a new nation. Jefferson was in the forefront of most of the great political developments of his age.

One of the many paradoxes of his life is that Jefferson should be remembered for the studied sentences of his public papers, for he was inclined to distrust rhetoric and oratory. Behind the words of his great state papers, however, are both the maturing of a great people and a deep faith in the integrity of the common man.

Summary View of the Rights of British America (1774) · "Autobiography" [up to 1790] (completed 1821; published 1829) · *First Inaugural Address* (1801) · *Second Inaugural Address* (1805)

SARAH ORNE JEWETT 1849-1909

Sarah Orne Jewett was born in the village of South Berwick, in the southwest corner of Maine, just ten miles from the seacoast. Although she became cosmopolitan, traveling in Europe and spending a good deal of time with friends in Boston (Annie Fields, William Dean Howells, Thomas Bailey Aldrich), South Berwick was her lifelong home, and she always returned there to write. Her formal schooling was irregular and fragmentary; her real education for writing came from riding and talking with her father, a country doctor, as he visited his many patients in the fishing villages and on the upland farms, and from reading in her father's library. Her first story appeared in the *Atlantic Monthly* in 1869, when she was only twenty. In 1877 she published *Deephaven*, a collection of stories and sketches about a Maine village, nominally Deephaven but really South Berwick. Miss Jewett wrote many such sketches and stories which appeared at frequent intervals in the *Atlantic* and were collected from time to time in book form. Though her work is not as great as Hawthorne's, her stories of New England are the best that have been written since Hawthorne. Her work is authentic literary art, and she adds to the New England spareness a needed delicate grace.

Deephaven (1877) · *Country By-Ways* (1881) · *A White Heron and Other Stories* (1886) · *A Native of Winby and Other Tales* (1893) · *The Country of the Pointed Firs* (1896)

JAMES WELDON JOHNSON 1871-1938

The son of a hotel headwaiter and a grade-school teacher, James Weldon Johnson was born in Jacksonville, Florida, on June 17, 1871. When he was killed in an automobile accident on July 26, 1938, in Wiscasset, Maine, he had served his people in many ways.

Johnson's mother gave him his first training. Later he won an A.B. (1894) and an M.A. (1904) from Atlanta University. While serving as principal of a black high school in Atlanta he read law and in 1897 was admitted to the Florida bar. In Atlanta, too, he collaborated with his brother, John Rosamond, a composer, on some songs. Encouraged by the success of these, the brothers in 1901 went to New York, there to write and publish many additional songs, a number of them for Broadway musicals. Johnson studied at Columbia University to enlarge his knowledge of literature. President Theodore Roosevelt in 1906 appointed him consul to Venezuela, later to Nicaragua, where he served until 1913.

In 1916, Johnson became active in the National Association for the Advancement of Colored People and served in important offices until 1930. Meanwhile, he became a noted anthologist and critic of Afro-American spirituals and poetry, as well as the author of volumes of his own poetry.

Johnson's only novel, *The Autobiography of an Ex-Coloured Man*, published anonymously in 1912, made some impact because it was taken to be a factual account of a light-skinned black's "passing"; when its authorship was acknowledged in 1927, it was even more widely read, and it was widely praised for its vivid representation of many aspects of Negro life.

Poetry: *Fifty Years and Other Poems* (1917) · *God's Trombones: Seven Old-Time Negro Sermons in Verse* (1927) · *St. Peter Relates an Incident of the Resurrection Day* (1930)

Novel: *The Autobiography of an Ex-Coloured Man* (1912)

Autobiography: *Along This Way: The Autobiography of James Weldon Johnson* (1933)

LEROI JONES (Imamu Amiri Baraka) 1934–

Like all black writers in America, LeRoi Jones has found himself torn between protest and art, between politics and poetry. His poetry ranges widely in its form and subject, related in some ways to jazz, clearly personal in its interior probings, and yet caught up too in the modern social unrest and agony. He was born in New Jersey in 1934, went to high school in Newark, and graduated from Howard University in Washington, D.C. After a stint in the Air Force, he turned to writing, and in 1961 published his first volume of poems: *Preface to a Twenty Volume Suicide Note*. This was followed in 1964 by *The Dead Lecturer*. He is also known for his drama, much of it considered angry and controversial, and he has also written fiction as well as nonfiction studies of black music and social issues.

Poetry: *Preface to a Twenty Volume Suicide Note* (1961) · *The Dead Lecturer* (1964) · *Black Arts* (1966)

Drama: *Dutchman* and *The Slave* (1964) · *Baptism* and *The Toilet* (1967) · *Slave Ship* (1967) · *Arm Yourself, or Harm Yourself* (1967)

Novel: *System of Dante's Hell* (1966)

Short Stories: *Tales* (1967)

Nonfiction: *Blues People: Negro Music in White America* (1963) · *Black Music* (1967) · *Home: Social Essays* (1966)

JACK KEROUAC 1922–1969

The "beat" or "hipster" movement had its origins in bohemianism but has adopted a metaphysical interest in Zen Buddhism. Jack Kerouac, born in Lowell, Massachusetts, and educated at Columbia University, was a leading writer in the group. He was interested in both aspects of the movement, as evidenced by the title of one of his books—*The Dharma Bums.* ("Dharma" is the Buddhist word for truth.) Kerouac, as R. W. B. Lewis remarks, "returned to the ever-expanding spirit, at once visionary and sensual, of Walt Whitman," and one of his books derives its title from Whitman's "Song of the Open Road."

The beat movement, at first centered in San Francisco, soon spread across the country. Kerouac lived the wandering life he describes in his books and, with Gregory Corso and Allen Ginsberg, helped bring attention to the beat phenomenon.

Novels: *The Town and the City* (1950) · *On the Road* (1957) · *The Dharma Bums* (1958) · *The Subterraneans* (1958) · *Doctor Sax* (1959) · *Tristessa* (1960) · *Big Sur* (1962) · *Visions of Gerard* (1963) · *Maggie Cassidy* (1959) · *Visions of Cody* (1960, 1973) · *Satori in Paris* (1965)
Poetry: *Mexico City Blues* (1959)
Nonfiction: *Lonesome Traveler* (1960) · *Book of Dreams* (1961)

MARTIN LUTHER KING, JR. 1929–1968

Martin Luther King was born in 1929 in Atlanta, Georgia, the descendant of a long line of Baptist ministers. He graduated from Morehouse College in Atlanta in 1948, and took a Bachelor of Divinity degree at Crozer Theological Seminary, Chester, Pennsylvania, in 1941. In 1955 he earned a Ph.D. at Boston University. It was during this period that he made the fateful decision to turn down the several opportunities to settle in the North, and chose instead to accept a church in the South where he could best serve his oppressed people. He became minister of the Dexter Avenue Baptist Church in Montgomery, Alabama.

He first gained national attention as the leader of a bus boycott that lasted for 381 days in 1955-1956, aimed as a protest against the requirement that blacks always sit in the back of the bus. This successful nonviolent boycott turned out to be the opening event of the black revolution of the 1950's and '60's. King provided the handbook for the nonviolent revolution in *Stride Toward Freedom: The Montgomery Story* (1958). And he provided the leadership for the movement as he became president of the Southern Christian Leadership Conference, an organization dedicated to his basic principles.

In 1964 King was awarded the Nobel Peace Prize. He was in great demand throughout the country, wherever there was confrontation on the issue of segregation, or civil rights, or racial prejudice, or injustice. He traveled ceaselessly, in both South and North, always finding a place of leadership in the front lines. His writings recorded his experiences and related them to his philosophy of love and nonviolence. He was assassinated on April 4, 1968, in Memphis, Tennessee. His death brought shock and grief to the nation and the world, and elevated him to martyrdom.

Stride Toward Freedom: The Montgomery Story (1958) · *Strength to Love* (1963) · *Why We Can't Wait* (1964) · *Where Do We Go from Here: Chaos or Community* (1967) · *Trumpet of Conscience* (1968)

SARAH KEMBLE KNIGHT 1666–1727

The daughter of a Boston merchant, Sarah Kemble Knight was a woman of enterprise and intelligence. After her husband's death, she efficiently attended to the business of the estate. In addition, she kept a dame's school, which Benjamin Franklin is said to have attended, did a good deal of legal work, and managed a rather large household. She lived in Boston until 1713; then she moved to New London, Connecticut, where she lived until her death. She is remembered today for her *Journal* (October 1704-March 1705), which was a record of a trip through Rhode Island and Connecticut to New York and thence back to Boston. Madame Knight's sense of comedy plus her flair for observation gave her little book added importance as an early humorous depiction of the characters and manners of rural New England and New York.

Journal (wirtten, 1704; published, 1825)

SIDNEY LANIER   1842-1881

Sidney Lanier was a Southerner, but he did not belong to the planter aristocracy. His background was urban and professional: his father was a lawyer, and the boy grew up in the little city of Macon, Georgia. When the Civil War broke out shortly after his graduation from Oglethorpe College, he enlisted as a Confederate soldier, and he served faithfully for the war's duration, spending the last five months in a federal prison.

Lanier wanted ardently to be a musician and a poet. Since there was little opportunity for the cultivation of music and poetry in the South during the reconstruction years, he sought a more favorable environment and found it in Baltimore. In that half-Northern, half-Southern city, in the 1870's, he played the flute with professional skill in the Peabody Symphony Orchestra. His studies at this time of Old and Middle English and of the Elizabethan period resulted in a series of lectures at Peabody Institute and in an appointment, in 1879, as lecturer on English literature at Johns Hopkins University. Before he was forty, death from tuberculosis cut short a career of promise.

Lanier's reputation as a poet does not stand nearly so high today as it did at the turn of the century. He has been found prudish and sentimental, vague and confused; some Southern regionalists have found him too sophisticated and "modern." However, he has written many lines that are felicitous and true, and the musical aspects of his verse are yet to be properly appreciated.

Novel: *Tiger Lilies* (1867)
Nonfiction: *The Science of English Verse* (1880) · *The English Novel* (1883) · *Shakespeare and His Forerunners* (2 vols., 1902)
Poetry: *Poems of Sidney Lanier*, ed. Mary Day Lanier (1884)

SINCLAIR LEWIS   1885-1951

Sinclair Lewis was born at Sauk Centre, in central Minnesota. His father was a physician; his mother died when he was only five. Small-town life was uncongenial to him. Yearning for the romance of the East, he spent six months at Oberlin to prepare himself for college entrance examinations and entered Yale with the class of 1907. There he earned much of his way by newspaper work, spent two summer vacations on the then-traditional cattle-boat tour to Europe, and gained some reputation as a writer for the college literary magazines. Dropping out of college at the beginning of his senior year, he joined the group at Helicon Hall, the Socialist community established by Upton Sinclair at Englewood, New Jersey, with the profits from *The Jungle*. A brief stretch as janitor ended in illness. When he recovered he spent some months as a free-lance writer and editor in New York City and then returned to Yale to graduate in 1908. Seven years of odd literary jobs followed—reporting, editing, reading for publishers, writing advertising. Meanwhile he was writing fiction in his spare time.

About the time that his third book was published, Lewis finally found himself selling his short stories; he promptly gave up his job as an advertising manager to begin the life of a professional writer. His success was almost immediate, although it was five years before he startled the literary world into heated debate on the merits of *Main Street* (1920). For *Arrowsmith* he was offered the Pulitzer Prize, which he dramatically refused; in 1930 he received the Nobel Prize, being the first American writer so honored. He died in Italy in 1951, and his body was returned for burial at Sauk Centre.

It is clear that the novels of Sinclair Lewis are the historical record of the crassness of an epoch. The United States between World Wars I and II had need of reformers, and in Lewis it had one of its most persistent, although by no means most virulent, gadflies. Life seemed so interesting to him that he seldom was discouraged about it, and he never plumbed the depths of pessimism as did Mark Twain.

Our Mr. Wrenn (1914) · *The Job* (1917) · *Main Street* (1920) · *Babbitt* (1922)· *Arrowsmith* (1925) · *Elmer Gantry* (1927) · *The Man Who Knew Coolidge* (1928) · *Dodsworth* (1929) · *It Can't Happen Here* (1935) · *Gideon Planish* (1943) · *Cass Timberlaine* (1945) · *World So Wide* (1951)

ABRAHAM LINCOLN 1809–1865

An autobiography which Abraham Lincoln wrote in 1859 tells the main details of his early life in his characteristic style. It reads, in part:

"I was born February 12, 1809, in Hardin County, Kentucky. My parents were both born in Virginia, of undistinguished families. . . .

"I was raised to farm work, which I continued till I was twenty-two. At twenty-one I came to Illinois, Macon County. Then I got to New Salem . . . where I remained a year as sort of clerk in a store. Then came The Black Hawk War; and I was elected a captain of volunteers, a success which gave me more pleasure than any I have had since. I went the campaign, was elected, ran for the legislature the same year (1832), and was beaten—the only time I ever have been beaten by the people. The next and three succeeding biennial elections I was elected to the legislature. . . . During this legislative period I had studied law, and removed to Springfield to practice it. In 1846 I was once elected to the lower House of Congress. Was not a candidate for reelection. From 1849 to 1854, both inclusive, practised law more assiduously than before. . . ."

Lincoln's account breaks off at the time of the repeal of the Missouri Compromise (1854), a political move which caused him to return to public life when the Republican Party was founded. In 1858 the Lincoln-Douglas debates on the subject of popular sovereignty attracted nationwide attention and led to Lincoln's becoming a dark-horse candidate for the presidential nomination. He was nominated in 1860, subsequently elected, and began to serve in 1861 as the Civil War was starting. His wartime leadership was rewarded by his reelection in 1864. About a month after his second inaugural, he was shot to death by John Wilkes Booth in a Washington theater. That Lincoln took great pains in his writing is evident in his most famous utterances—most of them masterpieces of American oratory.

The Collected Works of Abraham Lincoln, ed. R. P. Basler (9 vols., 1953)

VACHEL LINDSAY 1879–1931

Born and reared in Springfield, Illinois, Vachel Lindsay, from childhood, was a member of the intensely evangelical Disciples of Christ church and interested in oratory. After studying in Springfield and in Hiram College in Ohio, he lived in Chicago, attending the Art Institute (1900-1903) and working at various part-time jobs. He also studied at the New York School of Art (1904-1905). He went on tramping trips to various parts of the country, and he made still other tours as a lecturer for the Y.M.C.A. and the Anti-Saloon League. It was during a walking trip from Illinois to New Mexico in 1912 that he composed the poem "General William Booth Enters into Heaven," which won him his first national acclaim.

Shortly after this first success, Lindsay became a favorite of the lecture platform and traveled to every corner of the country. In the end he wearied of his appearances because he felt the theatrical quality of his reading obscured not only his message but also his lyric artistry. His later books of poetry, more lyrical in nature, did not succeed as had his earlier works. Always subject to occasional fits of melancholia, in his last years he gave way more and more frequently to a feeling of depression. He died by his own hand in 1931.

Better perhaps than any recent poet, Lindsay represented some of the important attitudes of the great Middle West—its agrarianism, its democracy, and its evangelism. His poems, in turn, reflect the man: not only his emotionalism and his religious and political convictions, but the robust humor and oratorical manner inherited from his rural background.

Autobiography: *Adventures While Preaching the Gospel of Beauty* (1914)
Poetry: *General William Booth Enters into Heaven and Other Poems* (1913) · *The Congo and Other Poems* (1914) · *The Chinese Nightingale and Other Poems* (1917) · *The Golden Whales of California and Other Rhymes* (1920) · *Going-to-the-Sun* (1923) · *Going-to-the-Stars* (1926) · *The Candle in the Cabin* (1926) · *Every Soul Is a Circus* (1929)

HENRY WADSWORTH LONGFELLOW 1807–1882

Henry Wadsworth Longfellow was born in Portland, Maine, and educated at Bowdoin and abroad. He taught modern languages at Bowdoin (1829-1835) and then, after a second trip abroad, at Harvard (1837-1857). Meanwhile his fame, which had begun to flourish when *Voices of the Night* was published, was augmented by such books as *Ballads and Other Poems* (1842) and *Evangeline* (1847). Carefully sheltered in childhood and early manhood, never worried by poverty, the poet lived most of his days in peaceful old Craigie House in Cambridge. Scholars had long thought of Longfellow's life as peaceful and placid, but a study by Lawrance Thompson has shown that Longfellow won such peacefulness only after a youth full of storm and struggle. His fight against odds to become an author, his desperate sorrow following the death of his first wife in 1835, and his torture of spirit during the seven-year courtship of his second wife, Frances Appleton, all left their imprint on his life and work. His works were always popular, and by the time he died, just a few weeks after his seventy-fifth birthday, he was clearly established as the most famous and loved poet of his day.

Critics who disapprove of a large share of Longfellow's verse do so because they feel that its thought is commonplace, its mood sentimental, and its form not well related to its substance. Such critics are likely to

admit, however, that at his infrequent best, he wrote poetry which deserves
to be treasured by even fastidious readers.

Poetry: *Voices of the Night* (1839) · *Ballads and Other Poems* (1842) ·
Poems on Slavery (1842) · *Poems* (1845) · *Evangeline* (1847) · *Hiawatha*
(1855) · *The Courtship of Miles Standish* (1858) · *Tales of a Wayside Inn*
(1863) · *Household Poems* (1865) · *Christus: A Mystery* (1872) · *Kéramos
and Other Poems* (1878) · *Ultima Thule* (1880) · *In the Harbor* (1882)
Fiction: *Outre-Mer* (1833-1834) · *Hyperion* (1839)

JAMES RUSSELL LOWELL   1819–1891

Of Brahmin background and training, James Russell Lowell was graduated
from Harvard in 1838, and in 1843 he began his first and very brief editorial venture with a journal called *The Pioneer.* After his marriage to Maria
White in 1844 he lived in Philadelphia, where he wrote for several liberal
periodicals, but within a year he went to Europe, where he spent fifteen
months in study. Five years after the death of his first wife in 1853, he
married Frances Dunlap. When Longfellow retired, Lowell took the distinguished chair which Longfellow had held at Harvard and served there from
1856 until 1877. He was not only a teacher, a critic, and a poet, but also
editor of the *Atlantic Monthly* (1857-1861) and of the *North American
Review* (1864-1872), a minister to Spain (1877-1880), and a minister to
England (1880-1885).

The wide range of activity represented in Lowell's life is paralleled by
the wide range in the writing of this most versatile of the Cambridge
authors. In the years before his appointment at Harvard, Lowell, largely because of the influence of his first wife, became a leading writer in behalf of
abolition. And in the field of belles-lettres, Lowell wrote both criticism and
poetry. Six years after the death of his second wife, he died at "Elmwood,"
the house of his birth.

Lowell's early criticism was frankly subjective and impressionistic, but
beginning with the 1850's it was much improved as he gradually became
more systematic while still expressing his judgments in memorable terms.
He did write some good poetry, although his versatility somewhat diffused
his energies. He was at his poetic best, perhaps, in some of his nature
poems and in some of his odes.

Essays: *Among My Books* (first series, 1870; second series, 1876) · *My
Study Windows* (1871) · *Democracy* (1884)
Poetry: *Biglow Papers* (first series, 1848; second series, 1867) · *A Fable
for Critics* (1848) · *The Vision of Sir Launfal* (1848) · "Ode Recited at the
Harvard Commemoration" (1865) · *The Cathedral* (1869)

ROBERT LOWELL   1917–

A member of the famous Lowell family which included Amy Lowell and
James Russell Lowell, Robert Lowell, born in Boston, was graduated *sum-
ma cum laude* from Kenyon College in 1940. He was an editorial assistant
at Sheed and Ward until 1942; in 1943 he was jailed as a conscientious ob-
jector. He was awarded the Pulitzer Prize in 1947 for his *Lord Weary's
Castle,* an apt reflection of his Roman Catholic convictions. That same year
he received a Guggenheim fellowship and was appointed consultant in
poetry for the Library of Congress. He has taught at Boston University, the
State University of Iowa, and Kenyon College.

Robert Lowell is generally considered one of the most significant of
modern American poets. The remarkable discipline which he exercises is

revealed in the conciseness and the biting precision of his statements. *Land of Unlikeness* (1944) · *Lord Weary's Castle* (1946) · *The Mills of the Kavanaughs* (1951) · *Life Studies* (1959) · *For the Union Dean* (1964) · *The Old Glory* (1965) · *Near the Ocean* (1967) · *Notebook of a Year* (1969) · *The Dolphin* (1973) · *For Lizzie and Harriet* (1973) · *History* (1973)

ARCHIBALD MACLEISH 1892–

Archibald MacLeish is a writer who has distinguished himself in the field of public service as well as that of literature. He was born and reared in Glencoe, Illinois. After graduating from Harvard Law School in 1920, he joined a law firm in Boston, and during three years there he found himself increasingly attracted to poetry. After deciding to become a writer, MacLeish went abroad with his family and for six years wrote poems and short stories. Returning to the United States in 1929 for financial reasons, he served on the editorial staff of the new business magazine *Fortune,* and his views on economics and politics achieved new dimensions. He came to believe that it was the responsibility of writers to take politics seriously, and he set an example himself in his writings and, subsequently, in his work in government offices. In 1939 he became Librarian of Congress and for two years worked on the reorganization of the library. During World War II, he helped establish the Office of Facts and Figures, which later became the Office of War Information. In 1944 he became Assistant Secretary of State and helped create in the American people an awareness of the importance of the United Nations. In 1946 Mr. MacLeish was in charge of the American delegation to the UNESCO organization conference in Paris.

Although creative work took second place during the time MacLeish worked for the government, when he resumed publishing after the war, his writings showed growth. He won the Pulitzer Prize three times—in 1933 for an epic poem *Conquistador;* in 1953 for *Collected Poems,* a volume of poetry written over a period of years from 1917 to 1952; and in 1958 for his play *J.B.* The modern adaptation of the story of Job in his play *J.B.* was produced in New York, across the country, and at the World's Fair in Brussels, winning widespread acclaim.

Poetry: *Tower of Ivory* (1917) · *Conquistador* (1932) · *Act Five and Other Poems* (1948) · *Collected Poems, 1917-1952* (1952) · *Songs for Eve* (1954) · *The Wild Old Wicked Man and Other Poems* (1968) · *The Human Season: Selected Poems 1926-1972* (1972)

Drama: *J.B.* (1958) · *Herakles* (1967) · *Scratch* (1971)

Essays: *Poetry and Opinion* (1950) · *Poetry and Experience* (1961) · *A Continuing Journey* (1968)

CARSON McCULLERS 1917-1967

Carson McCullers, born in Columbus, Georgia, has often been compared with such diverse writers of the South as William Faulkner and Katherine Anne Porter—proof that her writing is unique. Expecting to have a career in music, she studied in the Juilliard School of Music and Columbia University. She broke off her schooling, took up writing, and at the precocious age of twenty-two published her first novel. Immediately she was recognized as an important new talent, and readers eagerly awaited her relatively infrequent subsequent works. Her second novel, *Reflections in a Golden Eye,* an account of a grotesque adventure into the underworld of the emotions, was ranked high among writings in the new Gothic school. Her third novel, *The Member of the Wedding,* charmingly and wistfully portrayed a Southern family, in particular the adolescent girl through whose eyes the events were seen. Critics abroad as well as in the United States praised McCullers' sense of construction and character, her feeling, her lucidity, and her poetic symbolism. She died in Nyack, N.Y., in 1967, after a long illness.

The Heart Is a Lonely Hunter (1940) · *Reflections in a Golden Eye* (1941) · *The Member of the Wedding* (1946) · *The Ballad of the Sad Café* (1951) · *The Square Root of Wonderful* (1958) · *Clock Without Hands* (1961)

NORMAN MAILER   1923–

After graduating from Harvard in 1943, Norman Mailer spent two years in the army. His experience as a clerk and rifleman in the Pacific theater served as a background for a war novel which he wrote at the age of twenty-five, *The Naked and the Dead.* This was a best seller and was later made into a motion picture. He has since written several other novels, compiled an autobiographical collection of his early stories, newspaper pieces, and columns written for the *Village Voice* (of which he was co-founder) in *Advertisements for Myself,* and published a collection of poems, *Death for the Ladies.* More recently he has written reviews and feature articles for *Esquire* and other periodicals. He has come to be known as a "hipster" or a proponent of the "beat" trend in literature, as well as a practitioner of the "new journalism."

Novels: *The Naked and the Dead* (1948) · *Barbary Shore* (1951) · *The Deer Park* (1955) · *The Man Who Studied Yoga* (1956) · *An American Dream* (1965) · *Why Are We in Vietnam?* (1967)

Nonfiction: *Advertisements for Myself* (1959) · *The Presidential Papers* (1963) · *The Armies of the Night* (1968) · *Miami and the Siege of Chicago* (1968) · *Of a Fire on the Moon* (1970) · *The Prisoner of Sex* (1971) · *Existential Errands* (1972) · *Marilyn* (1973)

BERNARD MALAMUD   1914–

Bernard Malamud was thirty-eight when he published his first book, *The Natural,* in 1952. This first work, which is about a home-run hitting baseball player, is in contrast with most of his writing which concerns the world of Jewish small businessmen—shopkeepers, tailors, and salesmen—many of whom live in Brooklyn, where Malamud himself grew up. Most of his characters, in spite of grief, conscience, suffering, and heartaches, show their understanding of humanity because they have wisdom, humor, and compassion. Portrayed in a style which is simple and straightforward, the people he creates are both comic and pathetic.

Novels: *The Natural* (1952) · *The Assistant* (1957) · *A New Life* (1961) · *The Fixer* (1966) · *Pictures of Fidelman* (1969) · *The Tenants* (1971)

Short Stories: *The Magic Barrel* (1958) · *Idiots First* (1963) · *Rembrandt's Hat* (1973)

COTTON MATHER   1663–1728

Son of Reverend Increase Mather and grandson of John Mather, Cotton Mather received his B.A. from Harvard in 1678 when he was fourteen. Four years after taking his M.A. in 1681, also at Harvard, he was installed as his father's co-minister at the Old North Church in Boston. There he remained all his life, marrying three times, burying most of his fifteen children, preaching literally thousands of sermons, and writing untiringly. He published 444 separate items, and great quantities of material are still extant in manuscript. He wrote in an extensive variety of forms and cultivated and defended an elaborate, allusion-studded style. Although he has come to be known to later generations as a pedantic, neurotic, megalomaniac, reactionary, benighted witch hunter—with some truth, to be sure—to understand Cotton Mather is a way to explore intellectual America between 1680 and 1728.

The Wonders of the Invisible World (1693) · *Magnalia Christi Americana* (1702) · *Essays to Do Good [Bonifacius]* (1710) · *The Christian Philosopher* (1721) · *Manuductio ad Ministerium* (1726)

HERMAN MELVILLE 1819–1891

Herman Melville, born in New York City, moved with his family to Albany when he was eleven. Two years later his father died, leaving the family in debt. During the seven ensuing years the boy was occupied clerking and working on his uncle's farm at Pittsfield, Massachusetts. At the age of twenty he shipped as a sailor on a merchantman bound for Liverpool. Following his return he taught school in Albany and Pittsfield and tried his hand at writing.

The most decisive event of Melville's life came on January 3, 1841, when at the age of twenty-one he shipped from New Bedford on the *Acushnet*, a whaler, for the South Seas. Melville was gone three years and nine months. The exact details of his wanderings in the Pacific are in large measure still uncertain, but it is known that, after some eighteen months on the *Acushnet*, Melville deserted at the Marquesas Islands. After a month or two among the cannibals he escaped to Tahiti; further travels may have taken him to Japan. In 1843 he joined the crew of the frigate *United States* at Honolulu and remained with this ship until his arrival at Boston more than a year later.

The eight or nine years following his return from his voyage were Melville's great productive period when he poured forth a veritable torrent of books. From the summer of 1850 till the autumn of 1851, Melville and Hawthorne were near neighbors and frequent companions, the former residing at Pittsfield, the latter at Lenox. After Hawthorne left the Berkshires, however, their friendly intimacy was interrupted. In 1856, when Melville was on a recuperative journey to Italy and the Holy Land, the two men met again in England. From 1866 to 1885 Melville was Inspector of Customs in New York City. He was a prolific writer and at his death left several unpublished works, including the just completed *Billy Budd*.

Recent studies, like Richard Chase's, have found in Melville's writings a rich and inexhaustible mine of symbolic meanings. The conferences, lectures, library exhibits, and the like which marked in 1951 the centenary of the publication of *Moby Dick* testified to the current widespread recognition of Melville's importance.

Novels: *Typee* (1846) · *Omoo* (1847) · *Mardi* (1849) · *Redburn* (1849) · *White Jacket* (1850) · *Moby Dick* (1851) · *Pierre* (1852) · *Israel Potter* (1855) · *The Confidence Man* (1857) · *Billy Budd* (1924)
Short Stories: *The Piazza Tales* (1856)
Poetry: *Battle Pieces and Aspects of the War* (1866) · *Clarel* (1876)

HENRY LOUIS MENCKEN 1880–1956

Henry Louis Mencken was born in Baltimore of German ancestry. His education at Baltimore Polytechnic was augmented by some correspondence-school work, but he never attended college. After becoming a reporter at nineteen, he plied his trade so successfully that within a couple of years he became an editor. In those two years he had launched into creative work to produce some short stories and a book of mediocre poetry, *Ventures in Verse*, which was to appear in 1903. He worked as a journalist on the Baltimore *Herald* (1903-1906) and intermittently on the Baltimore *Sun* papers (1906-1941). When a book by Mencken on George Bernard Shaw (1905) and another on the philosophy of Nietzsche (1908) attracted attention beyond Baltimore, he became editor of a national magazine, *Smart Set* (1908-1914). His writings for this periodical and his syndicated weekly column for the *Evening Sun* won him a national following. In 1924, when the *American Mercury* was established, he became its editor, to serve until 1933. No one was much surprised when, with his retirement from the *Mercury*, Mencken began to write his reminiscences, for his influence was already on the wane. His followers, however, regarded him as a great emancipator, their leader in attacks upon old-fashioned conventions and values. The power and gusto of his style, inspired in part by his love for words, had much to do with his appeal.

Poetry: *Ventures in Verse* (1903)

Nonfiction: *George Bernard Shaw—His Plays* (1905) · *The Philosophy of Friedrich Nietzsche* (1908) · *Prejudices* (six series, 1919-1927) · *The American Language* (1919; revisions in 1921, 1923, 1936; supplements in 1945, 1948; condensation in 1963) · *Treatise on the Gods* (1930)

Autobiography: *Happy Days: 1880-1892* (1940) · *Newspaper Days: 1899-1906* (1941) · *Heathen Days: 1890-1936* (1943)

ARTHUR MILLER 1915–

After his graduation from high school in New York City, Arthur Miller worked for two years in Manhattan. He began his literary career when, interested in writing, he enrolled in the University of Michigan. Following his graduation in 1938 he returned to New York where he worked in the Federal Theatre Project. The theater did not last long, however, and Miller turned to radio script writing. It was not until 1947 that he achieved his first success in the legitimate theater with the production of *All My Sons*. He has won the Pulitzer Prize for *Death of a Salesman* and for *A View from the Bridge*.

Miller is seriously concerned with both the content and the form of his drama. To him the moral statements in his dramas and the quality of the structure of his plays are equally important. He has not only written in the classical Greek tradition in *A View from the Bridge*, but he has also consciously gone against the Greek tradition in *Death of a Salesman*, in which he seeks to demonstrate the significance and worth of even a nonheroic protagonist.

The Man Who Had All the Luck (1944) · *All My Sons* (1947) · *Death of a Salesman* (1949) · *The Crucible* (1953) · *A View from the Bridge* (1955) · *After the Fall* (1963) · *Incident at Vichy* (1964) · *The Price* (1967)

WILLIAM VAUGHN MOODY 1869–1910

William Vaughn Moody was born in Indiana, and as a boy he was fond of outdoor exercise, music, painting, and study; his liking for all these stayed with him. In 1889 he entered Harvard, and although he worked his way through, he found time for many contributions to the *Harvard Monthly*. Having satisfied the requirements for graduation in three years, Moody spent his senior year in Europe. Before he died, he returned to Europe five more times: like Howells and Henry James he found the other side of the Atlantic a second home. In 1893, however, he returned to Harvard for two years of graduate study and then taught at the University of Chicago. There he spent his free time editing textbooks and traveling on vacations. In addition, there was always writing, which he was coming to regard as his real profession. Beginning in 1902 he was able to give it his full time because of the success of a textbook, *A History of English Literature,* written in collaboration with his friend Robert Morss Lovett. His production in the remaining years of his life was not large, primarily because of the tumorous condition which caused his death.

Moody was, on the whole, traditional in his forms, although not slavishly so. Frequently reminiscent of the later English Victorians, his verses nevertheless reveal a sensitive and observant individual whose bookishness did not obscure his fresh perceptions. Although he did not like the characteristics of the progressive era in which he lived, his humanism enabled him to evaluate his world with detachment and quiet penetration.

Poetry: *The Masque of Judgment* (1900) · *Poems* (1901) · *The Fire-Bringer* (1904)

Drama: *The Great Divide* (produced, 1906) · *The Faith Healer* (1909)

Textbook: *A History of English Literature* (with Robert Morss Lovett, 1902)

MARIANNE MOORE 1887–1972

Marianne Moore, born in St. Louis, Missouri, was graduated from Bryn Mawr in 1909 and began publishing her poetry in the *Egoist,* edited by Richard Aldington and, during the war, by his wife "H.D." Her first associations, therefore, were with the Imagist group which stressed the importance of hard, clear, accurate images. Her first book of verse came out in 1920. She taught in the government Indian school in Carlisle, Pennsylvania, worked as an assistant at the New York Public Library, and was an editor of *The Dial* from 1925 to 1929.

Miss Moore's poetry won many awards, among them the Pulitzer Prize, the Bollingen Prize in Poetry, and the National Book Award. She created a very personal poetical style; her verse, elegant and brilliant, is rendered in exquisitely meticulous language.

Poetry: *Poems* (1921) · *Observations* (1924) · *Selected Poems* (1935) · *The Pangolin and Other Verse* (1936) · *What Are Years?* (1941) · *Nevertheless* (1944) · *Collected Poems* (1951) · *Like a Bulwark* (1956) · *O To Be a Dragon* (1959) · *The Complete Poems* (1967)

Essays: *Predilections* (1955)

THOMAS MORTON 1580?–1646

Little is known of Thomas Morton's life before 1625, when he became a part of a trading company at Mount Wollaston, near Plymouth, later renamed "Ma-re," or Merry, Mount. He had probably been a London lawyer, and made an earlier visit to New England. In 1627 he was arrested and deported, either for licentious and atheistic behavior, as reported by William Bradford, or because of his successful trade with the Indians and his support of the Church of England, as Morton himself maintained. He returned, and in 1630 was again deported.

Morton's single book, the *New English Canaan, or New Canaan,* was first printed at Amsterdam in 1637. It consists of three parts. The first concerns the Indians, their origin and customs; the second is essentially a promotion tract, with an account of the country and its commodities; the third is an account of the English settlement, as seen from Morton's anti-Puritan position. Morton appears to have fancied himself as a writer, and his book is unusual among works of its type for its allusive literary and sometimes overornamental style.

Morton was in America again in 1643, and was once more arrested. After many months in the Boston jail, he was released. He left Massachusetts, this time without being forced to, and found a retreat in Maine, where he died in 1646.

New English Canaan, or New Canaan, ed. C. F. Adams, Jr. (1883)

MARY NOAILLES MURFREE (Charles Egbert Craddock) **1850–1922**
Mary Noailles Murfree was born in middle Tennessee near the town of Murfreesboro (named for her great-grandfather, a Revolutionary officer from North Carolina). Her father was a successful lawyer, an owner of plantations in the delta country, and an admirer of Scott and Dickens. Miss Murfree was educated in the traditional Southern manner at young ladies' finishing schools—at the Nashville Female Academy and at Chegary Institute in Philadelphia. The Murfrees spent some fifteen summers at Beersheba Springs, a fashionable resort in the Cumberland Mountains; it was the country around Beersheba which furnished the materials for Miss Murfree's early stories, though she later visited, and utilized in her fiction, the wilder, more primitive Great Smokies, which lie to the east of the Cumberland range.

Miss Murfree's reputation rests chiefly on her earlier books, although she later wrote many volumes of mountain stories and of historical fiction dealing with the colonial Southwest and the Civil War, all under a pseudonym. Her work, like that of most of the writers of the local color school, seems much less important now than it did at the end of the last century.

In the Tennessee Mountains (1884) · *The Prophet of the Great Smoky Mountains* (1885)

FRANK NORRIS 1870–1902
Born in Chicago to well-to-do parents, Frank Norris moved with his family to San Francisco in 1884. Somehow, at the age of seventeen, he persuaded his family to allow him to study art in Paris. During his stay abroad, however, he changed his allegiance from the Atelier Julien to literature. Back in California as a student at the University of California (1890-1894), he discovered the appeal of the French naturalistic school led by Zola, and of Rudyard Kipling. His writings as a student at Harvard (1894-1895) showed this influence.

Gifted with a talent for friendship, Norris took great delight in becoming one of the Bohemian group in Paris and equal delight in becoming a friend of athletes, men-about-the-campus, and scholars in his college fraternity. At the same time he was very much a conscious literary artist, and his critical writings attest that he had thoroughly developed theories about technique. The career which came to an untimely end when Norris died in 1902 had been a promising one indeed. In his novels he foreshadowed some of the aspects of the writings of notable modern authors—the unflinching depiction of sordid detail of Faulkner, the brutality of Hemingway, and the poetic fervor of Wolfe.

McTeague (1899) · *The Octopus* (1901) · *The Pit* (1903) · *Vandover and the Brute* (1914)

O. HENRY: see William Sydney Porter

FLANNERY O'CONNOR   1925–1964
Flannery O'Connor was born in 1925, in Savannah, Georgia. She attended
Women's College of Georgia, in Milledgeville, began to try her hand at fiction, and graduated in 1945. On the basis of one of her stories she was
awarded a fellowship at the Writer's Workshop at the University of Iowa,
and took the Master of Fine Arts in Literature in 1947. By the time she
finished her studies, she had already begun to publish stories, and, shortly
after, she began to work on her first novel, *Wise Blood,* not published until
1952.

   Her novels and stories deal repeatedly with poor, illiterate Southerners
who are obsessed with religious visions rooted in fundamentalist beliefs.
These tortured prophets and crusaders are presented, however, not with
the usual emphasis on satire and comedy, but rather with understanding
and deep moral probing. In spite of the intensity of her interest in rural
fundamentalist folk, Flannery O'Connor was a committed Catholic and
considered herself a religious writer. It is a tribute to the sophistication of
her belief and the genius of her art that few of her readers learn of her
faith from her fiction.
Novels: *Wise Blood* (1952) · *The Violent Bear It Away* (1960)
Short Stories: *A Good Man Is Hard to Find* (1955) · *Everything That
Rises Must Converge* (1965)

JOHN O'HARA   1905–1970
John O'Hara was born in Pottsville, Pennsylvania, and graduated from
Niagara Prep School in 1924. When his father's death prevented him from
attending Yale University, he entered into a varied career as an engineer,
boat steward, call boy, freight clerk, guard in an amusement park, steel
worker, Hollywood press agent, private secretary, motion-picture writer,
critic, and feature writer.

   O'Hara's short stories and novels are noted for the accuracy with
which they report the conversation, manners, and morals of a certain seg-
ment of American society—the Hollywood, country club, and hotel-bar
sets. Edmund Wilson has called O'Hara the "outstanding master of *The
New Yorker* short-story sketch."
Novels: *Appointment in Samarra* (1934) · *Butterfield 8* (1935) · *A Rage
to Live* (1949) · *Ten North Frederick* (1955) · *A Family Party* (1956) ·
From the Terrace (1958) · *Ourselves to Know* (1960) · *Elizabeth Appleton*
(1963)
Short Stories: *Files on Parade* (1939) · *Pal Joey* [later a musical comedy,
1952] (1940) · *Sermons and Soda-Water* (1960) · *Assembly* (1961) · *Hat
on the Bed* (1963) · *Waiting for Winter* (1966) · *And Other Stories* (1968)

EUGENE O'NEILL   1888–1953
Son of popular actor James O'Neill, Eugene O'Neill was born in New York
City. The varied experiences of his youth included not only academic
study (at Princeton, 1906-1907, and at Harvard, 1914-1915) but also two
years at sea, a tour in vaudeville, and a turn at newspaper reporting. In
1912, forced into a year of convalescence because of tuberculosis, O'Neill's
interest in drama grew as he spent much of his leisure time reading plays,
especially those of the Greeks, Elizabethans, and moderns. He began his
career as a dramatist in 1916 with his first significant one-act play, *Bound*

East for Cardiff. His first full-length play, *Beyond the Horizon,* produced in 1920, won a Pulitzer Prize, the first of four he received. In his last years he suffered from Parkinson's disease and found it almost impossible to continue writing.

By common consent O'Neill is the greatest dramatist that America has produced. His plays are interesting both for their bold experimentation and their psychological insights. Although the degree to which he used Freudian psychology may prove injurious to his future reputation, there is no denying the originality and power of his best work.

Bound East for Cardiff (1916) · *Beyond the Horizon* (1920) · *The Emperor Jones* (1921) · *Anna Christie* (1922) · *The Hairy Ape* (1922) · *Desire Under the Elms* (1925) · *The Great God Brown* (1926) · *Strange Interlude* (1928) · *Mourning Becomes Electra* (1931) · *Ah, Wilderness!* (1933) · *The Iceman Cometh* (1946) · *Moon for the Misbegotten* (1952) · *Long Day's Journey into Night* (1956) · *A Touch of the Poet* (1957)

THOMAS PAINE 1737–1809

Thomas Paine was born in England, and after leaving school at thirteen he searched fruitlessly for a quarter of a century before he found an agreeable occupation. At thirty-seven, penniless and unknown, Paine met Benjamin Franklin, who gave him a letter of introduction to use when he went to America later that year. After a serious illness, he readied himself for a new profession by a series of contributions to the *Pennsylvania Magazine.* With the publication of *Common Sense* in January 1776, his career as a propagandist of genius was begun. His contributions to the Revolution included pamphlets, service in the Continental Army, and various kinds of work for the Continental Congress.

In April 1787 Paine sailed for France and became a supporter of the French Revolution. However, as an honorary citizen and member of the National Convention, he opposed the execution of Louis XVI; and by December 1793, he was imprisoned as a foreigner. *The Age of Reason,* his last "offering" to mankind, so shocked people that many were willing to burn Paine at the stake. After his return to America in 1802 he was shot at, insulted, and humiliated even on his deathbed.

No man of his time was better able to express, simply and clearly, the views which effected vast changes in the political, social, and religious constitution of Western civilization. The force, directness, and variety of his appeals to reason and emotion made him the foremost propagandist-agitator of his time.

Common Sense (1776) · *The American Crisis* (1776-1783) · *The Rights of Man* (Part I, 1791; Part II, 1792) · *The Age of Reason* (Part I, 1794; Part II, 1795)

SYLVIA PLATH 1932–1963

In spite of her brief life and slender output of poetry, Sylvia Plath has had a deeply felt impact on the modern imagination. Hers is a haunted poetry, and in reading it the sensitive modern reader feels the tremors that come from the shock of recognition—recognition, that is, of the horrors lurking in ordinary contemporary existence. She was born in Boston, went to Smith College, and in 1955 went to England on a Fulbright. There she met and married the British poet Ted Hughes. Her first book of poems, *The Colossus,* was published in 1960. After her death by suicide in 1963, her remaining poems were gathered together in a volume entitled *Ariel.* She also wrote an autobiographical novel, *The Bell Jar*, about a young woman's experiences with madness and attempted suicide.

Poetry: *The Colossus* (1960) · *Ariel* (1963)

EDGAR ALLAN POE   1809–1849

The son of a wandering theatrical family, Edgar Allan Poe was orphaned at two and became the ward of the John Allan family of Richmond, Virginia. Never legally adopted, he could not live quite the normal life of a son in a well-to-do family. Although in his early years both Mr. and Mrs. Allan did what they could to spoil him, friction grew between him and his foster father until he was withdrawn from the University of Virginia after less than a year of attendance. There followed a period of service in the army (1827-1829), an unhappy brief career at West Point (1830-1831), and a final break with Allan (1832).

Before the break Poe had published three books of poetry, none very successful financially. Driven to try to make a living with his pen, he began writing tales. A sign that he had some success was that one of them, "The MS. Found in a Bottle," won a one-hundred-dollar prize in 1833. Befriended by one of the contest judges, John Pendleton Kennedy, he began a career as editor, serving on the staff of the *Southern Literary Messenger* (1835-1837), *Burton's Gentleman's Magazine* (1839), *Graham's Magazine* (1841-1842), and other periodicals. Other tales won repute for him, and he was an alert and canny editor; but his poverty, his fiery temper, and his instability worked against his success. His pay as an editor was usually small, less than sixteen dollars a week, for instance, for his very successful work as editor of *Graham's*. Even in 1845, after he had won wide popularity, a collection of his verse, *The Raven and Other Poems*, and a volume of stories, *Tales of the Grotesque and Arabesque*, did not have financial success.

Although Poe was not at all times the brooding, gloomy person tradition has painted, his life was on the whole an unhappy one. In 1831 he found a home with Mrs. Maria Clemm, mother of Poe's cousin, Virginia— a home in which, although members of the family were devoted to one another, poverty and sickness made life hard. In 1835 he married thirteen-year-old Virginia, a fragile child who suffered from a devastating illness destined to end her life when she was twenty-six. He died in mysterious circumstances, in Baltimore, October 7, 1849.

Poe was outstanding as a critic, a fiction writer, and a poet. His discussions of contemporary writers and his treatises on poetry and fiction won him a place as the greatest critic of his day. Employing the principle of the single effect, he wrote masterful horror stories and invented the detective story as a genre. His musical poems, often creating strange and mysterious worlds, were highly influential on French poets, who in turn did much to shape modern English and American poetry.

Poetry: *Tamerlane and Other Poems* (1827) · *Al Aaraaf, Tamerlane, and Minor Poems* (1829) · *Poems* (second edition, 1831) · *The Raven and Other Poems* (1845)

Short Stories: "The MS. Found in a Bottle" (1833) · "The Fall of the House of Usher" (1839) · *Tales of the Grotesque and Arabesque* (1840) · "The Murders in the Rue Morgue" (1841) · "The Masque of the Red Death" (1842) · *Tales* (1845) · "The Cask of Amantillado" (1846) · *The Narrative of Arthur Gordon Pym* (1838)

Essays: "Review of *Twice-Told Tales*" [revision in "Tale Writing," 1847]
(1842) · "The Philosophy of Composition" (1846) · *Eureka: A Prose Poem*
(1848) · "The Poetic Principle" (1850)

KATHERINE ANNE PORTER   1894–

Katherine Anne Porter was born in Indian Creek, Texas, the great-great-
great-granddaughter of Daniel Boone, and spent her early life in Texas and
Louisiana. She was educated in various convent schools of the South. She
married in 1933 and was soon divorced; in 1938 she married Albert Russel
Erskine, Jr., and they were divorced in 1942. Miss Porter has lived in various parts of the world: in the South, in New York City, in Europe, in
Mexico. Using details from her experiences, she has therefore employed a
variety of backgrounds in her fiction. She was awarded a Guggenheim Fellowship for creative writing in 1931 and again in 1938. In 1944 she was
Fellow of Regional American Literature in the Library of Congress, and in
1958-1959 she was writer in residence at the University of Virginia. Although *Ship of Fools* is her major novel, she has written primarily short
stories and novelettes.

Throughout her career Miss Porter has worked scrupulously and painstakingly, refusing to print anything until completely satisfied with it. Her
devotion to her craft has been richly rewarded, for, although she has
published comparatively little, she has achieved high distinction in the art
of fiction.

Novel: *Ship of Fools* (1962)
Short Stories: *Flowering Judas and Other Stories* (1930, 1935) · *Pale
Horse, Pale Rider* (1939) · *The Leaning Tower and Other Stories* (1944) ·
The Collected Stories of Katherine Anne Porter (1965)

EZRA POUND   1885–1973

Ezra Pound was born in Idaho in 1885, studied at the University of Pennsylvania and Hamilton College, taught for a short time at Wabash College.
He lived much of his life abroad, in London from 1909-1920, in Paris from
1920-1924, and in Rapallo, Italy, from 1924 until the end of World War II.
Because of his support of the Fascists in radio broadcasts during the war,
he was captured and returned to America. But instead of standing trial for
treason, he was committed to a federal insane asylum. Upon his release in
1958 he returned to Italy.

When Pound published his first volume of verse in 1908 *(A Lume
Spento),* American poetry was generally in the doldrums. He was one of
the key figures in sparking the poetic renaissance that began shortly before
World War I. He championed the little magazines congenial to poetry, serv-
ing as the foreign editor for Chicago's *Poetry,* founded in 1912 by Harriet
Monroe. He promoted such writers as Robert Frost, T. S. Eliot, and James
Joyce, and such literary groups as the Vorticists and Imagists (both antiro-
mantic and neoclassical in outlook).

Pound's own poetry is characterized by its rich allusiveness and its
dense intellectual texture. While much of it is marred by opaque philosophy and pedantry, at its best it contains passages of immense power and
beauty—difficult to read, perhaps, but impossible to ignore.

Poetry: *Lustra* (1916) · *Hugh Selwyn Mauberley* (1920) · *Personae* (1926)
· *A Draft of XXX Cantos* (1933) · *Pisan Cantos* (1948; subsequent Cantos
were issued in 1954, 1956, and 1959)
Nonfiction: *Letters,* ed. D. D. Paige (1950) · *Literary Essays,* ed. T. S.
Eliot (1954)

EDWIN ARLINGTON ROBINSON 1869-1935
Edwin Arlington Robinson was born in the village of Head Tide, Maine, and spent his youth in nearby Gardiner, the "Tilbury Town" of his poems. After finishing the high-school course in Gardiner, he entered Harvard, but he left after two years, returning to Gardiner to devote himself to writing poetry. In 1897 he moved to New York, where he lived for the rest of his life, except for summers spent, after 1911, at the MacDowell Colony near Peterborough, New Hampshire. He went to Europe once, but never traveled in the United States beyond New England and New York City. Unmarried, shy, and with little money, he lived quietly and inexpensively. In his lifetime he published over twenty volumes of poetry and was awarded the Pulitzer Prize three times.

Although Robinson writes in the New England tradition, the Puritan accent in his poetry is neither strong nor triumphant. His poetry is, in fact, modern in temper and reflects the New England tradition in its decay. His poetry is also modern in its diction, even though it is written in nineteenth-century forms.

The Children of the Night (1897) · *Captain Craig* (1902) · *The Town Down the River* (1910) · *The Man Against the Sky* (1916) · *Merlin* (1917) · *Lancelot* (1920) · *Collected Poems* (1921) · *The Man Who Died Twice* (1924) · *Dionysus in Doubt* (1925) · *Tristram* (1927) · *Matthias at the Door* (1931)

THEODORE ROETHKE 1908-1963
Born in Saginaw, Michigan, Theodore Roethke grew up around his father's florist business and greenhouses. He attended the University of Michigan and Harvard, and taught at a series of schools, including the University of Washington in Seattle from 1947 until his death. His first book of poems, *Open House* (1941), incorporated many of his early experiences in his father's greenhouses and was filled with the wonder of growing things. Although he published other early collections, he really hit his stride in 1953 with *The Waking: Poems 1933-1953,* which won the Pulitzer Prize. He won the National Book Award twice, once in 1954 for *Words for the Wind* and again in 1964 for *The Far Field* (awarded posthumously).

There is a kind of child's delight of discovery in much of Roethke's poetry, not unlike the breathlessness of Emily Dickinson at her best. But, at the same time, there is a Whitman-like sense of identity with the natural world and the submerged impulses of the cosmos.

Roethke suffered a heart attack in August 1963, while he was relaxing at his swimming pool, and died at the age of 55.

Poetry: *Open House* (1941) · *The Lost Son* (1949) · *Praise to the End!* (1951) · *The Waking: Poems 1933-1953* (1953) · *Words for the Wind* (1958) · *I Am! Says the Lamb* (1961) · *The Far Field* (1964) · *Collected Poems* (1966)
Nonfiction: *On the Poet and His Craft* (1965)

J. D. SALINGER 1919-
Jerome David Salinger has been one of the most talked about but also one of the most retiring of contemporary authors. He has taken care to keep his private life out of view of reporters and photographers. He was born in New York City and went to school in that area. During World War II he served in France. He published his first story at the age of twenty-one and has since published frequently in *The New Yorker* and other magazines.

Although his works are few in contrast to those by other well-known authors, they have been the subject of numerous critical and scholarly articles. Salinger's works deal in many instances with the world of sensitive children and adolescents who see through the "phony" exterior of the adults in the world around them.

Novel: *Catcher in the Rye* (1951)
Short Stories: *Nine Stories* (1953) · *Franny and Zooey* (1961) · *Raise High the Roof Beam, Carpenters; and Seymour: an Introduction* (1962)

CARL SANDBURG 1878–1967

Born in Galesburg, Illinois, Carl Sandburg left school at thirteen to drive a milkwagon; later he was a porter and then a worker in a brickyard. He traveled a good deal (mostly on the underside of boxcars), stopping off to work here and there. During his enlistment for the Spanish-American War, he was persuaded by an alumnus that he ought to go to Lombard College at Galesburg. After working his way through Lombard, he became a traveling salesman of stereopticon slides, and he was engaged in this work when, in 1904, his first book, a little pamphlet called *In Reckless Ecstasy*, was published. A few years later Sandburg went to Milwaukee, working as labor reporter on Socialist Victor Berger's Milwaukee *Leader.* In 1908 he married Lillian Steichen, who, like him, was interested in the fortunes of laborers. In 1912 he and his wife drifted to Chicago, where he worked for several publications, notably the *Daily News.*

When *Poetry* was started in Chicago, Sandburg was one of its early contributors; and in 1916 his first book of poems to be put out by a nationally known publisher appeared. Sandburg was awarded the Pulitzer Prize for Poetry in 1950.

Meanwhile, Sandburg developed an interest in folklore. His great collection of ballads, gathered during his wide travels, was presented on many platforms and eventually published in 1927. Folklore also figured importantly when he turned to history and wrote his moving biography of an earlier midwesterner, Abraham Lincoln.

The poetry, ballad collection, and biography are all of a piece. They spring from Sandburg's desire to voice the thoughts and feelings he learned from the common people. His poetry is expressive of his times in both its form and its subject matter. It is free verse of the sort that was becoming fashionable when he started to write. He wrote in the American vernacular, the richness of which was being discovered in his youth. He, like others, was bewildered by the shift from the agrarian way of living to industrialization and was resentful of the abuses that accompanied the shift. But he, like others, found his hope and belief in the common man.

Poetry: *In Reckless Ecstasy* (1904) · *Chicago Poems* (1916) · *Cornhuskers* (1918) · *Smoke and Steel* (1920) · *Slabs of the Sunburnt West* (1922) · *Good Morning, America* (1928) · *The People, Yes* (1936) · *Complete Poems* (1950) · *Collected Poems* (1951) · *Harvest Poems, 1910-1960* (1960)
Songs: *The American Songbag* (1927)
Nonfiction: *Abraham Lincoln: The Prairie Years* (2 vols., 1926) · *Abraham Lincoln: The War Years* (4 vols., 1939)
Novel: *Remembrance Rock* (1948)
Autobiography: *Always the Young Strangers* (1953)

SAMUEL SEWALL   1652–1730
For nearly sixty years following his graduation from Harvard in 1671, Samuel Sewall was active in business and politics. For a period (1681-1684) he managed the colony's printing press; he spent a year in England (1688-1689), engaged in private business and assisting Increase Mather in his unsuccessful efforts to bring about the restoration of the colony's charter. He was captain, in 1701, of the Ancient and Honorable Artillery Company; and from 1718 to 1728 he was Chief Justice of the Superior Court of Massachusetts. Sewall was the only one of the three judges of the Salem witch trials ever to admit publicly that the court had been guilty of a grave error. But perhaps more worthy of note is his remarkably concise and suggestive *Diary* (1674-1729) which affords a rich and vivid picture of life in colonial Boston.
Autobiography: *Diary* (1674-1729; published, 1878-1882)
Nonfiction: *The Selling of Joseph* (1700)

KARL SHAPIRO   1913–
Karl Jay Shapiro was born in Baltimore, Maryland, the son of a Jewish father and a Catholic mother. A year at the University of Virginia, perhaps a shade more committed than most American colleges to the ancient cult of the "gentleman," was obviously painful. Shapiro was publishing poetry at twenty-one, and a slim collection, *Poems*, appeared in 1935. Between 1936 and 1940 he was a student at Johns Hopkins University. There he evidently read to good purpose, for his later verses reveal an acquaintance with a wide range of subjects and poetic devices. Selective Service caught him in 1941, and at the time Evelyn Katz, his fiancée, saw *Person, Place, and Thing* through the press in 1942, he was on active duty "somewhere in the Pacific." His postwar work has included a year as poetry consultant at the Library of Congress, teaching at Hopkins and at Nebraska and, 1950-1955, editing *Poetry, A Magazine of Verse*.

Shapiro's *V-Letter and Other Poems* (1944) won the Pulitzer Prize for him at thirty-one. It, with his other work, is among the best records thus far available of what the war has done to his generation. Some critics have complained of a certain superficial cleverness in Shapiro's work, but the lasting impression is of an honest and intelligent man probing the great questions of life.
Poetry: *Poems* (1935) · *Person, Place, and Thing* (1942) · *V-Letter and Other Poems* (1944) · *Essay on Rime* (1945) · *Trial of a Poet and Other Poems* (1947) · *Poems of a Jew* (1958) · *The Bourgeoise Poet* (1964) · *Selected Poems* (1968) · *White-Haired Lover* (1968)
Novel: *Edsel* (1971)
Essays: *A Bibliography of Modern Prosody* (1948) · *Beyond Criticism* (1953) · *In Defense of Ignorance* (1960) · *To Abolish Children* (1968)

HENRY WHEELER SHAW (Josh Billings)   **1818–1885**
Henry Wheeler Shaw was born in Lanesboro, Massachusetts. He prepared for college at Lenox Academy and then attended Hamilton College for about two years before he was expelled for a prank. At seventeen he migrated to the West. He was, at various times, a farmer, a coal operator, and a proprietor of an Ohio River steamboat before he returned to the East and settled down to be a real estate operator and an auctioneer in Poughkeepsie, New York. In the late 1850's, when some of his comic writings for newspapers were widely reprinted, he got off to a start as a successful funnyman.

He moved to New York City and remained there the rest of his life.

Josh Billings, Shaw's creation, was famous not for stories but for essays or single sentences packed with amusingly phrased common sense. His kinship with Poor Richard was obvious, but his use of idiosyncratic spellings showed that his writing was also related to that of such a contemporary as Artemus Ward.

Josh Billings, His Sayings (1865) · *Josh Billings on Ice and Other Things* (1868) · *Josh Billings' Farmer's Allminax* (1869-1879)

EDWARD ROWLAND SILL 1841–1887

Edward Rowland Sill, born in Windsor, Connecticut, was the descendant of a distinguished line of New England ancestors which included several ministers. He prepared for college at Phillips Exeter and attended Yale. Then followed a period of indecision which ended with his becoming a teacher and author at the University of California. In 1882 he retired from teaching and returned to the East, where he died in 1887.

With some differences in time and place, the pattern of Sill's living was reminiscent of the lives of earlier Brahmin poets, and he thought of poetry much as they had. Putting his beliefs into practice in creative writing, Sill produced a number of poems which were very much in the vein of Longfellow—"The Arch," for instance, and "Spring Twilight," and two very popular poems, "The Fool's Prayer" and "Opportunity." Sill, though a minor poet, merits attention as a representative poet of his period. However, he transcends most of his contemporaries, and was one of the first American poets to express in verse a metaphysical anxiety.

The Poetical Works of Edward Rowland Sill (published 1906)

WILLIAM GILMORE SIMMS 1806–1870

Though born in the most aristocratic of Southern cities, Charleston, South Carolina, William Gilmore Simms did not belong to the aristocracy. The death of his mother and his father's removal to Mississippi left the boy to the care of an impoverished grandmother. His schooling was irregular; for a time, he was apprenticed to a druggist. At the age of eighteen he visited his father in Mississippi, where he saw the mixed life of the frontier. After his return to Charleston, he first experimented in poetry and journalism and then turned to the writing of fiction, his first novel appearing in 1833. Two years later he achieved a popular success with *The Yemassee*. For a good while his works were more favorably received in the North than in his native city, where an eighteenth-century classical taste in literature persisted longer than almost anywhere else. By marriage in 1836 he connected himself with the planter aristocracy and acquired the country estate, midway between Charleston and Augusta, known as "The Woodlands." Here Simms wrote his books and entertained his friends.

In the 1850's he became the leader of a group of younger writers in Charleston, which included the poets Paul Hamilton Hayne and Henry Timrod; he was instrumental, together with the other members of the group, in founding the distinguished though short-lived *Russell's Magazine* (1857-1860). In the 1850's, also, he became an active opponent of abolitionism and contributed to the Southern manifesto, *The Pro-Slavery Argument* (Charleston, 1853). The Northern invasion of South Carolina inflicted severe personal hardships on Simms, among them, the burning of his house and the loss of a fine library.

Simms has often been regarded as a lesser Cooper, but this is an uncritical view because Simms' materials and methods were his own. Parrington compares Simms with the early English novelists, Henry Fielding and Tobias Smollett, and notes the element of the picaresque as particularly distinguishing his work from Cooper's.

Martin Faber (1833) · *Guy Rivers* (1834) · *The Yemassee* (1835) · *The Partisan* (1835) · *Mellichampe* (1836) · *Richard Hurdis* (1838) · *The Border Beagles* (1840) · *Katherine Walton* (1851) · *Woodcraft* (1854) · *The Forayers* (1855)

UPTON SINCLAIR 1878–1968

Upton Sinclair was born in Baltimore but brought up in New York, where he was graduated from the College of the City of New York in 1898. By then he was already earning his own living by selling stories and jokes. His first serious novel was published in 1901, shortly before he became active as a Socialist. The League for Industrial Democracy (formerly the Intercollegiate Socialist Society) and the American Civil Liberties Union are largely of his creation. Three times he ran for Congress and three times for the governorship of California. In *I, Governor of California and How I Ended Poverty* (1933) and other pamphlets he set forth his platform, EPIC (End Poverty in California). This program found wide public support in the early days of the New Deal, and he was very nearly elected. With eruptions of fascism and communism in Europe, Sinclair turned his attention to these phenomena.

Sinclair always wrote with amazing fluency and a consequent unevenness. As a propagandist, akin in spirit to Thomas Paine, he was considered radical and unsound by conservatives; and extreme left-wing thinkers condemned him for not adhering to the Marxist line. But of his earnestness and sincerity there is no question. He was master of the literary method of "exposure," best shown in *The Jungle* (1906).

Novels: *The Jungle* (1906) · *King Coal* (1917) · *Oil!* (1927) · *Boston* (1928) · *The Wet Parade* (1931) · *Dragon's Teeth* (1942) · *It Happened to Didymus* (1958) · *Affectionately, Eve* (1961)

Nonfiction: *The Brass Check* (1919) · *The Goose-Step* (1923) · *I, Governor of California and How I Ended Poverty* (1933)

Autobiography: *American Outpost* (1932)

JOHN SMITH 1579–1631

John Smith, known today mostly because of his lively travel accounts, in 1606 led the expedition which was to result in the first permanent British colony on this continent, and in 1614 he explored New England thoroughly from the Penobscot River to Cape Cod.

Smith's works are interesting for their characterization of the author, their description of events, and their style. The style is that of an educated —but not too educated—man, writing imaginatively about first-hand experiences. It has the varied rhythms, the homeliness fused with strangeness and stateliness, of prose in the age of the King James Bible.

A True Relation (1608) · *Map of Virginia* (1612) · *A Description of New England* (1616) · *The Generall Historie of Virginia, New England, and the Summer Isles* (1624)

SEBA SMITH (Jack Downing) 1792–1868

Seba Smith was born in Buckfield, Maine, and lived in Buckfield and other Down East towns until he was twenty-three. He left school to work at odd

jobs but eventually completed his education when, at twenty-six, he was graduated with honors from Bowdoin College. After some traveling he returned to Maine where he became assistant editor of the *Eastern Argus*. In 1829 he began his own newspaper, the Portland *Courier*, for which Smith invented the humorous character Jack Downing to say his say about contemporary politics. Jack was the first in the long line of common-sensible figures which included influential comic oracles such as Hosea Biglow, Josh Billings, Mark Twain, Mr. Dooley, and Will Rogers.
The Life and Writings of Major Jack Downing of Downingville (1833) · *My Thirty Years Out of the Senate* (1859)

W. D. SNODGRASS 1926–

William DeWitt Snodgrass was reared in Beaver Falls, Pennsylvania. He attended Geneva College in 1943, but his education was interrupted by two years of service in the Navy. In 1946 he returned to Geneva College, where he received his B.A. in 1947. At the State University of Iowa, where he studied under Robert Lowell, he received his M.A. in 1951 and his M.F.A. in 1953. He taught at Cornell University, the University of Rochester, and in 1959 became assistant professor of English at Wayne State University. In 1960 he won the Pulitzer Prize for his poems, *Heart's Needle.*

Though autobiographical in tone and nonacademic in spirit, the poetry of W. D. Snodgrass is polished and traditional in form. His undisguised concern with himself, the individual, is one of the unique and pleasing features of his poetry.
Heart's Needle (1959) · *After Experience: Poems and Translations* (1968)

SUSAN SONTAG 1933–

Born in 1933, Susan Sontag graduated from the University of Chicago in 1951 and took an M.A. from Radcliffe in 1952. She then studied at both Oxford in England and at the Sorbonne in Paris. Her varied career has included a period on the editorial staff of *Commentary* and teaching posts in philosophy at a number of places, including Sarah Lawrence College and Columbia University. She was Writer in Residence at Rutgers University, 1964-1965, and she was awarded a Guggenheim Fellowship in 1966.

Although she is known primarily as a critic, Sontag considers herself primarily a novelist; however, neither of her novels has been a popular success and both are regarded as in some sense experimental or avant-garde, exploring the thin line between dreams and actuality, and probing the ambiguous nature of reality.
The Benefactor (1963) · *Death Kit* (1967)

LINCOLN STEFFENS 1866–1936

Lincoln Steffens, a Californian whose father was indulgent up to a point, was graduated from the university of his native state in 1889. He spent three years in study in Europe, and while there he married a fellow American but neglected to inform his family of the fact. This caused him to lose his father's favor and financial assistance, but on his own he found a place, not too easily, on the New York *Evening Post* and was soon extraordinarily successful. By the investment of a small legacy from one of his Leipzig classmates he obtained financial freedom which enabled him to pursue with few restrictions the task he set himself—an understanding of the ethical implications of social and political processes.

Considered the founder of the school of "muckrakers," Steffens, in his explorations of corruption in government and business, came to believe that one could not lay all the blame for these abuses on "evil" individuals. He saw bribery and bossism, crime and organized vice as connected parts of a vast "System" for which citizens themselves, through their indifference and selfishness, were responsible.

Nonfiction: *The Shame of the Cities* (1904) · *The Struggle for Self-Government* (1906)

Autobiography: *Autobiography* (1931)

JOHN STEINBECK   1902–1968

John Steinbeck, born at Salinas, California, grew up in a rich but strike-tormented valley where he learned at first hand about the life of the agricultural and factory workers. From 1919 through 1925 he attended Stanford University, taking the courses that attracted him without worrying about degree requirements and dropping out now and then to work as a laborer. Already determined to be a writer, he contributed to the university magazines. After leaving Stanford, he worked briefly as a reporter in New York City. Illness caused him to return to California, where he became a caretaker on a mountain estate. His first published book, *Cup of Gold*, said to be the fourth that he wrote, appeared in 1929. Steinbeck's popularity began with *Tortilla Flat* (1935), rejected by nine publishers before it was accepted by Covici. In 1940 he received the Pulitzer Prize for *Grapes of Wrath*, and in 1962 he was awarded the Nobel Prize for Literature.

Steinbeck has been called a primitivist, and it is true that he tended to glorify rudimentary folk. Yet, as Frederick Ives Carpenter has pointed out, he combined several of the great skeins of American thought: Emerson's mystical monism, Whitman's sense of democracy, and a pragmatic belief in effective action. Though aware of human failure, Steinbeck created in his characters a zest in living which is perhaps more essential for survival than an understanding of life.

Novels: *Cup of Gold* (1929) · *To a God Unknown* (1933) · *In Dubious Battle* (1936) · *Of Mice and Men* (1937) · *The Grapes of Wrath* (1939) · *The Moon Is Down* (1942) · *The Wayward Bus* (1947) · *The Pearl* (1948) · *East of Eden* (1952) · *Winter of Our Discontent* (1961)

Short Stories: *The Pastures of Heaven* (1932) · *Tortilla Flat* (1935) · *Cannery Row* (1945) · *Sweet Thursday* (1954)

Autobiography: *Travels with Charley* (1962)

Nonfiction: *The Sea of Cortez* (1941) · *America and the Americans* (1966)

WALLACE STEVENS   1879–1955

Wallace Stevens was born in Reading, Pennsylvania. His mother was of Pennsylvania descent and his father, a lawyer, of Dutch ancestry. After attending Harvard and New York Law School, Stevens entered law practice in New York City, and it was during his years as a lawyer that he began to publish poems in the newly founded *Poetry* and the more avant-garde New York magazine, *Others.* In 1916 he moved to Hartford to work for an insurance company, continuing his writing of poetry but not publishing his first volume, *Harmonium,* until 1923. In 1931 he published a revised version of this first book, adding a few new poems. Stevens' period of greatest productivity, however, did not begin until after 1934, when he became vice-president of the insurance company by which he was employed.

Stevens' matter and manner, divorced as they frequently were from the mundane, had relevance to one of his major concerns—loss of belief and direction from man's life. Though he did not go unappreciated during his early years as a poet, it was not until the 1930's and 1940's that his originality, his artistry, and his insights won for him a large audience and a place as a leading American poet.

Harmonium (1923; revised, 1931) · *Ideas of Order* (1935) · *Owl's Clover* (1936) · *The Man with the Blue Guitar and Other Poems* (1937) · *Parts of a World* (1942) · *Notes Toward a Supreme Fiction* (1942) · *Transport to Summer* (1947) · *Three Academic Pieces* (1947) · *The Auroras of Autumn* (1950) · *Opus Posthumous* (1957)

HARRIET BEECHER STOWE   1811–1896

Litchfield, Connecticut, was the birthplace of Harriet Beecher. Her father was a New England Calvinist, and one of her brothers the famous pulpit orator, Henry Ward Beecher. At fourteen, after an education in private religious schools, she became a teacher. Seven years later her family moved to Cincinnati, where she taught in a seminary for a time. At twenty-four, she married Calvin Stowe, a member of the faculty, and in 1850 the Stowe family moved East.

From childhood, Mrs. Stowe escaped some of the grimness of her surroundings by imagining interesting adventures for herself. This imagination was of service to her when, in Cincinnati, she composed stories to be read to a literary club. The sale of some of these stories later brought important additions to the meager income of Professor Stowe. Somehow, while caring for her large family, Mrs. Stowe still found time to write numerous stories and sketches. Less sensational, but probably of more lasting value than her novels, were her works dealing with life in prewar New England, important contributions to the local color movement.

Novels: *Uncle Tom's Cabin* (1852) · *Dred* (1856) · *The Minister's Wooing* (1859) · *The Pearl of Orr's Island* (1862) · *Oldtown Folks* (1869) · *Poganuc People* (1878)

Short Stories: *Sam Lawson's Oldtown Fireside Stories* (1872)

WILLIAM STYRON   1925–

Although he has lived in the North for many years, William Styron, born in Newport News, Virginia, was reared in the South and regards himself as a Southerner. After graduating from Duke University, where he majored in English and was considered the "campus esthete," he worked for a few unhappy months as an associate editor in a publishing house. His first novel, *Lie Down in Darkness*, won him the Prix de Rome of the American Academy of Arts and Letters. It was the product of a short-story writing course at the New School for Social Research in New York City in which his teacher, Hiram Hayden, urged him to write a novel. Employing stream-of-consciousness he here recounts the downfall of a Southern middle-class family. The critics praised the book highly, comparing the young writer with Faulkner, Wolfe, and Joyce. In 1967, he was awarded the Pulitzer Prize for *The Confessions of Nat Turner*.

Lie Down in Darkness (1951) · *The Long March* (1952) · *Set This House on Fire* (1960) · *The Confessions of Nat Turner* (1967)

ALLEN TATE 1899–

Allen Tate, a distinguished member of the Nashville group headed by John Crowe Ransom, was born in Kentucky. He attended Vanderbilt, where he was graduated in 1922. Although engaged almost continuously in writing, he has found time for other employments: in the 1930's he was a member at different times of the English departments of Southwestern University at Memphis, the North Carolina Woman's College at Greensboro, and Princeton; in 1942-1944, he held the chair of poetry in the Library of Congress. Later, he taught at New York University. In 1951 he joined the English faculty of the University of Minnesota.

Tate and his Nashville associates are "reactionary" in the better sense of the word. They have sought to recover certain values of the past: the Southern cultural tradition, the religious point of view, and an intellectual fiber best exemplified in the poets of seventeenth-century England. The writings of this group have had wide influence on present literary criticism.

Poetry: *Poems: 1922-1947* (1948) · *Collected Poems* (1960) · *The Swimmers and Other Collected Poems* (1970)

Essays: *Reactionary Essays on Poetry and Ideas* (1936) · *"Narcissus as Narcissus"* (1938) · *Reason in Madness* (1941) · *Essays of Four Decades* (1969)

EDWARD TAYLOR c. 1645–1729

Very few biographical facts concerning Edward Taylor are known. He was born in Coventry, England. In 1668, at the age of twenty-two or twenty-three, he left England, presumably for liberty of conscience, and came to Boston, where he was cordially received by Increase Mather. He was admitted to Harvard College and was graduated in the class of 1671. A lifelong friendship with Samuel Sewall, of the same class, dates from his college years. Following his graduation, Taylor became pastor of the church at Westfield, Massachusetts. He lived quietly at Westfield during the remaining fifty-eight years of his life, serving the community for that long period both as minister and as physician. Twice married, he had seven children by his first wife and six by his second. Taylor's poetry takes rank not only as the best poetry written in America before the nineteenth century but also as one of the classics of New England literature.

The Poems of Edward Taylor, ed. Donald E. Stanford (1960)

WILLIAM TAPPAN THOMPSON 1812–1882

William Tappan Thompson was born in Ohio and orphaned at fourteen. With background experience as a printer's devil, as a political executive in Tallahassee, Florida, and in newspaper, magazine, and printing work in Augusta, he became an editor of a weekly newspaper, *The Southern Miscellany,* published in Madison, Georgia, in 1842. It was in this newspaper that Thompson introduced the naïve but sensible Major Jones, the Georgian imitation of Seba Smith's Jack Downing. The letters of Major Jones, with their accurate use of the vernacular speech of Georgia, were clearly related to the humor based on the oral tale, so popular in the Southwest at the time.

Major Jones's Courtship (1843) · *The Chronicles of Pineville* (1845) · *Major Jones's Sketches of Travel* (1848)

HENRY DAVID THOREAU 1817–1862

Henry David Thoreau, born in Concord, Massachusetts, was graduated without distinction from Harvard College in 1837. After graduation he assisted his brother John for a while in teaching a private school. He also helped his father manufacture lead pencils in the 1840's; but he gave up pencil making because of a desire for fresh experiences. In 1839 he and John went on a famous journey, the literary record of which, *A Week on the Concord and Merrimack Rivers,* appeared ten years later.

Thoreau was a frequent contributor to *The Dial* from 1840 to 1844. In 1841, and again in 1847-1848, he was a member of Emerson's household, doing odd jobs. In 1838 Thoreau had delivered before the Concord Lyceum his first lecture and continued lecturing for many years. However, he was not very successful as a lecturer—much less successful and less popular than Emerson.

In 1845 Thoreau began his famous residence at Walden Pond. Two years later he left Walden, not from a sense of failure or disappointment but because of a desire to explore new modes of living. In 1846, during his residence at Walden, Thoreau was arrested because of his refusal to pay the poll tax and spent a night in the Concord jail. The reason for his rebellion was his opposition to Negro slavery and the movement to increase slave territory in the Southwest. He helped at least one fugitive slave to evade the Boston police and escape into Canada. Along with Emerson, he gave active support to John Brown. When the selectmen of the village refused to sanction a memorial service to Brown, Thoreau rang the bell of the town hall himself.

Thoreau had traveled a good deal in many places. His excursions to the Maine Woods, Cape Cod, Monadnock, and the White Mountains furnished material for much writing which appeared in part in magazines during Thoreau's lifetime and which was collected after his death. In 1856 he visited Whitman in New York, and in 1861 he traveled as far west as Minnesota, but his health was already failing. He died of tuberculosis in Concord in 1862 just before he reached his forty-fifth birthday.

Only in comparatively recent times has Thoreau attained his present high reputation. The growth of his fame has no doubt been owed not only to a recognition of his fine literary qualities but also to various special appeals which his works make to modern readers. His lessons in simplicity and economy have appealed to those who are harassed by the complexity and expense of modern life.

Essays: "Civil Disobedience" (1849) · "Plea for John Brown" (1860)
Autobiography: *A Week on the Concord and Merrimack Rivers* (1849) · *Journal [The Journals]* (1837-1861; published, 1906) · *Walden; or Life in the Woods* (1854) · *The Maine Woods* (1864) · *Cape Cod* (1865)

THOMAS BANGS THORPE 1815-1878

Although he was the author of the most famous tall tale of the pre-Civil War Southwest, "The Big Bear of Arkansas," Thomas Bangs Thorpe was born in the East—in Westfield, Massachusetts, in 1815. He left Wesleyan University, in Middletown, Connecticut, in 1836, when ill health made it necessary for him to move to a milder climate, and settled down in Baton Rouge, Louisiana. In Louisiana and other parts of what was then the Far West, Thorpe gathered material for both paintings and writings which won a fine reputation for him.

Thorpe had a varied career. He painted various frontier scenes and numerous portraits, among the most admired of which were one of Jenny Lind and one of his friend, Zachary Taylor. He edited several newspapers and wrote a number of sketches detailing life in the backwoods which were widely reprinted. He was in the army during the Mexican War. After the war, he returned to the East—to New York, where he was an editor until his death in 1878.

The Mysteries of the Backwoods; or Sketches of the Southwest including Character, Scenery, and Rural Sports (1846) · *The Hive of the Bee Hunter* (1854)

JAMES THURBER 1894–1961

James Grover Thurber was born in Columbus, Ohio, where he attended grade school, then high school, and finally Ohio State University. When World War I began, Thurber quit the university without completing his work for the B.A. degree. Unable to enlist because an accident in boyhood had blinded him in one eye and because the sight of his other eye had deteriorated, Thurber became a code clerk in the State Department in Paris and served until 1920. He next became a journalist, first on the Columbus *Dispatch,* then on the Chicago *Tribune* in Paris, then on the New York *Evening Post.* In 1926 he began selling to *The New Yorker,* and in 1927 he became a member of its staff. He served briefly as managing editor but resigned to devote a larger share of his time to writing, most of which was featured in *The New Yorker.*

Thurber's humor, though whimsical, is far from sentimental. The unique outlook on which it is based may be one reason why many feel that Thurber is the greatest of modern American humorists. Certainly his clear style and versatility have also contributed to the admiration he has won.

Short Stories and Sketches: *Is Sex Necessary?* (with E. B. White, 1929) · *The Owl in the Attic* (1931) · *The Seal in the Bedroom* (1932) · *The Middle-Aged Man on the Flying Trapeze* (1935) · *Let Your Mind Alone* (1937) · *Fables for Our Times* (1940) · *The White Deer* (1945) · *The Beast in Me and Other Animals* (1948) · *The Thirteen Clocks* (1950) · *Further Fables for Our Times* (1956) · *Alarms and Diversions* (1957) · *Wonderful O* (1957)

Drama: *The Male Animal* (with Elliott Nugent, 1940)

Autobiography: *My Life and Hard Times* (1933) · *The Thurber Album* (1952) · *The Years with Ross* (1959)

HENRY TIMROD 1828–1867

Henry Timrod attended the Coates School in Charleston, South Carolina—his birthplace—and studied for a year and a half at the University of Georgia. After trying the law, he turned to tutoring in planters' families. Later he was a contributor to *Russell's Magazine* (1857-1860), a journal of literary promise published in Charleston and edited by his friend Paul Hamilton Hayne. In 1861 Timrod enlisted in the Confederate army, but because of ill health he was able to serve less than a year. Undertaking the work of a war correspondent, he observed at close range the battle of Shiloh. In 1864 he edited a newspaper in Columbia, South Carolina; this position ended abruptly when Columbia was taken by Sherman's army. The three last years of his life were a losing struggle against poverty and disease. His poems were collected, with a memoir, by Paul Hamilton Hayne in 1873. Timrod's early verses were imitative of Wordsworth. The war called forth his latent originality and inspired his best poems in which he achieved a distinctive fusion of romantic and classical elements.

Poems of Henry Timrod, ed. P. H. Hayne (1873)

JEAN TOOMER 1894-1967

Jean Toomer was born in Washington, D.C., the grandson of P. B. S. Pinch-back, a black man who for a brief time was Acting Governor of Louisiana. In 1922 Toomer wrote in a brief biographical sketch of himself: "Racially, I seem to have (who knows for sure) seven blood mixtures: French, Dutch, Welsh, Negro, German, Jewish, and Indian. Because of these, my position in America has been a curious one. I have lived equally amid the two race groups. Now white, now colored. From my own point of view I am natural-ly and inevitably an American." In this same sketch, Toomer indicated that he had lived in many cities (including Washington, New York, Chicago) and had worked at many jobs (including soda clerk, salesman, shipyard worker, schoolteacher). As for his education, he remarked: "Neither the universities of Wisconsin or New York gave me what I wanted, so I quit them."

Although the latter part of Jean Toomer's life is wrapped in mystery, it is known that he lived for a time in Carmel, California; Taos, New Mexi-co; and, finally, in Bucks County, Pennsylvania. And he continued to write —in quantity. He left at his death a large number of unpublished manu-scripts.

Cane, the work for which Toomer is remembered, has been compared to Sherwood Anderson's *Winesburg, Ohio,* but it includes poems and drama as well as short stories, and the scene shifts from the rural South in the first half of the book to the urban North in the latter half. It is, in fact, a recapit-ulation of the Afro-American experience, and is now regarded as an American classic.

Cane (1923, 1967)

MARK TWAIN: see Samuel L. Clemens

JOHN UPDIKE 1932-

John Updike, one of the youngest of the new novelists, was born in Skillington, Pennsylvania, served as an editor of the Harvard *Lampoon,* and was graduated from Harvard in 1954. He spent a year at the Ruskin School of Fine Arts in Oxford, and on his return to the United States he joined the staff of *The New Yorker;* he is still a frequent contributor of poems and stories to that magazine. Updike has been praised for his sensitivity to the "dislocations of modern life" and for his stylistic virtuosity. Probably his most interesting novel is *The Centaur,* a juxtaposition of classical myth with contemporary life; it won the National Book Award for fiction in 1964.

Poetry: *The Carpentered Hen* (1958) · *Telephone Poles and Other Poems* (1963) · *Midpoint and Other Poems* (1969)

Short Stories: *The Same Door* (1959) · *Pigeon Feathers* (1962) · *The Music School* (1966) · *Museums and Women and Other Stories* (1972)

Novels: *The Poorhouse Fair* (1959) · *Rabbit, Run* (1960) · *The Centaur* (1963) · *Of the Farm* (1965) · *Couples* (1968) · *Bech: A Book* (1970) · *Rabbit Redux* (1971)

DAVID WALKER 1785-1830

"This little book produced more commotion amongst slaveholders than any volume of its size that was ever issued from an American press." This assessment was made in 1848 by Henry Highland Garnet, himself an escaped slave and a leading abolitionist, of a pamphlet first published in

Boston in 1829—*Walker, David. Appeal, in Four Articles, Together with a Preamble, to the Coloured Citizens of the World. . . .*

The author of *Appeal* was born to a free mother in Wilmington, North Carolina, on September 28, 1785—the posthumous son of a slave father. As a boy (some accounts say at the incredible age of nine), Walker determined to leave the South, and eventually made his way to Boston. There he learned to read and write; he entered the clothing business; and he did much to further the abolitionist movement. His *Appeal* was distributed widely, and actions and utterances of officials and newspaper editors between 1829 and 1831 in Georgia, Virginia, Louisiana, North Carolina, and Mississippi provided striking evidence that it created panicky uneasiness in many slave states. Walker died in 1830 before he could learn how influential his pamphlet was to be. Addressed, of course, not only to blacks but also to whites, because of its very eloquent intensity it made a profound impression upon its readers and thus became a historic milestone in the Afro-American fight for freedom.

ARTEMUS WARD: see Charles Farrar Browne

ROBERT PENN WARREN 1905–
Robert Penn Warren was born in Guthrie, Kentucky, and took his B.A. at Vanderbilt (in the class of 1925), his M.A. at the University of California, and his B.Litt. at Oxford. He has taught at Vanderbilt, Louisiana State University, the University of Minnesota, and at Yale, first as Professor of Dramatic Composition and since 1961 as Professor of English. At Vanderbilt he was a member—along with John Crowe Ransom, Donald Davidson, Allen Tate, and others—of the now famous group of poets known as "Fugitives." At Louisiana State University, he was co-editor (with Cleanth Brooks) of the influential and important *Southern Review* (1935-1942) and co-author (also with Brooks) of a revolutionary textbook, *Understanding Poetry* (1938).

Though Warren is certainly an admirer of Faulkner, and though his fiction doubtless resembles Faulkner's in some ways, he is no mere disciple. He possesses certain advantages conveyed by a more academic and more cosmopolitan experience. He is in a sense, therefore, less provincial than Faulkner, but his truest work, like Faulkner's, is at once Southern in its origins and universal in its meanings.

Poetry: *Thirty-Six Poems* (1936) · *Brother to Dragons* (1953) · *Promises* (1957) · *Selected Poems New and Old, 1923-1966* (1966) · *Audubon: A Vision* (1969)

Novels: *Night Rider* (1939) · *At Heaven's Gate* (1943) · *All the King's Men* (1946) · *World Enough and Time* (1950) · *Band of Angels* (1955) · *The Cave* (1959) · *Wilderness* (1961) · *Flood* (1964) · *Meet Me in the Green Glen* (1971)

Short Stories: *The Circus in the Attic and Other Stories* (1947)

BOOKER T. WASHINGTON 1856?–1915
Booker Taliaferro Washington was born in a slave cabin on a Franklin County, Virginia, plantation, probably in 1856. In Malden, West Virginia, to which the family moved after their emancipation, the boy started the difficult business of getting an education by studying a few hard-gained hours a day or at night while working with his stepfather in a salt-furnace or a coal mine. In 1872 his eagerness to continue took him to Hampton

Institute, which—through work as a janitor—he was able to attend until graduation in 1875. His success as a teacher in Malden and then in Hampton led to his appointment to head Tuskegee Institute when it was founded in 1881. Under Washington's leadership, this normal and industrial school for blacks grew rapidly. His success won nationwide attention and within a decade and a half his influence was remarkable. "By the beginning of the new century," historian John Hope Franklin found, "Washington was one of the most powerful men in the United States," an influential adviser of leading industrialists and even of American presidents. "When he died in 1915," Franklin continues, "he was still firmly entrenched in the position of leading educator, leading racial adviser at many levels, and leading advocate of what Du Bois called 'the gospel of work and money.' "
Up from Slavery (1903)

EUDORA WELTY 1909–
A native of Jackson, Mississippi, Eudora Welty still makes her home in the town in which she was born. Although she remained close to home by attending the Mississippi State College for Women, she left the state to study at the University of Wisconsin and Columbia, and she worked at various writing and publicity jobs before she began to write seriously about the small-town Mississippi life so familiar to her. Her novels and short stories have won many awards.

Characteristic of Miss Welty's work is the accurate reproduction of colloquial speech for comic effect and the creation of characters whose personalities are a grotesque and at times symbolic combination of the ordinary and the eccentric.

Novels: *The Robber Bridegroom* (1942) · *Delta Wedding* (1946) · *The Ponder Heart* (1954) · *Losing Battles* (1970)
Short Stories: *A Curtain of Green* (1941) · *The Wide Net* (1943) · *The Golden Apples* (1949) · *The Bride of the Innesfallen* (1955) · *The Shoe Bird* (1964) · *The Optimist's Daugher* (1972)

PHILLIS WHEATLEY 1753?–1784
Phillis Wheatley was brought to America as a slave when she was a child and sold to John Wheatley, a Boston merchant. She was precocious and learned English quickly. The Wheatleys encouraged her learning, and eventually made her a member of the family and later gave her her freedom. Although her poetry is not highly regarded today—it is derivative, as is much of the American poetry of the period, patterned after English neoclassical rhythms and modes of thought—her *Poems on Various Subjects* was received with much acclaim when it was published. Certainly it was a significant accomplishment for the time.
Poems on Various Subjects, Religious and Moral (1773)

WALT WHITMAN 1819–1892
The son of a carpenter, Whitman was born on Long Island and spent his early life there, in Brooklyn, and in New York. He attended the public schools of Brooklyn, read omnivorously, and listened to Elias Hicks, a Quaker preacher. Other early experiences included participating in a debating society, working in printing offices, and teaching in country schools on Long Island and "boarding round." In the 1840's he was connected with various newspapers, including the Brooklyn *Daily Eagle,* which he edited in 1846-1847. His knowledge of American life was further enlarged in 1848

by a leisurely journey down the Ohio and Mississippi to New Orleans, a stay of two or three months in that city, and the return journey by way of Chicago and the Great Lakes. Upon his return to Brooklyn, he resumed journalistic work and assisted his father in building houses.

Whitman was not a soldier in the Civil War, but he was nonetheless one of the war's real heroes. He served indefatigably as a volunteer nurse in the Washington hospitals, distributing knickknacks among the soldiers, writing letters home, radiating cheerfulness and the will to live. He also visited the camp hospitals of the Army of the Potomac in Virginia. His hitherto magnificent health suffered under the strain and exposure. In the summer of 1864 he was ill with "hospital malaria," from the effects of which he never fully recovered. In 1873 he had a paralytic stroke, and he continued a partial invalid during the remaining nineteen years of his life.

Whitman's poetry was original and revolutionary and indisputably American. He broke with the conventions and traditions of English verse. He employed free rhythms, which are comparable with those of the Old Testament. There have been, and still are, sharp differences of opinion as to the absolute merit of his work as poetry. Intellectual critics object to his emotionalism and vagueness; formal critics to his lack of close structure; academic critics to his apotheosis of the uncultivated. But there can be no question of his power and influence.

Poetry: *Leaves of Grass* (1855; revisions, 1856, 1860, 1867, 1871, 1876, 1881-1882, 1889, 1891-1892) · *Drum-Taps* (1865) · *Sequel to Drum-Taps* (1865-1866)

Essays: *Democratic Vistas* (1871)

Autobiography: *Specimen Days and Collect* (1882)

JOHN GREENLEAF WHITTIER 1807–1892

Born on a farm near Haverhill, Massachusetts, educated in country schools, long a worker on his father's farm and at the cobbler's bench, John Greenleaf Whittier saw things through the eyes of a common man, and his words were drawn from nature rather than art. From Robert Burns, his first and most important model, he learned a simple style of versifying which pleased ordinary readers. A member of a religious sect which had contributed many great opponents of the slave system, Whittier followed the promptings of his Quaker Inner Light to work zealously for reform.

He was mostly self-educated and was an energetic man in spite of his poor health. For several decades Whittier devoted a large share of his energy to the antislavery cause. He was successful in practical politics, winning his own election to the Massachusetts legislature in 1835, acting as a lobbyist at the State House, and giving assistance to political leaders who were helpful to abolitionism. As a pamphleteer, as a poet, and as an editor of various periodicals, notably of the *National Era* (1845-1860), he attacked slavery ferociously.

After the war Whittier turned to a field of work in which he had already shown proficiency—the portrayal of the rural New England life which he knew so well. It was as a local colorist that he did his most distinguished work. In these poetic writings he followed the tradition represented before his birth by the poet of Scottish rural life, Robert Burns, and carried on in the work of Robert Frost.

Poetry: *Legends of New England* (1831) · *Mogg Megone* (1836) · *Poems Written During the Progress of the Abolition Question . . .* (1837) · *Lays of My Home and Other Poems* (1843) · *Voices of Freedom* (1846) · *Songs of*

Labor and Other Poems (1850) · *Home Ballads, Poems, and Lyrics* (1860) ·
In War Time and Other Poems (1863) · *Snow-Bound* (1866) · *The Tent on
the Beach and Other Poems* (1867) · *Among the Hills and Other Poems*
(1869) · *Ballads of New England* (1870) · *At Sundown* (1890)
Novel: *Leaves from Margaret Smith's Journal* (1849)

MICHAEL WIGGLESWORTH 1631–1705

Michael Wigglesworth, author of *The Day of Doom,* the most widely read
poem written in seventeenth-century New England, was born in Yorkshire
but was brought to Connecticut by his parents before he was seven. Precocious but frail, he was sent to the Latin school at New Haven but was taken
out when he was needed to help work his father's farm. Unfit by physique
and temperament for farm labor, he was sent back to school after three
years and in 1651 was graduated from Harvard College. He was uncertain
of his calling. He seems to have thought first of studying medicine, but
either the Cambridge environment or a religious experience turned him to
theology and the ministry. He stayed on at Harvard as a fellow and tutor,
began to preach occasionally, and from around 1654 had some assurance
of the church at Malden, a town about four miles north of Boston. He married, after much soul searching, in 1655, and is believed to have been
ordained at Malden two years later.

Afflicted apparently by "preacher's sore throat" and hypochondria,
and disturbed by strong sexual drives which he had difficulty in controlling,
he was hardly a successful minister. From 1657 until 1686, in fact, he
seems never to have performed regularly all the duties expected of a pastor,
although he preached occasionally and practiced medicine among his neighbors. For the last twenty years of his life, Wigglesworth recovered a large
measure of his health, and served his church effectively and faithfully, although he was remembered as "a little feeble shadow of a man."

Out of the travail of his long illness came three major poems and more
than a dozen lesser pieces, but Wigglesworth's future reputation probably
will rest in large part upon his diary, although we have only a fragment of
it. Partly written in shorthand, it was not printed until 1951, but no other
Puritan document is as revealing of the profound depths of religious and
personal insecurity.
Poetry: *The Day of Doom* (1662) · *Meat Out of the Eater* (1669) · "God's
Controversy with New England" (printed 1873)
Autobiography: *The Diary of Michael Wigglesworth,* ed. Edmund S.
Morgan (1951)

RICHARD WILBUR 1921 –

After graduating from Amherst College in 1942, Richard Wilbur went to
Harvard University, where he received his M.A. in 1947. From 1950 he was
Assistant Professor of English at Harvard; in 1954 he became Associate Professor at Wellesley; and in 1957 Professor at Wesleyan University. In 1957
he received the Pulitzer Prize for Poetry for his *Things of This World.* He
has translated some Molière, Guillén, and Quasimodo.

Though Wilbur is fundamentally an intellectual poet, his sophistication
has not cut him off from an understanding of things beyond his immediate
world. His poetry is always disciplined and often light in spirit, but his concern about the problem of atomic power has brought to his poetry very
serious moments.
The Beautiful Changes (1947) · *Ceremony and Other Poems* (1951) ·

Things of This World (1956) · *Poems 1943-1956* (1957) · *Advice to a Prophet* (1961) · *Walking to Sleep* (1969)

ROGER WILLIAMS   1603?-1683

Roger Williams, a Puritan and the first vigorous proponent of the separation of church and state, was originally a student of divinity in the Anglican Church, but, unable to tolerate the measures of Charles I, he eventually sailed for Massachusetts. Because of his independent thinking in religious matters and his defense of the rights of the Indians, he was forced to leave Massachusetts for what is now Rhode Island, where he set up the independent government of the Providence Plantation. Williams has an honored place in American history as the first vehement supporter, both in his actions and in his writings, of the principle of freedom of thought.

A Key into the Language of America (1643) · *The Bloudy Tenent of Persecution for the Cause of Conscience* (1644) · *George Fox Digg'd out of His Burrowes* (1676)

TENNESSEE WILLIAMS   1914-

Born in Mississippi, Thomas Lanier (Tennessee) Williams received part of his higher education in that state. However, he took his B.A. degree at the State University of Iowa in 1938. Even as a boy he was fond of reading and interested in writing, but not until 1940 did his writing ability gain recognition when he won a thousand-dollar fellowship to write a play. The outcome of his efforts was *Battle of Angels,* which, though itself unsuccessful, was later rewritten as *Orpheus Descending* (1957). Success came in 1945 with the production of *The Glass Menagerie.* He later won Pulitzer Prizes for both *A Streetcar Named Desire* and *Cat on a Hot Tin Roof.*

Williams' plays are characterized by their concern with the psychologically sick who often express themselves in violent actions. The significance of these plays, however, is based on their expression of the lack of love among men. His *Night of the Iguana* is the fullest statement of his philosophy.

Drama: *Battle of Angels* [*Orpheus Descending,* 1957] (1940) · *The Glass Menagerie* (1945) · *A Streetcar Named Desire* (1947) · *Summer and Smoke* (1948) · *The Rose Tattoo* (1951) · *Camino Real* (1953) · *Cat on a Hot Tin Roof* (1955) · *Suddenly, Last Summer* (1958) · *Sweet Bird of Youth* (1959) · *Period of Adjustment* (1960) · *The Night of the Iguana* (1961) · *The Eccentricities of a Nightingale* (1964) · *Slapstick Tragedy* (1965) · *The Seven Descents of Myrtle* (1967) · *Out Cry* (1971) · *Small Craft Warnings* (1972)

Novel: *The Roman Spring of Mrs. Stone* (1969)

Stories: *One Arm* (1948) · *Hard Candy* (1954)

WILLIAM CARLOS WILLIAMS   1883-1963

William Carlos Williams was born in Rutherford, New Jersey. After graduating from the University of Pennsylvania he continued into the medical school and received his M.D. in 1906. Following his internship and a year in Leipzig studying pediatrics, he set up practice in Rutherford, where he remained throughout his entire medical career. The year 1909 not only marked Williams' return to his home town; it was also the year that he published *Poems,* the first of many works that include poetry, fiction, plays, and translations.

Some have criticized Williams for his imagistic tendencies, but it is these tendencies which have contributed to his tight, clear style. Though Williams is a precise writer, he is by no means a traditionalist. His poetry, unrhymed, eccentric in meter, is, in fact, representative of the works of those poets who adopted free verse as the means of achieving the feeling of American speech. The quality of his attention to the simple descriptive statement won for him enthusiastic followers who in the 1930's organized into a group called the Objectivists.

Poetry: *Poems* (1909) · *Paterson* (Books I-IV) (1946-1951) · *The Collected Later Poems of William Carlos Williams* (1950, revised 1963) · *The Collected Earlier Poems of William Carlos Williams* (1951) · *The Desert Music* (1954) · *Journey to Love* (1955) · *Sappho* (1957) · *Paterson* (Book V) (1958) · *Pictures from Brueghel* (1962)

Autobiography: *The Autobiography of William Carlos Williams* (1951)

JOHN WINTHROP 1588-1649

John Winthrop, lawyer and author of his *Journal* or *The History of New England* (1630-1649), was the first governor of the Massachusetts Bay Colony and was eight times reelected. A devout Puritan, he shared his wealth with others and spent much of his time promoting the good of the colony. Though now he is read chiefly in his *Journal,* his series of letters to his third wife, Margaret, is worthy of note as perhaps the finest picture of a happy Puritan marriage in our literature.

"A Modell of Christian Charity" (1630) · *The History of New England [Journal]* (1630-1649)

THOMAS WOLFE 1900-1938

Thomas Wolfe was born and brought up in Asheville, North Carolina, which is situated high in the Smokies and is described with remarkable completeness in his *Look Homeward, Angel.* After graduating from the University of North Carolina, Wolfe studied at Harvard, taught at New York University, and traveled in England and France. On his visits to Europe he was able to concentrate on his writing. While still at the height of his career he became ill with pneumonia and died.

Wolfe was a great romantic genius with all the vitality, the exuberance, the undisciplined ardor which the name implies. He was Wordsworth's "creature moving about in worlds not realized." His closest affinities were with Coleridge, whom he often quoted, and with Whitman, whom he obviously emulated. His prose at its best has a lyrical exultation; at its worst, it is so unpruned as to verge on the bombastic. But more eloquently than any other writer since Whitman, Wolfe restated the American dream: the right of every man "to live, to work, to be himself, to become whatever thing his manhood and his vision can combine to make him."

Look Homeward, Angel (1929) · *Of Time and the River* (1935) · *The Web and the Rock* (1939) · *You Can't Go Home Again* (1940)

JOHN WOOLMAN 1720-1772

John Woolman was born on a farm on Rancocas Creek, midway between Burlington and Mount Holly, New Jersey. There he lived until he was twenty, learning to love the Quaker way of life in his family, the village school, and the weekly Meeting. He then went into a shop in Mount Holly, five miles away, and in his spare time learned the tailor's trade. Soon he felt the call to visit other Meetings, as was the custom of those Friends who wished to become ministers and elders in a sect which had no professional clergy. His tact, his literary skill, and, most of all, his unimpeachable sincerity made him successful in Quaker politics and action, and he was chiefly responsible for consolidating Quaker sentiment for the emancipation of Negro slaves. His inclination to help arouse the English Quakers to the importance of this cause sent him to England in 1772. He arrived in London in June, visited Friends there and in the neighborhood, and then, wishing to go to the North, chose characteristically to walk rather than have any part in the oppression of postboys and horses. He got as far as York, where he died of smallpox.

The sweet reasonableness of Woolman's writings and the apparent carelessness in their organization clothe a keen and penetrating intellect, stored with the rich wisdom of the Bible and of personal experience, and directed by convictions which are often revolutionary.

Some Considerations on the Keeping of Negroes (Part I, 1754; Part II, 1762) · *A Plea for the Poor* (1837) · *The Journal* (published, 1774)

RICHARD WRIGHT   1908–1960

Richard Wright was born near Natchez, Mississippi, grew up in Memphis, Tennessee, and arrived in Chicago in early youth. He began to publish stories which he brought together in 1938 under the title *Uncle Tom's Children,* winner of the annual award of *Story* magazine. His reputation was firmly established by the publication of *Native Son* in 1940, and he gained still more plaudits for an autobiographical volume, *Black Boy,* which appeared in 1945.

In spite of his success as a writer, Wright became increasingly disenchanted with American life. After World War II, he went to Paris where he lived as an expatriate until his death in 1960. Although he continued to write and publish, his later work did not seem to have the immediacy and agonizing authenticity of his early fiction. He came under the influence of the French existentialists, and his work became more philosophically complex and ambitious.

Richard Wright must be recognized as a kind of pioneer-leader in the black-literature movement in America. He commanded the attention of the country at large. Before him, excellent black writers were neglected. And after him, new black writers would displace him. His wide popularity made it easier for others to gain a hearing. It is not, however, his popularity, but his integrity as a writer for which he will be remembered.

Novels: *Native Son* (1940) · *Black Boy* (1945) · *The Outsider* (1953) · *The Long Dream* (1958)

Short Stories: *Uncle Tom's Children* (1938) · *Eight Men* (1961)

MALCOLM X   1925–1965

Malcolm X was born Malcolm Little in Omaha, Nebraska, the seventh child of a Baptist minister. The family lived a nomadic existence, moving from place to place—Omaha, Milwaukee, Lansing—and always on the edge of poverty. When Malcolm was six, his father was killed, and sheer existence became a challenge. It is not surprising that Malcolm early turned to a life of petty crime, and that he spent time in prison.

Attracted to the black nationalist movement, Malcolm joined the Black Muslims and became a brilliant recruiter, organizer, and spokesman in their ranks. A main tenet of the movement was segregation of the races in order that the black race might retain its purity; the main enemy of the blacks was clearly identified as the "white devils." Malcolm X (his Black Muslim name) rose quickly in the organization, and soon became second in command to the prophet, Elijah Muhammad. He was astonishingly successful in defending and expanding the movement throughout the country, but gradually a rift developed between Elijah and Malcolm X.

An open break came in 1964, and shortly thereafter Malcolm X repeatedly told his friends that his life was being threatened by the Black Muslims. In February 1965, at a meeting of his organization in Harlem, just as he was about to launch into his speech, he was shot and killed by a group of assassins, all of whom escaped.

His fascinating and moving autobiography was published after his death and quickly established itself as a classic chronicle of black life in America, as well as an engrossing account of the black nationalist movement. The book has helped to establish Malcolm X as one of the major mythmakers and heroes of the contemporary Black Revolution in America.
The Autobiography of Malcolm X (1965) · *Malcolm X Speaks: Selected Speeches and Statements* (1965)

GUIDE TO FURTHER READINGS
Two detailed histories of American literature by a number of leading scholars, both of which contain bibliographies, are *Cambridge History of American Literature* (New York, 1917-1921), 4 vols., ed. W. P. Trent and others, and *Literary History of the United States*, 3rd ed. revised (New York, 1973), ed. Robert E. Spiller and others. An excellent shorter account is Leon Howard, *Literature and the American Tradition* (Garden City, 1963). Clarence Gohdes, *Bibliographical Guide to the Study of the Literature of the United States*, 3rd ed. revised (Durham, 1970) is a useful handbook, as is the short *Reader's Guide to English and American Literature* (Glenview, 1970), ed. Andrew Wright. Three books, each made up of essays by scholars, direct students to special studies of leading authors: *Eight American Authors*, revised ed. (New York, 1971), ed. James Woodress, reviews scholarship and criticism of Emerson, Hawthorne, James, Melville, Poe, Thoreau, Mark Twain, and Whitman. *Fifteen American Authors Before 1900* (Madison, 1971), ed. Robert A. Rees and Earl N. Harbert, evaluates writings about Henry Adams, Bryant, Cooper, Stephen Crane, Emily Dickinson, Edwards, Franklin, Howells, Irving, Longfellow, James Russell Lowell, Frank Norris, Edward Taylor, Whittier, and "Writers of the Old and New South." *Fifteen Modern American Authors* (Durham, 1969), ed. Jackson R. Bryer, has bibliographical essays concerning Anderson, Cather, Hart Crane, Dreiser, T. S. Eliot, Faulkner, Fitzgerald, Frost, Hemingway, O'Neill, Pound, Robinson, Steinbeck, Stevens, and Thomas Wolfe. Beginning with the year's work for 1963, *American Literary Scholarship: An Annual* has provided evaluations by specialists of books and articles for previous years (Durham, 1965-   ).

Index

frontier, 156-157; as humorist and local colorist, 177, 179-182; and mechanistic philosophy, 162; and realism, 182-183; and social criticism, 150

Congregationalism, 5, 12, 13

Connecticut Wits, The, 51, 53, 68

Connelly, Marc, 211, 212

Constitution of the United States, The, 49, 50, 53, 54, 55, 107

Cooper, James Fenimore, 10, 51, 56, 60, 62, 66, 73, 292, 335; and romanticism, 64-65

Cotton, John, 28, 30

Cowboy songs, 175

Craddock, Charles Egbert; see Murfree, Mary Noailles

Crane, Hart, 221, 292-293

Crane, Stephen, 152, 163, 227, 229, 293, 310; and mechanistic philosophy, 162; and naturalism, 185-186; and poetry, 168, 209, 216

Crèvecoeur, Michel Guillaume St. Jean de, 10, 49, 50, 54, 55, 57, 62, 66, 70, 73, 293

Crockett, David, 123, 124, 125, 156, 294

Cullen, Countee, 202, 220, 294

Cummings, Edward Estlin, 218, 219, 260, 294

Day, Clarence Shepard, Jr., 295

Declaration of Independence, The, 49, 51, 52, 67

Deism, 14, 15, 57-58

Democracy: in the American Renaissance, 82-86, 100; after the Civil War, 151; in the colonies, 17-20; and Melville, 97; in the new republic, 48-54; and Poe, 98; and Whitman, 149-150, 170-171; after World War I, 199, 244, 246, 249-250

Depression, The, 201, 208

Detail: in frontier tales, 124-125; in modern fiction, 228-231

Determinism, 164, 184-185, 204-205

Dial, The, 93

Dialect, 51, 124, 125; in humor, 178; in poetry, 177

Diaries and autobiographies, 32-33, 67-68

Dickey, James, 295

Dickinson, Emily, 168-170, 209, 216, 293, 295-296; and religion, 161-162

Diction: of modern poetry, 216, 222-225; of oratory, 125

Dooley, Mr.; see Dunne, Finley Peter

Dos Passos, John, 198, 227, 230, 296; and the documentary method, 228, 259; and plot patterns, 232; and psychology, 234-235; and social criticism, 205

Douglass, Frederick, 296

Downing, Jack; see Smith, Seba

Drama: after the Civil War, 190-192; in the colonial period, 36-38; and the little theater movement, 209-210, 210-211; in the new republic, 70-71; after World War I, 210-214; since World War II, 271-277

Dreiser, Theodore, 204, 227, 228, 229, 297; and mechanistic philosophy, 163; and naturalism, 163, 184, 185; and social criticism, 152, 153, 200

Du Bois, W. E. B., 154-155, 202, 297-298

Dunbar, Paul Laurence, 168, 177, 298

Dunlap, William, 70-71

Dunne, Finley Peter *(Mr. Dooley),* 164-165, 298

Dwight, Timothy, 53, 54, 55, 57, 58, 66, 68, 71

Economics: in the American Renaissance, 87-88; after the Civil War, 147-149; in the Civil War, 110; in the colonies, 7-10, 21, 55; and the Negroes' quest, 154-155, 249-250; in the new republic, 50, 54-56; after World War I, 203; since World War II, 249

Education: in the American Renaissance, 80, 83-84, 87-88; college, 36, 130, 210; in the new republic, 50, 58-59; and race relations, 250; since World War II, 245, 248